RACE & RACISM

IN 21ST-CENTURY CANADA

RACE AND RACISM IN 21ST-CENTURY CANADA
Continuity, Complexity, and Change

edited by Sean P. Hier and B. Singh Bolaria

broadview press

LIBRARY AND ARCHIVES CANADA CATALOGUING IN PUBLICATION

Race & racism in 21st-century Canada : continuity, complexity, and change / edited by Sean P. Hier and B. Singh Bolaria.

Includes bibliographical references and index.
ISBN 978-1-55111-794-2

1. Canada—Race relations—Textbooks. 2. Pluralism (Social sciences)—Canada. 3. Racism—Canada—Textbooks. 4. Canada—Social conditions—1991– —Textbooks. I. Hier, Sean P. (Sean Patrick), 1971– II. Bolaria, B. Singh, 1936– III. Title: Race and racism in 21st-century Canada.

FC104.R312 2007   305.800971'09051   C2007-902670-2

NORTH AMERICA
Post Office Box 1243,
Peterborough, Ontario,
Canada K9J 7H5

Post Office Box 1015,
3576 California Road,
Orchard Park, New York, USA 14127
TEL: (705) 743-8990
FAX: (705) 743-8353

customerservice@broadviewpress.com

UK, IRELAND, & CONTINENTAL EUROPE
NBN International, Estover Road,
Plymouth, UK PL6 7PY
TEL: 44 (0) 1752 202300
FAX: 44 (0) 1752 202330
EMAIL: enquiries@nbninternational.com

AUSTRALIA & NEW ZEALAND
UNIREPS University of New South Wales
Sydney, NSW 2052 Australia
TEL: 61 2 96640999
FAX: 61 2 96645420
infopress@unsw.edu.au

BROADVIEW PRESS is an independent, international publishing house, incorporated in 1985. Broadview believes in shared ownership, both with its employees and with the general public; since the year 2000 Broadview shares have traded publicly on the Toronto Venture Exchange under the symbol BDP.

We welcome comments and suggestions regarding any aspect of our publications—please feel free to contact us at the addresses above or at broadview@broadview press.com/www.broadviewpress.com.

Broadview Press acknowledges the financial support of the Government of Canada through the Book Publishing Industry Development Program (BPIDP) for our publishing activities.

Cover design and interior by Em Dash Design
Copy-edited by Betsy Struthers

Printed in Canada

This book is printed on paper containing 100% post-consumer fibre.

In memory of my late parents, Gurbax and Davinder Bolaria.
—Singh Bolaria

To Mary Elizabeth, Jacob, Sam, and Sara.
—Sean Hier

CONTENTS

PREFACE

Canadian history is fraught with explicit forms of institutional racism. Since 1945, however, the racist character of Canadian social structure has been transformed. Although racism persists in Canadian institutions and in everyday life, there have been significant changes to levels of institutional participation among and within Canada's diverse ethnic, racial, cultural, and religious populations. These progressive, albeit uneven, changes can be observed in institutional domains including immigration practices, educational attainments rates, labour market participation, and patterns of civic-democratic participation. It is crucial to realize, too, that the changes taking place in Canada are not simply outcomes of interrelated social-structural transformations underway since the 1960s; rather, they are also catalysts for interrelated changes that continue to transform the country. While many researchers offer important studies laying claim to the pervasiveness of institutional or systemic forms of racism in Canada, there is an important body of evidence that also contests the extent to which the social categories of race and ethnicity function as categorical determinants for the inequitable distribution of services and resources.

As the ethnic, racial, cultural, and religious composition of the country continues to diversify, and as the number of Canadians who are politically classified as "visible minority" continues to grow, social research must address the complex material relations and social relationships that accompany demographic, political, economic, and cultural change. Significant collective gains for "visible" and "non-visible" minority groups have been made over the past 45 years, and there are important differences to be discerned within and among minority groups in terms, for example, of class position, gender, immigration status, age, and region. At the same time, claims to racism in all areas of Canadian social life continue to be articulated, the most recent of which pertain to media reporting following the terrorist attacks of 11 September 2001 (New York City and Washington, DC) and 7 July 2005 (London)—and following the apprehension of the so-called "Toronto 17" on 3 June 2006. Our goal is not to argue that racism ceases to be a significant force that negatively affects the life chances of Canada's diverse populations but to examine different forms of evidence to understand the continuity and complexity of racism and social change in the country.

We bring together analysts from a variety of backgrounds—sociology, economics, literary studies, women's studies, and public policy work. We are not interested in comparing different research findings to render a final verdict on which body of evidence is "correct." Our purpose is to demonstrate some of the ways in which researchers produce different forms of knowledge about racism and social incorporation in Canada and how these different sets of knowledge can be reconciled and applied to anti-racist and equity policies in contemporary Canadian society. To this end, the book examines diverse and, at times, conflicting research findings to clearly understand what racism is, how it manifests, and, importantly, how it affects social groups differently. We also take care to conceptualize key analytical concepts and to identify future research directions based on important changes taking place in the country. These analyses, we believe, are important, timely, and necessary for achieving a full understanding of racism and social change in Canada.

The book opens with an analytical essay addressing research on race and racism in 21st-century Canada. This is followed by three chapters that assess various theories, concepts, and ways of knowing about race and racism. Taken collectively, the chapters in Part I: Theories, Concepts, Politics, and Identification address established and emerging themes in ethnic and racial studies, including standpoint, critical realism, and whiteness studies. They also critically assess the ways in which knowledge about racism in Canada is produced.

Part II: Racism and Structural Patterns of Incorporation in Canada presents four chapters that demonstrate the diversity of structural incorporation within and between Canada's ethno-racial minority groups and shed light on the complexity of Canadian labour market incorporation. Importantly, they demonstrate that there is significant diversity among groups of people who trace their ancestral origins to locations other than Europe (or people of colour born in the Western world), and they pose serious questions pertaining to Canadian public policy on equity hiring practices, Aboriginal training, foreign credential recognition, settlement and immigration services, and responsible immigration legislation. The chapters also flesh out enduring empirical contradictions between immigrants' education and training, labour market incorporation, and patterns of social mobility.

In Part III: Articulations of Race and Gender, four chapters gauge the cultural and experiential dimensions of race and gender in Canada. Guided by the general orientation of anti-racist feminism, the authors explore the significance of racial and gender distinctions in the context of labour, education, law, immigration, and social services. Each author takes care to establish a link between Canada's colonial past and the present structure of relations of ruling in the country; thus, they complement the analyses appearing in Part II. Specifically, the chapters highlight the importance of moving beyond the race-class-gender triad, and they problematize the reductionism that tends to characterize otherwise well-meaning social justice research.

In Part IV: Multiculturalism, Anti-Racism, and Public Policy, key issues pertaining to multiculturalism and anti-racism are addressed. The authors in this section recognize, in different ways, the potential of ant-racist work for achieving equity and justice. The first two chapters address the gains made following the introduction of multiculturalism as national policy in the country, while the last two probe anti-racism on a local and international scale.

Taken collectively, contributors to the volume share an interest in exposing and interrogating the continuity of racism in Canada, but they differ in the ways in which they study racism and social change and, consequently, in the solutions they offer for achieving a just and equitable society. What we find in the analyses contained in these 16 chapters is complexity, continuity, and change pertaining to race and racism in Canada. Important variation among Canada's visible minority groups is clearly established but so, too, are the subtle and not-so-subtle nuances of racism, sexism, class stratification, and social inequality. *Race and Racism in 21st-Century Canada* aims to stimulate debate about what racism is, where it requires institutional attention, and how it has been successfully addressed. It also raises crucial questions concerning what Canadian policy-makers should do to achieve a society free of racist restrictions.

NOTE FROM THE EDITORS

In *Race and Racism in 21st-Century Canada*, we present 16 papers over four sections: Theories, Concepts, Politics, and Identification; Racism and Structural Patterns of Incorporation in Canada; Articulations of Race and Gender; and Multiculturalism, Anti-Racism, and Public Policy.

Not only will this strategy generate debate and force us to sharpen our data and argument, but it will also put us in a better collective position to influence and develop effective policy frameworks. In the end, regardless of methodological, conceptual, personal, or professional differences, all the contributors to this book are committed to ending racism and to forging sound anti-racist and social justice policy awareness.

Although a considerable body of conceptual literature on race and racism is now available, a number of arguments still need to be made. In particular, there exists a pervasive tendency in the literature to conceptualize race as a social construct and racialization as the process of socially designating racial identities. However, this conceptual thinking is not able to sustain itself when followed through to its logical conclusion. Throughout the book, we also rehearse basic lessons on racism that are all but ignored in the contemporary literature, namely, that the social practice of racism is not constitutional to any one group of people. In short, before sound empirical work can be done—work to inform policy—we need clarity on what we are dealing with.

PART ONE
Theories, Concepts, Politics, and Identification

INTRODUCTION

Over the last two decades, scholarly debate about the analytical value of the race concept has persisted. On the one hand, there is a group of writers who reject the concept of race analytically on the grounds that it is a scientific myth whose continued use in scholarly analysis hides more than it reveals about human variation. They conceptualize race as a temporal historical construct caught up in material forces of production, and they seek to explain why, and under what conditions, racial identities become salient. While these writers are not oblivious to the experiential, everyday significance of race and racism, they are foremost concerned to explain how understandings of race change, what social forces encourage groups of human beings to lay claim to racial identities, and what changing forms of race categorization tell us about patterns of human group classification and distinction.

On the other hand, a second group of researchers seeks to explain the ways in which racial identities are experienced, internalized, and lived. While they accept the argument that race is a historical, scientific myth and that the contents of race classification change through time, they nevertheless invoke Thomas and Thomas's (1928) dictum that if men [sic] define social situations as real, then these situations are real in their consequences. For this group of writers, it matters neither if race is "real" in a biological sense nor if cultural understandings of race change. What does matter is that people believe that race is real in the present context and that they use race as an organizing principle of social life. Race, in this latter regard, is understood as "socially real" even if there is no biological justification to divide the world's population into discrete racial categories; for this group, current patterns of race signification are the primary focus of research.

In this section, four chapters explore the complexity of racial identification and analysis. In the first, Sean P. Hier offers a broad assessment of research on race and racism in 21st-century Canada. Encouraging a comprehensive framework that makes the best of "race retention" and "race rejection" approaches, Hier contends that contemporary debates about the status of race and the prevalence of racism are a place to begin dialogue and debate. For Hier, there should be no disagreement about the meaning of race and racism, although researchers should assess the multidimensional realities of racial categorization and race-based patterns of incorporation.

In Chapter 2, Robert Carter situates conceptual debates about the analytical value of race in the context of wider debates about the influences of social structure and human agency. He points out that it is foolish for researchers to deny race as a social reality. People have ideas about race, he explains, just as they have ideas about class and gender. This does not mean that race is real in a biological or scientific sense, however. Ideas about race, just like ideas about class or gender, are simply ideas. Race ideas matter to people in their everyday affairs, and this makes ideas about race a significant concern for social analysis. Focusing on race in social analysis does not mean that race is real in an analytical or ontological way. The scientific community has come to this conclusion, says Carter, but social scientists have confused the analytical significance of race with its experiential significance.

After exploring certain popular perspectives in ethnic and racial studies, Carter introduces critical or sociological realism as a viable alternative to remedy the conceptual and theoretical problems with current approaches. Sociological realism is particularly useful, he explains, because it is able to differentiate levels or domains of analysis. This differentiation is crucial in ethnic and racial studies because it allows us to theorize the mutually influential relations between structure and agency. Up to this point, social analysts have not adequately addressed agency in studies of race and racism, and this has as much to do with continuing debates about the race concept as it does with continuing debates about the power of the social sciences.

Whereas Carter foregrounds social scientific analysis in the study of race and racism, placing in the background the experiential dimensions of race, George Dei turns the tables in the next chapter. For Dei, race is an epistemic reality that cannot be silenced by the "intellectual gymnastics" of certain researchers. Although he recognizes the importance of historical and theoretical work, Dei affirms that race retains a salience that must be acknowledged and spoken about. He also affirms that it is indispensable to analyses of racism. He points to the dangers of anti-essentialist scholarship—namely, the silencing of diverse voices—and he maintains that neither race nor racism can be separated in scholarly analyses.

1 | STUDYING RACE AND RACISM IN 21st-CENTURY CANADA[1]

Sean P. Hier

A PLACE TO BEGIN

In his assessment of current issues in ethnic and racial studies, Michael Banton (2005) argues that the field lacks coherence. Too often, he says, research is influenced by interrelated personal, political, conceptual, and methodological biases that do not fully address the complexity of racism and ethno-racial categorization. There is nothing new about situated knowledge or disciplinary-specific ways of knowing, Banton acknowledges; what is new, he contends, is the dearth of scholarly exchange between researchers with opposing if not antagonistic points of view. This lack of exchange is problematic: without progressive open discussion and debate to counterbalance one another's biases—a hallmark of the production of scholarly knowledge—groups of researchers with increasingly narrow research interests pose only certain kinds of questions and generate only certain kinds of answers (often outside the pages of refereed periodicals). For Banton, deeper levels of understanding in ethnic and racial studies will only be realized if researchers stop distancing themselves from evidence and ways of knowing that do not fit comfortably with their own data and argumentation.

The substance of Banton's arguments was not lost on John Stuart Mill (1991 [1859]) when he ruminated about the liberty of thought and discussion in the mid 19th century. According to Mill, in order to achieve clarity of thought and conviction of opinion, we must seek out and engage with opposing points of view. The dangers of failing to engage with viewpoints that are incompatible with our own are two-fold: first, true opinions or arguments might be silenced by authoritative bodies or the "tyranny of the majority" (Mill 1991 [1859]: 20–61); second, those who hold true opinions might not fully understand the reasons why their opinions are true. In the first case, when a group of people silences opposing viewpoints and argumentation, or when they refuse to engage in discussion and debate with people who voice arguments different from their own, they assume that their own arguments are infallible. For Mill, a person or group of people cannot claim to espouse an irrefutable opinion by silencing dissent or ignoring contradictory forms of evidence; rather, they must subject their own arguments and evidence to discussion and debate. In the second case, the struggle to achieve conviction of opinion does not only involve proving one's own arguments, it also involves disproving others' arguments. In the process of engaging with counter-argumentation, Mill insisted, opposing parties, equally confident of their infallibility, should come to realize that their own opinions and the opinions of others only partially capture the complexity of social reality. To realize higher degrees of insight, or to more fully understand social phenomena in their complexity, he concluded that liberty of thought and discussion is indispensable to sound intellectual inquiry.

Mill's lessons about the liberty of thought and discussion are an instructive place to begin addressing research on race and racism in 21st-century Canada. On the one hand, many researchers lay claim to the pervasiveness of "institutional" or "systemic" racism in Canadian cultural and institutional life. Guided by a general set of assumptions that racism traces foremost to cultural and normative patterns of misrecognition or devaluation, yet also reverberates throughout the political-economic structure of society, they argue that race and racism are lived or experiential everyday realities. For these researchers, race cannot be subordinated to any other social indicator (e.g., class); to question the significance of race or the pervasiveness of racism is, for them, a rationalization or denial (Henry and Tator 2006). On the other hand, a second group of researchers is producing a growing body of evidence that contests the extent to which the social category of race functions as an irrefutable determinant for the inequitable distribution of services and resources in Canada. Guided by a general set of assumptions that racism traces foremost to political-economic structures, yet also reverberates throughout the cultural and normative codes of society, they argue that participation in Canadian institutional life is not in any absolute sense shaped by racial designations. For these researchers, race is often overplayed at the expense of class differences; they contend that there is as much variation among members of the same visible minority groups as there is between different groups (Levitt 1997; Satzewich 1998). Although both sets of researchers share an interest in addressing, exposing, challenging, and overcoming racism, they differ in the ways in which they measure racism and, consequently, the extent to which they acknowledge racism as a determinant of the life chances of members of Canada's diverse populations.

It is true that many studies convincingly demonstrate the lived or experiential realities of racism in different Canadian institutional spaces such as education, immigration, labour, and cultural production (Das Gupta 1996; Henry, Tator, and Mattis 1997; Kelly 1998; Calliste and Dei 2000). It is equally true that many studies convincingly demonstrate that the degree of participation in institutional spaces is not uniformly determined by ancestral origin or skin colour (Li 1996; Simmons and Plaza 1997; Davies and Guppy 1998; Hum and Simpson 1999; Walters, White, and Maxim 2004). While both research orientations offer valuable insights into some of the ways that race and racism manifest in Canada, it is counterproductive to assume that one orientation offers forms of evidence that are better or more objective than the other. Too often, we favour certain forms of evidence in order to arrive at the "truth" about social life (e.g., statistical data over interview data), and too often we assume that certain ways of knowing are better or more reliable than others (e.g., interpretive or experiential social research conducted by people of colour versus research conducted by "white" people). Competing claims about the extent of racism in Canada are not ends in themselves; they are a place to begin asking deeper and more challenging questions. Why, for example, do contradictions exist in the empirical literature on race and racism? How do research assumptions produce different kinds of knowledge about racism in Canada? What is racism and how does it operate in different social domains? Are there connections to be established between different groups of research findings? How or in what ways are different forms of evidence compatible? And how do our understandings of racism influence anti-racist interventions?

The purpose of this book is to bring greater clarity to the study of race and racism in 21st-century Canada. Assembling contributions that are not commonly considered side by side, *Race and Racism in 21st-Century Canada* illustrates that the problem with continuing to frame research on racism in either/or terms—racism either exists in a certain area of Canadian life or it does not— is that researchers fail to achieve a depth of insight that is otherwise obtainable. By staging debate among researchers who interact infrequently, the book makes an effort to clarify arguments, refine concepts, and address data and evidence that are otherwise treated discretely in social research. As noted above, there is an impulse for researchers to assume the mantle of truth and to lay claim to how things "really are"—a tendency shared with areas of study outside ethnic and racial studies. The ways in which such claims are arrived at, however, are rarely balanced or empirically holistic (cf. Hier and Walby 2006). There is also a growing impulse on the part of some scholars of colour to claim that their voices are the only voices that should be heard in research on race and racism. It matters who speaks about certain aspects of race and racism, and it matters that we take seriously the social and cultural contexts in which discourse on race and racism unfolds. But research on race and racism is not a zero-sum game: as more scholars focus their research attention on race and racism, the project of anti-racism and social justice will only be strengthened. Rather than moralizing on who is able to ascertain "the truth" about racism, under what conditions, and in what contexts, and rather than excluding forms of evidence that do not support our respective positions, anti-racist and social justice advocates are encouraged to come together as one group of researchers to shed light on different dimensions of race, racism, and social inclusion or exclusion in the country. This is not to suggest that one group of researchers can or should speak *for* other groups but rather that we can and should speak *to* one another.

WAYS OF KNOWING

Countless studies begin with the assumption that racism is a fact of Canadian social life. This study is no different. Racism is a serious, enduring fact requiring sustained analytical and political attention. Acknowledging racism as a fact of social life, however, is not an end in itself. It is, rather, a place to begin to ask deeper, more analytical questions about the nature of race and racism. Too often researchers implicitly assume that racism is a single phenomenon or an objective state of affairs that can be studied and known through the application of only certain research methods (e.g., interviews, opinion surveys, discourse analysis, analyses of quantitative data sets). This tendency persists despite the current obsession with the concept of "racisms" to signify the many ways that racism manifests and, by implication, the multiple research strategies required to capture its complexity. Documenting the different manifestations of racism is undoubtedly crucial for achieving a full understanding of racism in Canada. As we develop policy recommendations and strategies of resistance, we must also document the multidimensional existence of racism. But documenting racism—an exercise that yields inconsistent results—is only one part of the process, no matter which methods (or how many) are used. It is equally important to develop general explanations for what racism is, to theorize the complex and multifaceted processes under study (e.g., racial classification, class formation, racialization), and to formulate strategies for what can and should be done to achieve a fair and equitable society. In other words, it is important to assess "what is," but it is also important to develop a comprehensive understanding of what we are studying, how we are able to ascertain knowledge about it, and what can be done to improve our communities and societies.

Research findings are influenced by the questions we pose. These, in turn, are influenced by the theoretical and conceptual assumptions we make about phenomena being studied and, concomitantly, by the efficacy of certain research methods to reveal answers to our questions. While these explanatory issues are by no means unique to contemporary ethnic and racial studies, investigations of race and racism increasingly lack serious attention granted to theoretical, conceptual, and, consequently, methodological matters. Although important conceptual and theoretical debates defined the field of ethnic and racial studies in the 1980s and early 1990s (see, for example, Miles 1982, 1989; Rex and Mason 1986; Anthias 1990; Collins 1990; Allahar 1993), theories and concepts are increasingly glossed over or referenced in a perfunctory manner. At the very least, the lack of care granted to epistemology—the presuppositions and foundations for how we know what we know—limits the extent to which research is able to document and explain the complexities of race and racism. At the very worst, it obscures the field of inquiry, restricts the effectiveness of policy development, and contributes to the further polarization of empirical research findings.

To make sense of these tensions in the empirical literature on race and racism, it is useful if somewhat overly simplistic to differentiate two analytical research orientations that predominate in social research generally: social critique versus social comment. The distinction should be construed to denote the basic constitution of two general analytical frameworks that inform the ways in which empirical research is conducted. The intellectual orientation of social critique is concerned to explain *why* the social world is configured the way it is. Critique involves rigorous theoretical, conceptual, empirical, and methodological analyses, and it seeks cultural, historical, and physical explanations for why people do the things they do. Scholars interested in social critique are not content to explain reality exclusively on the basis of individuals' subjective accounts or on the basis of aggregate patterns of group social incorporation; rather, they pursue wider and more complicated explanations for why individuals understand reality the way they do and why the social world is stratified in certain inequitable ways.

The intellectual orientation of social comment, by contrast, entails the collection and dissemination of information about how people experience, interpret, and live in the world. Some scholars working with this general orientation document what people say and how they interpret their claims using qualitative research strategies, and they invoke the interpretivist logic that what is real is only what people experience as real. Others working in this field use quantitative research strategies to attempt to document the degree to which groups of people with certain shared characteristics (e.g., skin colour) are able to access valued resources (e.g., jobs, income). For this latter group, what is real is only what can be documented statistically.

Although the general research orientations of social comment and social critique entail investigative strategies that are indispensable to gaining a complete understanding of race and racism in Canada, neither encompasses a standard set of processes that can be used to discover "truths" in an objective social world. Instead, both orientations are comprised of diverse assumptions that enact "the social" in ways that enter into every stage of the research process. However, despite the importance of both research strategies, social comment has increasingly overshadowed social critique as a framework for scholarly investigation. This predominance applies to both qualitative and quantitative research orientations. It is often the case that qualitative researchers are accused of abandoning the principles of social critique under the guise of "race essentialism" and the politicization of difference, but quantitative researchers who use "race" as a categorical variable in regression analyses with little care for the historical, cultural, and experiential nuances of racial designations are also guilty of race essentialism. Quantitative empirical research cannot ignore the insights of theoretical and qualitative research, but qualitative research cannot remain blind to the insights gleaned through quantitative analyses. Both kinds of analysis, moreover, cannot ignore wider historical, theoretical, and conceptual issues pertaining to race, racism, and the multiple dimensions of social incorporation.

It is often the case that data gleaned from studies capturing only one portion of social reality are presented in the absence of other forms of data in order to generalize or make grand claims about racism in Canada. Scholars too readily accept the partial perspective as a valid way of knowing about race and racism *sui generis*. This has the effect of obscuring the value of the partial perspective, whose significance is realized in conjunction with other partial perspectives, whether qualitative or quantitative in orientation. While the empirical quantitative and qualitative realities of race and racism are indisputably important to investigators, both research orientations too readily confuse what requires explanation with an explanation itself. That is, they accept the manifestations or effects of a deeper and more endemic set of relations as ends themselves, and they take as fact what actually requires explanation. Again, this is not to deny the significance of lived reality in its textured or demographic forms but rather to affirm that partial perspectives cannot be used to close down further argumentation and debate.

We find ourselves, therefore, confronted with certain dilemmas in the exercise of conducting social research on race and racism. Do we develop explanations for *why* discourses of race and patterns of racism persist? Or do we document and observe *how* people experience racial identities and patterns of racist exclusion? Do we examine why people adopt certain racial identities and are constrained by certain racist exclusions at particular historical moments? Or do we accept historically specific racial identities and racist exclusions as given and design our studies to measure the effects of racial designation? In short, is the purpose of scholarly inquiry into race and racism social critique or social comment?

Our responses to these questions must break from the logic of duality transmitted through "either/or" thinking to embrace the logic of complexity captured in "both/and" thinking. We require explanations for *both* why racism persists and how or in what ways it manifests at particular historical moments, *and* we require attention to many other historically informed dimensions as well. Among these latter are the questions of how race became a viable concept in qualitative and quantitative analyses, how it has changed over time, and what benefits and limitations are associated with using race in social research. A second issue is to address and explain contradiction within qualitative and quantitative research interventions. In other words, it is crucial to document and explain the different ways in which people individually and collectively experience and are constrained or enabled by the everyday world (social comment), but it is equally important to resist the temptation to explain social phenomena on a single historical articulation exclusively, ignoring other partial perspectives. This argument is not presented with the expectation that researchers interested in contemporary patterns of race and racism will abandon partial perspectives in favour of producing comprehensive, multidimensional investigations. It is presented, however, with the hope that researchers have the courage, strength, and humility to address ways of knowing and forms of evidence that are different from their own without resorting to rhetorical arguments, politicized identities, moralized research strategies, and dogmatic claims that fail to advance scholarship and understanding in a holistic manner.

CONCEPTUAL PARAMETERS

It will become clear throughout this book that cleavages in the empirical literature on racism in Canada are at least partially influenced by the ways in which the race concept is applied and understood in scholarly research (i.e., epistemological assumptions). While epistemological disagreement about the significance and usefulness of race in scholarly research is widespread, there should be no disagreement about the basic conceptual parameters of race, racism, and related concepts. That is, scholars might not agree on how to study race or measure racism, and they might not agree on the political importance of certain ways of knowing. We must, however, develop a general set of conceptual parameters to understand the basic foundations of what we are investigating, irrespective of what specific dimensions of race and racism we seek to gauge in our individual research projects. We also must develop an agreed-upon set of concepts so we all mean the same thing by race, racialization, racism, etc. To this end, we now turn to a general overview of key concepts and terms. The nuances and complexities to be found within these conceptual parameters—nuances that pose implications for empirical research findings—are worked out in the chapters to follow.

The Signification of Difference

There is a scholarly consensus that race is neither a natural nor biological feature of groups of human beings. Biologists, physical anthropologists, and population geneticists generally agree that there is little empirical value to be derived from using the race concept to infer the social, intellectual, moral, and political aptitude of groups of human beings. What this means is that there is no convincing evidence that biological or genetic inheritance constitutes the parameters for one's social or cultural capabilities. From the writings of William Edward Burghardt Du Bois to the contributions of Cornel West, influential thinkers in the social sciences and humanities have been quick to reproduce these arguments and contend that the category of race is a social construct whose significance is bound up with history, Western European science, and the cultural signification of diverse groups of people. Race, in other words, is neither a natural nor scientifically accurate way to classify and order the world's human population; it is a cultural signifier that hides more than it reveals about human variation.

However, many of those same thinkers in the social sciences and humanities who denounce race as a Western European social construct and as a product of 19th-century pseudo-science call upon the race concept to signify human group differences. That is, although a wide range of scholars associated with anti-racist and social justice movements denounces race as a cultural scientific myth, many retain race on the basis of its utility as an organizing social principle. They argue that even though race is a biological myth, it nevertheless has social value in the context of European post-colonial relations of oppression and exploitation.

As Vic Satzewich notes in Chapter 4, while almost all researchers acknowledge that the race category is a social construct, they part company in their interpretations of what the social construction of race implies. One group of scholars, noted above, retains race as an analytical category. They tend to adopt a normative or interpretive approach to the study of race, and they attempt to measure the experiential dimensions of living in a society that places great faith in racial distinctions. The normative deployment of the race concept, moreover, applies equally to qualitative and quantitative research designs. A second group of researchers rejects race as an analytical category on the grounds that deploying race in scholarly research reproduces and validates the dangerous pseudo-scientific ideological belief system that the world's population can be meaningfully and accurately separated along racial lines. Given the enduring rift over the analytical utility of race, it is crucial to begin by developing a general understanding of the basic conceptual parameters of race beyond any single application.

Contrary to popular belief, the concept of race is not very old. The first recorded use of race in the written English language traces to 1508 AD (Banton 1998). What this means is that race, as one of many discourses used to represent human diversity, is no more than 500 years old (significantly less than 1 per cent of the time of human existence on the planet). Race classifications originated from, but have not necessarily remained, dialectical Western European discourses of human categorization, whereby social groups are "imagined" to be different from one another, usually based on the signification of somatic or phenotypic characteristics (Miles and Brown 2003). The differences are "imagined" because the vast majority of people whom we conceptualize as racially different from (and similar to) ourselves are people we have never actually encountered. For example, when 16th-century European explorers and colonists encountered groups of human beings whom they perceived to look and act differently than they did, these others were "experienced others" (Miles and Brown 2003: 24) for the explorers and colonists. When explorers and colonists shared their knowledge with fellow Western Europeans (e.g., through personal accounts, visual depictions, newspaper reports), however, the experience of otherness for a wider audience was based on imagination. Representations of others, racial or otherwise, are usually based on imagined differences, and the imagination of difference is just as significant today as it was in the 16th century. We only need to consider contemporary media representations of al-Qaeda terrorist cells to appreciate this point. It is possible that some readers have had first-hand, immediate experiences with members of al-Qaeda, but it is probable that most of us rely on our imaginations of difference to comprehend and represent these others.

The discourse of race, then, is only one of many discourses used to represent self and imagined/experienced others. Although race appeared in the English written language in the 16th century, it did not become popular or ubiquitous until the 19th century (less than 200 years ago). For much of the 16th to 18th centuries, the race concept was not commonly used to classify and order human beings. Based largely on colonial and imperial interactions, Western European writings were more likely to classify the peoples of Africa, Asia, and the Americas using concepts such as pagan, heathen, uncivilized, barbarian, and, particularly, non-Christian. While many of these representations were negative, some involved positive attributions based on the characteristics of strength, agility, and courage (Miles and Brown 2003). Although used infrequently during this period, the discourse of race denoted the common history or shared lineage of a group of people (Banton 1998). Skin pigmentation and other physical features (e.g., hair type) were used to signify difference and to classify groups of human beings living in geographically dispersed areas of the world. But so fluid were race discourses leading up to the 18th century that the French aristocracy employed the race concept prior to the revolution of 1789 to denote their common ancestry in France (Guillaumin 1995), and the bourgeoisie in Victorian England constructed the British working class as an inferior race (Bonnett 1998).

By the mid 19th century, there were discernable changes in the ways in which discourses of race were deployed in scientific and popular analysis. A movement generally recognized as scientific racism began to develop around 1850 that conceptualized race in terms of discrete natural biological differences between groups of human beings based on the signification of certain human physical features (most commonly skin colour). That is, after 1850 certain Western European writers and politicians increasingly used a limited range of human bodily features to signify fixed group characteristics such as morality and intelligence. The significations used to delineate different and discrete races, based on the belief in inherent differences or attributes, involved hierarchical social constructions that dialectically pitted the Western European self against the non-Western European other as, respectively, superior and inferior socially, culturally, and/or intellectually. For this reason, arguing that the only "race" is the "human race" actually negates the process by which racial representations are formed. Race classification is always dialectical: to categorize or define racial others as different from oneself is necessarily to categorize and define oneself in racial terms (cf. Miles and Brown 2003).

Still, several centuries prior to the 19th century, and surely before the year 1508, groups of human beings who were perceived by each other to look and act differently came into contact and represented one another in a variety of ways. Predating northwestern European expansion in the 15th century, for example, the ancient Mediterranean cultures of Greece and Rome were attuned to colour differences; they readily distinguished among Ethiopians, Egyptians, and certain Asian populations (cf. Hier and Bolaria 2006). But the Greeks and Romans also held Ethiopians (and Egyptians), with whom they enjoyed frequent contact, in high regard (Snowdon 1983), and representations found in Greek and Roman poems, writings, philosophy, and art do not approximate modern understandings of race and natural difference. Similarly, Egyptians in the 14th century classified human collectivities along the Nile based on hair type, and ancient Egyptian representations of Nubians (Ethiopians) clearly demarcate the latter's darker skin tone (Hier and Bolaria 2006).

Given the fact that diverse groups of human beings came into contact and represented one another on the basis of physical appearance long before the discourse of race appeared in the English language, it is crucial to understand that the signification of race difference is a specific kind of representation of self and other that takes place in a wider social process of human biological/somatic/physical differentiation. Before the race concept was popularized, groups of human beings used physical features of the body (e.g., hair texture, eye shape, body type, skin pigmentation) to classify self and others. Miles and Brown (2003: 101) identify this process as racialization: "those instances where social relations between people have been structured by the signification of human biological characteristics in such a way as to define and construct differentiated social collectivities." Considering the connotative meaning of the word, it is understandable that almost all contemporary researchers conceptualize racialization as the process of "racial" assignment or the social construction of "racial" groups. This, however, is logically and conceptually mistaken.

In Miles and Brown's assessment, racialization refers to a dialectical process of human differentiation, whereby human biological/physical characteristics are signified to define and construct "differentiated social collectivities." Those collectivities could easily be represented discursively as "ethnic groups," "religious groups," or "cultural groups." That is, we could use the physical features of the body to construct "Jews" and "Muslims," for example, without recourse to the concept of race. From a contemporary vantage point, it might be tempting to classify all of these instances of human social differentiation as racial. However, we must be aware that many of these instances of human classification predate the race discourse. To classify them as racial would be to impose a relatively recent historical discourse on social relations that predate race—a distorted form of "historical presentism." Added to which, Miles and Brown's definition can also be used to socially differentiate "men" from "women." What their definition requires is the additional stipulation that socially constructed collectivities (not races) are understood in terms of, or perceived as, real or imagined ancestral groups. The latter stipulation has nothing inherently to do with racial groups, and it is able to discern ancestral differentiations from sexual ones.

Whereas race is a specific discourse whose origins trace to the 16th century, therefore, racialization is the dialectical social process of using the physical features of the body to classify human populations along real or imagined ancestral lines. Racialization does not imply any moral judgement or evaluative assessment (i.e., positive or negative attributions). Some instances of racialization surely involve negative evaluations, but there is nothing in the definition that requires this. The concept of racialization is important analytically because if we fail to resist the temptation to conflate race and racialization, we are left with no way of differentiating historically specific, fluid discourses of race from the trans-historical social process of racialization. Put simply, racialization can be a misleading concept because it neither depends on nor does it have to be associated with a discourse of race.

Although race is a specific kind of historically variable representation that can but does not necessarily involve racialization, there are many instances in our world where cultural characteristics are used to socially construct and represent "racial groups." One of the classic examples is the attribution of Jews as victims of racial conflict based on Jewish religion and culture. The latter, of course, does not fit the definition of racialization if it involves significations based on human features other than bodily/physical characteristics. This necessitates a second concept to denote the use of socio-cultural signifiers such as religion to construct human collectivities. Miles and Brown (2003: 99) define ethnicization as "a dialectical process by which meaning is attributed to socio-cultural signifiers of human beings, as a result of which human beings may be assigned to a general category of persons that reproduces itself biologically, culturally, and economically." In a manner similar to the process of racialization, ethnicization does not only entail the social construction of distinct collectivities but also involves collectivities defined on the basis of ancestry. And in a manner similar to the race/racialization couplet, the term ethnicity is a discourse that is not required for the process of ethnicization to take place. Ethnicization is an important analytical concept to discern those instances where real or imagined ancestral groups are dialectically constructed on the basis of socio-cultural signifiers, and ethnicization can manifest in the discursive form of "race" (e.g., representing orthodox Jews as a racial group based on their dress).

To summarize, for purposes of gaining analytical clarity we need to differentiate four central concepts. Race and ethnicity are discourses or signs whose historical meaning is neither fixed nor stable. Racialization and ethnicization, by contrast, are dialectical processes of human signification involving biological or socio-cultural characteristics, respectively, in such a way as to define and construct social collectivities along real or perceived ancestral lines. Based on these conceptual distinctions, it is empirically possible to use socio-cultural characteristics (e.g., language) to discursively construct "races," and it is empirically possible to use bodily characteristics to discursively construct "ethnic groups." It follows that racialization does not rely on an explicit discourse of race (although it can invoke the race concept), and ethnicization does not rely on an explicit discourse of ethnicity (although it can invoke the ethnic concept). While racialization or ethnicization are necessary processes to classify by race or ethnicity—that is, racialization or ethnicization is involved in race and ethnic classification—processes of racialization and ethnicization are *analytically distinct* from discourses of race and ethnicity. Finally, although race discourses became popular as 19th century Western European discourses used to subordinate racially defined others, those social groups who at different moments in history have been subordinated on the basis of race have subsequently inverted its negative historical evaluation and adopted the term as a discourse of resistance (e.g., "black is beautiful"). Discourse, in short, is never fully referential in the sense that it is never final or absolute, although we should pay close attention to the ideological history of, and enduring connotations associated with, the race concept.

Racism

What, then, is racism? As Miles and Brown (2003) explain, racism should be defined by its representational content(s), not its function(s). The reason why racism is defined in terms of its representational contents is that there needs to be certain distinct features that qualify social phenomena as racism as opposed to sexism or homophobia (that is, criteria to distinguish what precisely qualifies an instance of social life as racism). When racism is defined on the basis of its functions rather than its representation content(s), we run the risk of inflating, deflating, or obscuring the meaning of the term (see Miles and Brown 2003: 57–86). For example, more than a few analysts aggregate statistical data on income levels of visible minorities to find that visible minorities as a whole earn less than Canadians generally. They conclude from these analyses that racism functions to structure inequitable pay scales in the country. This might be true, but nothing in this example has been said about what racism actually is, what specific processes produce these outcomes, and how we can address the underlying causes of inequitable pay distributions. In other words, in this example racism is understood on the basis of a function of the labour market. It is possible that factors such as immigration status, gender, ancestry, and language proficiency produce variation among the millions of people lumped together as "visible minority" (see Hum and Simpson 1999; Chapter 5 of this book). Scholars need to be open to the possibility that it might not be blanket racism that functions to drive income returns down, although that is a possibility. And they need to be aware that we cannot explain social phenomena exclusively on the basis of their effects. The latter is simply a place to begin.

Based on the representational contents of racism, certain human physical, somatic, and/or socio-cultural features are signified to identify and designate human social collectivities on the basis of ancestry or lineage, whether real or imagined. This is the process of racialization and/or ethnicization. Through these processes, one of the racialized or ethnicized populations is evaluated negatively (a negative racialization or ethnicization). This negative racialization or ethnicization involves a dialectical process of self and other, whereby the racialized or ethnicized self is attributed positive characteristics based on the signification of cultural and/or biological features and the racialized or ethnicized other is attributed negative characteristics based on similar assumptions. This set of representational processes could take the form of coherent (e.g., scientific racism) or less coherent (e.g., stereotypes or jokes) ideological articulations or institutional practices that can be demonstrated to have originally been structured by the components identified previously (and that continue to be) but which no longer articulate as an explicit ideological structure (i.e., institutional racism).

According to Miles and Brown, for negative instances of ethnicization or racialization to qualify as instances of racism, they must take place in the context of unequal social or material relations. They contend that ideologies are produced and reproduced in the context of material relations of superiority and inferiority involving one racialized or ethnicized group representing themselves more positively than others. Although the stipulation that representations of self and other must take place in the context of material relations is an important one—it helps us to explain where ideas and representations come from—it is useful to substitute "unequal material relations" with "material struggles." The rationale for this substitution is simple: if ideologies are produced and reproduced in the context of material inequality, as Miles and Brown contend (2003: 104), an inadvertent universal condition of unequal relations of power is imposed on the formation of ideology. Social inequality, however, does not presuppose ideology in an *a priori* manner. Rather, ideologies are produced in and through material struggle, and by understanding ideology in terms of struggle rather than on the basis of a universal, trans-historical condition of "material inequality," we are in a better position to theorize social change—including ideological change.

Racism, therefore, is an ideological phenomenon that is defined by its representational content (not function). It involves a negative signification (racialization/ ethnicization), whereby cultural and/or biological human characteristics are attributed to a real or perceived ancestral population on the basis of somatic, physical, or socio-cultural features. For purposes of simplification, it could be argued that racialization and ethnicization are theoretically horizontal processes of evaluation, whereas racism is a vertical process. These representational processes take place in the context of material struggle(s). They are formed through dialectical processes of self and other, to the extent that evaluations of inferiority and superiority are produced and reproduced to varying degrees of ideological articulation, intentionality, and practical adequacy. To reiterate, it is crucial to note that this definition does not allude to the function(s) of racism. It is not reducible to, nor is it dependent on, the concept of race. It allows for historically specific manifestations of racism, and it establishes a conceptual foundation for all manifestations of racism. That is, no matter how racism manifests, from instances of murder to racial stereotyping, we need to agree on a general set of criteria to diagnose racism *qua* racism (Miles and Brown 2003). In the absence of a clear conceptual understanding of race, racialization, and racism to inform empirical research, our concepts quickly become subject to indiscriminate and widespread use, they lose their precise meaning, and our analyses fail to realize their full potential.

CONCLUSION

The significance of the preceding analysis is that we need to understand clearly the terms and concepts we employ in our research and that we cannot turn away from conflict, complexity, and debate. As scholars interested in matters pertaining to race and racism, we all have different interests, goals, and political agendas. This is a positive characteristic of the diversity of scholarly inquiry. There are many ways of knowing about the social world, and there are many dimensions to the complex realities that we seek to explain. But we cannot remain blind to the fact that the literature is filled with sloppy conceptualization, narrow research interventions, and excessive claims-making that is more politically-charged than empirically and conceptually grounded. The chapters to follow paint a complex picture concerning patterns of racism and anti-racism in Canada. The time has come to embrace the complexity of research on race and racism in 21st-century Canada and to enter into a collective alliance to forge the most efficacious social policies informed by a variety of different research findings. The time has also come to embrace healthy interactive debate and to scrutinize one another's arguments in a progressive manner. The conceptualization worked out in this chapter—which is in its infancy—is one place to begin. If nothing else, the time of counterproductive polemical claims-making has past.

NOTE

1 Thanks to Kevin Walby and Hari Alluri, for taking the time to carefully critique the first draft, and to Mary Leighton for pointing out my grammatical and syntactical errors.

REFERENCES AND FURTHER READINGS

Allahar, A. 1993. More Than an Oxymoron: The Social Construction of Primordial Attachment. *Canadian Ethnic Studies* XXVI(3): 18–33.

Anthias, F. 1990. Race and Class Revisited: Conceptualizing Race and Racisms. *Sociological Review* 38(1): 19-42.

Banton, M. 1998. *Racial Theories*. Cambridge: Cambridge University Press.

——. 2005. Finding, and Correcting, My Mistakes. *Sociology* 39(3): 463–79.

Bonnett, Alastair. 1998. How the British Working Class Became White: The Symbolic (Re)formation of Racialized Capitalism. *Journal of Historical Sociology* (11)3: 316–40.

Calliste, A., and G. Dei. 2000. *Anti-Racist Feminism: Critical Studies in Race and Gender*. Halifax: Fernwood.

Collins, P. 1990. *Black Feminist Thought: Knowledge, Consciousness, and the Politics of Empowerment*. New York: Routledge.

Das Gupta, T. 1996. *Racism and Paid Work*. Toronto: Garamond.

Davies, S., and N. Guppy. 1998. Race and Canadian Education. In V. Satzewich, ed., *Racism and Social Inequality in Canada*. Toronto: Thompson Educational Publishing. 131–55.

Dei, G.J.S. 1996. Black/African Canadian Students' Perspectives on School Racism. In M. Ibrahim, ed., *Racism in Canadian Schools*. Toronto: Harcourt-Brace. 241–57.

Guillaumin, C. 1995. *Racism, Sexism, Power, and Ideology*. London: Routlege.

Henry, F., and C. Tator. 2006. *The Colour of Democracy: Racism in Canadian Society*. 3rd ed. Toronto: Harcourt-Brace.

Henry, F., C. Tator, and W. Mattis. 1997. *Challenging Racism in the Arts*. Toronto: University of Toronto Press.

Hier, S., and S. Bolaria. 2006. Identities Without Guarantees. In S. Hier and S. Bolaria, eds., *Identity and Belonging: Rethinking Race and Ethnicity in Canadian Society*. Toronto: Canadian Scholars' Press. 1–18.

Hier, S., and K. Walby. 2006. Competing Analytical Paradigms in the Sociological Study of Racism in Canada. *Canadian Ethnic Studies* 26(1): 83-104.

Hum, D., and W. Simpson. 1999. Wage Opportunities for Visible Minorities in Canada. *Canadian Public Policy* 25(3): 379–94.

Kelly, J. 1998. *Under the Gaze: Learning to be Black in White Society*. Halifax: Fernwood.

Levitt, C. 1997. The Morality of Race in Canada. *Society* 34(6): 40–47.

Li, P. 1996. *The Making of Post-War Canada*. Toronto: Oxford University Press.

MacInnis, J. 2004. The Sociology of Identity: Social Science or Social Comment? *British Journal of Sociology* 55(4): 531–44.

Miles, R. 1982. *Racism and Migrant Labour*. New York: Routledge.

——. 1989. *Racism*. London: Routledge.

Miles, R., and M. Brown. 2003. *Racism*. 2nd ed. London: Routledge.

Mill, J.S. 1991 [1859]. *On Liberty and Other Essays*. Oxford: Oxford University Press.

Rex, J., and D. Mason (eds.). 1986. *Theories of Race and Ethnic Relations.* Cambridge: Cambridge University Press.

Satzewich, V. 1998. *Racism and Social Inequality in Canada: Concepts, Controversies, and Strategies of Resistance.* Toronto: Thompson Educational Publishing.

Simmons, A., and D. Plaza. 1997. Breaking Through the Glass Ceiling: The Pursuit of University Training Among African-Caribbean Migrants and their Children in Toronto. *Canadian Ethnic Studies* 30(3): 99–120.

Snowdon, Frank. 1983. *Before Color Prejudice: The Ancient View of Blacks.* Boston: Harvard University Press.

Walters, D., J. White, and P. Maxim. 2004. Does Postsecondary Education Benefit Aboriginal Canadians? An Examination of Earnings and Employment Outcomes for Recent Aboriginal Graduates. *Canadian Public Policy* 30(3): 283–302.

2 | PROSPECTS FOR A POST-RACE SOCIOLOGY

Robert Carter

INTRODUCTION

Concepts of race continue to be extensively used to describe human populations in North America and the United Kingdom (UK). For example, in a speech considering the bombings in London on 7 July 2005, the Chair of the Commission for Racial Equality, Trevor Phillips, wondered how much these events had "changed the prospects for race relations in Britain?" (Phillips 2005). In the United States (US), the American Sociological Association (ASA) recently published its deliberations on whether social researchers should continue to use concepts of race. Their report, entitled "The Importance of Collecting Data and Doing Social Scientific Research on Race" (ASA 2003), concluded that they should. More recently still, Dawkins (2004) has argued for the evolutionary relevance of race categories on the grounds that they act as guides in mate selection.

In this chapter, I argue that the discredited ontological status of race raises doubts about the continued use of the race concept in sociological research; once discredited as a scientific description of objective features of human populations, its employment as a sociological category unavoidably entails a conflation of structure and agency, making a sociological account of the structure-agency interplay impossible. I begin by considering two popular sociological accounts using a concept of race—one focused on agency and the other on structure. I shall argue that the differentiation of agency and structure leads to an individualized and oversocialized account of social reality. In the next section, I suggest that sociological realism better explains the structure-agency relation and that realism is able to analyze the mutually influential relations among structure and agency. I conclude that the resources for a post-race sociology are available, but that their exploitation depends as much on the readiness of sociologists to defend the relevance of social science as it does on the explanatory advantages of sociological realism.

SOCIOLOGY AND THE CONCEPT OF RACE

What does "race" mean? "Race" is a concept used in the description of human differences; it is a constituent of various propositions or claims about the world. Whether the concept is a significant constituent of such propositions, and whether it is explicitly formulated, is a matter for empirical judgements. However, such judgements are difficult for a variety of reasons. People frequently disguise their motives, mostly intentionally but sometimes not; they may not be able to formulate their ideas in a readily accessible way; and the relation between behavioural outcome and motivational intent is commonly opaque.

Note that in this account there is no need to agree on a definition of what is meant by the term *race* beyond what people have generally taken it to mean, namely, the division of human populations into discrete groups (i.e., "races") whose characteristics are, to an important degree, unalterable and unique. This description of human differences *as a description* is no more a cognitive error than, say, a description of such differences in terms of income, sexual orientation, religion, attitudes towards global warming, or abortion. It is merely one of the many resources by means of which people negotiate a social world comprising all sorts of differences.

However, social research is a task (like many other tasks) requiring that we discriminate between descriptions. Indeed, when social researchers fail to discriminate, they are involved in a radical performative contradiction: to fail to discriminate is to deny any epistemic authority to social research itself (surely a matter of central interest to funders and sponsors); in researching topics such as racism and discrimination, they seem to be committed to the view that a racist description of the world is epistemically indistinguishable from a non-racist one, a conclusion unlikely to reassure those who wish for a more engaged and public role for social science.

Key to avoiding this contradiction—that is, by providing us with the means (albeit not straightforward or effortless) to discriminate between concepts and theories—is sociological discourse itself, the broader context of reasoning within which sociological concepts and theories are located. "Scientists are confident in their usage of particular terms," notes Pawson (1989: 236), "not because they have some once-and-for-all conceptual anchorage, but because they are entrenched in a formal network of concepts." The validity of sociological concepts, then, is defined by their capacity to explain and analyze social reality, not to their employment in everyday life or their capacity to evoke understanding based on commonsense usage. It is at this point that the concept of race comes unstuck.

The Collapse of the Ontological Status of Race

Race ideas have a relatively recent provenance, only coming to occupy a prominent place in both popular and scientific discourses during the 18th and 19th centuries (Kohn 1996; Malik 1996; Miles 1989). The racial taxonomies developed by Victorian scientists were based either on phenotypes (broadly speaking, physical features) or on loose notions about "blood" and descent. However, it proved difficult to ground these taxonomies in a coherent and convincing set of principles, a difficulty that arose directly from the failure to identify how a person's race might be determined. Evolutionary theory, by demonstrating that phenotypical features were merely a consequence of adaptive evolutionary strategies, revealed the concern with phenotypes to be radically misplaced: phenotypical features were a contingent, superficial, and wholly unreliable basis for scientific classification.

If races could not be defined on the basis of observable physical characteristics, then only some internal, non-observable criterion would do. The central difficulty with this scheme was that science was unable to locate a genotypical basis for classifying races. Indeed, it has become evident with the growth in genomic knowledge that existing models of racial categorizations cannot accommodate either the complexity of human genetic variation or the universality of humankind. Hence the now banal observation that individuals from one "race" are often more similar genomically speaking to individuals in other "races" than they are to other individuals in the same "race." In essence, it had become clear in the scientific community that race had no certain referent and that for scientific purposes the term was at best confusing and at worst misleading and tendentious (Jones 1997; Jorde and Wooding 2004; Rose and Rose 2005). Consequently, scientists have largely abandoned race ideas on the grounds that they are unhelpful and inaccurate descriptions of human social and cultural variation.

The conclusions of natural scientists concerning the ambiguous ontological status of races also carried implications for social scientists. Given that the idea of race was no longer viewed by scientists as a compelling part of the scientific lexicon, should sociologists review their use of the term? Broadly speaking, the responses of sociologists to the demise of race as a scientific concept have taken two forms. The first response is to insist that race concepts are a key part of the interpretative strategies employed by people to negotiate everyday social life. In so far as this is the case, it is argued that social researchers can legitimately and without confusion refer to the study of such strategies as the study of race. The second response is that race ideas are discursively produced and, thus, socially constructed descriptions whose effect is to produce particular sorts of objects (races are a product of discourses about race), particular modes of understanding, and particular forms of subjectivity. Of course, these approaches are neither discrete nor mutually exclusive (they are even sometimes conjoined; see Knowles 2003), but they are distinctive in their emphasis.

The first response identified above I shall term the phenomenological or interactionist approach. It focuses on the crucial role of meaning in the management and negotiation of social life. Although this stress on the meaningful nature of social action derives principally from the work of Max Weber, it was Robert Park who applied it to the study of social relations between people marked out politically as belonging to distinct groups. Park insisted that, while the term race had scant scientific credibility, it nevertheless enjoyed widespread popular use (Park 1950) and was profoundly embedded in everyday life—in school curricula, political commentary, social policy, and the mass media. As a result, "race" was deployed as a powerful organizing principle of everyday experience. Not only did this mean that ideas about race and races held a quotidian, taken-for-granted status, but also that such ideas provided a motivational basis for social action. W.I. Thomas observed years ago that if men [sic] define situations as real, they are real in their consequences (Thomas and Thomas 1970). This insight proved both seductively straightforward (many people believe in notions of race and in the idea of races and, in so far as they do, may act on the basis of such beliefs) and academically productive, since debates about the ontological status of race could be disregarded. What mattered was whether, and in what circumstances, people believed "races to be real."

The appeal of this strategy has been far reaching. For instance, in its document explaining why sociologists should continue to study what they refer to as race, ASA argued that:

> Individuals and social institutions evaluate, rank, and ascribe behaviours to individuals on the basis of their presumed race ... Sociologists are interested in explaining how and why social definitions of race persist and change. They also seek to explain the nature of power relationships between and among racial groups, and to understand more fully the nature of belief systems about race. (ASA 2003: 5)

There is a distinctively Parkian tone to this statement, expressed in the move from the unexceptionable observation that many people negotiate the social world on the basis of presumptions about "race" to the wholly contentious claim that there are power relationships between "racial groups."

As I have argued elsewhere (Carter 2000), the phenomenological approach, especially in the form developed by Park, is mistaken. It conflates an empirical claim—namely, that people use ideas about race both to interpret social situations and settings, and to assess, and possibly discriminate against, other people—with an assertion that researching this empirical claim is research into *race* rather than research into people's *beliefs* about race. The implication that race is a real phenomenon into which research might be conducted carries important consequences: it reaffirms popular notions about the continuing relevance of race ideas to the understanding of contemporary social relations, a relevance further emphasized by the incorporation of these notions into social policy ("race relations legislation," "racial equality programs"; see, for example, Morning and Sabbagh 2005 and Potvin 2005). It also reduces explanations of the social world to the interpretations people have of that world. In the ASA statement, as in Park's work, there is no account of how we get from the ideas people might have about particular forms of human difference to the existence of "racial groups" (a similar argument can also be made about ethnicity).

The second common sociological response to the ontological collapse of the race concept—race ideas are discursively produced (and thus socially constructed) descriptions whose effect is to produce particular sorts of objects—avoids this difficulty. However, it does so at the expense of what is the strength of the interactionist approach, namely, its concern with what people think and how this shapes their social interactions and influences the social networks that they form on the basis of such interactions. A theory of racism and discrimination that is compelling should be able to determine who is doing what to whom; it requires a sociologically adequate notion of human agency. This is conspicuously lacking in the "race as discourse" approach. Nevertheless, the approach does have merits of its own.

To begin with, old debates about whether race differences are natural or real are displaced in favour of an emphasis on exploring the discursive construction of race ideas in different social and political settings. Not only does this strategy historicize the deployment of such ideas, challenging simple notions about their purity or the uniqueness of the political projects they are used to pursue, it also emphasizes that categories of race are social constructions and products of social and scientific discourses. The possibilities for challenging the fixity of race categorizations and developing less rigid descriptions of human differences are thus enhanced, while the central difficulty facing the interactionists, that of accounting for the formation of "racial groups," is resolved: race concepts and their cognates—racial groups, race relations, mixed-race people—are the effects of particular sorts of discourses.

Despite these advantages, the "race as discourse" approach runs into similar problems, and it reproduces similar shortcomings to the "race as everyday experience" line. And this is because it uses notions of race (and ethnicity) in very much the same way. For example, Omi and Winant's popular text, *Racial Formation in the United States*, is concerned with "how concepts of race are created and changed, how they became the focus of political conflict, and how they have come to permeate US society" (Omi and Winant 1994: vii). They argue that "race is a concept which signifies and symbolises social conflicts and interests by referring to different types of human bodies" (55). Unquestionably, then, race is a social construct: races are discursively produced "imagined communities." Yet, Omi and Winant suggest that race is a social construct capable of cutting across class lines as well as dividing classes internally (32); it has its own dynamics which "must be understood as determinants of class relationships and indeed class identities, not as mere consequences of these relationships" (34); and race is "One of the first things we notice about people when we meet ... them ..." (59).

These are extraordinary powers to claim for a social construct. Indeed, as Banton (2005) has recently acknowledged, a social construct cannot serve as the basis of a social theory. The same author has also pointed out that no-one has ever seen another person's race (Banton 1997): you may "see" a person with somatic or physiognomic features different from your own, but it is the racist who insists that such features are a person's "race." In fact, despite Omi and Winant's self-conscious distancing from Marxism, their account has some family resemblances to its more structuralist forms, most notably in their theory of "racial formation." As they argue:

society is suffused with racial projects, large and small, to which all are subjected. This racial "subjection" is quintessentially ideological. Everybody learns
some combination, some version, of the rules of racial classification, and of her
own racial destiny, often without obvious teaching or conscious inculcation.
Thus we are inserted in a comprehensively racialized social structure. (Omi and
Winant 1994: 60)

As with forms of mechanistic Marxism, "we" are inculcated into thinking
"racially"; a racialized social structure determines human agency. We now have
the obverse of the lacuna facing the phenomenologists and interactionists: whereas
they found it difficult to move from how people interpreted the world to the
structural forms and features of that world, Omi and Winant find it difficult to
move in the opposite direction. To insist that everybody is inserted into a racialized
social structure is to fashion too broad a sword for filleting out the complexities
of human agency and the many ways in which it has the capacity for modifying
social contexts.

More recently, Goldberg has developed related ideas into the notion of the
"racial state." In Goldberg's account, the racial state is defined in "racial terms"
(Goldberg 2002: 34), that is, a state which is ordered "by, in, and through race"
(96). It is not clear what exactly this might mean, however, since the race concept
itself is undefined. The central point that Goldberg presumably wishes to establish is that ideas about race can become embedded in dominant forms of representation and modes of signification. In this way, such ideas powerfully influence
social action, and so shape social policy and the operation of state institutions.
These are important insights, but they are concealed under claims about the
omnipotent reach of the racial state, whose invincibility is vividly recognized by
Goldberg himself:

> In states that are racially conceived, ordered, administered, and regulated, the
> racial state could be said to be everywhere. And simultaneously seen nowhere.
> It (invisibly) defines almost every relation, contours virtually all intercourse. It
> fashions not just the said and the sayable, the done and doable, possibilities
> and impermissibilities, but penetrates equally the scope and quality, content
> and character of social silences and presumptions. The state in its racial reach
> and expression is thus at once super-visible in form and force and thoroughly
> invisible in its osmotic infusion into the everyday, its penetration into common
> sense, its pervasion (not to mention perversion) of the warp and weave of the
> social fabric. (Goldberg 2002: 98)

The behemoth of the racial state represents the elimination of human agency;
human subjectivity is the product of an ensemble of discourses and practices so
deeply embedded in "the warp and weave of the social fabric" (Goldberg 2002:
98) that it is neither possible to comprehend it (since comprehension is formed by
the state itself) nor to resist it (since this would require as a necessary condition
an account of what was to be resisted). This is a pessimistic conclusion, but one

that reflects a sociological approach that has a weak account of human agency and hence imputes powers and influences to the social order far in excess of those that it actually possesses.

In summary, the two major sociological responses to the collapse of the onto-logical status of race—what I have characterized as interactionist and discursive approaches to race—have significant shortcomings. For the interactionist, the formation of "racial groups" and the persistence of structured inequalities and injustice remain unexplained; for the discourse theorist, the identification of politi-cal constituencies with an interest in, and the resources to challenge, racist poli-cies and representations has proved elusive. Put more formally, both responses are unable to come to grips with the problem of structure and the problem of agency, respectively. Discourse approaches lead to an oversocialized conception of human agency, one in which the capacity of people to modify the social world is significantly underestimated or rendered nugatory. Interactionist approaches tend to reverse the emphasis, providing an undersocialized conception of human agency, one in which the capacity of people to modify the social world is signifi-cantly exaggerated.

RACE CONCEPTS AND SOCIOLOGICAL REALISM

A central element in the inability to provide a convincing account of the structure-agency relation is the common use of a concept of race whose referent is indeter-minate. It is not necessary for everyday purposes of social interaction that people agree what they mean by a term, but it is necessary that sociologists agree about the descriptive parameters of sociological terms (even if they may disagree about its accuracy or relevance as a description). There may be intense debate about how a concept such as social class may be operationalized in social research; there may be widely different accounts of what social class may be held to refer to; and theo-rists may draw on very divergent traditions of sociological theory to establish the credibility or plausibility of their particular use of the concept. Systemic concepts such as social class—bureaucracy, rationalization, gender, and capitalism are other examples—"refer primarily to the reproduced social relations which represent the historically emergent standing conditions of an ongoing society"; thus, the pri-mary reference point for these concepts is "the reproduced social relations (and the powers and practices which underpin them) that form the settings and contexts in which social behaviours are enacted" (Layder 1998: 88). Importantly, such con-cepts refer not only to the empirical world but also to theoretical networks from which the concepts are constructed and from which they take their meaning. They are assessed, therefore, not in terms of their popularity with lay speakers or their presence in everyday life but rather by the broader context of reasoning in which they are embedded and their relation to other competing or complementary con-cepts or theories. And here, as I have already argued, the concept of race fails mis-erably: discredited in natural science, the best defence of it that can be managed in social science is that some people use the term in non-sociological contexts.

Even where the concept has retained some favour—usually as a means of describing sub-species with systematic hereditable difference—it is in contexts where its irrelevance for interpreting social and political differences is made unequivocally clear (Jones 1997). Conversely, critiques of race concepts from within sociology, accelerated by the postmodern emphasis on reflexivity and the "linguistic turn," have drawn attention to their contested, symbolic nature (see, for example, Gilroy 1993; Hall, Held and McGrew 1992; Smaje 1997; Modood 2005). Taken together, these two developments raise doubts about the theoretical status of a concept of race and its appropriateness for sociological analysis.

None of this would matter very much if it were not for, firstly, the consequences of employing the concept of race in sociological analysis and, secondly, the fact that recent developments within the social and natural sciences have altered significantly the prospects for notions of race. As to the consequences, there are three in particular that I wish to address. First, when pressed into service in sociological accounts, race concepts conflate structure and agency, making an analysis of their interplay impossible. This leads directly to the instability of key categories, such as "racial group," and to confusion about the relations between these and other explanatory sociological terms such as racism and discrimination. Second, the persistent use of the race concept in social science undermines the credibility of sociological critiques of the concept; indeed, in many instances, criticism of race ideas is seen as inappropriate since the content of such ideas is less significant than their function in everyday life. Third, without a critique of race ideas, and a compelling account of their relations with political projects, discrimination, and other forms of structured inequalities, sociologists would appear to have little to contribute to public policy debates about how best to challenge and combat racism and discrimination.

Such a callow attitude is not ineluctable. Other responses to the demise of race categories are possible, and in the remainder of this chapter I want to consider one of these. I also wish to explore how it might afford a different view of some contemporary debates about racism, discrimination, and ethnicity. Clearly, in view of the arguments adduced earlier, an alternative response to the collapse of the ontological status of race requires a plausible view of the structure-agency relation, one that recognizes their distinctive characteristics, holds them to be distinctive sorts of entity, and so is able to analyze their mutually influential relations. Such a view has been advanced by a number of writers over the last decade or so (see, for example, Archer 1988, 1995; Carter 2000; Layder 1997, 1998; Porpora 1989; Sayer 1992), and it is their work, which may be broadly described as "sociological realism," that I shall draw on in the argument that follows.

An alternative realist account of race and racism might begin from the recognition that ideas about race and ethnicity are concepts in a formal theoretical sense, devised to describe accurately certain features of human populations. As with all concepts, once they are embodied in a symbolic code of some sort—a written text, for example—they attain an independence from their originators and become occupants of what Archer (1988) terms the "cultural system."

Archer takes culture "to refer to all intelligibilia, that is to any item which has the dispositional capacity of being understood by someone" (Archer 1988: xvi). Culture in this view is the limitless realm formed by the products of human consciousness, from electric toasters to the Taj Mahal, and from McDonald's to Beethoven's symphonies. One's mobility within this realm, as well as one's access to its resources, is of course powerfully shaped by one's social location and the opportunities it makes available. This is a radically different notion of culture than is often proposed in debates about multiculturalism, for example. In Archer's model, one's cultural coordinates at any given moment are flexible and agency-driven, circumscribed by the enablements and constraints of one's social location, though not deterministically so. One does not "have a culture"; one has, rather, access to cultural resources whose horizons may expand or contract depending on circumstances and context.

The cultural system, for Archer, is the "sub set of items to which the law of contradiction can be applied" (Archer 1988: xvi), namely, propositions about the nature of the world which assert truth or falsity. This is the realm of ideas *as* ideas—that, for instance, there are races whose relationship to each other is hierarchical such that one race is superior to others in significant respects. While the cultural system at any given time is the product of previous socio-cultural interaction, that is, of what previous social actors have accomplished, its elements will at any specific historical moment share two essential qualities. They will, first, have a relative independence or autonomy from social actors (race ideas continue to inhabit the cultural system whether or not I choose to recognise them) and, second, will have a relative autonomy from each other (claims about the superiority of one race to other races remain distinct from claims about, say, capitalism and the growth of democratic polities).

Consequently, ideas about race or ethnicity may be linked to all sorts of other ideas within the cultural system (e.g., civil rights or national identity). There are also many ideas with which it has little or no connection at all, such as your preferred make of car or the shrubs you choose to plant in your garden. Furthermore, ideas can have two sorts of logical relation to other ideas: contradiction or compatibility. If an individual believes that certain groups of people are inferior, this will be a view compatible with other ideas (e.g., about colour, culture, and inequality). On the one hand, there will be an incentive to preserve the compatible ideas, since they are mutually reinforcing, by seeking out further evidence for these beliefs. On the other hand, if an individual believes in a hierarchy of races with different degrees of assimilability to a national "way of life," but is also committed to the idea that discriminatory behaviour is unacceptable, there will be an incentive for them to rectify the extent to which these ideas are contradictory.

Consequently, ideas are not reducible to individual beliefs, and there may be contested interpretations by different groups with different material interests. In this sense, we may say that ideas about race and ethnicity are used as cultural resources in ordinary or routine social interactions (the partial truth of the interactionist approach). Racism as a property of the cultural realm can thus be deployed as a motive for actions, as a rationalization of anxieties, as a sincerely held account of how the world works, and so on, by anybody with access to the relevant ideational resources. However, it remains dependent on human reflexivity to be socially effectual, and its relationship to human behaviour, to what actual human beings do, is complex and mediated by social relations. In particular, the connection between racism and discrimination is not a necessary one: in some contexts, discriminatory outcomes may be explicable in terms of racist beliefs held by certain groups. In other contexts, such outcomes will be the result of a combination of features of which racist beliefs may be one but equally may not. Often, people will frequently accept such ideas and imaginings as common sense, using them routinely as interpretative devices. It follows from the partially autonomous nature of race ideas, however, that when expressed as propositions, they will have logical relations with all sorts of other ideas, such as a belief in tolerance, or equality, or rationality; to the extent that individuals seek to fashion a plausible account of their world and a consistent self-narrative, these relations will have a shaping force.

Postulating theories, ideas, and conjectures as relatively independent from each other and from their provenance has several advantages. Firstly, it allows a view of theories as having logical relations with other theories on the basis of the propositional claims they make. Our deployment of cultural resources is thus not without constraints. It is difficult, for example, to reconcile a belief in equality with a claim that one should discriminate against certain people because of where they come from or where they were born. Such relations are distinct from the question of individual belief and from the reasons why, and to what extent, people hold particular ideas. False or bad arguments can be sincerely held. This is why it is rarely possible to make race theories vanish by demonstrating their falsity to specific individuals, since ideas are ontologically distinct from the individuals who may adhere to them. So, individuals will find their ideational choices shaped by the effects of the logical relations between beliefs. Such relations do not of course determine actions; they are merely conditions that actors have to take into account.

Secondly, as propositions about the world, ideas of race are as vulnerable to criticism as any other description of social reality that proposes certain things to be the case. Such criticisms will have all sorts of intended and unintended consequences. The efforts of Victorian scientists to found a notion of race scientifically led to the emergence of a scientific critique of race ideas, as scientists found it unexpectedly difficult to ground race ideas in science (Barkan 1991; Banton 1997). Over the last decade or so, less attention has been paid to the propositional forms of, and the distinctions between, race ideas (e.g., anti-semitism and anti-Irish racism) because of the focus in much contemporary discussion on race as a generic object. The discursive force of race, rather than the actual content of the ideas as such, has become a central concern of theorists. This partially has to do with the realization that the rational criticism of racist propositions is usually insufficient to bring about a change of conviction (although I think this insufficiency is sometimes exaggerated). More significant, though, has been the conflation of *ideas about race* with the *notion of race*, and the analytical confusion this entails between culture and social action.

Domains of the Social

The view of culture and agency proposed here rests on a view of the social world as comprising analytically distinct elements or, to use Layder's helpful term, "social domains" (Layder 1997). Layder identifies four such domains: psychobiography, situated activity, social settings, and contextual resources. His model attempts to capture the social and temporal distancing of social relations from lived experience, while recognizing that, at the same time, every lived experience is embedded within the other domains.

The first domain, "psychobiography," refers to the unique biographies of human beings in which "personal feelings, attitudes and predispositions" contribute to a continuing selfhood, which is "embedded in their daily routines and experiences." Thus "the notion of 'psychobiography' points to the development of the self as a linked series of evolutionary transitions, or transformations in identity and personality at various significant junctures in the lives of individuals" (Layder 1997: 2–3, 47).

The second domain, "situated activity," also focuses on human agency. Despite the unique quality of our psychobiographies, human beings are pre-eminently *social* actors, much of whose lives involve the negotiation of face-to-face interaction. "Situated activity" refers to these experiences of social life. The situated activity of face-to-face conduct, however, is itself embedded within what Layder identifies as the domain of "social settings," the third domain. Here the focus shifts from agency—that is, what actors do and experience—to structures: the social context within which these interactions are situated. Social settings are the physical and social contexts "of social activities and specific social practices", such as workplaces, schools, or places of worship, and their routinized ways of doing things (Layder 1997: 87).

The final domain, "contextual resources," is the most distant from people's experiences. "Contextual resources" refers to the anterior distributions of material and cultural capital that social actors inherit as a consequence of being born in a particular place at a particular time. While individuals have no choice about this, the distributions of these resources are systematically reproduced. It is not being claimed that we experience these domains in this stratified way as we live from moment to moment and day to day. What is being claimed is that our lives are constantly being shaped in each domain and that we are aware of certain domains more than others. Structural domains involve institutional constraints and enablements that are themselves partly the product of the distribution and allocation of economic, political, and cultural resources (children from poor backgrounds rarely become professors). This means that they may be more opaque to actors' knowledgeability.

So far, so good, one might say. But what do we get if we apply these ideas to the analysis of racism and discrimination, race ideas and ethnicity? In the remainder of this chapter I shall point to three important benefits of adopting a realist approach to the study of racism and race ideas, and I will illustrate these with some practical examples.

APPLYING SOCIOLOGICAL REALISM

The first important benefit to be gained from a realist social science is a plausible view of agency-structure relations. This is important because it allows for identification of agency and makes possible an assessment of policy outcomes in terms of who is responsible for doing what to whom. For example, a major debate, both in North America and in the UK, has concerned "racial profiling" in policing. There is a large body of evidence that demonstrates that police forces tend to use stop and search powers disproportionately against particular sectors of the population, sectors frequently defined in terms of somatic or other physiognomic features (see, for example, 1990 Trust 2004; Dodd 2005; Fitzgerald 1999; Harris 2002; Office of the Attorney General of the State of New York 1999; Cole 1999). A number of explanations for this disproportionality have been advanced, but one that has proved popular both with politicians (see the Macpherson report in the UK; Macpherson 1999) and with some academic commentators is institutional racism. According to this approach, the police force is a racist institution, and disproportionality in stop and search procedures (as well as in arrests and prosecutions) reflects this feature of policing.

A number of criticisms of the concept of institutional racism have been made (see, for instance, Bridges 2001; Fitzgerald 1999), but I want to examine the notion of institutional racism in the light of the perspective outlined above. First, the term *institutional racism* conflates the structure-agency distinction: institutions, as structures of roles, practices, and procedures, cannot be intentional since structured social relations do not possess the property of intentionality any more than they possess the property of reflexivity that would enable them to hold ideas about race. Secondly, as a direct consequence of the conflation of structure and agency, the concept of institutional racism makes it difficult to identify the targets for policy change. It does so because institutional practices are held to be mysteriously agent-free and a product of larger structural forces such as "canteen culture" in the UK Macpherson report, or a "racist world order" in Goldberg's (2002) account.

However, stop and search policing, as Delsol (2006) has noted, is a prime example of low visibility policing; it takes place on the street, away from the gaze of supervisory officers, and so allows a considerable degree of discretion to the officers involved. In other words, the social locus of stop and search policing is the domain of situated activity, of face-to-face interaction. Policy intervention, therefore, would need to focus initially on this domain, perhaps by introducing greater levels of scrutiny or accountability. In whatever way this was done, the central point remains that the issue in challenging the disproportional use of stop and search has to be the regulation of individual behaviour, whether that is directly attributable to racist beliefs or not.

However, although stop and search policing consists primarily of face-to-face interaction, its context is shaped by factors operating in other domains. On the one hand, for instance, in the psychobiographical domain, an individual police officer may be strongly committed to racist beliefs, and this may be the major factor determining the nature of her stop and search interactions; her notion of what counts as reasonable suspicion will be configured by racist assumptions about appearance. On the other hand, several writers (see, for example, Quinton *et al.* 2000; Waddington *et al.* 2004; Dixon *et al.* 1989) have pointed to the ways in which police judgements about what counts as suspicious behaviour are rooted in the culture of police work, forming an important element of the social setting domain of policing. Social settings are more remote from individual experience, they are relatively durable compared to face-to-face encounters, and they are, consequently, often very resistant to efforts directed towards influence and change. Such efforts require political will and a commitment to change from those occupying senior positions within the organization if they are to have any likelihood of success. They also require a different form of policy intervention from that directed at the level of situated activity, one that also recognizes that the impact of policies directed toward one domain will necessarily be mediated by the other (racist police officers will disguise their racism more effectively; the police officers on the street will search for ways of evading scrutiny; those responsible for formulating policy within a police force will seek to avoid identifying individuals and disciplining them). These are difficult concerns, but a non-conflationary view of the structure-agency relation renders them less opaque. It can also identify with greater precision the potentially most relevant objects of policy intervention.

The second benefit of the realist approach is that it favours the robust rejection of conceptions of race. Race ideas, concepts, and imaginings are denizens of the world of human knowledge, and, like all such denizens, they are mediated through human agency. Race ideas carry no intentions, nurture no ambitions, and cannot determine social action: without human beings to believe in them and act upon them, they are as inert and ineffectual as any other ideas in the contemporary world. The interesting sociological questions are those that address the social contexts and conditions under which a belief in ideas about race and ethnicity comes to be socially significant. But this, of course, is not the study of something called "race," but the study of the relations between power, interests, and ideas and between structure and agency. In my view, sociology, and social science more generally, still has much to offer the study of these relations.

The rejection of race as a category of sociological analysis is especially significant given recent developments within the social and natural sciences, and within Western societies more broadly, which have altered significantly the prospects for notions of race. Most pertinently, within the natural sciences there has been the advent of the Human Genome Project with its remit to identify and map the human DNA sequence, generating a range of debates about, among other things, what it is to be human, the genetic relations between human beings and other animals, and the connections between disease and genetic populations (see Carter 2007). These debates have not been confined to geneticists and other science professionals but have converged into wider debates about social policy and governance in which race concepts are being reinvigorated through their association with genomically based claims about human populations. Moreover, the linking of genetics with genealogy has often served to reinforce popular notions of ancestry, descent, and belonging—notions that have occasionally overlapped with those underpinning immigration legislation in the UK and elsewhere. The tracing of ancestry has become an expanding business (Tutton 2004), which both reflects and generates an "obsession with provenance" (Bywater 2004: 86) that draws implicitly, and often explicitly, on notions of race. This can result in a view of history and human endeavour based on a "genetic reductionism" of the sort found in evolutionary psychology, but it also has implications for sociological conceptions of both race and ethnicity.

Although genomics provides an uncertain basis for claims about the distinctiveness of the human and about the uniqueness of the individual, newer forms of identity politics have emerged that combine genomics and genetics in a powerful way with popular notions of descent, ancestry, race, and ethnicity to reaffirm and rearrange classifications of human beings according to genetic characteristics. This is what Hauskeller (2004) has aptly termed the "geneticization of identity," the belief that individual uniqueness is guaranteed by some sort of "real" physical matter, that is, a specific genomic sequence. In effect, genomics dissolves race categories only to reinsert them at a deeper genetic level so that they reappear as a new truth about human identity. This emphasis on physical matter as a guarantee of individual uniqueness reaffirms the trait-based classification associated with much race thinking and effects a form of genetic reductionism in which a person's authenticity of social status and belonging becomes a matter of biology.

Finally, the third benefit from the application of realist sociology is the distinctive view of current debates about identity and multiculturalism that it generates. Space does not permit a full examination of these topics, but I shall point to two implications of the realist approach, touching on the topics of ethnicity and identity and the debates concerning recognition and redistribution. It should be clear from the above discussion that the term *ethnicity* faces similar difficulties to that facing the term *race*, namely, that its referent is unstable (and so its ontological status is unclear) and its use in sociological analysis is inextricably entangled with its various lay meanings (so that its epistemological fitness for social research is seriously compromised). The customary defence of ethnicity echoes that for the defence of the concept of race: people perceive themselves (sometimes) and others (often) as possessing ethnicity, or as having an ethnic identity, or as belonging to an ethnic group. However, the stratified social world, and the opacity of social relations that results from it, make people's accounts of that world significant but partial. What people think they are and how they place themselves in relation to others (or how they describe others in relation to themselves) is an important element of a sociological explanation, but it is only one element. Indeed, if it were the only element, social research would amount to no more than an accumulation of narratives, as its detractors sometimes allege.

Social science, then, should consider eschewing notions of ethnicity in favour of research that seeks to examine the conditions under which people come to see themselves and others in ethnic terms. As Fenton (2003: 2) puts it, "a theory of ethnicity has to be a theory of the contexts under which it is 'activated.'" This would not be a theory of ethnicity (any more than the study of the contexts in which race concepts are activated amounts to a theory of race) but a theory of the material and cultural contexts in which the expression of ethnic forms of identification become relevant for significant social actors or for a significant number of social actors. Such forms of identification are distinguished by their emphasis on some notion of "shared culture" or "shared descent," notions with an extremely dubious past that should be firmly cold-shouldered. "People or peoples do not just possess cultures or share ancestry," notes Fenton, "they elaborate these into the idea of a community founded upon these attributes" (Fenton 2003: 3) and it is the conditions under which they do this that should be the object of sociological study (see Mann 2005 for a compendious illustration of such an approach). Analogous arguments about the equally confused notion of identity have been proposed by Brubaker (2004: 37), who notes again that the adoption for analytical purposes of a category of everyday experience and political practice entails "a series of deeply problematic assumptions," most or all of which get reproduced in debates about identity politics.

CONCLUSION

Goldthorpe (2000) suggested several years ago that sociologists had lost their nerve when it came to defending the relevance of their own discipline and had abandoned any claim to epistemic authority in the analysis of the social world. One area of social research where this development is most marked is in the study of racism and discrimination. Here the reluctance to abandon concepts of race as analytical tools has led to a smothering concern with difference in which "culture" and "religion," in Ali's words, "are softer, euphemistic substitutes for socio-economic inequality ... as if diversity, rather than hierarchy, were the central issue in North American or European society today" (Ali 2003: 337). I have suggested that the resources for a post-race sociology, one in which sociological theorizing might again be made relevant, are available in sociological realism. Whether sociologists can find the nerve to use them is another matter.

REFERENCES AND FURTHER READINGS

1990 Trust. 2004. *Stop and Search: The Views and Experiences of Black Communities on Complaining to the Police.* London: Metropolitan Police Authority.

Ali, T. 2003. *The Clash of Fundamentalisms: Crusades, Jihads, and Modernity.* London: Verso.

American Sociological Association [ASA]. 2003. *The Importance of Collecting Data and Doing Social Scientific Research on Race*. New York: American Sociological Association.

Archer, M.S. 1988. *Culture and Agency: The Place of Culture in Social Theory*. Cambridge: Cambridge University Press.

——. 1995. *Realist Social Theory: A Morphogenetic Approach*. Cambridge: Cambridge University Press.

Banton, M. 1997. *Ethnic and Racial Consciousness*. Harlow: Addison Wesley Longman.

——. 2005. Finding, and Correcting, My Mistakes. *Sociology* 39(3): 463–79.

Barkan, E. 1991. *The Retreat of Scientific Racism: Changing Concepts of Race in Britain and the United States Between the World Wars*. Cambridge: Cambridge University Press.

Bridges, L. 2001. Race, Law and the State. *Race and Class* 43(2): 61–76.

Brubaker, R. 2004. *Ethnicity Without Groups*. Cambridge, MA: Harvard University Press.

Bywater, M. 2004. *Lost Worlds: What Have We Lost and Where Did It Go?* London: Granta.

Carter, R. 2000. *Realism and Racism: Concepts of Race in Sociological Research*. London: Routledge.

——. 2007. Genes, Genomes and Genealogies: The Return of Scientific Racism? *Ethnic and Racial Studies*.

Cole, D. 1999. *No Equal Justice: Race and Class in the American Justice System*. New York: New Press.

Dawkins, R. 2004. Race and Creation. *Prospect* 103. <http://www.prospect-magazine.co.uk>.

Delsol, R. 2006. *The Police, Stop and Search, and Institutional Racism: A Comparative Study of Stop and Search at a Local Level in the UK and USA*. PhD thesis. University of Warwick, UK.

Dixon, D., K. Bottomley, *et al*. 1989. Reality and Rules in the Construction and Regulation of Police Suspicion. *International Journal of the Sociology of Law* 17: 185–206.

Dodd, V. 2005. Surge in Stop and Search of Asian People after July 7. *The Guardian*.

Fenton, S. 2003. *Ethnicity*. Cambridge: Polity.

Fitzgerald, M. 1999. *Searches in London, Under s1 of the Police and Criminal Evidence Act 1984*. London: Metropolitan Police Service.

Gilroy, P. 1993. *The Black Atlantic: Modernity and Double Consciousness*. London: Verso.

Goldberg, D.T. 2002. *The Racial State*. Oxford: Blackwell.

Goldthorpe, J.H. 2000. *On Sociology: Numbers, Narratives and the Integration of Research and Theory*. Oxford: Oxford University Press.

Hall, S., D. Held, and T. McGrew (eds.). 1992. *Modernity and its Futures*. Milton Keynes: Oxford University Press.

Harris, D.A. 2002. *Profiles in Injustice: Why Racial Profiling Cannot Work*. New York: New Press.

Hauskeller, C. 2004. Genes, Genomes, and Identity. Projections on Matter. *New Genetics and Society* 23(3): 285–99.

Jones, S. 1997. *In the Blood: God, Genes and Destiny*. London: Flamingo.

Jorde, L.B., and S.P. Wooding. 2004. Genetic Variation, Classification, and "Race." *Nature Genetics* 36(11): S28–33.

Knowles, C. 2003. *Race and Social Analysis*. London: Sage.

Kohn, M. 1996. *The Race Gallery: The Return of Racial Science*. London: Vintage.

Layder, D. 1997. *Modern Social Theory*. London: UCL Press.

——. 1998. *Sociological Practice: Linking Theory and Social Research*. London: Sage.

Macpherson, S.W. 1999. *The Stephen Lawrence Inquiry.* CM4262-1. London: HMSO.

Malik, K. 1996. *The Meaning of Race: Race, History and Culture in Western Society.* London: Macmillan.

Mann, M. 2005. *The Dark Side of Democracy: Explaining Ethnic Cleansing.* New York: Cambridge University Press.

Miles, R. 1989. *Racism.* London: Routledge.

Modood, T. 2005. *Multicultural Politics: Racism, Ethnicity and Muslims in Britain.* Edinburgh: Edinburgh University Press.

Morning, A., and D. Sabbagh. 2005. From Sword to Plow-Share: Using Race for Discrimination and Antidiscrimination in the United States. *International Social Science Journal* 57(183): 57–73.

Office of the Attorney General of the State of New York. 1999. *The New York City Police Department's "Stop and Frisk" Practices: A Report to the People of the State of New York from the Office of the Attorney General.* New York: Office of the Attorney General.

Omi, M., and H. Winant. 1994. *Racial Formation in the United States: From the 1960s to the 1990s.* New York: Routledge.

Park, R.E. 1950. *Race and Culture.* New York: The Free Press.

Pawson, R. 1989. *A Measure for Measures: A Manifesto for Empirical Sociology.* London: Routledge.

Phillips, T. 2005. *After 7/7: Sleepwalking to Segregation.* Speech, Manchester Community Relations Council, UK, 25 September. <http://www.cre.gov.uk>.

Porpora, D.V. 1989. Four Concepts of Social Structure. *Journal for the Theory of Social Behaviour* 19(2): 195–211.

Potvin, M. 2005. The Role of Statistics on Ethnic Origin and "Race" in Canadian Anti-Discrimination Policy. *International Social Science Journal* 57(183): 27–42.

Quinton, P., N. Bland, *et al.* 2000. *Police Stops, Decision-Making and Practice.* London: Home Office.

Rose, S., and H. Rose. 2005. Why We Should Give Up on Race. *The Guardian* 9 April.

Sayer, A. 1992. *Method in Social Science: A Realist Approach.* London: Routledge.

Smaje, C. 1997. Not Just a Social Construct: Theorising Race and Ethnicity. *Sociology* 31(2): 307–27.

Thomas, W.I., and Thomas, D.S. 1970 [1928]. Situations Defined as Real are Real in Their Consequences. In G. Stone and H. Farberman, eds., *Social Psychology Through Interaction.* Waltham, MA: Ginn-Blasidell. 154–55.

Tutton, R. 2004. "They Want To Know Where They Came From": Population Genetics, Identity, and Family Genealogy. *New Genetics and Society* 23: 105–20.

Waddington, P.A.J., K. Stenson, *et al.* 2004. In Proportion: Race and Police Stop and Search. *British Journal of Criminology* (44): 889–914.

3 SPEAKING RACE
Silence, Salience, and the Politics of Anti-Racist Scholarship[1]

George J. Sefa Dei

THE SALIENCE OF RACE

This chapter outlines the relationship between race as an illusory Eurocentric scientific concept and race as a function of, and for, inequity and oppression in the Canadian and international contexts. I examine the socio-political underpinnings of the ways in which we speak and do not speak about race, both currently and historically. The idea of the scientific racial category is investigated with an eye for how such definitive scholarship conflates the social and the scientific. Critical anti-racist discourse is posited as a framework that works with the salience of race and that offers an intellectual basis for understanding, researching, and developing positive action-oriented solutions to oppression. I argue that silence around race is far from neutral and that the anti-racist discourse, despite those who blame it for bringing race to the table, is a necessary strategic perspective for addressing that which by all means already exists.

In writing a chapter on the sociological concept of race, I feel it is important to state from the outset where I am coming from and why an anti-racist lens offers a more fruitful entry point for me to engage this discussion. In fact, we cannot honestly discuss the sociological concept of race as a lived reality without addressing the denial and silences around race as a valid concept of analysis. An anti-racist lens requires that we not only speak of the salience and centrality of race but that we also point to some of the subtle ways that even progressive scholarship can silence race through supposedly acknowledging racism (and not race) as the problem. Omi and Winant (1993: 5) once opined that race is "... a fundamental principle of social organization and identity formation.... Our society is so thoroughly racialized that to be without a racial identity is to be in danger of having no identity at all. To be raceless is akin to being genderless." In a later work, the same authors also argued that race is, in fact, present in every individual social relationship and institution. We must critically evaluate our perceptions and understandings of our personal and collective lived experiences to see how we are constantly compelled to think racially and to use racial codes, categories, meaning systems, and signifiers (Omi and Winant 1994).

In reflecting on these ideas, it is puzzling that denials and silences around race persist. Given the ways we have been socialized to think and act, it is neither possible nor desirable to remain "colour-blind." Unfortunately, and understandably, there is a discomfort in speaking race, but this must not be confused with the urgency of addressing racial problems. I say this because of the ways in which the analytical validity, or lack thereof, of the race concept continues to be privileged in our understanding of race and racism. In my anti-racist scholarship, one of the intellectual frustrations I encounter stems from attempts by well-meaning progressive scholars to argue that the notion/idea of race is "conceptually bankrupt." This is personally frustrating, largely because anti-racism has some particular non-negotiable principles. One such principle is the salience or centrality of race in the axis of difference for understanding social oppressions. In the analysis of asymmetrical power relations, the utility of social categories in understanding social oppressions (e.g., race, gender, class, sexuality, etc.) is critical.

The concept of race has always been a part of modern human history, although our understandings of it have shifted over the years. From some of the early writings of Banton (1977a, 1977b), for example, we learn how Social Darwinism conceived of original races as pure and biologically determined. In fact, the sociologist Ludwig Gumplowicz (1838–1909) argued that societies were socially constructed dialogues between inferior and superior races. In his many writings, Gumplowicz also advanced notions of ethnocentrism in which he argued that all peoples seek dominance—a sort of eat or be eaten philosophy—which lends itself to a notion that is still with us: "everyone is racist if given the chance, and it's all just a matter of who is on top" (see Gumplowicz 1875, 1881, 1883, cited in Banton 1977a). In later scientific scholarship on race, physical as well as social anthropological approaches attempted to find physical explanations and justifications for racial differentiation and thus inequality. These approaches used phenotypical variation such as head, nose, and body size/shape as measurements of racial differences among groups. Racial antagonism was often understood as innate in these frameworks (Banton 1967, 1977a, 1977b), and, in fact, modern science must be understood as having shaped modern understandings of race.

In this chapter, I conceptualize race as a social relational category defined by socially selected physical and cultural characteristics (see also Li 1990). I do not think that the discomfort of speaking race is merely due to the fact that race lacks analytical significance or conceptual clarity as a "real" attribute of human beings. After all, race is already on the table, and our discomfort in acknowledging it does not make it go away. Unfortunately, the significance of race is repeatedly denied and masked by other forms of difference. I find it hard to believe that one can take a stand that denies race and simultaneously can challenge racism effectively. Denying race is both theoretically and politically suspect. This stance merely privileges a form of Western scientific knowledge to the exclusion of other epistemic realities. How, for instance, does science account for the power of an illusion? Do we simply dismiss race because it is an illusion? Within this dominant perspective, action-oriented questions become muddled. Where, for example, does one place the call for keeping race-based statistics to understand institutional racism (see Dei and Kempf 2005)? How do we call for representation of diverse faculty in our schools, colleges, and universities? Are white identities and whiteness not both racial and racialized categories? How do we render visible the racialized relationships that we often take for granted (see also Duncan 2002, 2005)? In the face of black and Aboriginal youth disengagement from school, racist profiling of black and Asian bodies, and the dominant propensity to encode black and racial minority bodies with criminality, how far can a critic go in transformative praxis with an unending zeal to complicate racial identities? For far too long, liberal ideologies have rendered the colour line, as well as race, invisible. Any critical anti-racist writing must challenge these silences.

The intellectual gymnastics around the race concept have taken many forms. Even in early, so-called progressive scholarship, we can point to works by Cox (1948, 1976), Miles (1989, 1993), Miles and Torres (1996), Solomos (1986), and Solomos and Back (1995) that have attempted to reduce or subsume race under class. I contend that it is dangerous to subsume race under class, especially in anti-racist work (Dei 1996; see also Gabriel and Ben-Tovim 1978, 1979). If we do not speak of race as the central entry point to anti-racist practice, we cannot address the problem of racism. It is a delusion to think otherwise. While I share the desire to bring an historical-materialist lens to understanding anti-racist work, we must be careful not to simply locate race and racism in material conditions/ existence. Race and class are inextricably linked, perhaps more so today than ever before, but the functions of a phenomenon do not adequately explain its origins. No doubt, class may be a more relevant formal analytical category than race, but to argue that class is the most important perspective for analyzing social oppression negates the utility of race as a social organizing principle. In other words, although linked, racism does not always substitute for race and vice versa. Scholarly attempts to offer a class/materialist-based analysis of race run the risk of failing to engage with the non-material dimensions of social existence, as captured through the lens of Indigenous knowings or knowledges such as equity/anti-racist work as flowing from spirituality. It is legitimate to query the limitations of a strictly class-based, historical-materialist analysis of racism. For example, is there a form of subtle racism inherent in class-based analysis? What is being denied and why? How do we account for the intellectual agency of raced subjects who resist the amputation of race as a significant part of their identity, one that makes them whole alongside other identities? Is there not intellectual purpose in working with the power of illusion?

In this vein, it is highly problematic for scholars to place race in commas, either figuratively or literally. Similar arguments can be advanced in support for other social categories of identification (e.g., gender, sexuality, and class). Anti-racism is a political engagement and not merely an intellectual/discursive undertaking. The issue is not merely deciding whether or not a concept has an analytical status or validity. For example, how do we understand the process of racialization in the absence of the race concept? How is race situated and refracted in our understanding of the historical processes of racialization? Racialization also works with other categories such as class, gender, and sexuality. The power of dominant consciousness is so deeply rooted that it is not simply the product of material conditions or forces.

The denial of race and racial difference is at the heart of the failure to acknowledge racism (see also Winant 1994). The existence of races and racial differences do not themselves constitute the problem of racism in the first place. There is an important understanding of difference beyond the hegemonic and often Eurocentric understanding of difference as hierarchical. It is more than just the way(s) in which such categories are evoked or constructed. A critical reading of race brings a political, ideological, and spiritual reality to the understanding of our myriad identities. The non-recognition of identities is as problematic as the misrecognition of our identities (May 1999). Understanding race as a social construct can only go so far without negating the material consequences of evoking language. Put bluntly, there are times when we must separate the metaphor from the real. Working with the race concept does not translate *a priori* into an objectification and reification of the concept, particularly when most anti-racists point to the historically fluid, contested, and contextualized nature of our concepts. While race is not a fixed or static concept, it works in "broadly predictable ways and through well-rehearsed narratives to position Whites as superior to non-Whites" (Howard, 2004: 4). This is the underlying power of white supremacy. Furthermore, and specifically, African anti-racism offers a powerful way of knowing that black bodies experience race differently than other non-white bodies.

When we fail to acknowledge the power of white racial identity, whiteness, white supremacy, and their critical linkages, we also fail to uncover how race plays out beyond racism. For example, Apartheid, the system of institutional racism in South Africa, was not based exclusively on material or economic interests. It was also based on an ideology of black inferiority and hatred. If the roles had been reversed, I do not believe it would have been tolerated for any length of time by the major European superpowers, even if the hypothetical black minority controlled the political, material, and economic forces in the interest of global capital. Unfortunately, some may want to dismiss this.

At one level, it could be argued that racism produces race(s) and not vice versa. This may be a powerful thought. However, since social practices and constructs are inextricably linked, where does this proposition lead us? Constructs themselves are constitutive of social practices. We can, similarly, argue that classism and sexism produce social classes and sexes/genders, respectively. An acknowledgment of this should not translate to abandoning the social categories of race, class, and gender. Sure, there is a connection between racism and race, but the link cannot simply be understood as unidirectional. Can there be racial designations without imbuing/encoding negative racist meanings to difference? Can there be race without the existence of racism? The answer is both yes and no. History indicates that this is what happened because of Eurocentric understandings of "difference." Race is about difference. Racial differences *per se* are not the problem. In fact, they are sources of potential opportunities. There are Indigenous communities that bring varied, positive (as in solution-oriented) meanings to difference. At the same time, the existence of perceived racial differences has also fostered differential and unequal treatment. It is precisely because of this connection (perhaps conundrum) that we cannot choose discursively to separate race and racism. We thus instead argue that, analytically and discursively, the focus must be on racism and not on race. When race is ignored, however, racism is further reproduced.

The power of naming race and privilege is an important act in decolonization projects. Similarly, the power to self-define is also a form of resistance. In order to deal with race and difference positively, we must be able to speak about race in different ways. Silence and avoidance is unproductive. We cannot separate the "politics of difference" from the "politics of race" because this practice merely helps dominant bodies to deny and refuse to interrogate white privilege and power. We need to be acutely aware of how anti-essentialism can serve white power and privilege, bringing them to the centre of supposedly critical political pursuits (see also Doyle-Wood 2002). In other words, the emphasis on individual and dispersed myriad identities can be paralyzing to the extent that it can deny the ways centralized dominant systems of power work to establish and sustain particular advantages. The articulation of white hegemonic power can also deny and silence the experiential realities of bodies of colour.

In making these assertions, I do not mean to suggest that we should ignore the fact that gender, ethnicity, and social class demarcate whiteness or that it is unproblematic to generalize white privilege. A critical approach to understanding the questions of power and difference from an anti-racist lens requires, however, that we speak of the salience of race, even as we recognize the intersections of race with other forms of difference. What is notable is that whiteness is often rendered invisible through a process of normalization. Johal (2005: 273) is particularly instructive when he declares that "as much as White folks across differences of class, gender, sexuality, ethnicity, or religion may be oppressed in relation to the dominant white middle class heterosexual male subject, they hold a pigmentary passport of privilege that allows sanctity as a result of the racial polity of whiteness." This is a luxury bodies of colour across all our differences do not enjoy.

RACE AS AN EXPERIENTIAL REALITY

To better understand the sociological concept of race as a contemporary lived or experiential reality, I focus briefly on what Kempf (2006) has termed five conversations of the current race discourse. It is important to recognize that race occupies more than one space at a time. What this means is that there is no monolithic discourse within which, or from which, race can be understood. It is taken up in different historical, social, and geopolitical contexts, with each of these factors affecting discourses of race. The following "five conversations" bring together the well-established fields of anti-racism discourse and multiculturalism, and they contextualize anti-racism and multiculturalism within historical and social contexts. What follows is a brief "state of the union" summary of five key discourses on race.

The first conversation identified by Kempf is "The Old Debate." Despite overwhelming scientific proof that scientific conceptualizations of race conceal more than they reveal, the debate about the biological underpinnings of race persists through the efforts of numerous scholars and funding agencies whose research and efforts advance a social agenda wrapped in a (Eurocentric) scientific package. Inherent to the argument that there is credible evidence supporting a biological division of the human population by race is the notion of different racial intelligences. Arguments of this nature can be found in works such as Rushton (1994, 2001) and Murray and Herrnstein (1994). They demonstrate how the "old debate" continually resurfaces as part of the lived reality of raced bodies. For example, there is a hypervisibility to peoples of African descent that is not accorded to any other community of colour (Deliovsky 2005). Almost everyone else is designated by his or her established ethnic/geographic location. This conflation of colour and racial/ethnic origins has applied only to Africans and Europeans. To a large extent, the use of a colour descriptor has fed, and has fed on, a black/white binary. It has been a source of contention even among black groups. The politics of racial/ethnic categorization has led to a black/white Manichaeism that shapes aesthetic and moral valuations and which is operative in the determination of power and privilege in North American society (Deliovsky 2005: 9). Such Manichean moral frameworks have symbolized positional tensions between racialized groups (see also Hoch 1979), and they have served as the *raison d'être* for the primordial conflict between light/darkness, good/bad, and goodness/evil dualisms. In such dualism, European or whiteness is mythologized as goodness and blackness is mythologized as devilish and evil (see also Deliovsky 2005: 9).

The question, then, is what to do with these racial terms and their ideological and political baggage without reinscribing their concomitant ideological heaviness? As I have already argued, the answer lies in avoiding the reification of these terms by putting them in inverted commas or in contexts that might lead to dismissing or disregarding them. We need to find a way to come to grips with the problematic and socially constructed nature of these terms as they speak to and for lived reality.

The second conversation that is taking place in the contemporary context is about "Multiculturalism." As, perhaps, the dominant paradigm in minority and, increasingly, in majority world contexts, multiculturalism works with principles of symbolic equality at the expense of material and cultural equity. Taking a top-down approach, the multicultural idea works with acts of tolerance in place of acts of valuing difference. Characterized by the "Samosas and Saris" version of understanding difference, multiculturalism fits tightly into a capitalist paradigm of rights in place of responsibilities, and it relies on myths pertaining to social mobility. It focuses on recognition of the positive contributions of different groups in society, and it problematizes issues as resulting from misunderstanding and miscommunications among segments of a population. Multiculturalism celebrates cultures and their diversity without necessarily responding to power issues of difference. Its emphasis is on rooting out intolerance, discrimination, and a lack of goodwill.

The third conversation about race is unfolding under the auspices of the "Binary Conceptions Within the Current State of the Empire." This colonial framework has characterized all Euro-American colonial encounters; its current metaphorical articulation pits Islamophobia against Americanism. This is not simply "good" versus "bad," but rather "safety" versus "insecurity." While Eurocentric science has taken pre-emptive strikes in defining and pathologizing non-white bodies, imperialist military strategy invades and occupies the "other" under the not-so-hidden guise of a civilizing mission. Indeed, this is a pre-emptive strike on otherness! In this context, race is seemingly conflated with the rise of religious fundamentalism guiding policy in various contexts. Class, gender, and sexuality intersect with race as contestations arise around identity, power, and self-definition. This has implications on micro and macro levels as, globally, Euro-American colonialism moulds trade and migration, and, locally, people struggle for voice against an increasingly smaller number of dominant bodies acting as custodians of knowledge. The implications for endangered cultures are particularly grave.

In the "local" context of Canadian consciousness, we see the emerging question of youth violence and the subsequent representation of black cultures today. Apart from the fact that the pejorative term "black on black violence" stereotypes a whole community as violent, the identities of black and African peoples are scripted in very limited ways by institutional forces, particularly the media and police. There is a constant juxtaposing of whiteness and blackness, and it is one that achieves its full effects and intended impact when the evils/transgressions/criminality of other black bodies are served simply to sanctify the benevolence/goodness/morality and humanity of white bodies. Again, we can see some analogies in the local contexts of the lived realities of the racialized identities of so-called immigrant and other minority populations in Canada. Such identities are paired with punishment and repulsion. Consider, for instance, current discussions regarding racist profiling, testimonies of the Ontario Human Rights Commission, and how brown/Asian bodies and Muslim identities were, and continue to be, branded as "terrorists."

The fourth conversation about race is found within the "Critical Anti-Racism Discourse." Anti-racism has become an action-oriented political strategy to confront the problem of race and myriad forms of racism, as well as their intersections with other forms of oppressions that reproduce and sustain white dominance, power, and privilege (Dei 2000; Dei and Kempf 2005). There is a crucial link between the "Critical Anti-Racist Discourse" and the "Multiculturalism" and "Binary Conceptions Within the Current State of the Empire" discourses. Working with the anti-colonial framework, critical anti-racism resists the hegemony of multiculturalism and imperialism. It seeks to connect broader questions about structural racism to social oppression, domination, and the marginalization of peoples in society. It interrogates the underlying assumptions of empathy, commonality, and goodwill, and shifts the discourse to challenging and changing values, structures, and behaviours that perpetuate *systemic* racism and other forms of oppression. The entrenched inequities and power imbalance among social groups are addressed. Critical anti-racism also works with the idea of situational and contextual variations in intensities of oppressions, alongside recognition of the relative saliencies of different identities. There is the severity of issues for certain bodies. In Euro-American society, race demarcates life chances in very profound ways (see Dei 1996).

Finally, the fifth conversation of the current race discourse identified by Kempf is "Minority Bodies React: Resistant Dialogues." In 2005, a number of important events brought race to the forefront of mainstream media attention. Internationally, Hurricane Katrina, the uprising of minoritized French youth, and the Sydney race riots at the very least stimulated numerous conversations about race that would not otherwise have occurred. Gun violence in Toronto has also produced a highly racialized response from the popular press. These events are not to be celebrated or championed. They have, however, forced dialogue on race, and they have exposed structural and individual forms of racism in at least four dominant nations (i.e., the US, France, Canada, and Australia). It also tells those who did not know it before that people understand their oppression and that they are much closer to doing something about it than many might otherwise think. In the US, Jon Bon Jovi and Oprah Winfrey debated class and race on television, while President George W. Bush patted colleagues on the back for the swift response that left thousands dead. In France, youth took up whatever arms they could against the state—and this uprising spread to neighbouring countries as quickly as it had begun. Using the latest technology, white youth in Australia organized lynch mobs. Women were assaulted and used as racial currency in the ensuing battles between dominant and non-dominant bodies. The responses to these crises are most informative about the state of race and racism in our world. As thousands of poor black citizens remain unaccounted for in the US after the hurricane, a number matched only by the death toll, authorities continue to deny the role of race in the response to the aid effort. In France, official representatives re-enacted 50-year-old laws first implemented to quell the Algerian revolution. Colonialism has never ceded! As a response to the uprising, French authorities are deporting dozens of protestors on shaky legal ground. Indeed, rights run thin when power is threatened. In Australia, the prime minister, like many white Australians, continues to deny that Australia is a racist country.

What are the implications of these events for understanding the lived realities of raced subjects? Despite pretensions to the contrary, there persists pointed discursive and political pursuits aimed to preserve a racial hierarchy in the absence of slavery. Racial minorities continue to experience a process of historical, ideological, and symbolic signification in the white imagination alongside a subordinate positioning in contemporary social formation. This process has been referred to as racialization. It is a process that attributes a racial consciousness/awareness to even a previously unclassified racial relation and which entails the notion of biological determinism—the concept of particular human traits as biologically determined and thus as consistent both for individuals and for the group to which those individuals may belong. The most important point here is that racialization is an historical construction, one that allows for white supremacist systems of power to suppress racial minority resistance.

In looking at racialization today, we see how certain historical and contemporary processes and trajectories have allowed dominant groups to call upon culture, ethnicity, language, religion, and, of course, race and skin colour as a way of distinguishing groups for differential and unequal treatment. Closely aligned with the processes of racialization is the production of racialized subjects. As Lawson (2004) argues, we must use the notion of "racialize" as a verb, that is, the act of doing something to the body based on its phenotypical features. In the broader sense, the production of racialized subjects refers to how bodies are read or scripted according to skin colour and other features. For example, when we associate black skin with dishonesty or when we associated brown skin with terrorism, we are engaged in the process of racialization. In framing the issue in terms of the "racialized subject," we place the gaze on the people doing the "racializing" rather than on the people being "racialized." The process of racializing is thus external and strategic, and it is not the responsibility of the person who is targeted. This distinction is important because of the tendency for some to argue that those who do anti-racist work actually create the problem by engaging with race. Anti-racist workers do not speak of race to create it but rather to acknowledge what already exists.

Biologically determined (and thus racist) ideas of behaviour, values, beliefs, cultural practices, etc. are grafted onto particular social relations and issues such as immigration, education, and crime. In this sense, dominant systems of racialized power construct ideas of criminality. For example, some see crime and "gang violence" largely through (and in terms of) black and brown bodies and communities because they believe it is these bodies who have been invested with a biological propensity towards violence and crime.

As mentioned, particular bodies are now invested with the notion of terrorist—they are viewed as a group possessing certain biological traits that lead to the nurturing of suicide bombers, fanatical hatred of the West, sexist oppression, etc. The process of racialization and the making of racialized subjects are indicative of larger cultural and social forces. We need to ask, for example, why is it that Canadian families largely constitute themselves as white? What does this practice tell us about race and racism in Canadian history and contemporary politics and culture?

THE POLITICS OF ANTI-RACIST SCHOLARSHIP

Again the racialized context of everyday non-material and discursive realities; and challenges to the positivists' goals of value-free detachment and objectivity as not merely impossible but undesirable. Research must start with personal implication in the subject of inquiry and draw connections between personal experiences and the larger social mechanisms that organize society. It must subvert dominant/taken-for-granted knowledge. For example, race is not the exclusive property and epistemic knowledge of bodies that the dominant group has marked with racial difference. Consequently, a basic principle of anti-racist research is also to subvert the idea that the dominant group is an unnamed, unmarked racial category. We work with the understanding that all groups are raced and that they are raced differently.

The racial identity of the researcher is as significant as her class, gender, and sexual identifications. Both the researcher and the research subjects have the power to influence the direction of research. This speaks to a complex power dynamic in the field, the question of how power is negotiated. Also, both the researcher and the researched bring situated knowledges to the research process. As situated knowers, we must be critical and self-reflective. For example, the location of the research may influence the data-gathering process or the site of data gathering. These of course have a bearing on the content of the information.

In discussing race as a lived reality, I have allowed myself to be informed by "embodied knowing." I have worked with the relationship between questions of embodiment and subjectivity as separate but related concerns. Although there is an epistemic significance of the body, "embodiment" largely works with the understanding of the self, the inner environment, and one's aspirations, desires, and anxieties. There is a relationship between bodies and embodied selves, but it is also important to know that the racialized body may not necessarily be working with embodied knowing. "Embodied knowing" is crucial to understanding the ontological nature of racism (particularly white racism) because of the danger that comes with ignoring or denying the embodied nature of racial ideologies (Howard 2005). The "sociology of embodiment" addresses ways we come to know, through our social and individual interactions, practices, experiences, histories, and bodies. We can speak of moral agency and how certain understandings of our bodiliness simultaneously help produce and resist hegemonic knowledge. I allude to embodiment in order to challenge the certainties of knowing, particularly but not exclusively binary thinking.

What, then, to do with race? There is the "mythology of racelessness" that has been a hallmark of Canadian historical tradition (see Backhouse 1999). Canada has cultivated a national persona (ostensibly free from systemic racial exploitation) as a "raceless" society (Deliovsky 2005: 29). The Canadian refusal to see what is there is more than complacency. It speaks of our desire to avoid complicities while claiming innocence. We need to subvert the constant juxtaposition of the US when racial issues emerge in Canadian contexts. For example, in dealing with silences around race, we must "return the gaze" and problematize how Canadians can see race and class at play in the aftermath of Hurricane Katrina in New Orleans yet fail to acknowledge any systemic neglect of our own communities.

All social identities morph into complex configurations. Racial identities are historically contingent/specific, calling into focus the history and context of their evocations. But while identities are transient we must also recognize the "permanence" of skin colour as a salient marker of identity through human history. The significance of colour in the mind of the racist cannot be dismissed. This has served to perpetuate not only the material but also the psychic injury of invisibility and insignificance of an important reality—the racial identity of the minoritized. We must also be aware of the structural dynamics of whiteness, that is, the socio-economic forces and the institutional aspects of structure/society that work alongside everyday discursive practices and social scripts/texts to place whites in a "positional superiority" (Said 1979) over "Others." The positional superiority of whites is also fed constantly by the ideological system of white supremacy. Relations of domination are not shaped by history, politics, culture, and materiality alone. They are also shaped by local actions and daily discursive practices (see also Deliovsky 2005: 12; Hall 1997).

NOTE

1   I would like to thank Arlo Kempf, Ph.D. candidate in the Department of Sociology and Equity Studies of the Ontario Institute for Studies in Education of the University of Toronto (OISE/UT), for reading through and commenting on drafts of this paper. The many conversations with him when I began the process of writing greatly influenced my thoughts in most directions. I also thank the editors of this special collection for their reviews and commentary, and also for extending an invitation to me to be part of the cause and the project.

REFERENCES AND FURTHER READINGS

Backhouse, C. 1999. *Colour-Coded: A Legal History of Racism in Canada: 1900–1950.* Toronto: University of Toronto Press.

Banton, M. 1967. *Race Relations.* New York: Basic Books.

——. 1977a. Social Darwinism. In M. Banton, ed., *The Idea of Race.* London: Tavistock. 89–100.

——. 1977b. The Intellectual Inheritance. In. M. Banton, ed., *The Idea of Race.* London: Tavistock.

Cox, O. 1948. *Caste, Class and Race: A Study in Social Dynamics.* New York: Monthly Review Press.

——. 1976. *Race Relations: Elements and Social Dynamics.* Detroit, MI: Wayne State University Press.

Davy, K. 1995. Outing Whiteness. *Theatre Journal* (47): 189–205.

Dei, G.J.S. 1995. Integrative Anti-Racism and the Dynamics of Social Difference. *Race, Gender and Class* 2(3): 11–30.

——. 1996. *Anti-Racism Education in Theory and Practice.* Halifax: Fernwood.

——. 1999. The Denial of Difference: Reframing Anti-Racist Praxis. *Race, Ethnicity and Education* 2(1): 17–37.

——. 2000. Towards an Anti-Racist Discursive Framework. In. G. Dei and A. Calliste, eds., *Power, Knowledge and Anti-Racism Education.* Halifax: Fernwood. 23–40.

Dei, G.J.S., and A. Kempf. 2005. *The Application and Impact of Race-Based Statistics to Effect Systemic Change and Eliminate Institutional Racism.* Paper presented at the Canadian Race-Relations Foundation Policy Dialogue, Novotel Hotel, North York, Ontario, 21 October.

Deliovsky, K. 2005. *Elsewhere From Here: Remapping the Territories of White Femininity.* Ph.D. dissertation. Department of Sociology, McMaster University, Hamilton.

Doyle-Wood, S. 2002. Personal Communication. Department of Sociology and Equity Studies in Education, OISE/University of Toronto. Toronto.

Dubois, W.E.B. 1975. *The World and Africa: An Inquiry into the Part Which Africa has Played in World History*. New York: International Publishers.

Duncan, G.A. 2002. Critical Race Theory and Method: Rendering Race in Urban Ethnographic Research. *Qualitative Inquiry* 8(1): 85–104.

——. 2005. Critical Race Ethnography in Education: Narrative, Inequality and the Problem of Epistemology. *Race, Ethnicity and Education* 8(1): 93–114.

Dyer, R. 1997. *White*. London: Routledge.

Foucault, M. 1979. *Discipline and Punish: The Birth of Prison*. New York: Vintage Books.

Gabriel, J., and G. Ben-Tovim. 1978. Marxism and the Concept of Racism. *Economy and Society* 7(2): 118–54.

——. 1979. The Conceptualization of Race Relations in Sociological Theory. *Ethnic and Racial Studies* 2(2): 190–212.

Gumplowicz, L. 1875. *Rasse und Staat: Eine Untersuchung Uber Das Gesetz Der Staatenbilding*. Vienna: Verlag Der Manzschen Buchhandlung.

——. 1881. *Rechtsstaat und Socialismus*. Innsbruck: Verlag Der Wagner Schen Universtaets-Buchhandlung.

——. 1883. *Der Rassenkampf: Sociologische Untersuchungen*. Innsbruck: Verlag Der Wagner Schen Universtaets-Buchhandlung.

Hall, S. 1997. *Representations: Cultural Representations and Signifying Practices*. London: Sage Publications.

Hoch, P. 1979. *White Hero Black Beast: Racism, Sexism and the Mask of Masculinity*. London: Pluto Press.

Howard, P. 2004. Reflections on a Reading Course: Interrogating Whiteness in Critical/Anti-racist and Other Ostensibly Equitable Spaces. Unpublished Paper, Department of Sociology and Equity Studies in Education, OISE, University of Toronto.

——. 2005. Ph.D. Comprehensive Examination. Unpublished Paper, Department of Sociology and Equity Studies in Education, OISE, University of Toronto.

Johal, G. 2005. Order in K.O.S.: On Race, Rage and Method. In G.J.S. Dei and G. Johal, eds., *Critical Issues in Anti-Racist Research Methodology*. New York: Peter Lang. 269–93.

Kempf, A. 2006. Unpublished Paper (untitled). Department of Sociology and Equity Studies in Education, OISE, University of Toronto.

Lawson, E. 2004. Notes on Racialization and Racialized Subjects. Department of Sociology and Equity Studies in Education, OISE, University of Toronto.

Li, P. 1990. Race and Ethnicity. In P. Li, ed., *Race and Ethnic Relations in Canada*. Toronto: Oxford University Press. 3–17.

May, S. (ed.). 1999. *Critical Multiculturalism: Rethinking Multicultural and Anti-Racist Education*. London: Falmer Press.

Miles, R. 1980. Class, Race and Ethnicity: A Critique of Cox's Theory. *Ethnic and Racial Studies* 3(2): 169–81.

——. 1989. *Racism*. London: Tavistock.

——. 1993. *Racism After "Race Relations."* London: Routledge.

Miles, R., and R. Torres. 1996. Does Race Matter? Transatlantic Perspectives on Racism after Race Relations. In V. Amit-Talai and C. Knowles, eds., *Re-Situating Identities: The Politics of Race, Ethnicity and Culture*. Peterborough, ON: Broadview. 24–46.

Murray, C., and R. Herrnstein. 1994. *The Bell Curve*. New York: The Free Press.

Omi, M., and H. Winant. 1993. On the Theoretical Concept of Race. In C. McCarthy and W. Crichlow, eds., *Race, Identity and Representation in Education*. New York: Routledge. 3–17.

———. 1994. *Racial Formation in the United States*. 2nd ed. New York: Routledge.

Rushton, J.P. 1994. *Race, Evolution, and Behaviour: A Life History Perspective*. New Brunswick, NJ: Transactions Publishers.

———. 2001. Is Race a Valid Taxonomic Construct? Internet Essay, 14 December. <http://www. charlesdarwinresearch.org/TaxonomicConstruct.pdf>.

Said, E. 1979. *Orientalism*. New York: Vintage Books.

Shiva, V. 1997. Western Science and its Destruction of Local Knowledge. In M. Rahnema and V. Bawtree, eds., *The Post-Development Reader*. London: Zed Books. 161–67.

Smith, J. 1995. In Search of John Ogbu. Paper delivered at the annual conference of the American Educational Research Association (AERA), San Francisco, CA, 12 April.

Solomos, J. 1986. Varieties of Marxist Conceptions of "Race," Class and the State: A Critical Analysis. In J. Rex and D. Mason, eds., *Theories of Race and Ethnic Relations*. Cambridge: Cambridge University Press. 84–109.

Solomos, J., and L. Back. 1995. Marxism, Racism and Ethnicity. In J. Stanfield, ed., *Theories of Ethnicity*. Thousand Oaks, CA: Sage Publications. 407–20.

Winant, H. 1994. Racial Formation and Hegemony: Global and Local Implications. In A. Rattansi and S. Westwood, eds., *Racism, Modernity and Identity*. London: Polity Press. 266–89.

4 WHITENESS STUDIES
Race, Diversity, and the New Essentialism[1]

Vic Satzewich

INTRODUCTION

Twenty years ago, many North American and European social scientists would have scratched their heads in confusion if they were told that a colleague or graduate student was doing "white studies." Whiteness, for most scholars, was obvious, invisible, self-evident, and hardly worth wondering about. Today, however, there are white studies programs in universities, some academic job advertisements in the social sciences and humanities are addressed to experts in white studies, and a variety of academic disciplines call for disciplinary and interdisciplinary research agendas on whiteness (see, for example, Roediger 1991; Wing Sue 2004; Peake and Ray 2001; Brodkin 1998; McDonald 2005; King 2005). Still, despite the institutionalization of whiteness studies, snickers continue to be heard in academic corridors, and some scholars consider the analysis of whiteness as simply one more example of political correctness run amok.

In social science literature, there are two broad, interrelated approaches that scholars adopt to study and explain whiteness. I call these the historical and experiential approaches to whiteness, although the distinction should be construed primarily as analytical rather than empirical. Advocates of the historical approach conceptualize whiteness as a set of claims and counter claims about individual and group identity and status. This branch of research involves historical and contemporary studies of how diverse groups of people have claimed the mantle of whiteness and of how claims to whiteness have been contested, negotiated, accepted, and rejected. Historically oriented scholars do not conceptualize whiteness as a single, homogeneous attribute of a specific group of human beings that exists outside of the forces of history and social change. Rather, they understand whiteness as historically variable and constantly changing. They argue that many groups of people that are today commonly identified as "white" (e.g., Ukrainians, Italians, Jews, Celts, Slavs, and Irish) did not enjoy membership in this category as little as two or three generations ago and that it is historically inaccurate to apply the concept of whiteness to all people of European ancestry uncritically, collectively, and trans-historically.

While supporters of the experiential approach also acknowledge that whiteness has an historical dimension, they focus their attention elsewhere to conceptualize whiteness as an objective condition of a group of human beings that needs to be acknowledged, studied, and overcome. The experiential approach emerged out of debates within feminist theory, and it now involves a wide range of scholarship and activism associated with anti-racism and anti-colonialism. White people, so the argument goes, enjoy everyday privileges on the basis of their skin tone that non-white people are denied. A key aspect of combating racism, they maintain, is for white people to become aware of their privileges, their "white gaze," and the oppressive nature of their white culture. While scholars using an experiential approach wish to draw attention to the normative dimensions of Euro-Christian culture, they do so by conceptualizing "whiteness" as a synonym for "European" on the basis of the visibility of the white body. This has the effect of reducing the moral and intellectual essence of all people of European ancestry, however remote, to the pigmentation of their skin tone and of attributing a range of characteristics to white people, not least of which is an inability to see beyond skin privileges and cultural norms.

At first blush, it appears that both approaches to whiteness are grounded in a social constructionist approach to race. Fundamentally, social constructionism challenges biological and essentialist understandings of race and race difference. Rather than conceptualizing race as a fixed, biological attribute of human beings, social constructionists explain racial categories as historically variable and socially, politically, and economically constructed (Miles and Brown 2003). There are undoubtedly physical and genetic differences between people, but social constructionists maintain that these differences are not natural or biological "race" differences. Instead, they explain race as a social or cultural construct that has been used to describe and explain various patterns of physical and genetic difference (e.g., skin colour). What constitutes race and race difference, as well as the creation, application, and maintenance of racial labels and group boundaries, then, are matters of social definition, claims-making activities, and differential power relations. While many scholars apply the social constructionist approach to understand negative historical and contemporary constructions of black people and blackness, the constructionist approach has more recently been applied to historical and contemporary constructions of white people and whiteness. In this way, processes of racialization are accurately and usefully understood to occur not only when individuals and groups are socially constructed as "black" or "visible minority," for example, but also when they are socially constructed as "white."

Challenging the notion that the study of race and racism is most appropriately directed at black and other racialized minorities, whiteness studies has opened a broader field of analysis. Questions have been raised about how and why certain groups assert whiteness as an identity claim, about how and why groups become socially accepted as white, and about the correlates and consequences of whiteness. In this chapter, I critically assess some of the strengths and weaknesses associated with the historical and experiential approaches to whiteness. I point to certain contradictions in the research on whiteness, and I urge caution in conceptualizations of whiteness as an objective condition of human social groups. After examining each approach in some detail, I argue that, although the experiential approach, in combination with the historical approach, has effectively problematized whiteness, it often digresses into a new form of essentialism that is neither intellectually progressive nor empirically accurate. I conclude by encouraging a critical research agenda that simultaneously recognizes the everyday currency of socially perceived whiteness and that resists the temptation to conflate whiteness to the pale European body and to an essential character of human beings, many of whom have probably never seen Europe.

HISTORICAL CONSTRUCTIONS OF WHITENESS

Whiteness has entered into scholarly and political debate in part based on work on the new social history of immigration and race (e.g., Roediger 1991; Brodkin 1998; Ignatiev 1995; Iacovvetta 1992; Panayi 1994). In this literature, whiteness is analyzed as an assigned racial category and a self-adopted racial identity (Brodkin 1998). Whiteness is not regarded as a monolithic, permanent, and enduring racial category and identity but rather as a category and identity that is historically, geographically, and socially contingent. In other words, interesting historical and sociological questions are posed regarding how and why certain groups become accepted as "white," how and why they adopt white identity claims, and what consequences white identity claims have for social relations.

Much of the stimulus behind the development of this approach is grounded in the recognition that the current tendency to equate whiteness with European origin or ancestry masks a complex social and historical process of racialization. Omi and Winant (1986: 65), for instance, claim that the processes of class and racial formation in American political culture produced "the institutionalization of a racial order that drew a colour line *around* rather than *within* Europe." However, Jacobson (1998: 7) counters that, in the US between the 1840s and the 1920s, "it was not at all clear just where that line ultimately *would* be drawn." Many of the European groups that are now uncritically accepted as "white" were far from being considered white as little as two or three generations ago. For much of the late 19th and early 20th centuries, scholars, politicians, trade union leaders, captains of business, and members of the public in North America and Europe thought of Europe as being made up of a plurality of "races" that were inherently different from each other (Lorimer 1978). Whether one analyzes the images and discourses of science, common sense, politics, or popular culture, there was considerably less certainty about the "racial" homogeneity of Europeans than there is now. Groups from the southern and eastern periphery of Europe were particularly prone to racialized othering, but so too were members of the working class and peasantry in various Western European countries (Guillaumin 1995; Miles and Brown 2003; Balibar and Wallerstein 1991; Bonnett 1998). The subsequent transformation of classes and nationalities of "Europeans" into "whites" was neither natural nor inevitable; it was, rather, the outcome of political, economic, and ideological struggles.

The racial otherness of peripheral Europeans has been long recognized by American scholars. Historian John Higham notes that during the late 19th century there was an

> extension to European nationalities of that sense of absolute difference which already divided white Americans from people of other colors. When sentiments analogous to those already discharged against Negroes, Indians, and Orientals spilled over into anti-European channels, a force of tremendous intensity entered the stream of American nativism. (Higham 1955: 132)

Higham's classic study sought to demonstrate that the "racial ferment" of the late 19th and early 20th century in the US infected both popular culture and the world of science. Groups from the southern and eastern periphery of Europe were constructed as racially different from dominant whites and as one more racialized threat to the future stability of the American nation. However, as Jacobson argues, Higham was incorrect in emphasizing that the late 19th century saw a shift "toward racism." Questioning Higham's characterization of the timing of the racialization of Europeans from southern and eastern Europe, Jacobson argues that "race" was central to the entire history of European migration to the United States, not just a product of the late 19th century:

> "Fitness for self-government," a racial attribute whose outer property was whiteness, became encoded in a naturalization law that allowed Europeans unrestricted immigration and their unhindered male civic participation. It is solely because of their race that they were permitted entrance. But the massive influx borne of this "liberal" immigration policy, in its turn, generated a new perception of some Europeans' *un*fitness for self-government, now rendered racially in a series of subcategorical white groupings—Celt, Slav, Hebrew, Iberic, Mediterranean and so on—white Others of a supreme Anglo-Saxondom. (Jacobson 1998: 42)

Much of the recent literature on the social and historical transformation of peripheral Europeans into whites comes from the US. Irish immigrants are the archetypes of the process of becoming white, although research has also focused on Italians (Jacobson 1998; Gabaccia 1997) and Jews (Brodkin 1998). In the early 19th century, the social, intellectual, cultural, and political capacities of Irish immigrants and their descendants were racially defined in ways that were little different from the ways in which the American black population was defined. In the popular culture, politics, and racial science of the day, the Irish were regarded as racial others whose presence constituted a significant threat to American democracy. As Roediger (1991: 133) puts it: "*low browed*, and *savage*, *groveling* and *bestial*, *lazy* and *wild*, *simian* and *sensual*—such were the adjectives used by many native-born Americans to describe the Catholic Irish 'race' in the years before the Civil War."

The Irish, however, underwent a rather remarkable transformation during the course of the nineteenth century. They were able to renegotiate their externally imposed racial otherness, assert a white identity, and come to be accepted as members of the "white race." Having been accepted as white, they turned around and became some of the most vigorous defenders of whiteness. In many cases, their defence of a newly acquired whiteness put them at the forefront of hostilities and conflicts with black people.

Whiteness as an Elastic Concept

The case of the Irish in the US offers a compelling account of how and why a racialized group of peripheral Europeans was able to renegotiate their status within the American white/non-white racial dichotomy. To what extent should the Irish experience of whiteness in the US form the template by which we understand the social construction of whiteness for other peripheral Europeans? Was whiteness a universal aspiration for the peripheral Europeans who were subject to various kinds of racisms in the late 19th and early 20th centuries? And to what extent does the analysis of whiteness in the US form the template for understanding the social and historical constructions of whiteness in Canada?

Regarding the issue of peripheral Europeans, David Roediger expresses caution about over-generalizing from the Irish case. He and Barrett argue that in the US, the Irish became leaders in the crusade for white supremacy. However,

> New immigrant leaders never approximated that path. With a large segment
> of both [political] parties willing to vouch for the possibility of speedy, orderly
> Americanization and with neither party willing to vouch unequivocally for their
> racial character, Southern and Eastern Europeans tried to change the subject
> from whiteness to nationality and loyalty to American ideals.

They go on to suggest that "what might be termed an *abstention from whiteness* ... characterized the practice of rank-and-file East Europeans" when it came to their making claims about their identities and political loyalties (Barrett and Roediger 1999: 158).

While not fully developed, their observation raises important questions about the role of homeland politics in the creation of identities for groups from southern and eastern Europe. It also raises questions about the theoretical relationship between racism and nationalism (Miles and Brown 2003). Theorists like Anderson (1983) and Nairn (1981) argue that racism and nationalism are contradictory ideologies. Whereas racism speaks of inherent and eternal differences between peoples, they contend, nationalism, despite class, gender, or other similarities, speaks of the inherent unity of a people. Miles (1993), however, notes the possibility of the articulation of racism and nationalism, pointing out that in some historical circumstances nationalist identity claims can be overlaid with racism. What this suggests is that the two ideologies may be more complementary than conceived of by Anderson and Nairn. In some circumstances, externally imposed racial assignments may lead to the development of self-generated national identity claims. The social construction of a group as racial others does not necessarily lead members of that group to develop an identity that seeks inclusion within the dominant racializing group. In other words, groups might be labelled as racial others but they may respond to this racial otherness by advancing national identity—rather than race-based claims.

The analysis of historical constructions of whiteness in the US offers useful insights into how white identity claims are made and not made, negotiated and contested, but we should be cautious about how this kind of analysis is extended to countries like Canada. Canada and the US do share certain similarities in their immigration histories. Even though Canada has a history of slavery, it has a weaker historical imprint here than it does south of the border. That is, much of the politics pertaining to the claiming of whiteness in the US was based on European groups attempting to differentiate themselves from blacks and from the institution of slavery. Many of the early political and economic divides in Canada were, however, framed in the context of French-English and Catholic-Protestant relationships. To be sure, racialized othering was central to the formation of Canada and to the contemporary understanding of French-English relations, but racial otherness was complicated. Sometimes it was constructed around skin colour and biological superiority; at other times it was constructed around language, religion, and culture.

Added to which, as some American-based critics of historical studies of whiteness have argued, it is not at all clear that immigrants and racialized peripheral Europeans were not "white" upon their arrival in North America. In Canada, immigrants from eastern and southern Europe were certainly regarded as "uncivilized" and of questionable value for the purposes of nation building in a settler capitalist society. As one source from the 1920s noted,

> A line drawn across the continent of Europe from northeast to southwest, separating the Scandinavian Peninsula, the British Isles, Germany, and France from Russia, Austria-Hungary, Italy, and Turkey, separates countries not only of distinct races but also of distinct civilizations. It separates Protestant Europe from Catholic Europe; it separates countries of representative institutions and popular government from absolute monarchies; it separates lands where education is universal from lands where illiteracy predominates; it separates manufacturing countries, progressive agriculture, and skilled labour from primitive hand industries, backward agriculture, and unskilled labour; it separates an educated, thrifty peasantry scarcely a single generation removed from serfdom; it separates Teutonic races from the Latin, Slav, Semitic, and Mongolian races. (cited in Osborne 1991: 85)

Although the "Latin" and "Slav" immigrants who were on the wrong side of "the line" were racialized and attributed with a variety of negative cultural, economic, religious, and political traits, it is not clear that they were actually regarded in Canada as "not white" (see also Hartman 2004; Kolchin 2002). In Canada at the time, "race" was arguably understood in a way that was different from the way it is today, with many groups being regarded as racially different from Anglo Saxons and members of the "Teutonic race." Race difference, however, was not necessarily based on differences in skin colour.

Finally, potential immigrants in early 20th-century Canada were evaluated on the basis of a racialized hierarchy of desirability, with immigrants ranked as "preferred," "non-preferred," and "inadmissible." Although immigrants from the European periphery were generally regarded as "non-preferred," they were nevertheless admitted to Canada. This was unlike the case of inadmissible groups like immigrants from China and India, who were subjected to near blanket exclusion. The latter groups were regarded as racially inferior and non-white. Peripheral Europeans, while also regarded as racially inferior, were perceived by many elite Canadians to be capable of assimilation and cultural change. They were, therefore, deemed to be less of a threat to the reproduction of settler capitalist relations. It is not exactly clear what considerations made them less of a threat, but it is possible that their common or emerging whiteness played a role. In addition, although southern and eastern Europeans faced prejudice, racism, and discrimination, they did not face the same scale of racist exclusions that were faced by Chinese and East Indian workers who managed to arrive in Canada before near complete bans on their further immigration were implemented.

What these observations suggest is that caution should be exercised in the historical analysis of race difference and of white identity claims and counter claims. Although the Irish experience in the US constitutes an important example of how white identity claims are made and negotiated, care needs to be taken in extending this line of analysis to other groups and other national contexts. It is true that there are important differences in the way peripheral European immigrants and immigrants from China and India were received in Canada. It is equally true that there are important differences to be respected in the ways in which British and non-British Europeans were received. The latter speaks to the fluidity of white identity claims as a continual historical process and to the problems of conceptualizing whiteness as a resolute fact of history.

EXPERIENTIAL CONSTRUCTIONS OF WHITENESS

As noted above, the second approach to whiteness considered in this chapter, the experiential approach, conceptualizes whiteness as a condition that needs to be acknowledged, exposed, and fought against. While the historical approach to whiteness shares these goals—as both a research program and anti-racist strategy—the experiential approach foregrounds the claim that the elimination of racism is contingent on the simultaneous recognition and overcoming of whiteness as a social condition (Bonnett 2000).

A number of social scientists and anti-racist activists argue that an essential part of the anti-racist struggle is for whites to understand and expose their own white privilege, their white culture, and their white gaze (Henry and Tator 2006: 47). According to Ruth Frankenberg, there are three dimensions to whiteness that need to be taken into consideration in both scholarly analysis and in the struggle against anti-racism:

> First, [whiteness] ... is a position of structural advantage, associated with "privileges" of the most basic kind, including for example, higher wages, reduced chances of being impoverished, longer life, better access to health care, better treatment by the legal system, and so on.... Second whiteness is a "standpoint" or place from which to look at oneself, others and society. Thirdly, it carries with it a set of ways of being in the world, a set of cultural practices, often not named as "white" by white folks, but looked upon instead as "American" [and Canadian?] or "normal." (Frankenberg 1993: 52)

Within this framework, challenging whiteness is both praxis and a research agenda. It is only when white privilege is understood, and when white culture and the white gaze are exposed as racist, that societies like Canada will be able to genuinely deal with the issues that lie at the heart of racism.

Although Frankenberg treats the notions of a white gaze and white culture separately in her characterization of whiteness studies, I treat them here as interlinked. As she noted, the other dimensions of whiteness that scholars and activists argue need to be studied, and challenged, are the white standpoint (or the white gaze) and white culture. There are a number of interrelated explanations in the literature for what is meant by a white standpoint/gaze and white culture. For example, Kobayashi and Peake (2000: 394) contend that the standpoint of whiteness is: "a place from which to look at ourselves and the surrounding society, a position of normalcy, and perhaps moral superiority, from which to construct a landscape of what is same and what is different." Dalton's take on the notion of a white gaze or standpoint emphasizes a particular reaction to issues of racism. He argues that racism persists, in part, because white people do not perceive themselves as having a "race." By not thinking in racial terms about themselves, white people will never be able to confront racism. According to Dalton, the failure of white people to think of themselves in racial terms "leaves them with huge blind spots," which

> » ... leave them [Whites] "baffled" by the amount of energy that many Black people pour into questions of racial identity.
> » ... make [Whites] ... incapable of understanding why many blacks have a sense of group consciousness that influences the choices they make as individuals.
> » blind ... [Whites] to the fact that their lives are shaped as much by race as the lives of black people. (Dalton 2002: 17–18)

And in Dyer's (2002: 10) assessment, "the assumption that white people are just people, which is not far off saying that whites are people whereas other colours are something else, is endemic to white culture."

What are the contours of white culture that lie at the heart of calls within the anti-racist movement to recognize whiteness and white privilege? Geographers Audrey Kobayashi and Linda Peake argue that whiteness is a

... set of cultural practices and politics based upon ideological norms that are lived but unacknowledged. As a result, it "forecloses [a] broader examination of the present and thereby precludes action to transform it" (West 1993: 39). Whiteness is indicated less by its explicit racism than by the fact that it ignores, or even denies, racist indications. It occupies central ground by deracializing and normalizing common events and beliefs, giving them legitimacy as part of a moral system depicted as natural and universal .... Geographically, human beings reciprocally shape and are shaped by their surrounding environments to produce landscapes that conform similarly to ideals of beauty, utility, or harmony, values not immediately associated with "race" but predicated upon whitened cultural practices. (Kobayashi and Peake 2000: 394)

According to this definition, there are two fundamental dimensions to white culture. The first is characterized by systematic and generalized denial of racism. In this way, Kobayashi and Peake's definition of white culture is consistent with the argument by Henry and Tator (2006: 22; see also Razack 1998) that white Canadians are democratic racists: people who value justice, equality, and fairness but at the same time hold attitudes and engage in behaviours that negatively affect the lives and life changes of people of colour. The second dimension refers to the built environment and the way that the environment reflects white cultural aesthetics: white ways of valuing buildings, public spaces, art, and, indeed, wider events in the world.

In the remainder of this section, I want to critically evaluate each of the claims made about whiteness in this anti-racist academic research agenda. In doing so, I am not questioning the existence of racism in Canadian society. Instead, my concern about portraying whiteness as an objective condition that needs to be overcome is that it tends to essentialize the category of white and to homogenize the positions, attitudes, and experiences of diverse groups of people. While whiteness is a useful analytical concept, there is a difference between conceptualizing whiteness as an essential attribute of a group of people and conceptualizing it as an historically based articulation of identity claims and counter claims.

White Privilege and White Socio-Economic Advantage?

Let us first consider the notion of white privilege or white structural advantage. As noted by Frankenberg above, white people, as a collectivity, are seen to operate from a position of structural advantage over black people and other racialized minorities. Whites, in short, are seen to have more political and economic power, and more socio-economic resources than other groups in society. What evidence is there that white people in Canada, as a collectivity, have a consistent structural advantage over people who are not socially defined as white?

To answer this question, we should clarify the people we are referring to when we refer to "whites." Statistics Canada has only recently started to collect data on the "race" of Canadians. While post-World War II census questionnaires have consistently asked Canadians for information about their "origins," for the first time in the 1996 census Statistics Canada asked questions about the "racial" origins of Canadians. It asked whether Canadians were: white, Chinese, South Asian, black, Arab/West Asian, Filipino, South East Asian, Latin American, Japanese, Korean, or other. In Canada, all of these groups, save for the first, are collectively referred to as "visible minorities." Whites, by default, are arguably all those who are not included in the above list. They are sometimes referred to as the "not visible minority," and they encompass groups like Australians, Americans, and individuals who trace their ancestry to Europe—Scots, Greeks, Poles, and Belgians, for example (Stelcner 2000).

The categories of "white" and "visible minority" are arguably too crude to accurately disentangle social stratification and the nature of structural advantage and disadvantage. They lump together a wide variety of different groups of people with differing migration histories and differing structural positions in Canadian society. Even though some claim that there is a new, racialized vertical mosaic in Canada, with European groups at the top of the socio-economic hierarchy and visible minorities at the bottom (Fleras and Elliott 2003: 117), research on the socio-economic performance of different groups in Canadian society offers a rather mixed picture of systematic advantage and disadvantage that does not fall clearly along a white/non-white divide. For example, young Chinese and Filipino men and women in Canada tend to have higher rates of university degrees than most European origin groups (Davies and Guppy 1998; Ali and Grabb 1998). In Toronto, immigrants from the former Soviet Union, Poland, and the former Yugoslavia have annual wage incomes that are below those of Caribbean, South and Central American, African, Filipino, and Indian immigrants (Jansen and Lam 2003: 118–19). When considering social class, white Canadians are not consistently over-advantaged compared to their non-white counterparts. Visible minority and European-origin Canadians are distributed across the range of class sites as workers, managers, supervisors, professionals, the self-employed, and employers (Liodakis 2002).

To be sure, many authors have noted that white privilege is mediated by the categories of class and gender:

> Whiteness does not confer on all White people the same access to privilege. The White mother on welfare, the homeless White male do not form a homogeneous community with White journalists, judges, educators, and CEOs and clearly do not enjoy equal access to White privilege. (Henry and Tator 2006: 46)

More often than not, however, these concessions to class-based disadvantage are symbolic and are not taken seriously in the analysis of the patterns of privilege in Canadian society. While there is an almost ritualistic admission that "race," class, and gender are intersecting bases of inequality, the class relations are often dropped when it comes to characterizing the fundamental nature of privilege in Canada.

In short, the notion of white privilege as a proxy for whiteness does not offer an accurate picture of social inequality because there is no clear-cut pattern of white structural advantage and non-white structural disadvantage when it comes to education, income, and social class in Canada (Stelcner 2000).

Following are three critical observations about notions of white culture and the white gaze that are at the heart of calls to acknowledge whiteness.

Double Standards

First, there is a double standard associated with anti-racist calls for whites to recognize and take responsibility for their white culture. As a number of activists and scholars have pointed out, black culture is not homogenous, and there are differences among black people in terms of their migration histories, beliefs, cultures, and values. Black people from the Caribbean do not necessarily believe in the same things, or have the same values, as black people from Africa or from other parts of the world. And further, among African immigrants, cultural diversity and intra-group conflicts "undermine ... any serious movement towards Black unity in this country" (Mensah 2002: 127). Indeed, because black people are so diverse, it makes little sense to speak of a unified and homogenous black culture that holds black people together as blacks. Indeed, some have written powerfully of the "myth" of a unified and homogeneous black culture (Gilroy 1987: 16–17; Lawrence 1982: 95–142).

Similar reservations have been expressed about the concept of "visible minority" in Canada. Synnott and Howes argue that there are a number of conceptual problems associated with the notion of "visible minority." In their view,

> 1) It homogenizes the singular, the specific, and the unique. 2) It sacralizes sight and vision. 3) It ignores the significance of language, history, religion and cultural, sounds, tastes and smells which also create identification. 4) It is an imposition by the majority, by "the Other," by the center (whichever metaphor you prefer) on "the Other." 5) It "racializes" many types of ethnic identification. 6) It "biologizes" the social in the social construction of reality. (Synnott and Howes 1996: 156–57)

If notions of a unified black culture are a myth, if part of the anti-racist agenda is to expose the myth of a unitary and essential black culture, and if the concept of "visible minority" uncritically and illegitimately racializes and biologizes the socially constructed nature of ethnic identification, then should white culture be attributed with a reality that is immutable, deterministically held, and negatively evaluated? The category of "white" is arguably just as diverse as the categories "black" or "visible minority." The irony is that, at the same time that there have been effective challenges to the notion of black culture and the homogeneity of visible minority, notions of white culture have become essentialized. As explained by Hartigan (1999: 185), the notion of white culture that forms part of the discourse about whiteness comes "close to undermining the basis of social constructionist views of race because the conviction that there are no inherent affinities between people sharing a collective racial identity is destabilized by such a singular, unified definition of whiteness."

A Unified White Gaze?

The second observation focuses on the notion of a "white" gaze. Do all white people have the same attitudes, or gaze, when it comes to "racial" issues? Are all white people blind to the realities of racism? To be sure, some white people do not see that racism is a problem in our society. At the same time, however, others do. In fact, in various surveys, significant proportions of white people in Canada do recognize that racism is a problem in our society and that minority groups experience racism and discrimination. For example, the 1995 *Final Report of the Commission on Systemic Racism in the Ontario Criminal Justice System* found that a significant proportion of white residents of Toronto believed that judges do not treat black and white people the same. In one of their surveys the commission found that 52% of black respondents, 31% of Chinese respondents, and 36% of white respondents believed that judges do not treat black people the same as white people. Among those who felt that there was differential treatment of blacks and whites, 87% of black, 85% of Chinese, and 80% of white respondents felt that judges treat black people worse or much worse than white people. Combined, these figures indicate that 45.2% of black, 26.4% of Chinese, and 28.8% of white Torontonians in the survey felt that judges treated blacks worse or much worse than whites (Commission on Systemic Racism in the Ontario Criminal Justice System 1998: 181). The fact that nearly three in 10 white people in the survey felt that judges treated black offenders worse than white offenders needs to be taken seriously and indicates that whites do not have a singular "gaze" when it comes to perceptions of racial issues.

Furthermore, there are other findings from the survey that also question whether there are homogenous racialized gazes on issues of racism and unequal treatment. Over half of the black respondents, and nearly 75% of Chinese respondents, did not feel that black offenders were treated worse than white offenders (Commission on Systemic Racism in the Ontario Criminal Justice System 1998: 181). This suggests that there is diversity in the "gaze" of black and Chinese respondents about differential treatment and that white respondents were not the only group to question whether there was racially based unequal treatment within the Ontario justice system.

The survey also examined the perceptions of different professionals within the justice system regarding the extent of unequal treatment. While it did not differentiate between professionals of different backgrounds, it did find that 10% of general division judges, 10% of provincial judges appointed before 1989, 13% of crown attorneys, 33% of provincial judges appointed after 1989, 34% of defence lawyers with less that 40% racial minority clientele, and 52% of defence lawyers with 40% or more racial minority clientele thought that white and racial minority accused are not treated the same in the justice system (Commission on Systemic Racism in the Ontario Criminal Justice System 1998: 198–99).

Other evidence suggests that some white Canadians recognize and acknowledge that Aboriginal peoples experience significant problems with racism and discrimination. A 1994 survey found, for example, that 23% of responses to a Canada-wide survey indicated that alcohol or drugs was the most serious problem facing Aboriginal people in Canada, but that nearly the same proportion (21%) felt that racism or discrimination was the most serious problem they faced. Put differently, nearly the same proportion of Canadians who blamed the victim also blamed dominant society racism as the main source of Aboriginal peoples' problems (Ponting 1998: 289).

When it comes to characterizing the "white gaze," therefore, one of the problems with experiential approaches to whiteness studies is that it conflates a wide variety of attitudes towards issues of racism and racial inequality. While the notion of a white gaze may be a convenient rhetorical tool for describing a collectivity, it is not a useful sociological category because it homogenizes the attitudes and values of people who appear "white." In effect, the logic of this argument makes no distinction between the views and opinions of members of organized racist groups (see Barrett 1987) and ordinary "white" Canadians. Moreover, white supremacists do seem to recognize their white privilege and their white gaze, but they do so not in ways that anti-racist activists would like them to.

White Landscapes

The third critical observation about whiteness as a condition pertains to claims about "white" landscapes and a "white" built environment. Clearly, urban and rural landscapes bear the imprints of past generations and their aesthetic and cultural values. Immigrants build and paint houses, decorate their yards, and try to organize their neighbourhoods in ways that reflect their socio-economic and culturally based aesthetic values. Urban and rural landscapes are not ethnically neutral but rather reflect certain socially conditioned standards of beauty and good taste. The question, however, is whether Canadian historical landscapes and features of the built environment are economic and ethnocultural artifacts or simply racial artifacts that reflect whiteness.

There have been a number of recent and well-publicized controversies in Canada about the ways that immigration is contributing to changes to urban landscapes. The debate about monster houses in Vancouver in the 1980s and 1990s and the spread of Asian shopping malls in Markham, Ontario, both involved conflicts over the use, organization, and design of urban space (Li 2003). In both cases, Chinese immigrants have been targets of hostility for their attempts to transform urban spaces.

In the case of Vancouver, wealthy Chinese businesspeople, actively recruited by the federal government under the business immigration program, came to Canada, bought properties in established neighbourhoods, and proceeded to change their properties in ways that reflected their culturally and economically driven aesthetics. Geographer Katharyne Mitchell (2004:187) argues that the resulting debate reflected a complex mix of racial and class-based politics. While there were undoubtedly racist elements to the concerns about monster houses, she uncritically conflates historically specific cultural aesthetics with white racial aesthetics. She argues that much of the west side of the city of Vancouver was built using British architectural and landscape symbols. Even though she characterizes the urban landscape of parts of Vancouver as rooted in a particular historical English/British ethnicity, she equates this British culturally inspired landscape not only with "whiteness" but also with racism. In referring to Chinese business immigrant resistance to critiques about their housing and property aesthetics, Mitchell argues that

> The newcomers actively contested these narratives. They did so by exposing the British-inflected and racist cultural norms of historical Vancouver spaces, and also by practicing (and occasionally advocating) alternative dispositions of home, landscape and territory. (Mitchell 2004: 215)

While the debate about monster houses was unquestionably informed by racism, it is not obvious that the dominant Vancouver landscapes that were being defended by longer settled residents of Vancouver were *white* landscapes. Mitchell's analysis tends to conflate certain class-based, English/British-inspired landscapes with white landscapes. As earlier sections of this chapter have shown, there is diversity within the category of "white" and analytical claims about the existence of white landscapes hide and suppress that diversity.

Richard Harris, in his book *Creeping Conformity: How Canada Became Suburban, 1900–1960*, effectively documents the historical origins of "suburbia" in Canada. In his analysis, it is clear that before World War II, there were distinct class differences in suburban types. Anglo-American, upper-class suburbs were clearly one form of suburban life, but there were others. Middle-class suburbs were different, and working-class "shacktown" suburbs were "different again" (Harris 2004: 157–60). Harris traces the increasing convergence of suburban landscapes and architectural styles in the postwar period to federal government lending policies and to corporate decision-making rather than to a common desire on the part of European-origin Canadians to create "white" social spaces.

Furthermore, in many large Canadian cities there remain clearly identifiable pockets of architectural and landscape difference that reflect ethnically based urban aesthetics. These pockets are neither "white" nor in complete conformity to their wider surroundings. Nor are they simply the stereotypical "Little Italies," "Greektowns," or "Little Portugals" that are sometimes deliberately marketed by city governments or ethnic elites for the purposes of promoting ethnic tourism. The pockets are evident in the everyday ways in which at least some individuals of different backgrounds, particularly first-generation immigrants, organize their lives and relationships to the urban environment. In *Eh, Paesan! Being Italian in Toronto*, Nicholas Harney describes travelling to an interview north of Toronto and the gradual transformation of the landscape in ways that pointed to his entry into an identifiable Italian, or Italian-Canadian, neighbourhood:

> As I drove these first tentative kilometers, I was struck by the walled hous-
> ing tracts to the north, interspersed with the occasional business, and the low
> sprawling malls on the streets just to the south. The architectural style of the
> homes, with their marble, brick or stone patios, and stretches of wood beam
> arbours hinted at the ethnocultural make-up of the neighbourhood. The rela-
> tionship between Italian immigrants and nature became a shorthand for me as
> I navigated settlements in the city. Backyards flush against formed-stone walls
> revealed the tops of fruit tress and the weathered wood of shacks for storing
> equipment and tomato stakes and bean poles. I learned later that there is one
> practical reason, aside from the political, why many Italian-Canadian front
> lawns are dotted with the signs of several political parties during election cam-
> paigns: the wooden stakes are handy, sturdy, and free support for the summer's
> harvest. (Harney 1998: 27)

In sum, claims about white landscapes that are also at the centre of whiteness studies need to be treated with care. Historically urban landscapes have been con-structed and marked as much by social class, corporate interests, and government policy as by ethnicity and a desire to construct and preserve white social spaces. Nor do there seem to be agreed-upon urban landscapes, aesthetics, and hous-ing designs that are universally accepted as "white" by individuals of European background.

CONCLUSION

The problematization of "whiteness" in recent scholarship about race and racism has opened up new areas of inquiry that have increasingly caught the attention of a wide variety of social scientists. In this chapter, I have considered literature on historical and experiential approaches to whiteness. The former considers white-ness as an identity claim, while the latter treats whiteness as an objective condition that shapes the structural position, attitudes, and culture of a group of people, usually defined by their common European origins and purportedly common skin tone. While both perspectives on whiteness have generated considerable amounts of research and scholarly and political debate, this chapter has suggested that care should be taken in how whiteness is used as an analytical category.

In particular, the notion that whiteness is an objective condition that needs to be overcome is premised on a simplistic understanding of social inequality and of advantage and disadvantage in capitalist societies. The conceptualization of whiteness as an objective condition that carries with it a certain gaze, culture, and set of aesthetics is problematic because it homogenizes a group of people with a diverse set of attitudes about racial issues. Individuals with purportedly white skin tones or of European origin do not hold uniform beliefs about minority and racism related issues, nor do they appear to have uniform preferences about urban designs, landscapes, and public spaces.

The aim of this chapter has not been to discredit certain analyses of whiteness. Rather, some of the pitfalls of both approaches to whiteness have been identified in order to help clarify research and analytical issues. As the historical approaches to whiteness have made abundantly clear, groups that are now considered in common sense as white were not necessarily considered as white as little as two or three generations ago. Furthermore, it is also clear that some individuals and groups claim whiteness as a marker of identity and group boundaries, and so experiential approaches to whiteness can offer an interesting and useful perspective on how those identity claims are made and negotiated, and of how processes of inclusion and exclusion operate. However, experiential approaches to whiteness need also be sensitive to history. Historical context is important because it reminds us that analytical and descriptive categories like "whiteness" are not invariable attributes or conditions of groups of people. One of the most valuable contributions of constructionist approaches to the issue of race has been to undermine essentialist and primordial understandings of human difference. By focusing on whiteness as a form of racialization that is both historically specific and socially negotiated, experiential approaches to whiteness can offer a unique lens by which to understand identity formation and the formation and maintenance of group boundaries.

NOTE

1   A section of this chapter first appeared in Satzewich 2000.

REFERENCES AND FURTHER READINGS

Ali, Jennifer, and Edward Grabb. 1998. Ethnic Origin, Class Origin, and Educational Attainment in Canada: Further Evidence on the Mosaic Thesis. *Journal of Canadian Studies* 33(1): 3–21.

Allen, Theodore. 1994. *The Invention of the White Race: Volume One: Racial Oppression and Social Control.* London: Verso.

Anderson, Benedict. 1983. *Imagined Communities: Reflections on the Origin and Spread of Nationalism.* London: Verso.

Balibar, Etienne, and Immanuel Wallerstein. 1991. *Race, Nation and Class: Ambiguous Identities.* London: Verso.

Banton, Michael. 1987. *Racial Theories.* Cambridge: Cambridge University Press.

Barrett, James, and David Roediger. 1999. In Between Peoples: Race, Nationality, and the "New Immigrant" Working Class. In N. Yetman, ed., *Majority and Minority: The Dynamics of Race and Ethnicity in American Life.* Boston: Allyn and Bacon.

Barrett, Stanley. 1987. *Is God a Racist? The Right Wing in Canada.* Toronto: University of Toronto Press.

Bonnett, Alastair. 1998. How the British Working Class Became White: The Symbolic (Re)formation of Racialized Capitalism. *Journal of Historical Sociology* (11)3: 316–40.

———. 2000. *Anti-Racism*. London: Routledge.

Brodkin, Karen. 1998. *How Jews Became White Folks & What That Says About Race in America*. New Brunswick, NJ: Rutgers University Press.

Commission on Systemic Racism in the Ontario Criminal Justice System. 1998. Racism in Justice: Perceptions. In Vic Satzewich, ed., *Racism and Social Inequality in Canada*. Toronto: Thompson Educational Publishers.

Dalton, Harlon. 2002. Failing to See. In Paula Rothenberg, ed., *White Privilege: Essential Readings on the Other Side of Racism*. New York: Worth Publishers.

Davies, Scott, and Neil Guppy. 1998. Race and Canadian Education. In Vic Satzewich, ed., *Racism and Social Inequality in Canada*. Toronto: Thompson Educational Publishers.

Dyer, Richard. 2002. The Matter of Whiteness. In Paula Rothenberg, ed., *White Privilege: Essential Readings on the Other Side of Racism*. New York: Worth Publishers.

Fleras, Augie, and Jean Leonard Elliott. 2003. *Unequal Relations: An Introduction to Race and Ethnic Dynamics in Canada*. 4th ed. Toronto: Prentice Hall.

Frankenberg, Ruth. 1993. Growing Up White: Feminism, Racism, and the Social Geography of Childhood. *Feminist Review* 45: 51–84.

Gabaccia, Donna. 1997. The "Yellow Peril" and the "Chinese of Europe": Global Perspectives on Race and Labor, 1815–1930. In Jan Lucassen and Leo Lucassen, eds., *Migrations, Migration History, History: Old Paradigms and New Perspectives*. Bern: Lang.

Gilroy, Paul. 1987. *There Ain't No Black in the Union Jack*. London: Hutchinson.

Guillaumin, Collette. 1995. *Racism, Sexism, Power and Ideology*. London: Routledge.

Harney, Nicholas DeMaria. 1998. *Eh, Paesan! Being Italian in Toronto*. Toronto: University of Toronto Press.

Harris, Richard. 2004. *Creeping Conformity: How Canada Became Suburban, 1900-1960*. Toronto: University of Toronto Press.

Hartigan, John. 1999. Establishing the Fact of Whiteness. In Rodolfo Torres, Louis Miron, and Jonathan Xavier Inda, eds., *Race, Identity, and Citizenship: A Reader*. Oxford: Blackwell.

Hartman, Andrew. 2004. The Rise and Fall of Whiteness Studies. *Race and Class* 46(2): 22–38.

Henry, Frances, and Carol Tator. 2006. *The Colour of Democracy: Racism in Canadian Society*. 3rd ed. Toronto: Thomson-Nelson.

Higham, John. 1955. *Strangers in the Land: Patterns of American Nativism*. New York: Atheneum Press.

Iacovetta, Franca. 1992. *Such Hardworking People: Italian Immigrants in Post-War Toronto*. Toronto: University of Toronto Press.

Ignatiev, Noel. 1995. *How the Irish Became White*. London: Routledge.

Jacobson, Matthew Frye. 1998. *Whiteness of a Different Color: European Immigrants and the Alchemy of Race*. Cambridge, MA: Harvard University Press.

Jansen, Clifford, and Lawrence Lam. 2003. Immigrants in the Greater Toronto Area: A Sociodemographic Overview. In Paul Anisef and Michael Lanphier, eds., *The World in a City*. Toronto: University of Toronto Press.

King, Richard. 2005. Cautionary Notes on Whiteness and Sports Studies. *Sociology of Sport Journal* 22: 397–408.

Kobayashi, Audrey, and Linda Peake. 2000. Racism out of Place: Thoughts on Whiteness and an Anti-Racist Geography in the New Millennium. *Annals of the Association of American Geographers* 90(2): 392–403.

Kolchin, Peter. 2002. Whiteness Studies: The New History of Race in America. *Journal of American History* 89: 145–73.

Lawrence, Errol. 1982. In the Abundance of Water the Fool is Thirsty: Sociology and Black "Pathology." In Centre for Contemporary Cultural Studies, *The Empire Strikes Back: Race and Racism in 70s Britain*. London: Hutchinson.

Li, Peter. 2003. *Destination Canada: Immigration Debates and Issues*. Toronto: Oxford University Press.

Liodakis, Nick. 2002. *The Vertical Mosaic Within: Class, Gender and Nativity Within Ethnicity*. Ph.D. dissertation. Department of Sociology, McMaster University, Hamilton.

Lorimer, Douglas. 1978. *Colour, Class and the Victorians: English Attitudes to the Negro in the Mid-Nineteenth Century*. New York: Holmes and Meier Publishers Inc.

McDonald, Mary. 2005. Mapping Whiteness and Sport: An Introduction. *Sociology of Sport Journal* 22: 245–55.

Mensah, Joseph. 2002. *Black Canadians: History, Experiences, Social Conditions*. Halifax: Fernwood.

Miles, Robert. 1993. *Racism After "Race Relations."* London: Routledge.

Miles, Robert, and Malcolm Brown. 2003. *Racism*. 2nd ed. London: Routledge.

Mitchell, Katharyne. 2004. *Crossing the Neoliberal Line: Pacific Rim Migration and the Metropolis*. Philadelphia, PA: Temple University Press.

Nairn, Tom. 1981. *The Break-up of Britain*. London: Verso.

Omi, Michael, and Howard Winant. 1986. *Racial Formation in the United States*. London: Routledge.

Osborne, Brian. 1991. "Non-Preferred" People: Inter-war Ukrainian Immigration to Canada. In Lubomyr Luciuk and Stella Hryniuk, eds., *Canada's Ukrainians: Negotiating an Identity*. Toronto: University of Toronto Press.

Panayi, Panikos. 1993a. Anti-German Riots in Britain During the First World War. In Panikos Panayi, ed., *Racial Violence in Britain: 1840–1950*. Leicester: Leicester University Press.

——. 1993b. Anti-Immigrant Riots in Nineteenth- and Twentieth-Century Britain. In Panikos Panayi, ed., *Racial Violence in Britain: 1840–1950*. Leicester: Leicester University Press.

——. 1994. *Immigration, Ethnicity and Racism in Britain, 1815–1945*. Manchester: Manchester University Press.

Peake, Linda, and Brian Ray. 2001. Racializing the Canadian Landscape: Whiteness, Uneven Geographies, and Social Justice. *Canadian Geographer* 45(1): 180–86.

Ponting, J. Rick. 1998. Racism and Stereotyping of First Nations. In Vic Satzewich, ed., *Racism and Social Inequality in Canada*. Toronto: Thompson Educational Publishers.

Razack, Sherene. 1998. *Looking White People in the Eye: Gender, Race, and Culture in Courtrooms and Classrooms*. Toronto: University of Toronto Press.

Roediger, David. 1991. *The Wages of Whiteness: Race and the Making of the American Working Class*. London: Verso.

Satzewich, Vic. 2000. Whiteness Limited: Racialization and the Social Construction of "Peripheral Europeans." *Histoire sociale/Social History* 33(66): 271–90.

Stelcner, Morton. 2000. Earnings Differences Among Ethnic Groups in Canada: A Review of the Research. *Review of Social Economy* LVIII(3): 295–317.

Synnott, Anthony, and David Howes. 1996. Canada's Visible Minorities: Identity and Representation. In Vered Amit-Talai and Carolyn Knowles, eds., *Re-Situating Identities: The Politics of Race, Ethnicity, and Culture*. Peterborough: Broadview.

West, Cornell. 1993. *Keeping Faith: Philosophy and Race in America*. London: Routledge.

Wing Sue, Derald. 2004. Whiteness and Ethnocentric Monoculturalism: Making the "Invisible" Visible. *American Psychologist* (November): 761–69.

PART TWO
Racism and Structural Patterns of Incorporation in Canada

INTRODUCTION

In 1965, Canadian sociologist John Porter published *The Vertical Mosaic: An Analysis of Class and Power*. *The Vertical Mosaic* was a comprehensive effort to bring conceptual coherence to the relationships among power, ethnicity (race), and social class relations in Canada. Porter argued that the economic and political mobility of subordinated ethno-racial groups entering Canada develops in relation to "charter group" power and privilege. He believed that an "entrance status" is assigned to less preferred immigrant groups that restricts collective gains in education, income, and membership among Canada's elite. For Porter, an entrance status derives from charter group prejudices that are reinforced by the retention of certain cultural practices (such as language or custom). He believed that an entrance status was powerful enough to become a "caste-like" barrier, restricting the extent to which social mobility among ethno-racial minority group members is possible.

As Hier and Walby (2006) observe, the imagery of the vertical mosaic continues to resonate strongly with many Canadian sociologists, but numerous sociological research findings since its publication have challenged the extent to which Porter's original arguments can be generalized. The three decades following World War II brought considerable social-structural change in Canada, and the influence of those changes may be observed consistently, albeit unevenly, across Canadian institutional spaces. Significant collective advances in education, labour, and social mobility have been made among members of Canada's visible minority groups, but social position, language proficiency, place of birth, and immigration status remain important correlates of social incorporation within and among visible minority groups in Canadian institutions.

This section presents four chapters concerned with racism and social structural incorporation. Derek Hum and Wayne Simpson, in the first chapter of this part, begin their analysis by observing that, although all visible minority groups in Canada show lower earnings than non-visible minority groups, there is considerable variation among them. Using data from the master file of the Survey of Labour and Income Dynamics, they seek to better understand variation in wage differentials among visible minority groups in the country. Through a series of regression analyses, Hum and Simpson find that, with the exception of black and Latin American men, there are no significant wage differentials between visible and non-visible minority groups where native-born workers are concerned. While differences are greater for foreign-born workers, they maintain that it is too simplistic to attribute these to skin colour. Hum and Simpson conclude by reflecting on the significance of their findings for employment equity practices in Canada, and their analysis warns of the dangers of homogenizing visible minority groups in public policy debate on earning differentials and labour market incorporation.

In the following chapter, Li Zong observes another generalizing tendency in the literature: the assumption that Chinese immigrants to Canada are increasingly wealthy, prosperous, and possessed of large amounts of capital. Zong points out that most recent Mainland Chinese immigrants are well-trained, experienced professionals who are welcomed by Canadian immigration officials, but he contends that many new Chinese immigrants experience disappointment after immigrating to Canada because they fail to achieve satisfactory social and economic status (see also Chapter 12). Zong presents data from Statistics Canada to illustrate the dramatic growth of Chinese immigration over the past decade. Based on longitudinal survey data, however, he maintains that recent immigrants are not achieving parity in the Canadian labour market compared to their previous occupations in China. Importantly, he contends that upward mobility is a function of factors such as immigration status, credentials, and proficiency in the English language, but he also devotes considerable attention to covert forms of racism in Canada. His chapter raises important questions about policy formation on foreign credentials and the significance of covert forms of systemic racism.

In Chapter 7, Terry Wotherspoon assesses the incorporation of Aboriginal labour, which has become a key policy debate in Canada. As the Canadian workforce ages and the economy becomes increasingly globally competitive, education, skills training, and aptitude for labour market participation have taken on a new urgency where younger Aboriginals are concerned. Wotherspoon begins by demonstrating how First Nations economies have been transformed from relatively autonomous spaces into an interdependent web of capitalist relations. Marginalization of First Nations communities gave rise to concerted efforts on the part of government and non-government agencies to advance the social and economic status of Aboriginal peoples (involving on and off reserve programs). While Aboriginal peoples have occupied a range of structural positions in the Canadian labour market, Aboriginal organizations in Canada and internationally are consolidating their interests. These efforts are diverse, and Wotherspoon pays attention to how class differences associated with global capitalism produce uneven and, at times, conflicting outcomes for Aboriginal people.

The final chapter in this section takes up the class dimensions of labour market incorporation in seasonal labour migrations. Ricardo Trumper and Lloyd Wong suggest that the labour of guest workers in Canada is flexible from employers' points of view, but it is "precarious" from the labourers' points of view. They contend that the structure of global capitalism does not purposefully create race and gender barriers but that race and gender are salient factors in the outcome of differential labour market incorporation in Canada. Examining the plight of agricultural labourers (farm workers), live-in caregivers (domestic workers), and highly skilled hi-tech workers who come to Canada under the provisions of the Temporary Foreign Worker Program, Trumper and Wong show how Canada's historical pattern of importing temporary labour to fill positions in the labour market has remained constant. They also observe that the point system designed to attract high-end immigrants has created barriers for workers in occupations that do not require high skill levels and formal training. Because of Canada's aging workforce and population, combined with the influence of neo-liberalism, domestic workers are becoming more important. Nevertheless, Trumper and Wong argue, contradictions in the incorporation of workers and citizens persist along class and, related but not uniform, ethno-racial lines.

The papers in this section collectively paint a complex picture of racism and structural incorporation in Canada. The data suggest that visible minority groups can be homogenized neither by experience nor class position and that there are important mediating factors beyond ethnicity or race in patterns of incorporation. They also suggest that policy-makers must rethink the targeting of specific groups of people in the realm of equity hiring, skills training, and citizenship. Not one of the authors in this section is oblivious to the impact of racism in its various forms, but they are primarily concerned with the interaction effects of ethno-racial designation and income, labour market participation, training, gender, class, credential devaluation, and immigration status.

REFERENCES

Hier, Sean P., and K. Walby. 2006. Competing Analytical Paradigms in the Sociological Study of Racism in Canada. *Canadian Ethnic Studies* 26(1): 83–104.

Porter, John. 1965. *The Vertical Mosaic: An Analysis of Social Class and Power in Canada.* Toronto: University of Toronto Press.

5 | REVISITING EQUITY AND LABOUR
Immigration, Gender, Minority Status, and Income Differentials in Canada[1]

Derek Hum and Wayne Simpson

INTRODUCTION

In North America, the performance of visible minority groups in the workplace is a major policy concern. The median family income of blacks in America, for example, is only 60% of the median family income of whites. Hispanic families earn about 68% of what white families in America earn, and Puerto Ricans earn as little as 45% of what whites do (Levitan *et al.* 1981: 238, 246). The median incomes of Japanese and Chinese Americans, conversely, are 132% and 112% of the national average, respectively (Sowell 1982: 46). Economic disparity in labour markets, observed between and among racial groups, is often attributed to racial discrimination on the basis of skin colour. The extent to which income disparity can be attributed to productivity-related considerations such as education, work experience, or language proficiency is a matter for empirical investigation.[2]

In Canada, the federal government attempts to alleviate disadvantages in labour markets for particular designated groups using the Canadian Employment Equity Act (Short Title, assented to 15 December 1995). The purpose of the Act is

> ... to achieve equality in the workplace so that no person shall be denied employment opportunities or benefits for reasons unrelated to ability and, ... to correct the conditions of disadvantage in employment experienced by women, aboriginal peoples, persons with disabilities and members of visible minorities.... (Section 2).

The Act defines "visible minorities" as "... persons, other than aboriginal peoples, who are non-Caucasian in race or non-white in colour."

While skin colour is the primary signifier used to designate disadvantage among members of visible minority groups, other important factors to consider include place of birth and, if foreign-born, the length of time a person has lived and worked in Canada. There is ample evidence to demonstrate that immigrants face economic disadvantage upon arrival in Canada. Evidence also shows, however, that disadvantage declines as individuals assimilate in the workplace (Borjas

1994). It is, therefore, necessary to account for immigration circumstances when examining economic opportunities for visible minorities. It is important because two out of every three new immigrants to Canada now belong to a visible minority group. The significance of immigration status is only enhanced when we consider that the visible minority population will grow more rapidly than Canada's total population by 2016 (Kalbach *et al.* 1993: 8, 24ff.).

Table 5.1 presents annual earnings and hourly wage rates for non-visible minority groups and for various visible minority groups in Canada.[3] Visible minorities as a whole show annual earnings of $25,880 and an hourly wage rate of $17.89. Non-visible minorities, by contrast, show annual earnings of $29,992 and an hourly wage rate of $19.43. What this means is that visible minorities as a group suffer close to a 9% wage disadvantage and a 16% earnings disadvantage when compared to non-visible minority groups. The implication that is often drawn from these data is that Canadian employers discriminate on the basis of colour.

TABLE 5.1 | SELECTED CHARACTERISTICS OF CANADIANS BY VISIBLE MINORITY (VM) GROUP

GROUP	ANNUAL EARNINGS	HOURLY WAGE	ANNUAL HOURS	AVERAGE AGE	% MALE	% IMMI-GRANT
Non-VM	$29,992	$19.43	1,474	43.91	50.94	10.56
VM	$25,880	$17.89	1,433	41.92	47.57	86.07
Black	$24,741	$16.93	1,416	41.95	41.80	79.00
Indo-Pakistani	$26,855	$17.37	1,429	41.18	48.39	92.26
Chinese	$25,913	$20.05	1,379	43.59	50.08	83.33
Non-Chinese Orientals[1]	$28,244	$16.82	1,608	41.11	46.04	85.29
Arab	$21,089	$18.13	1,198	41.60	47.48	88.00
Latin American	$25,314	$15.99	1,545	39.27	52.08	96.47

1. The Non-Chinese Oriental group is comprised of persons of Korean, Japanese, South East Asian, Filipino, and Oceanic ancestry. The sample size for each of these groups individually is relatively small.

Note: Results are weighted by the cross-sectional weight to provide estimates for the Canadian population.

Source: Survey of Labour and Income Dynamics (SLID) 2002 internal master file.

While all visible minority groups presented in Table 5.1 show lower earnings than non-visible minorities, and all but the Chinese show lower hourly wages than non-visible minorities, there is clear variation among the visible minority groups.[4] One immediate complication posed by these data is found in the difference in the number of hours worked. For example, non-Chinese Orientals show lower wage rates than most other visible minority groups, but they work a substantially greater number of hours. Arabs, by contrast, work fewer hours than non-Oriental and visible minorities as a whole, and they earn much lower amounts than non-

Chinese Orientals ($21,089 for Arabs compared to $28,244 for non-Chinese Orientals). Still, they show a higher wage rate than non-Chinese Orientals. Wage rates are a better measure of labour market opportunity for paid workers than annual earnings (Christofides and Swidinsky 1994: 35) because earnings represent a combination of individual effort (i.e., hours worked) and offered rates of pay.

Table 5.1 also reveals little variation in average age, but it reveals greater variation in the proportion of males in each visible minority group. Considering that men are generally paid more than women in Canada, this disparity is reflected in the hourly wage rate and earnings amounts. More noteworthy, there is extremely wide variation in immigration status; only 10.6% of the non-visible minority sample is comprised of immigrants, while the immigrant composition of visible minority groups ranges between 79% and 96.5%. If immigration status is a proxy for numerous labour market disadvantaging factors, then these factors, visible minority membership aside, may be responsible for the observed wage differentials. In short, Table 5.1 is a salutary warning against hasty generalization about the wage structure of the Canadian labour market based upon a simple comparison of non-visible and visible minorities.

Although employment equity in Canada includes Aboriginal peoples and persons with disabilities, this chapter assesses wage differentials by visible minority status in conjunction with the social categories of gender and immigration status.[5] Specifically, we investigate recent wage gaps among visible minority groups in Canada, as well as wage differentials over the past decade, using data from the master file of the Survey of Labour and Income Dynamics (SLID). In addition to considering the usual determinants of wages, such as age, education, and residential location, we also include gender in our analyses. Women are a designated group in the Employment Equity Act, and it is important to investigate the "double negative," that is, whether women who belong to a visible minority group experience disadvantages in addition to or beyond disadvantages experienced on the basis of gender. We also explore immigration status among visible minorities in Canada. Our results pose implications for employment equity policy, as well as immigration policies in Canada.

PREVIOUS RESEARCH IN CANADA

In this section, we selectively examine previous research on wage differentials and social location in Canada. In their investigation of the wage implications of visible minority status and gender status in Canada, Christofides and Swidinsky (1994) use data from the 1989 Labour Market Activity Survey (LMAS). They find that minority women are especially disadvantaged in the Canadian labour market. They use a dichotomous (dummy) variable derived from a self-perception question to capture visible minority membership, acknowledging that their " ... data do not allow [them] to conduct an analysis of individual minority groups" (Christofides and Swidinsky 1994: 46).[6] As a consequence, it is not possible to determine whether certain visible minority groups earn less than non-visible minorities or whether some visible minority groups earn more than others. Furthermore, it is important to determine what proportion of any earnings differential is due to productivity-related factors (e.g., education and work experience) and what proportion might be ascribed to discrimination based upon colour or immigrant status. Christofides and Swidinsky (1994: 39) conclude that immigrants are "generally not disadvantaged in the Canadian labour market."

These findings appear at odds with Bloom *et al.*'s (1995) research findings. Bloom *et al.* apply a model developed by Chiswick (1978) and Borjas (1985) to pooled Canadian census data from 1971, 1981, and 1986 to examine immigrants' earnings. The Chiswick-Borjas model explains earnings as a function of human capital factors, such as education and potential experience (age less years of education), labour market effort (number of weeks worked and the number of hours worked per week), and immigration variables. The latter include a dummy indicator distinguishing those born outside Canada to measure "the entry effect" and the number of years since migration to Canada to measure "the assimilation effect."[7] Bloom *et al.* find a negative entry effect—that is, earnings for immigrants upon entry into Canada are less than native-born Canadians—and a positive assimilation effect—that is, earnings of immigrants tend to grow faster than average Canadian earnings. Their estimates imply that earnings of immigrants "catch up" to the native-born in about 25 years (the assimilation effect). The authors comment, however, that the Canadian labour market has had difficulty assimilating more recent cohorts of immigrants. Possible reasons suggested include a reduced absorptive economy, a reduction in immigrant skills, and "increased discrimination as the composition of immigrants changed towards more visible minorities" (Bloom *et al.* 1995: 1000). But, as these authors do not incorporate visible minority status in their analysis, it is not possible to confirm their suggestion of discrimination towards visible minorities.

In another study, DeSilva (1996) uses census data to examine the earnings of immigrants, many of whom are visible minorities. He concludes that earnings differences for visible minority immigrants can be explained by differences in the quality of seemingly identical educational qualifications. His conclusion is based upon the fact that virtually no earnings differential (and hence discrimination) was found between Canadian-born visible minorities and Canadian-born non-visible minorities. Similar to previous findings, DeSilva makes no distinction among different visible minority groups, and it therefore remains possible that positive and negative earning differentials for different visible minority groups offset one another.

Finally, Beach and Worswick employ the Job Mobility Survey for females aged 25–64 to determine if there exists a "double-negative" effect, that is, whether immigrant women suffer a disadvantage in addition to any disadvantage due to gender. Although they find no "across the board" effect, they do report a double-negative effect that is "quite marked for highly educated immigrant women" (Beach and Worswick 1993: 35). Consequently, the gender dimension of employment opportunities in Canada cannot be ignored.

Some authors have explored differences among visible minority groups themselves. Pendakur and Pendakur (1998) employ the 1991 Public Use Microdata File (PUMF) and report considerable differences in earnings between whites and visible minority groups, as well as among visible minority groups. Black males (native-born and immigrants) face large earnings penalties. However, Canadian-born black women face no earnings penalty. Hum and Simpson (1999) employ the 1993 SLID for similar purposes, but they focus on wage offers.

In summary, research in Canada that explores labour market disadvantages often focuses on visible minority status, gender, or immigrant adjustment. Increasingly, immigrants to Canada belong to visible minority groups, and a consensus is emerging that recent immigrants are not experiencing the same success in the labour market as in the past. The reasons suggested for this finding are numerous, and the specific contribution of employment equity policies themselves remains largely unevaluated.

DATA AND SAMPLE DESCRIPTION

Using the SLID for 2002, we revisit some of our earlier results (1999) concerning wages and visible minorities, and we describe what changes have taken place during the past decade.[8] We use the SLID rather than census data because, although census data are useful to enumerate and characterize the visible minority population, they are limited in labour market details. Not only does SLID provide more detailed information on labour market activity, but the master file also allows a finer grain examination of visible minority groups.

Our sample consists of 26,759 respondents with reported earnings in 2002 and who were not students or Aboriginal peoples.[9] We have the following information on respondents:

» annual earnings and a composite wage rate for all jobs held in 2002;
» labour market activity (hours worked per week and weeks worked);
» human capital characteristics (full-time equivalent years of schooling completed, place of education, and full-year full-time equivalent years of work experience);
» gender;
» mother tongue;
» location (region of residence and size of community);
» visible minority status by group; and
» immigration details (including years since immigration and age at immigration).

The weighted sample means are reported in Table 5.2.

TABLE 5.2 | SAMPLE MEANS FOR THE WORKING POPULATION IN SLID

Composite Hourly Wage	$19.27
Log Hourly Wage	2.84
Visible Minorities?	10.24%
Black?	1.60%
Indo-Pakistani?	1.96%
Chinese?	2.81%
Non-Chinese Oriental?	2.44%
Arab?	0.82%
Latin American?	0.60%
Immigrant?	16.21%
Years since Migration	3.43
Age at Migration	3.60
Years of Schooling	13.64
Educated primarily outside Canada?	11.55%
Years of work experience	17.79
Hours paid per week	36.82
Weeks worked per year	49.44
Male?	53.02%
English as mother tongue?	52.34%
French as mother tongue?	21.34%
Reside in: Atlantic provinces?	7.70%
Quebec?	23.93%
Prairies?	16.43%
British Columbia?	12.64%
City over 500,000?	51.76%
Rural area?	10.89%
Sample size (weighted)	12,184,514
Sample size (unweighted)	26,759

Source: SLID 2002

Table 5.2 represents a fairly comprehensive profile of Canadians. Not only is there classification by visible minority group, but there is also detail on immigration status, particularly the number of years spent in Canada since immigration. This is particularly important, as there is invariably a period of adjustment for immigrants. It is also important because adjustment patterns differ across visible minority groups. Additionally, information on the age at immigration, and whether or not an immigrant was educated in Canada, may be important considering DeSilva's (1996) suggestion that earning differentials are due to quality differences between Canadian-acquired and foreign-acquired education. The SLID

also contains superior information on labour market activity. Rather than rely-
ing on age (minus years of schooling) as a proxy for potential work experience,
SLID provides a direct measure of full-time full-year equivalent work experience
that takes into account interrupted work careers.[10] Finally, SLID contains detailed
demographic information and a composite wage determined from all jobs held
over an entire year, not merely a single job during a reference week.

These details enable us to explore visible minority status and wages in depth.
In particular, we can account for characteristics pertaining to accumulated human
capital, current labour market activity, immigration, gender, language, and location that affect wage rates. As a result, we are able to confront generalizations
about the relationship between visible minority status and wages glimpsed from
simple comparisons such as those displayed in Table 5.1.

A PRELIMINARY LOOK AT VISIBLE MINORITY WAGES

We indicated earlier that a simple tabulation of earnings for different visible
minority groups in Canada ignores many factors that also determine wages and
earnings. Some of the factors include education, work experience, age, and place
of residence. How would incorporation of these considerations change the data
presented in Table 5.1?

Multiple regression analysis can be used to determine what wage gaps exist
when factors in addition to visible minority status are taken into account.[11] We
consider the combined effect for men and women using, first, a simple dummy
variable to indicate visible minority status and, alternatively, a series of dummy
variables to represent different visible minority groups.[12] We find that visible
minority status results in wages about 6% less than other Canadians after allowing for the effects of accumulated human capital, current labour market activity,
immigration, gender, language, location, etc. This estimate is significantly different from zero.[13] For particular visible minority groups, we find the following
statistically significant results: blacks receive 13% less than non-visible minority
Canadians, Indo-Pakistani persons receive 5.5% less, Latin Americans receive
12% less, and non-Chinese Orientals receive about 8% less. Chinese, however, do
not receive less than non-visible minorities in Canada.

These wage differences are quite different for some groups than those depicted
in Table 5.1. For example, the "gross" differences in that table for the Indo-
Pakistani group (-21%) and the Latin American group (-23.1%) are much larger
than the respective "net" differences of -5.6% and -12% estimated by our multi-
variate analysis. This suggests that much of the gross difference (of Table 5.1) can
be explained by factors other than visible minority membership.[14]

A CLOSER LOOK AT THE WAGE DIFFERENCES

In exploring the above results more closely, one obvious refinement is an examination of men and women separately. This is needed because labour market experiences undeniably differ for men and women. Another required enhancement is comparison of different visible minority groups to determine the relative magnitude of disadvantage for each group. Accordingly, we estimate separate wage regressions for men and women by visible minority status. In addition to better measures for selected variables, our results also differ from earlier research by including information on the circumstances of immigrants. This omission from earlier studies is important because immigrant status is found to be (highly) significant only for visible minority men.[15] The wages of immigrants who do not belong to visible minority groups converge most quickly, reaching equivalence with their native-born Canadian counterparts for both women and men. For visible minorities, however, convergence is slower. Therefore, while visible minority status affects the speed of convergence of immigrant wages to those of the native-born, it is clearly immigration status that is important in determining wage differences between members of visible minorities and other Canadians.[16] We also estimate separate regressions for immigrants and for native-born Canadians while allowing for differences in visible minority membership.

TABLE 5.3 | ESTIMATED WAGE GAP BETWEEN NON-VISIBLE MINORITY MEMBERS AND MEMBERS OF VISIBLE MINORITY GROUP: 2002 VS. 1993

		MEN		WOMEN	
	VISIBLE MINORITY GROUP	IMMIGRANT	NATIVE-BORN	IMMIGRANT	NATIVE-BORN
2002	All	12.7% ***	6.9%	-0.5%	-0.8%
	Black	22.2% ***	21.9% ***	2.8%	8.0%
	Indo-Pakistani	13.1% **	6.3%	0.6%	-26.7% ***
	Chinese	2.1%	-1.8% 1	-6.0%	0.4%
	Non-Chinese Oriental	14.0% ***	6.2%	-0.2%	5.9%
	Arab	13.7% *	6.0%	-0.5%	-22.5%
	Latin American	17.7% *	38.8% ***	3.1%	-11.0%
1993	All	14.6% ***	3.1%	5.5%	2.7%
	Black	16.6% **	25.6% ***	-1.1%	-13.0%
	Indo-Pakistani	19.0% ***	-8.0%	2.3%	8.5%
	Chinese	17.3% **	-4.7%	9.9%	-2.4%
	Non-Chinese Oriental	23.9% ***	1.6%	11.5% **	17.2%
	Arab	11.2%	-29.3%*	-15.7%	23.4%
	Latin American	-18.2% a	32.6%*	9.2%	9.3%

1. Negative sign denotes wage difference in favour of the visible minority group.

Notes: *** denotes significance at the 1% level; ** significance at 5%; * significance at 10%.

Wage difference calculated as eß-1 where ß is the coefficient from the log wage regression in Table 5.4.

Source: Tables 5.4 (2002) and 5.5 (1993).

Our results are summarized in Table 5.3, which captures the most interesting and important findings. (Full details are presented in Tables 5.4 and 5.5 below.) After we account for other factors, including immigrant status, membership in a visible minority (in 2002) is significant principally for immigrant men. For Canadian-born men, visible minority membership is generally insignificant (at the conventional 5% significance level), as it is for both immigrant and native-born women. Among visible minority groups, there is a significant wage disadvantage for black men of approximately 22%, whether immigrant or native-born. There are also significant disadvantages for immigrant men who are members of the Indo-Pakistani group (13.1%) and the non-Chinese Oriental group (14.0%). Adopting a less strict level of significance—using a 10% level of significance rather than a 5% level—reveals disadvantage for Arab men (13.7%) and Latin American male immigrants (17.7%). But note that native-born Latin American men experience disadvantage of 38.8% at the highest level of significance. Therefore, Canadian-born Latin American men currently suffer a disadvantage that is even larger than that of blacks in Canada. Interestingly, native-born Indo-Pakistani women enjoy a large wage premium of nearly 27%. All other groups are individually insignificant.

The economic circumstances of blacks in Canada deserve further comment, especially since the results appear so startling and robust. Past empirical studies of the Canadian labour market have not especially concentrated on blacks *per se*. They have examined the earnings of all visible minority groups in the context of changing origins and the racial composition of immigration to Canada since the 1970s, specifically the shift towards visible minority immigrants from non-English-speaking nations. Baker and Benjamin (1994) compared black men to native-born men using the 1971, 1981, and 1986 census PUMF. They found significantly lower earnings for blacks as a group, combining both immigrants and native-born workers, but they could not distinguish a specific black immigrant effect in a pooled sample of those who were foreign and native-born. A subsequent study by Pendakur and Pendakur (1998) using the 1991 PUMF data, also found significant earnings penalties for black men, whether Canadian-born or immigrant. These results are consistent with Hum and Simpson (1999), who find significant lower earnings for visible minority men as a group relative to native-born men and significantly lower earnings for native-born black men compared to white men in the SLID. That is, they find significantly lower earnings for both immigrant and native-born black men, although they do not test to see if these differences are distinctive.[17] The situation of blacks (especially native-born men) in Canada is in much need of high quality empirical research, especially since recent findings confirm that, even after accounting for immigrant status and gender, Canadian-born black men face, by far, the largest (statistically significant) earnings disadvantage.

TABLE 5.4 | REGRESSIONS TO EXPLAIN LOG WAGE FOR MEN AND WOMEN BY IMMIGRANT STATUS, 2002

	(1)	(2)	(3)	(4)
	IMMIGRANT MEN		**CANADIAN-BORN MEN**	
Visible Minority?	-0.136***		-0.071	
	(3.69)		(1.08)	
Black?		-0.251***		-0.247***
		(3.95)		(3.21)
Indo-Pakistani?		-0.140**		-0.065
		(2.03)		(0.60)
Chinese?		-0.021		0.018
		(0.42)		(0.14)
Non-Chinese Oriental?		-0.151***		-0.064
		(3.22)		(0.54)
Arab?		-0.147*		-0.062
		(1.92)		(0.18)
Latin?		-0.195*		-0.491***
		(1.77)		(2.91)
Yrs since migration	0.016***	0.016***		
	(3.15)	(3.24)		
Yrs since mig sqd	-0.000	-0.000		
	(0.15)	(0.21)		
Age at migration	0.021***	0.021***		
	(4.10)	(4.36)		
Age at mig sqd	-0.000***	-0.000***		
	(2.64)	(2.97)		
Years schooling	0.043***	0.042***	0.052***	0.052***
	(9.52)	(9.40)	(26.25)	(26.53)
Educ ex Canada?	-0.012	-0.014	-0.088	-0.099
	(0.25)	(0.29)	(0.65)	(0.78)
Yrs work experience	0.008	0.008	0.031***	0.031***
	(1.52)	(1.52)	(20.93)	(20.99)
Yrs work exp sqd	-0.000	-0.000	-0.001***	-0.001***
	(1.52)	(1.55)	(14.43)	(14.49)
Hours paid per week	0.001	0.001	0.001*	0.001*
	(0.61)	(0.62)	(1.93)	(1.91)
Weeks worked per yr	0.007***	0.007***	0.008***	0.008***
	(3.75)	(3.68)	(11.78)	(11.80)
English?	-0.054	-0.025	0.088***	0.090***
	(1.42)	(0.63)	(6.17)	(6.47)
French?	0.098	0.109	0.098***	0.100***
	(0.87)	(1.00)	(4.62)	(4.78)
Atlantic?	-0.065	-0.059	-0.143***	-0.144***
	(0.81)	(0.75)	(11.02)	(11.12)
Quebec?	-0.085	-0.065	-0.076***	-0.077***
	(1.45)	(1.09)	(3.66)	(3.74)

	(1)	(2)	(3)	(4)
	IMMIGRANT MEN		**CANADIAN-BORN MEN**	
Prairies?	-0.038	-0.040	-0.061***	-0.062***
	(0.98)	(1.04)	(4.94)	(5.01)
British Columbia?	0.008	-0.013	0.018	0.015
	(0.18)	(0.32)	(1.03)	(0.90)
Cities > 500,000?	-0.009	-0.012	0.064***	0.064***
	(0.27)	(0.34)	(6.15)	(6.15)
Rural?	-0.044	-0.047	-0.022*	-0.022*
	(0.58)	(0.64)	(1.66)	(1.65)
Constant	1.501***	1.496***	1.371***	1.375***
	(9.29)	(9.22)	(30.59)	(30.92)
IMR	-0.296***	-0.296***	0.080***	0.079***
	(5.35)	(5.23)	(4.81)	(4.82)
Wald ^{2}	326.13***	350.67***	2235.20***	2259.14***
Sample size	1,312	1,312	12,439	12,439

	(1)	(2)	(3)	(4)
	IMMIGRANT WOMEN		**CANADIAN-BORN WOMEN**	
Visible Minority?	0.005		0.008	
	(0.15)		(10.19)	
Black?		-0.028		-0.083
		(0.45)		(0.98)
Indo-Pakistani?		-0.006		0.237***
		(0.11)		(3.52)
Chinese?		0.058		-0.004
		(1.18)		(0.07)
Non-Chinese Oriental?		0.002		-0.061
		(0.04)		(0.84)
Arab?		0.005		0.203
		(0.05)		(1.35)
Latin?		-0.031		0.104
		(0.44)		(1.24)
Yrs since migration	0.019***	0.019***		
	(4.23)	(4.32)		
Yrs since mig sqd	-0.000***	-0.000***		
	(2.90)	(2.96)		
Age at migration	0.003	0.002		
	(0.53)	(0.47)		
Age at mig sqd	-0.000	-0.000		
	(0.36)	(0.36)		
Years schooling	0.042***	0.043***	0.061***	0.061***
	(10.34)	(10.28)	(24.81)	(24.76)
Educ ex Canada?	-0.062	-0.061	-0.147***	-0.129
	(1.35)	(1.34)	(1.84)	(1.45)

	(1)	(2)	(3)	(4)
	IMMIGRANT WOMEN		**CANADIAN-BORN WOMEN**	
Yrs work experience	0.005	0.004	0.017***	0.017***
	(1.02)	(0.86)	(9.36)	(9.36)
Yrs work exp sqd	-0.000	-0.000	-0.000***	-0.000***
	(0.17)	(0.05)	(3.55)	(3.54)
Hours paid per week	-0.000	0.000	0.000	0.000
	(0.10)	(0.03)	(0.38)	(0.41)
Weeks worked per yr	0.006***	0.006***	0.008***	0.008***
	(4.51)	(4.50)	(15.00)	(14.97)
English?	0.046	0.059*	0.001	0.002
	(1.39)	(1.70)	(0.05)	(0.13)
French?	0.050	0.057	-0.008	-0.008
	(0.56)	(0.63)	(0.35)	(0.32)
Atlantic?	-0.011	-0.010	-0.157***	-0.156***
	(0.20)	(0.17)	(11.93)	(11.89)
Quebec?	-0.049	-0.038	-0.075***	-0.074***
	(0.82)	(0.59)	(3.31)	(3.28)
Prairies?	-0.106***	-0.109***	-0.076***	-0.077***
	(3.01)	(3.08)	(5.79)	(5.84)
British Columbia?	0.035	0.025	0.014	0.016
	(0.91)	(0.64)	(0.85)	(0.92)
Cities > 500,000?	0.068***	-0.066**	0.101***	0.101***
	(2.21)	(2.13)	(8.93)	(8.94)
Rural?	-0.126*	-0.133**	-0.016	-0.016
	(1.91)	(1.99)	(1.30)	(1.30)
Constant	1.464***	1.460***	1.278***	1.279***
	(11.44)	(11.21)	(23.50)	(23.52)
IMR	-0.049	-0.045	0.017	0.016
	(0.68)	(0.57)	(0.62)	(0.61)
Wald χ^2	266.08***	269.97***	1858.15***	2270.98***
Sample size	1,239	1,239	11,769	11,769

Notes: Robust z statistics in parentheses; * significant at 10%; ** significant at 5%; *** significant at 1%. Regressions are weighted using the cross-sectional weights in SLID to reflect the Canadian population. Sample size reflects uncensored (reported) wage observations. Adjustment for sample selection bias derived from a sample selection model with schooling, experience, experience squared, regional dummies, gender, English and French, city size, visible minority, immigration status, years since migration, years since migration squared, age, family size, and other family income as explanatory variables.

Source: SLID 2002.

TABLE 5.5 | REGRESSIONS TO EXPLAIN LOG WAGE FOR MEN AND WOMEN BY IMMIGRANT STATUS, 1993

VARIABLE	(1) IMMIGRANT MEN	(2)	(3) CANADIAN-BORN MEN	(4)
Intercept	1.769 (10.9)	1.797 (11.1)	1.678 (35.2)	1.677 (35.1)
Visible Minority?	-0.158 (3.5)		-0.032 (0.7)	
Black?		-0.181 (2.0)		-0.296 (2.7)
Indo-Pakistani?		-0.211 (3.2)		0.077 (0.3)
Chinese?		-0.190 (2.5)		0.046 (0.6)
Non-Chinese Oriental?		-0.273 (3.6)		-0.016 (0.2)
Arab?		-0.119 (1.2)		0.257 (1.7)
Latin American?		0.167 (1.5)		-0.394 (1.8)
Yrs since migration	0.023 (4.1)	0.020 (3.6)		
Yrs since mig sqd	-0.0004 (4.1)	-0.0004 (3.5)		
Age at migration	0.012 (1.6)	0.014 (1.8)		
Age at mig sqd	-0.0002 (1.4)	-0.0002 (1.6)		
Years schooling	0.048 (10.9)	0.049 (11.2)	0.046 (27.0)	0.046 (26.9)
Educ ex Canada?	-0.078 (1.2)	-0.097 (1.5)	0.080 (1.0)	0.068 (0.8)
Yrs of experience	0.018 (4.5)	0.018 (4.3)	0.025 (31.3)	0.025 (31.1)
Yrs of exp sqd	-0.0002 (4.8)	-0.0002 (4.6)	-0.0002 (30.1)	-0.0002 (29.9)
Hours paid per week	-0.005 (2.8)	-0.007 (3.4)	-0.002 (3.2)	-0.002 (3.2)
Weeks worked per yr	0.002 (1.1)	0.002 (1.4)	0.004 (7.7)	0.004 (7.8)
English?	0.067 (1.6)	0.067 (1.5)	0.054 (1.9)	0.061 (2.2)
French?	0.235 (2.1)	0.233 (2.1)	0.042 (1.3)	0.049 (1.5)
Atlantic?	-0.153 (1.3)	-0.137 (1.1)	-0.109 (5.5)	-0.111 (5.6)
Quebec?	0.041 (0.6)	-0.051 (0.8)	0.027 (1.2)	-0.028 (1.3)

VARIABLE	(1) IMMIGRANT MEN	(2)	(3) CANADIAN-BORN MEN	(4)
Prairies?	-0.080 (1.6)	-0.067 (1.4)	-0.066 (4.1)	-0.066 (4.1)
British Columbia?	0.052 (1.1)	0.068 (1.4)	0.074 (3.9)	0.072 (3.8)
Cities > 500,000?	-0.084 (2.0)	-0.079 (1.9)	0.021 (1.6)	0.020 (1.6)
Rural?	-0.069 (1.0)	-0.086 (1.2)	-0.026 (1.8)	-0.026 (1.9)
R2	0.376	0.392	0.259	0.261
F	16.497	13.819	127.480	96.461
Sample size weighted	679,527	679,527	3,787,808	3,787,808
(unwtd)	(540)	(540)	(5,497)	(5,497)

VARIABLE	(1) IMMIGRANT WOMEN	(2)	(3) CANADIAN-BORN WOMEN	(4)
Intercept	1.376 (9.5)	1.359 (9.3)	1.130 (24.0)	1.127 (23.8)
Visible Minority?	-0.057 (1.4)		-0.027 (0.4)	
Black?		0.011 (0.1)		0.122 (0.9)
Indo-Pakistani?		-0.023 (0.3)		-0.089 (0.5)
Chinese?		-0.104 (1.5)		0.024 (0.2)
NonChinese Orientals?		-0.122 (2.0)		-0.189 (1.3)
Arab?		0.146 (1.2)		-0.267 (1.0)
Latin American?		-0.097 (0.9)		-0.098 (0.3)
Yrs since migration	0.016 (3.1)	0.015 (2.9)		
Yrs since mig sqd	-0.0002 (2.4)	-0.0002 (2.2)		
Age at migration	-0.0016 (0.3)	-0.0026 (0.4)		
Age at mig squared	-0.0000 (0.2)	0.0000 (0.0)		
Years of schooling	0.060 (11.7)	0.061 (11.6)	0.068 (33.3)	0.068 (33.3)
Educ ex Canada?	-0.004 (0.1)	0.018 (0.3)	0.079 (0.9)	0.080 (0.9)

VARIABLE	(1) IMMIGRANT WOMEN	(2) IMMIGRANT WOMEN	(3) CANADIAN-BORN WOMEN	(4) CANADIAN-BORN WOMEN
Years of experience	0.018 (5.4)	0.018 (5.1)	0.018 (18.2)	0.018 (18.2)
Yrs of exp squared	-0.0002 (5.2)	-0.0002 (5.1)	-0.0002 (17.4)	-0.0002 (17.5)
Hours paid per week	-0.006 (3.5)	-0.006 (3.4)	-0.001 (1.9)	-0.001 (1.9)
Wks worked per year	0.004 (2.1)	0.004 (2.4)	0.006 (12.4)	0.006 (12.4)
English?	0.006 (0.2)	-0.018 (0.4)	0.041 (1.4)	0.044 (1.5)
French?	0.045 (0.4)	0.029 (0.3)	-0.019 (0.5)	-0.016 (0.5)
Atlantic?	0.120 (1.0)	0.087 (0.7)	-0.139 (6.4)	-0.139 (6.4)
Québec?	-0.273 (4.2)	-0.301 (4.5)	-0.002 (0.1)	-0.002 (0.1)
Prairies?	-0.135 (2.7)	-0.126 (2.5)	-0.086 (5.0)	-0.086 (5.0)
B.C.?	-0.011 (0.2)	-0.004 (0.1)	0.046 (2.4)	0.047 (2.4)
Cities > 500,000?	0.087 (2.1)	0.087 (2.1)	0.093 (6.8)	0.093 (6.8)
Rural?	0.006 (0.1)	0.010 (0.1)	0.000 (0.0)	0.000 (0.0)
R_2	0.439	0.446	0.311	0.312
F	19.822	15.993	144.241	108.348
Sample size weighted (unwtd)	630,486 (502)	630,486 (502)	3,185,507 (4,805)	3,185,507 (4,805)

Source: SLID 1993 (internal master file).

REVISITING VISIBLE MINORITY OPPORTUNITIES: QUO VADIS?

A decade has passed since the 1995 Employment Equity Act became part of Canada's economic policy culture. Canada continues to be an immigrant-receiving country. How have things changed? Do visible minorities fare better or worse today than a decade ago?

Our earlier examination of wage disadvantage of visible minorities, using the 1993 SLID master file data (sample size = 11,344), can provide a short historical perspective (Hum and Simpson 1999). The data from 1993 provide a benchmark snapshot immediately prior to the 1995 Employment Equity Act, while this chapter examines 2002 data.[18] That earlier study reported similar findings in the sense that visible minority immigrants faced economic disadvantages to various degrees. However, disadvantages for Arabs and Latin Americans were not statistically significant (at the conventional 5% level) in 1993. A conventional statistically significant wage penalty of 17.3% was found for Chinese immigrants (but not native-born Chinese men) in 1993 (see Table 5.3, lower panel). In contrast, the 2002 data find slightly statistically significant penalties of 13.7% and 17.7% for Arab and Latin American men, respectively, as well as a significant penalty of 38.8% for native-born Latin American men (see Table 5.3, upper panel). These results, we believe, are primarily due to the larger sample size (of 26,759) available for the present study rather than to the "sudden" emergence of penalties for these two groups since 1993. To highlight this feature, we note that estimated wage gaps for Latin American and Arab male immigrants were statistically insignificant (at 5% level) in 1993. In 2002, however, these wage penalties were statistically significant at the 10% level. Furthermore, the wage penalty for native-born Latin American men is not only statistically significant at the 1% level, but also large. In short, Latin American men, whether they are native-born or immigrant, are now experiencing substantial wage penalties, though not to the degree faced by black men in Canada. As previously noted, black men have a wage penalty of about 22%, whether immigrant or native-born.

Chinese male immigrants no longer appear to have a wage penalty in 2002. This result cannot simply be due to larger sample size, however, since the smaller sample available a decade earlier was sufficient to establish conventional statistical significance. Rather, we believe this change is due to aspects of "selection" in the intervening period with respect to Chinese immigrants. Chinese immigrants to Canada since 1993 appear to possess education and human capital skills, as well as financial and entrepreneurial capital means that contributed to their economic performance level, and that are not fully captured by the explanatory variables included in our regressions.[19] As a result, the "selective" immigration by this visible minority group may have eliminated the previously conventional significant wage penalty. While this is unlikely to be the entire explanation, we suggest that this "composition effect" is a large part of it.

The general view that wage penalties are more problematic for men than they are for women has not appreciably changed. However, inspection of Table 5.3 (both panels) reveals that non-Chinese oriental women immigrants no longer have a wage penalty. That immigrant women do not experience wage penalties now appears to be unambiguously supported for all visible minority groups. At the same time, while few visible minority native-born women have a (statistically significant) advantage or penalty, it is fascinating to discover that native-born Indo-Pakistani women now receive a wage premium of nearly 24% (and highly significant at 1%). This warrants more detailed research on the labour market experiences of this particular group.

If we were to summarize the changes over the last decade in terms of a "score-card of progress," Chinese male immigrants have made positive gains, and Arab and Latin American men are now shown to be disadvantaged. As in the past decade, black males continue to experience substantial disadvantage, whether Canadian-born or not. Indeed, there is no longer any distinguishable difference in the amount of wage disadvantage between immigrant and native-born black men in 2002, whereas previously native-born black males fared slightly better than immigrant black males.

SUMMARY AND POLICY IMPLICATIONS

The extent to which visible minorities participate in the Canadian economy is an important public policy issue. Together with women, Aboriginal peoples, and persons with disabilities, visible minorities are a designated disadvantaged group under federal employment equity legislation. While these four social groups are very different, the matter of racial discrimination is central to visible minorities and strikes at the heart of Canada's image as a tolerant and liberal democracy. At the same time, immigrants to Canada increasingly come from "non-white" countries of origin; hence Canada's image as an accommodating, immigrant-welcoming nation is also at stake.

Our research reveals the danger of merely collating information on visible minorities to draw inferences concerning discrimination by colour. This type of exercise, typified by Table 5.1, is incomplete and, worse, misleading, because it combines all visible minority individuals without distinguishing their colour, ethnic origin, education, work experience, or degree of assimilation into the Canadian labour stream. A more accurate picture is presented in Table 5.3, where it is apparent that, with the exception of black and Latin American men, there is no significant wage gap between visible minority and non-visible minority group membership for native-born workers. For all others, it is predominantly among immigrants that the question of wage differentials for visible minority status arises. But because two of every three new immigrants to Canada claim membership in a visible minority group, it is too easy to conflate disadvantage due to colour with disadvantage arising from immigration circumstances. At a conceptual level, appropriate ameliorative effort would require different policy responses according to whether the disadvantage is associated with colour or immigration adjustment.

What implications do these findings have for public policy? In this chapter, we have attempted to disentangle some of the determinants of wages for visible minority Canadians. It is primarily an economic—not a sociological or anthropological—examination of visible minority group membership. Yet, our findings should sound a warning bell with regards to treating visible minorities as a homogeneous group for public policy formation, particularly employment equity. With more and more of Canada's immigrants belonging to a visible minority group, and with our evidence that the issue of skin colour is largely bound up with immigrant status, it may now be time to rethink Canada's emphasis on achieving equal opportunity in the labour market. Our findings suggest that efforts to achieve a colour-blind labour market, offering opportunities for all Canadian workers, may have to focus more on helping immigrants adjust and integrate rather than on the traditional prods embodying employment equity legislation. The caveat is the urgent need to examine the economic circumstances pertaining to native-born black men. Complacency that black-white differentials are more an issue for Americans than they are for Canadians should be forthrightly abandoned. American research has understandably framed the issue in terms of black-white comparisons for social and cultural reasons specific to that country's historical past. In Canada, we tend to approach the issue of race within a multi-ethnic and multicultural discourse, silently acknowledging the percolating issue of colour but remaining reluctant to privilege one non-white group over another. Yet, history shows that progression from economic and social marginalization towards full economic participation and social integration has been markedly different for Chinese and Japanese Canadians, for East Asians, and for blacks.

The persistent disadvantage facing black men in Canada (and, now, Latin American men) should neither be submerged in a multicultural discourse nor confined exclusively within a "visible minority" context. The situation of native-born black Canadians can no longer be regarded as simply one extreme end of the variation that exists across all visible minority groups in this country. The size of differential for native-born black men in Canada is too large, and too long lasting, to be viewed as a statistical outlier. Rather, the evidence is clear that economic disadvantage for blacks in Canada stems from unique structural features of Canadian society and economy, and it is hard to resist the suggestion that racial discrimination is an important factor. The statistically significant (and large) penalty for native-born Latin American men is also disturbing in this context. Will Latin American men, over time, imitate the trajectory of Chinese male immigrants or that of native-born black men? These questions must be at the top of research agendas and policy priorities. Nonetheless, the necessary leitmotif of all enquiry concerning both race and immigrants in Canada bears repeating: visible minorities are an extremely heterogeneous category and should not be conflated in either statistical analysis or public policy.

NOTES

1   This research was partly funded by the Prairie Centre of Excellence for Research in Immigration and Integration (PCERII). We thank the Research Data Centre (Manitoba) of Statistics Canada for technical support. The views expressed are solely those of the authors.

2   American blacks speak English, but they still earn only 60–70% of what whites earn. Therefore, productivity factors beyond language are obviously important. Language is a perennial issue in Canada, but it is not our main concern in this paper. We do, however, allow for linguistic differences in our analysis of earnings. For an assessment of earnings differentials by linguistic groups in Quebec, see Shapiro and Stelcner 1997.

3   The data are taken from Survey of Labour and Income Dynamics (SLID). We describe the data in a later section.

4   Our groupings also mask considerable variation. For example, Japanese have annual earnings well above the comparable figure for whites, although the small sample size makes comparison unreliable. Small sample sizes for Koreans, Japanese, Southeast Asians, Filipinos, and Oceanic members force us to group them together as non-Chinese Orientals.

5   There are unique labour market issues associated with Aboriginal peoples. Additionally, there are too few Aboriginal peoples in our sample to afford statistical analysis. Also, the issue of immigrant Aboriginal peoples is not relevant. We have examined persons with disabilities elsewhere (Hum and Simpson 1996).

6   A "dummy variable" simply indicates the presence or absence of a particular qualitative trait such as female gender, disability status, or, in this case, visible minority membership. While useful for determining whether the particular characteristic trait is statistically important, dummy variables do not capture any degree or extent of the characteristic trait. Thus, a dichotomous or dummy variable indicates whether or not a person is a visible minority, but it cannot distinguish among different visible minority groups such as Chinese or Arabs.

7   The entry effect is the difference in wages between immigrants upon first landing (when years since migration is zero) and those who are native-born. The assimilation effect is the annual rate of decline in this difference after entry. Bloom *et al.* (1995) also use a series of dummy variables to estimate cohort effects for immigrants. In our study, which is confined to a single cross-section, we can only use years since migration (YSM) since YSM is perfectly collinear with cohort effects at any given point in time.

8   See Hum and Simpson 2004a for a recent survey of empirical evidence on the economic assimilation of immigrants in Canada.

9   Students are traditionally excluded from studies of earnings because their primary activity is education rather than work. Aboriginal peoples are excluded because of incomplete coverage, particularly of the population on reserves.

10 Hum and Simpson (2004b) demonstrate that using potential experience rather than actual experience exaggerates both the disruption and recovery caused by immigration.

11 The logarithm of the wage rate provided a better fit than the wage rate level in preliminary results that are available from the authors upon request.

12 These basic results are not reported but available from the authors on request. Results of an even more detailed nature are given in Tables 5.4 and 5.5.

13 We indicate different levels of significance in this study. The 5% level is adopted as "conventional" with the 10% level termed "slightly" significant and the 1% level "highly significant." This may be confusing to some readers, but we believe it is necessary to adopt various levels to distinguish changes that occurred over time and results that differ due to sample sizes and varying conventions.

14 We also corrected for any bias arising from considering only workers as opposed to potential workers (those willing to work). After this adjustment, the estimated effects of visible minority status are much the same.

15 We ignore here the well-understood bias arising from heterogeneous immigrant cohorts and what Borjas (1985) terms "declining cohort quality" since we are only using immigrant status as a control variable to improve our estimates of wage differences by visible minority status. See Hum and Simpson (2004a) for a proper discussion of this bias and a survey of its implications for the analysis of immigrant labour market integration for Canada.

16 These results do not adjust for "across cohort bias" or bias associated with the different experiences of successive immigrant cohorts. See Hum and Simpson (2004a) for a discussion of this issue.

17 Duleep and Regets (1992) find from the 1981 Census that the entry earnings of Chinese immigrants are 53% below native earnings while the entry earnings of British immigrants are 13% above native earnings, suggesting substantial differences in cohort effects related to language and visible minority status. Schaafsma and Sweetman (2001) show that members of a visible minority who immigrate at a younger age have higher age-earnings profiles than their older counterparts, particularly immigrants after the age of 35, suggesting that acculturation plays an important role in determining immigrant economic success. Because the changing composition of migrants toward non-European immigrants conflates language, visible minority status, and a host of economic and cultural differences, distinguishing these

different effects is a demanding, but potentially important task for future research on visible minority earnings.

18 This discussion should not be read as an evaluation of the Employment Equity Act. Rather, we are content with a modest general description of the change in circumstances of visible minorities in the past decade. A full evaluation of the Employment Equity Act or an analysis of how different visible minority groups have fared in the labour markets in the past decade is beyond the scope of this chapter.

19 We realize that some may regard this as too sweeping a statement, but the flight of people and capital from Hong Kong prior to 1997 as China prepared to reclaim it, as well as new investment from Chinese entrepreneurs encouraged by Canadian immigration policies, must certainly be factors on casual inspection. Detailed examination of the pattern of immigration to Canada by Chinese during this period is beyond the scope of this chapter. We merely note that there are "candidate" explanations for why Chinese male immigrants are no longer disadvantaged in the 2002 data while being so in the 1993 data. The proportion of the Chinese population in Canada that is immigrant increased from 72.5% (authors' calculation) to 83.3% (Table 5.1). Li (1993) provides a discussion of investment and business in Canada by Chinese immigrants, but his discussion ends just before the 1993 Employment Equity Act.

REFERENCES AND FURTHER READINGS

Baker, M., and D. Benjamin. 1994. The Performance of Immigrants in the Canadian Labor market. *Journal of Labor Economics* 12(3): 369–405.

Beach, C., and C. Worswick. 1993. Is There a Double-Negative Effect on the Earnings of Immigrant Women? *Canadian Public Policy/Analyse de Politiques* 19(1): 36–53.

Bloom, D.E., G. Grenier, and M. Gunderson. 1995. The Changing Labour Market Position of Canadian immigrants. *Canadian Journal of Economics* 28(4): 987–1005.

Borjas, G. 1985. Assimilation, Changes in Cohort Quality and the Earnings of Immigrants. *Journal of Labor Economics* 3: 463–89.

——. 1994. The Economics of Immigration. *Journal of Economic Literature* 32(4): 1667–1717.

Carlson, L.A., and C. Schwartz. 1988. The Earnings of Women and Ethnic Minorities, 1959-1979. *Industrial and Labor Relations Review* 41(4): 530–46.

Chiswick, B. 1978. The Effect of Americanization on the Earnings of Foreign-born Men. *Journal of Political Economy* 86: 897–921.

Christofides, L.N., and R. Swidinsky. 1994. Wage Determination by Gender and Visible Minority Status: Evidence from the 1989 LMAS. *Canadian Public Policy/Analyse de Politiques* 20(1): 34–51.

DeSilva, A. 1996. *Discrimination Against Visible Minority Men.* Hull: Human Resources Development Canada.

Duleep, H., and M. Regets. 1992. Some Evidence on the Effects of Admissions Criteria on Immigrant Integration. In B. Chiswick, ed., *Immigration, Language and Ethnicity: Canada and the United States.* Washington, DC: AEI Press.

Heckman, J. 1979. Sample Selection Bias as a Specification Error. *Econometrica* 47(1): 153–61.

Hum, D., and W. Simpson. 1996. Canadians with Disabilities and the Labour Market. *Canadian Public Policy/Analyse de Politiques* 22(3): 285–99.

——. 1999. Wage Opportunities for Visible Minorities in Canada. *Canadian Public Policy/Analyse de Politiques* 25(3): 379–94.

——. 2004a. Economic Integration of Immigrants to Canada: A Short Survey. *Canadian Journal of Urban Research* 13(1) 46–61.

——. 2004b. Reinterpreting the Performance of Immigrant Wages from Panel Data. *Empirical Economics* 29: 129–47.

Kalbach, W., *et al.* 1993. *Population Projections of Visible Minority Groups, Canada, Provinces and Regions, 1991–2016.* Interdepartmental Working Group on Employment Equity Data. Ottawa: Statistics Canada.

Levitan, S., G. Mangum, and R. Marshall. 1981. *Human Resources and Labor Markets.* New York: Harper and Row.

Li, P. 1993. Chinese Investment and Business in Canada: Ethnic Entrepreneurship Reconsidered. *Pacific Affairs* 66(2): 219–43.

Pendakur, K., and R. Pendakur. 1998. The Colour of Money: Earnings Differentials Among Ethnic Groups in Canada. *Canadian Journal of Economics* 31(3): 518–48.

Schaafsma, J., and A. Sweetman. 2001. Immigrant Earnings: Age at Immigration Matters. *Canadian Journal of Economics* 34(4): 1066–99.

Shapiro, D., and M. Stelcner. 1997. Language and Earnings in Quebec: Trends over Twenty Years, 1970–1990. *Canadian Public Policy/Analyse de Politiques* 23(2): 115–40.

Sowell, T. 1982. Weber and Bakke, and the Presuppositions of Affirmative Action. In W.E. Block and M.A. Walker, eds., *Discrimination, Affirmative Action, and Equal Opportunity.* Vancouver: The Fraser Institute. 36–63.

6 | RECENT MAINLAND CHINESE IMMIGRANTS AND COVERT RACISM IN CANADA

Li Zong

Between 2000 and 2004, over 30,000 to 40,000 immigrants from mainland China entered Canada each year (Citizenship and Immigration Canada 2002, 2004), making that country the largest immigration source country for this one. Most recent mainland Chinese immigrants, especially those arriving in the 1990s and 2000s, have been well-trained and experienced professionals seeking new opportunities. Canada welcomes these immigrants mainly because of their potential to contribute to the country's population and economic growth. However, many mainland Chinese immigrants, particularly skilled/professional immigrants, are disappointed and frustrated because they have not been able to achieve a satisfactory social and economic status in Canadian society.

This chapter reviews the trends of recent mainland Chinese immigration to Canada and examines obstacles that these immigrants face in integrating into Canadian society. Theoretical debates on the issue of occupational attainment for professional immigrants and covert racism will be addressed. The chapter emphasizes the diversity of mainland Chinese immigrants, and it distinguishes between business and skilled/professional immigrants: business immigrants, who make up only a small part of the mainland Chinese immigration pool, are chosen because of their business experiences and the amount of capital they possess; the skilled or professional class of immigrants are admitted mostly on the basis of their educational level. Chinese professional immigrants with higher education trained outside of Canada often experience disadvantages in obtaining professional jobs in the Canadian labour force. These disadvantages are related to many factors such as linguistic abilities, Canadian experience, labour market, non-recognition or devaluation of foreign credentials, and work experiences. The chapter highlights some of the individual and structural barriers these immigrants face, and it examines how foreign-trained Chinese professional immigrants perceive the devaluation of their foreign credentials. It is argued that institutionalized barriers relating to devaluation of foreign credentials may affect foreign-trained mainland Chinese professionals in accessing professional jobs and that individual barriers cannot be seen in isolation from social conditions and structural arrangements.

IMMIGRATION TRENDS FROM MAINLAND CHINA

Immigration from mainland China to Canada was small in the 1950s and early 1960s. Those who came were mainly family members joining close relatives in Canada, particularly wives and children coming as family members of Chinese men already in Canada (Li 1998: 96). For example, between 1956 and 1965, only 4,890 mainland Chinese immigrated to Canada (see Table 6.1). In 1967, Canada changed its immigration policy by adopting a "point" system (Privy Council, 1967: 1350–62) to screen independent immigrants. The point system provided an equal opportunity for immigration from Asian countries. At the same time, the Cultural Revolution, particularly in its early years (1966–70), brought social turbulence to mainland China, and many mainland Chinese who had relatives in Canada wanted to leave China to seek a more stable future in this country. Both pulling and pushing factors motivated a relatively large number of mainland Chinese (32,534) to immigrate to Canada between 1966 and 1970 (see Table 6.1). However, between 1971 and 1978, the number of immigrants from mainland China decreased because of political pressure and restricted migration control in China. It was not until 1979, after China adopted an open-door policy and began to relax its restrictions on the exit of Chinese citizens, that many mainland Chinese were able to leave for Canada and the immigration flow to Canada began to increase again.

Between 1979 and 1989, 35,366 mainland Chinese immigrated to Canada. The 1989 student protest movement in China, which led to the tragic incident at Tiananmen Square, triggered a sudden increase in mainland Chinese immigrants. The Canadian government enacted a special program (known as OM-IS-339) to protect Chinese students and visiting scholars who were in Canada at the time and who participated in demonstrations in Canada to support the student movement in China. The policy allowed thousands of Chinese students, visiting scholars, and their family members to obtain landed immigrant status on compassionate grounds. Table 6.1 shows that in the two years between 1990 and 1991, 22,319 mainland Chinese became landed immigrants in Canada. In the following two years (1992–93), another 21,998 mainland Chinese immigrated to Canada. After 1994, annual immigration from mainland China continued to increase, reaching 40,315 in 2001. In total, for the decade of 1994–2004, 293,680 mainland Chinese immigrated to Canada (see Figure 6.1).

These mainland Chinese immigrants can be classified in three broad catego-ries:[1] 1) economic class, 2) family class, and 3) humanitarian class. Between 1980 and 1989, the annual number of economic-class immigrants (principal applicants and their dependants) from mainland China was small. However, starting in 1990, it has increased dramatically (see Figure 6.2). The economic class of immigrants includes entrepreneurs, investors, self-employed people, and skilled workers and professionals. Although the annual number of immigrating entrepreneurs, inves-tors, and self-employed people increased between 1980 and 2002, as indicated in Figures 6.3, 6.4, and 6.5, the total annual numbers of these categories were rela-tively very small compared to the numbers of skilled workers and professionals (see Table 6.2). For example, from Table 6.2, we can observe that the numbers of principal applicants who were entrepreneurs, investors, and self-employed people immigrating into Canada peaked at 197, 1,038, and 67, respectively, in 2001. However, the peak for principal applicants who were skilled workers and professionals in 2001 was a staggering 13,342. Thus, most economic-class immigrants from mainland China were skilled workers and professionals. Between 1980 and 1989, the total number of principal applicants who immigrated to Canada from mainland China as skilled workers/professionals was only 5,909 (about 96% of the 6,127 economic-class mainland Chinese immigrants). Between 1990 and 2002, this number increased to 77,185, which is about 94% of the total number (82,354) (see Table 6.2 and Figure 6.6). The same trend also applied to the economic-class immigrants who were dependants (see Table 6.2). This is expected because, as the number of principal applicants for the economic-class immigration increases, the number of their dependants as immigrants also increases (see Figure 6.2) due largely to those principal applicants who are immigrating as a family unit.

TABLE 6.1 | MAINLAND CHINESE IMMIGRANTS IN CANADA BY LANDING YEAR, 1956–2004

YEAR	N	YEAR	N	YEAR	N	YEAR	N	YEAR	N
1956	1,516	1966	4,094	1976	833	1986	1,905	1996	17,532
1957	856	1967	6,409	1977	798	1987	2,625	1997	18,524
1958	894	1968	8,382	1978	644	1988	2,770	1998	19,781
1959	519	1969	8,272	1979	2,058	1989	4,415	1999	29,113
1960	183	1970	5,377	1980	4,947	1990	8,116	2000	36,716
1961	118	1971	47	1981	6,552	1991	14,203	2001	40,315
1962	244	1972	25	1982	3,571	1992	10,548	2002	33,231
1963	179	1973	60	1983	2,220	1993	9,485	2003	36,236
1964	184	1974	379	1984	2,220	1994	12,513	2004	36,411
1965	197	1975	903	1985	1,883	1995	13,308		

Sources:

Numbers for 1956–76 can be found at F.H. Leacy, (ed.), *Historical Statistics of Canada* (Ottawa: Statistics Canada, 1999). Cat. #11-516-XIE Series, A385-416 Immigration to Canada by Country of Last Permanent Residence, 1956–1976. <http://www.statcan.ca:8096/bsolc/english/bsolc?catno=11-516-X&CHROPG=1>.

Number for 1977 can be found at 1977 Immigration Statistics (Ottawa: Employment and Immigration Canada, 1978). Cat. #MP22-1/1977: 6, Table 3, Country of Last Permanent Residence and Destination of Immigrants. <http://www.cic.gc.ca/english/pdf/pub/1977stats.pdf>.

Number for 1978 can be found at 1978 Immigration Statistics (Ottawa: Employment and Immigration Canada, 1980). Cat. #MP22-1/1978: 6 Table 3, Country of Last Permanent Residence and Destination of Immigrants. <http://www.cic.gc.ca/english/pdf/pub/1978stats.pdf>.

Number for 1979 can be found at 1979 Immigration Statistics (Ottawa: Employment and Immigration Canada, 1981). Cat. #MP22-1/1979: 6 Table 3, Country of Last Permanent Residence and Destination of Immigrants. <http://www.cic.gc.ca/english/pdf/pub/1979stats.pdf>.

Numbers for 1980–2002 are compiled based on data from Landed Immigrant Data System, 1980–2002 [datafile], Citizenship and Immigration Canada (provided on CD).

Numbers for 2002–04 can be found at Facts and Figures 2004: Immigration Overview—Permanent and Temporary Residents (Ottawa: Citizenship and Immigration Canada, 2005). Cat. #Ci1-8/2004E-PDF: 34, Table: Canada-Permanent Residents from Asia and Pacific by Top Source Countries. <http://www.cic.gc.ca/english/pdf/pub/facts2004.pdf>.

FIGURE 6.1 | MAINLAND CHINESE IMMIGRANTS IN CANADA BY LANDING YEAR, 1956–2004

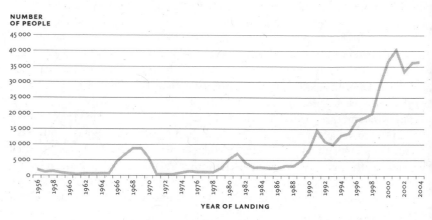

We can also see from Table 6.2 that the majority of immigrants from the family class were primarily parents and/or grandparents and spouses. Between 1980 and 2002, 29,415 immigrants in this category (about 31% of the total number during the same period) were parents or grandparents, while 43,507 (about 46%) were spouses.

For the humanitarian class, the numbers were relatively low compared to the other two classes between the years 1980 and 1989 (see Table 6.2). In 1990, however, numbers began to increase with the highest number of immigrants to Canada in this class occurring in 1996 and 1997 (see Figure 6.7). This has to do with the regularization program implemented between 1994 and 1998 by the Canadian government. In 1994, the Deferred Removal Order Class (DROC) was announced, allowing applications for landed status from refused refugee claimants who had not been removed after three years, subject to certain conditions. DROC was particularly aimed at resolving the situation of over 4,500 Chinese claimants waiting in limbo, usually because they were from moratorium countries—countries that the federal government considered too dangerous to deport people to. China was one of these countries, and Chinese community organizations in Canada began to advocate for permanent residency for failed refugee claimants. Groups from Toronto, Montreal, and Vancouver, including many non-status immigrants, drew public attention to this issue. Approximately 3,000 applicants from China, Iran, and other countries were regularized through this program, but many more were rejected because they did not meet residency requirements or had criminal records or serious medical conditions. In July 1999, a boat with 123 Chinese passengers arrived off the West Coast, the first of four such boats to arrive over the summer. The public response was virulently hostile.[2] Most of the Chinese were kept in long-term detention, and some were irregularly prevented from making refugee claims.

Mainland Chinese immigrants to Canada tend to locate themselves in large urban centres for settlement. Table 6.2 shows that 66.6% of mainland Chinese immigrants who entered Canada between 1980 and 2000 chose Toronto (41.3%)

and Vancouver (25.3%) as their intended destinations. Other favoured cities were Montreal (7.3%), Ottawa (4.2%), Calgary (3.8%), and Edmonton (3.2%). Only a small proportion of the mainland Chinese immigrants chose small cities located in Atlantic Canada and the Prairie provinces of Saskatchewan and Manitoba.

There has been a lot of hype about the successful integration of Chinese business immigrants, and government statistics have generally shown the success of its business immigration program in terms of capital invested and jobs created. However, as indicated above, the business class is only a small part of the mainland Chinese immigration pool. In fact, most mainland Chinese immigrants are skilled or professional immigrants who are not fairing so well, and they are experiencing downward mobility in Canada. The following section focuses on foreign-trained mainland Chinese professional immigrants and examines obstacles to their occupational attainment in the Canadian labour market.

OBSTACLES FOR OCCUPATIONAL ATTAINMENT IN CANADA

Between 1990 and 2002, over 77,000 well-trained and experienced principal applicants who were skilled workers or professionals immigrated to Canada from mainland China (Table 6.2) to seek better opportunities in Canada. However, after entering the country, many of them found difficulties in obtaining the professional jobs they expected, and consequently they experienced downward occupational mobility. According to a survey of 1,180 recent mainland Chinese professional immigrants[3] conducted in the cities of Vancouver, Toronto, Ottawa, Calgary, Edmonton, and Saskatoon between 1997 and 1999 (the 1997–99 Survey),[4] 79% of respondents reported having worked as professionals in China before immigrating to Canada. However, only 31% reported that they worked or had worked as professionals in Canada. Although about 6% of the respondents became proprietors, managers, supervisors, and administrators, 41% had lower social status in non-professional jobs, and 22% had never worked in Canada. About 75% of respondents reported that their occupations in their home country matched their professional qualifications well, while only 23% reported that their current (or last) occupation in Canada matched their professional qualifications. About 41% of respondents reported that they were overqualified for their current occupations, and 29% said they have not worked since their arrival (Zong 2004: 82–83).

There are two approaches in the literature to occupational attainment of immigrants. The first focuses primarily on individual barriers experienced by immigrants, including the inability to meet occupational entry requirements, a lack of Canadian work experience, and an inadequate command of English (Ornstein and Sharma 1983). In the 1997–99 Survey, 49% of respondents reported that they experienced difficulties with their command of English, and 34% also experienced difficulties in adapting to Western culture. Among those who answered "difficult" or "very difficult" with regard to command of English, 70% experienced downward occupational mobility. Among those who answered "difficult"

TABLE 6.2 | IMMIGRANT CATEGORIES FROM PEOPLE'S REPUBLIC OF CHINA BY YEAR OF LANDING IN CANADA, 1980–2002

	1980	1981	1982	1983	1984	1985	1986	1987	1988	1989	1990	1991	1992	1993	1994	1995	1996	1997	1998	1999	2000	2001	2002
FAMILY CLASS[1]																							
Spouse	310	280	454	336	286	248	233	321	303	307	338	731	2355	3143	1942	1144	953	1791	1895	2445	2480	3258	3862
Fiancé	48	144	297	411	390	290	316	421	487	460	531	673	1056	1069	972	729	306	310	299	293	84	54	100
Son or daughter	178	199	44	28	28	12	17	33	37	511	454	378	642	523	365	147	116	151	173	243	261	314	472
Parent or Grandparent	875	1109	827	936	1060	990	959	1184	950	1644	2002	2495	2173	2186	4053	3723	2188	2154	1787	1884	2313	2244	3771
Other family member	43	78	38	23	33	20	12	6	10	8	11	45	316	328	483	673	684	523	913	694	605	610	811
Subtotal	1454	1810	1660	1734	1797	1560	1537	1965	1787	2930	3336	4322	6542	7249	7835	6416	4247	4929	5067	5559	5743	6480	9016
ECONOMIC CLASS[2]–PRINCIPAL APPLICANT																							
Entrepreneur	4	1	8	19	59	0	4	5	15	14	21	19	20	22	32	71	103	128	153	159	179	197	117
Self-employed	0	5	14	14	21	5	3	4	4	15	12	15	14	21	27	38	49	41	50	48	55	67	40
Investor	0	0	0	0	0	0	0	1	0	3	12	13	11	38	20	33	64	130	228	271	665	1038	681
Skilled Workers	1509	1798	676	127	80	161	212	353	418	575	2819	6234	1742	808	1904	2497	4582	5132	5945	10072	12759	13342	9349
Live-in caregivers	0	0	0	0	0	0	0	0	0	0	0	0	0	1	7	26	24	7	11	3	2	3	1
Provincial/Territorial Nominee	0	0	0	0	0	0	0	0	0	0	0	0	0	0	0	0	5	0	0	12	27	70	68
Subtotal	1513	1804	698	160	160	166	219	363	437	607	2864	6281	1787	890	1990	2665	4827	5438	6387	10565	13687	14717	10256
ECONOMIC CLASS–DEPENDANT																							
Entrepreneur	4	2	9	20	35	0	3	5	18	11	18	26	44	49	63	135	211	273	289	310	362	407	252
Self-employed	0	3	10	25	19	3	0	2	4	20	15	21	23	32	38	58	71	56	76	94	84	95	68
Investor	0	0	0	0	0	0	0	0	0	3	7	11	28	55	66	88	187	303	525	635	1500	2388	1646
Skilled Workers	1961	2913	1135	174	65	84	132	269	505	792	1710	2636	961	776	2376	3075	4936	5777	6007	11190	14650	15484	10738

Category	1980	1981	1982	1983	1984	1985	1986	1987	1988	1989	1990	1991	1992	1993	1994	1995	1996	1997	1998	1999	2000	2001	2002
Live-in caregivers	0	0	0	0	0	0	0	0	0	0	0	0	0	0	1	3	11	12	16	1	0	1	0
Subtotal	1965	2918	1154	219	119	87	135	276	527	826	1750	2694	1056	913	2546	3367	5417	6425	6898	12230	16596	18374	12704
HUMANITARIAN CLASS[3]																							
Government Assisted Refugees	4	8	22	19	18	18	11	8	7	13	32	39	10	13	3	1	0	4	0	2	4	6	3
Privately Sponsored Refugees	11	4	8	10	4	1	0	0	4	13	121	433	536	169	14	7	5	0	2	0	0	3	32
Asylum Refugees	0	0	0	0	0	0	0	0	0	0	0	399	584	218	118	305	261	152	237	269	426	392	643
Dependent Abroad[4]	0	0	0	0	0	0	0	0	0	0	0	0	0	2	17	175	237	143	210	205	206	328	571
DROC & PDRCC[5] –Principal Applicant	0	0	0	0	0	0	0	0	0	0	0	0	0	0	0	324	1874	878	583	151	35	9	3
DROC & PDRCC –Dependent	0	0	0	0	0	0	0	0	0	0	0	0	0	0	0	47	663	555	397	132	19	6	3
Subtotal	15	12	30	29	22	19	11	12	11	26	153	871	1130	402	152	859	3040	1732	1429	759	690	744	1255
OTHER CATEGORY																							
Retireds–Principal Applicant	0	7	16	44	64	25	1	5	6	14	8	18	12	9	2	0	1	0	0	0	0	0	0
Retireds–Dependent	0	1	13	34	58	26	2	4	2	12	5	17	21	22	8	1	0	0	0	0	0	0	0
Subtotal	0	8	29	78	122	51	3	9	8	26	13	35	33	31	10	1	1	0	0	0	0	0	0

Source: Landed Immigrant Data System, 1980–2002 [datafile], Citizenship and Immigration Canada. (Provided on CD) 2004 Annual Report to Parliament on Immigration (2004), Minister of Public Works and Government Services Canada, 2004, Cat. no. Ci1-2004 http://www.cic.gc.ca/english/pub/immigration2004.html#500 1. The family class includes the following persons: spouses; common-law partners; conjugal partners; dependent children; the sponsor's parents and grandparents; children under 18 years of age whom the sponsor intends to adopt in Canada; orphaned brothers, sisters, nephews, nieces, and grandchildren under 18 years of age; and any other relative if the sponsor does not have any of the previously listed relatives abroad or in Canada; 2. The economic class includes skilled workers, business immigrants, provincial nominees, live-in caregivers, and their immediate family. There are three types of business immigrants: investors, entrepreneurs, and self-employed workers; 3. The humanitarian category includes Convention refugees (those selected abroad to resettle in Canada) and persons who were granted permanent residence after claiming asylum once in Canada; 4. "Dependents Abroad" refers to "dependents abroad of protected persons landed in Canada." (2004 Report to Parliament on immigration, 2004); 5. "DROC & PDRCC" stands for "deferred removal order and post determination refugee." (1980–2002 Landed immigrant Data Sysyem).

FIGURE 6.2 | ECONOMIC CATEGORY—PRINCIPAL APPLICANT & DEPENDANT

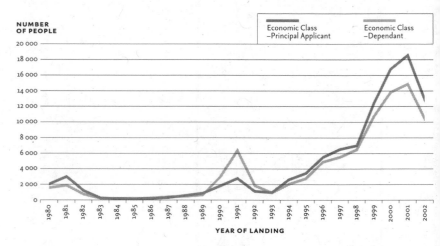

FIGURE 6.3 | ENTREPRENEUR

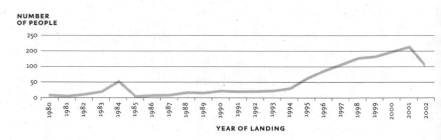

FIGURE 6.4 | SELF-EMPLOYED

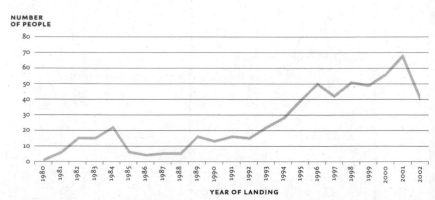

FIGURE 6.5 | INVESTOR

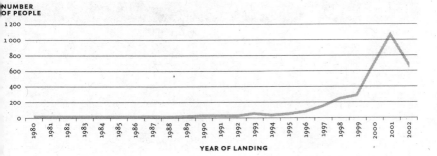

FIGURE 6.6 | SKILLED WORKERS

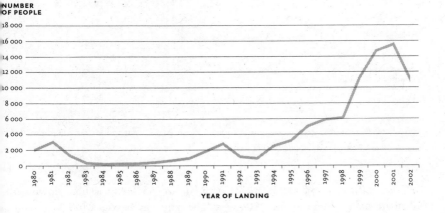

FIGURE 6.7 | HUMANITARIAN CLASS

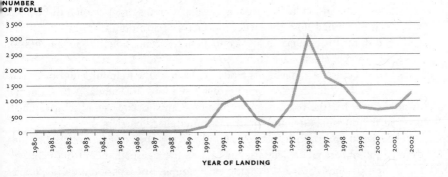

TABLE 6.3 | MAINLAND CHINESE IMMIGRANTS IN CANADA BY INTENDED DESTINATION, 1980–2000

INTENDED DESTINATION	N	%
Toronto	89,653	41.3
Vancouver	55,003	25.3
Montreal	15,806	7.3
Ottawa	9,184	4.2
Calgary	8,344	3.8
Edmonton	6,929	3.2
Winnipeg	3,658	1.7
Hamilton	2,710	1.2
Victoria	2,343	1.1
Saskatoon	1,783	0.8
London	1,669	0.8
Halifax	1,485	0.7
Regina	1,043	0.5
Quebec City	871	0.4
Other areas	16,549	7.7
CANADA	217,030	100.0

Source: Citizenship and Immigration Canada, 2001.

or "very difficult in adaptation to Western culture, 65% experienced downward occupational mobility (Zong 2004: 83). The language barrier can be overcome in time through personal effort. The survey shows that as the length of time in Canada increases, the percentage of downward mobility rate decreases (Zong 2004: 84). This suggests that the linguistic abilities and level of adaptation of new immigrants improves the longer they stay.[5]

Although the individual approach has elucidated some personal difficulties, it has not explained how the structural factors pertaining to policies, criteria, and procedures for evaluation also contribute to occupational disadvantages for foreign-trained professionals. Failure to locate individual barriers in social conditions and structural arrangements tends to assign blame to immigrant professionals themselves for failing to acquire professional jobs in Canada. A fundamental debate is whether the responsibility for immigrants' occupational disadvantages is on such individual attributes or on institutionalized barriers.

The second approach stresses structural barriers such as unequal opportunity, devaluation of foreign credentials, and racism. It suggests that control of entry to the professions has caused systematic exclusion and occupational disadvantages for professional immigrants (Boyd 1985: 393–445; McDade 1988; Trovato and Grindstaff 1986: 569–687; Rajagopal 1990: 96–105; Ralston 1988: 63–83; Beach and Worswick 1989: 36–54). For instance, Boyd provides an analysis of differences between Canadian-born and foreign-born workers in the acquisition of occupational status. She argues that the Canadian-born receive a greater return for their education compared to the foreign-born because of "difficulties of transferring educational skill across national boundaries" (Boyd 1985: 405). In their research, Fernando and Prasad (1986) report that among professional immigrants interviewed, particularly doctors and engineers, 71% had perceived barriers to full recognition.

Many mainland Chinese immigrants perceived some structural barriers that affect their occupational attainments in Canada. The 1997–99 Survey shows that 73% of respondents believed that they could not enter into professional occupations in which they were trained because there is unequal opportunity for visible minority immigrants. About 77% reported that it was difficult for them to find professional jobs because of a shortage of opening positions in the Canadian labour market. However, the major systemic barrier identified by respondents is that their foreign credentials and work experience were devalued by professional organizations, government evaluation agencies, and educational institutions (Zong 2004: 84): 69% of respondents reported that they experienced difficulties in having their foreign credentials recognized in Canada. Based on their own experience and observation, about 78% of respondents reported that "the difficulty in having their foreign qualifications or credentials recognized" was a major factor that affected or might have affected their chances to practice in their chosen professions (Zong 2004: 83).

Many Chinese immigrants thought that the greater the number of years of professional experience, the better their chance of getting a job in their field in Canada. This assumption, however, turned out to be an illusion. In the 1997–99 Survey, 94% of Chinese professional immigrants reported that they had professional work experience in China before immigrating to Canada, 50% had five to ten years of professional work experience, and 21% had more then ten years of professional work experience. Interestingly, Chinese professionals with more professional experience were more likely to experience downward mobility: 47% of respondents did not believe that "the foreign work experience is compared to Canadian standards fairly" (Zong 2004: 83). Thus, professional immigrants encounter a difficult situation in the Canadian labour market. On the one hand, non-recognition of their foreign professional work experience disqualifies their entry into professional jobs, leaving them no chance to get Canadian work experience; on the other hand, the emphasis on Canadian work experience as a requirement for professional employment makes it difficult for them to qualify for professional jobs.

COVERT RACISM IN MULTICULTURAL SOCIETY

The racism experienced by mainland Chinese immigrants in their everyday life is often expressed in a hidden form, which can be called "covert racism" (Zong 1997). This can be defined as a contemporary expression of hostility toward racial minorities that goes undetected by conventional measures (Weigel and Howes 1985).

Since the implementation of the multiculturalism policy in 1971, there has been a debate on whether or not multiculturalism promotes national unity in Canada. While Canadians generally support the values of equality and democracy, many have exhibited a remarkable degree of intolerance toward the increased presence of visible minorities in their midst. In the past two decades, the dramatic influx of refugees and immigrants from the Third World and a large volume of business and professional immigrants from Asian countries have produced renewed racial attitudes and a resurgence of racism. According to the 2003 Ipsos-Reid survey conducted by the Centre for Research and Information on Canada and the *Globe and Mail*, 74% of respondents expressed the view that there is still considerable racism in Canada.

Racism has been generated and reproduced within complex historical and social contexts. Before World War II, overt racism based on the belief in racial superiority was dominant in Europe and North America. It was widely accepted that the Caucasian "race" was physically and genetically superior to other races and was characterized by an inherent capacity for freedom and the ability to create democratic institutions, capacities which they could impose on many other parts of the world (Horsman 1976: 387–410; Horsman 1981: 9–77; MacDougall 1982: 2–3, 31–130). With the expansion of capitalism and colonialism, the "innate superiority" of whites and the "natural inferiority" of blacks and other non-white peoples was used to legitimate and justify racial oppression. Racism arose from initial unequal relationships as a dominant group sought to subjugate a subordinate group for the purpose of acquiring land, resources, and/or cheap labour. In Canada, racism was maintained towards racialized minorities such as the Aboriginal peoples and Asian immigrants; discriminatory laws, programs, and policies were entrenched in a social order that made prejudicial views appear as though they were natural and justifiable (Zong 1994: 122–34).

After World War II, many changes contributed to the weakening of notions of racial superiority or inferiority based on biological and genetic factors. These changes include the struggle against colonial rule, the rise of nationalism, the development of sciences, and the abrogation of discriminatory laws and policies in many advanced capitalist countries. Thus, overt racism has become less acceptable in Western societies. The traditional idea of genetic inferiority or superiority may still be important in the fabric of racism (Duster 1990), but the discourse of racial inferiority is increasingly reformulated as cultural deficiency, social inadequacy, and technological underdevelopment (Rodney 1982). An example is cultural ethnocentrism, which is a tendency to evaluate minorities' cultures based on the dominant group's imposed standards (Li 1994b). According to a survey conducted by the Angus Reid Group, about 13% of Canadians can be considered as "ethnocentrists," based on their negative attitudes towards immigrants and refugees. The basis of negative attitudes appeared to be largely cultural, as those expressing them were concerned with a threat to Canadian culture that they saw coming from an emphasis on multiculturalism and from a rapidly changing population resulting from high immigration levels (Angus Reid Group 1989: 7–8). In recent years, many scholars in North America (Elliott and Fleras 1992; Gaertner and Dovidio 1986; Henry *et al.* 1995; Katz, Wackenhut, and Hass 1986: 35–60; McConohay 1986: 91–126; Weigel and Howes 1985: 117–38) have drawn attention to the emergence of a form of racism in contemporary social settings which can be described as new racism.

The new racism often contains an oblique attack on visible minorities in a covert or disguised form. Different from the past when blatant and stereotypic forms of prejudice and discrimination were routinely directed at racial minorities with explicit hatred, the new racism usually disguises racist attitudes through behaviours that appear non-prejudicial or discriminatory on the surface. To avoid embarrassing situations or possible physical or legal retaliation, racism now is usually expressed in somewhat more muted or polite tones that are less likely to provoke outrage or indignation. Some scholars (Elliott and Fleras 1992; Henry *et al.* 1995) suggest that this new racism reflects a conflict of interest between opposing values in Canadian society. "On the one hand is a commitment to abstract equality and justice (egalitarianism); on the other, an equal but often conflicting endorsement of meritocracy and universalism (individualism)" (Elliott and Fleras 1992: 60).

Since World War II, Canada has witnessed the abolition of overt exclusionary policies and laws such as the repeal of the Chinese Immigration Act in 1947, the adoption of the multiculturalism policy in 1971, and constitutional guarantees of individual rights and freedoms in 1982. These changes help to promote a democratic and tolerant society, and the value of equality in Canadian society is widely propagated. However, economic, political, and social inequalities along racial and ethnic lines still exist, and covert expressions of bigotry and stereotyping remain (Bolaria and Li 1988; Satzewich 1992). The contradiction between democratic principles and racial inequalities at the structural level is reflected in the conflict between the egalitarian values of justice and racist attitudes. This is the basis of what Henry *et al.* call "democratic racism"—a new ideology held by the public in contemporary Canadian society "in which two conflicting sets of values are made congruent to each other. Commitments to democratic principles such as justice, equality, and fairness conflict but coexist with attitudes and behaviours that include negative feelings about minority groups and differential treatment of and discrimination against them" (Henry *et al.* 1995: 21).

The 1995 Vancouver survey conducted in Vancouver confirms the coexistence of these contradictory values, and the findings demonstrate the basis of a new ideology shared by many respondents in their attitudes towards Chinese immigrants. Although people generally accept the value of racial equality, many were not prepared to accept non-white immigrants such as Chinese. About 79% of the respondents agreed that "immigrants should have exactly the same job opportunities as Canadians"; and 82% of the respondents agreed that "minority groups in Canada should have equal opportunity for occupation, education, and promotion in society." However, European immigrants and Chinese immigrants were not equally supported by the public. About 73% of respondents supported admitting more European immigrants, while only about 47% supported admitting more Chinese immigrants. The negative attitude towards Chinese immigrants was not so much based on colour or biological differences but on perceived cultural differences.

It is widely held that different cultures brought by immigrants undermine the national unity. The 1995 Vancouver survey showed that about 50% of respondents disagreed with the statement that "the establishment of multiculturalism policy has promoted a democratic and tolerant society in Canada." Many respondents argued that multiculturalism encourages cultural diversity and denies the existence of Canadian culture, therefore creating and reinforcing separateness and racial conflict. This concern is reflected in public attitudes towards recent Chinese immigrants in Vancouver. The following are some comments made by respondents:

> Less emphasis should be placed on a multiculturalism policy. Effort and funds should go towards emphasizing assimilation into the Canadian way of life as my family did 90 years ago. (Male; German-Canadian; Age 59)

> "Multiculturalism" should be replaced by a new goal "Uniculturalism." The old saying applies "United we stand divided we fall." (Male; English-Canadian; Age 73)

> I am against any individualized multiculturalism. Canada is a country with two cultures (English and French). Any other immigrants of other culture have to adjust. Only by way of assimilation can Canada become one nation. (Female; German-Canadian; Age 79)

> Immigrants should be prepared to adapt to the Canadian way of life—become Canadians. They should not expect Canada or Canadians to adapt to them. (Female; English-Canadian; Age 60)

> I believe that Chinese immigrants should make [a] real effort in not only adopting but rather integrating their culture with other Canadian cultures and respect other cultures and stop imposing their own standards, and creating Chinese ghettos. It is also unfortunate that most of them can hardly speak English, reducing their degree of interaction with other cultures. (Male; French-Canadian; Age 49)

> Part of the Chinese-Canadian conflict exists because of the attitude of "non-integration" that the Chinese community often holds; they have no reason to attempt to enter into any activities relating to Canadian culture when their

community is self-contained. I would like to see Chinese make an honest effort towards learning English. (Male; English-Canadian; Age 19)

I think multiculturalism creates friction and intolerance. This is Canada and everything Canadian must and should be promoted to create unity. (Male; Dutch-Canadian; Age 53)

These comments reflect the common belief still held by many Canadians that nglo-Saxon culture as Canadian culture is the basis of national unity in this ountry and that immigrants must make conscious efforts to become "Canadian" y accepting and adopting behaviours of the dominant group. Most people would eny that race is important and almost unanimously would condemn racism as eing wrong. In the 1995 Vancouver survey, about 59% of respondents thought 1at ethnic origin should not be used as a criterion in admitting immigrants to ;anada, and over 82% agreed that minority groups in Canada should have equal pportunity for occupation, education, and promotion in society. Yet, at the same me, many people accepted visible minorities and immigrants only on the basis 1at they can adapt to Anglo Canadian culture. The same survey shows that about 9% of respondents agreed that "Chinese immigrants should adapt themselves to ;anadian culture in order to become a real Canadian."

Cultural diversity has always been a part of Canadian society; it is an existing act of life and not something that can be changed artificially. Despite cultural dif-erences, different racial and ethnic groups in Canadian society share core values uch as democracy and equality. Some scholars (Breton 1984: 123–44; Li 1994a: 4–33; Li 1994b: 365–91; Mercer 1995: 169–84) suggest that although there is o empirical evidence to indicate that immigrants and their cultural diversity are osing any real threat to the dominant culture of Canada, visible minorities and immigrants are often perceived as undermining a British-dominated traditional ymbolic order, on the grounds that they are seen as carriers of foreign cultures nd norms which are believed to be different, if not incompatible, with Canadian eritage and core values" (Li 1996: 24). As Li points out:

> the apparent growth of opposition to increased immigration to Canada and the intensification of negative sentiments towards immigrants, especially those from non-European origins, stem from the perceived threat to an established symbolic order and status hierarchy that are distinctly British dominated, and not necessarily from real conflicts between core Canadian values and the nor-mative and linguistic diversities that recent immigrants are supposedly to have imported with them. (Li 1996: 23)

Culture is dynamic and complex. The notion of "Anglo-Saxon Canadian cul-ure" is vague and ambiguous, and the concept of "acculturation" or "assimila-ion" stressed in national unity is misleading and ill-defined. Assimilation implies hat there are certain objectives and widely agreed-upon standards of behaviours that are indicative of social and structural integration. However, in practice, it is unclear what types of behaviours indicate a person is assimilated.

Cultural diversity does not in itself create racial tension and conflict. It is differential power and unequal treatments that do so. Members of the dominant group often use their "standards" as a frame of reference for interpreting and evaluating behaviours of other groups. As Elliott and Fleras (1992: 55) point out "Not surprisingly, these groups are rated inferior, backward, or irrational. It can be seen that although favouritism towards one's own group can promote cohesion and morale, it can also contribute to intergroup tension and hostility, ... [and] to a proliferation of stereotypes about outgroup members."

Finally, as regards the multiculturalism policy, the real issue is not whether it harms or enhances national unity, but how it promotes mutual understanding and a respectful relationship among different racial groups, and how it achieves national solidarity and harmony within a culturally diversified society.

CONCLUSION

In the past 25 years, the number of mainland Chinese immigrants to Canada increased dramatically, and they have brought significant financial and human capital resources to Canada. However, this study shows that new Chinese immigrants have experienced great difficulties in accessing education-related professions in Canada. The problem of transferring educational equivalences and work experience across international boundaries results in mainland Chinese professional immigrants taking jobs for which they are overtrained, resulting in downward occupational mobility relative to their occupations held before their immigrating to Canada. Recent mainland Chinese immigrants face both individual and institutional barriers to entry into their respective professions. Individual barriers such as linguistic ability and cultural adaptation can gradually improve over time through their personal efforts, community support, and programs and services provided by the Canadian government. However, immigrants themselves cannot resolve institutionalized obstacles, such as the devaluation of foreign credentials and work experience, unequal opportunity, and racism.

This chapter indicates that there are contradictory social values within a multicultural society that become an important ideological basis of new racism. On the one hand, Canadian people generally accept "racial equality" and "democracy" as central values in a social democratic society; on the other hand, cultural ethnocentrism prevails in society as reflected in negative attitudes towards Chinese immigrants. The author criticizes the discourse that cultural diversity threatens national unity and argues that national unity can be achieved in the context of cultural diversity. To make full use of the talents and skills of Chinese immigrants, Canadian governments at different levels should consider providing more assistance, including delivery of effective settlement services, to help them adapt to Canadian society. A better understanding of how these human resources are actually used after the immigrants' arrival in Canada is needed. It is essential for federal and provincial governments and professional organizations to understand how highly educated, foreign-trained professional immigrants establish themselves in the labour force and what systemic barriers they encounter. The chapter suggests that in order for Canada to fully benefit from international human capital transfer, a policy is needed to ensure that the credentials of foreign-trained professional immigrants are properly and fairly evaluated.

NOTES

1 Immigrants to Canada are officially grouped into more than 10 classes, but the various classes can be generalized into the three broad categories. The economic category includes (1) skilled workers/professionals who are admitted on the basis of skills, education, language ability, and occupational background; (2) business immigrants (investors, entrepreneurs, and self-employed) who must bring with them sufficient capital to start a business in Canada and either provide jobs for themselves or employ other Canadians; and (3) live-in caregivers. The family category refers to family members including spouses, fiancé/fiancée, dependent children, parents, grandparents, and assisted relatives of Canadian citizens or landed immigrants. The humanitarian category includes refugees, deferred order removal class (immigrants who at one time were ordered to leave Canada but subsequently had their deportation order cancelled), and designated class (immigrants admitted under a special government program, usually in response to political upheavals in their home countries). The retired class in this study is not included in the three categories, and it is listed separately as the "Other" category.

2 Hier and Greenberg (2002) provide an analysis of the problematization of undocumented Fujianese migrants who arrived on Canada's western shores from July–September 1999.

3 "Mainland Chinese professional immigrants" refers to those who received their professional training in China and worked as doctors, engineers, school/university teachers, and other professionals; who entered Canada as immigrants; and who were residents in Canada at the time of the survey.

4 The data were obtained through self-administered questionnaires, which included 71 questions on credentials, work experience before and after immigration, personal difficulties and perceived structural barriers in accessing professional jobs in the Canadian labour force, opinions on policy issues, and general respondent information. Findings of the survey were reported in Zong 2004.

5 The result is consistent with previous research findings. For example, Ramcharan (1976) in his study on the economic adaptation of West Indians in Toronto, found that the length of residence is an important factor affecting their economic success.

REFERENCES AND SUGGESTED READINGS

Angus Reid Group. 1989. Immigration to Canada: Aspects of Public Opinion. Winnipeg.

Basran, Gurcharn, and Li Zong. 1998. Devaluation of Foreign Credentials as Perceived by Visible Minority Professional Immigrants. *Canadian Ethnic Studies* 30(3): 6–23.

Beach, Christopher, and Charles Worswick. 1989. Is There A Double-negative Effect on the Earnings of Immigrant Women? *Canadian Public Policy* 16(2): 36–54.

Bolaria, B.S., and P.S. Li (eds.). 1988. *Racial Oppression in Canada*. 2nd ed. Toronto: Garamond.

Boyd, Monica. 1985. Immigration and Occupation Attainment in Canada. In Monica Boyd, ed., *Ascription and Achievement: Studies in Mobility and Status Attainment in Canada.* Ottawa: Carleton University Press.

Breton, Raymond. 1984. The Production and Allocation of Symbolic Resources: An Analysis of the Linguistic and Ethnocultural Fields in Canada. *Canadian Review of Sociology and Anthropology* 21(2): 123–44.

Citizenship and Immigration Canada. 2002. Landed Immigration Data System, 1980–2002 [Data File] (Provided on CD).

———. 2004. Facts and Figures 2004: Immigration Overview. Cat. No. Cil-8/2004E-PDF, pp. 34.

Duster, T. 1990. *Backdoor to Eugenics.* New York: Routledge.

Elliott, Jean Leonard, and Augie Fleras. 1992. *Unequal Relations: An Introduction to Race and Ethnic Dynamics in Canada.* Scarborough, Ontario: Prentice-Hall.

Fernando, Kamal K., and Tissa Prasad. 1986. *Multiculturalism and Employment Equity: Problems Facing Foreign-Trained Professionals and Tradespeople in British Columbia.* Vancouver: Affiliation of Multicultural Societies and Service Agencies of BC.

Gaertner, Samuel L., and John F. Dovidio. 1986. The Aversive Forms of Racism. In John F. Dovidio and Samuel L. Gaertner, eds., *Prejudice, Discrimination, and Racism.* New York: Academic Press.

Henry, Frances, Carol Tator, Winston Mattis, and Tim Rees (eds.). 1995. *The Colour of Democracy: Racism in Canadian Society.* Toronto: Harcourt Brace.

Hier, Sean P., and Joshua L. Greenberg. 2002. Constructing A Discursive Crisis: Risk, Problematization, and Illegal Chinese in Canada. *Ethnic and Racial Studies* 25(3): 490–513.

Horsman, R. 1976. Origins of Racial Anglo-Saxonism in Great Britain before 1850. *Journal of the History of Ideas* 37(3): 387–410.

———. 1981. *Race and Manifest Destiny.* Cambridge, MA: Harvard University Press.

Katz, Irwin, Joyce Wackenhut, and R. Glen Hass. 1986. Racial Ambivalence, Value Duality, and Behaviour. In J.D. Gaertner and S.L. Gaertner, eds., *Prejudice, Discrimination, and Racism.* New York: Academic Press.

Li, Peter. 1994a. Unneighbourly House or Unwelcome Chinese: The Social Construction of Race in the Battle over "Monster Homes" in Vancouver, Canada. *International Journal of Comparative Race and Ethnic Studies* 1(1): 14–33.

———. 1994b. A World Apart: the Multicultural World of Visible Minorities and the Art World of Canada. *The Canadian Review of Sociology and Anthropology* 31(4): 365–91.

———. 1996. *Literature Review on Immigration: Sociological Perspectives.* Ottawa: Citizenship and Immigration Canada.

———. 1998. *Chinese in Canada.* Toronto: Oxford University Press.

———. 2005. The Rise and Fall of Chinese Immigration to Canada: Newcomers from Hong Kong Special Administrative Region of China and Mainland China, 1980–2000. *International Migration* 43(3): 9–32.

MacDougall, H.A. 1982. *Racial Myth in English History: Trojans, Teutons, and Anglo-Saxons.* Montreal: Harvest House.

McConohay, John B. 1986. Modern Racism, Ambivalence, and the Modern Racism Scale. In J.D. Gaertner and S.L. Gaertner, eds., *Prejudice, Discrimination, and Racism.* New York: Academic Press.

McDade, Kathryn. 1988. *Barriers to Recognition of the Credentials of Immigrants in Canada.* Ottawa: Institute for Research on Public Policy.

Mercer, John. 1995. Canadian Cities and Their Immigrants: New Realities. *Annals of the American Academy of Political and Social Science* 538: 169–84.

Ornstein, Michael, and Raghubar D. Sharma. 1983. Adjustment and Economic Experience of Immigrants in Canada: An Analysis of the 1976 Longitudinal Survey of Immigrants. A Report to Employment and Immigration Canada. Toronto: York University Institute for Behavioural Research.

Privy Council. 1967. *Canada Gazette* Part II. 101(17): 1350–62.

Rajagopal, Indhu. 1990. The Glass Ceiling in the Vertical Mosaic: Indian Immigrants to Canada. *Canadian Ethnic Studies* 22(1): 96–105.

Ralston, Helen. 1988. Ethnicity, Class, and Gender among South Asian Women in Metro Halifax: An Exploratory Study. *Canadian Ethnic Studies* 20(3): 63–83.

Ramcharan, Subhas. 1976. The Economic Adaptation of West Indians in Toronto, Canada. *The Canadian Review of Sociology and Anthropology* 13(3): 295–304.

Rodney, W. 1982. *How Europe Underdeveloped Africa*. Washington, DC: Howard University Press.

Satzewich, Vic (ed.). 1992. *Deconstructing A Nation: Immigration, Multiculturalism and Racism in '90s Canada*. Halifax: Fernwood.

Trovato, Carl F., and Frank Grindstaff. 1986. Economic Status: A Census Analysis of Immigrant Women at Age Thirty in Canada. *Review of Sociology and Anthropology* 23(4): 569–687.

Weigel, Paul W., and Russel H. Howes. 1985. Conceptions of Racial Prejudice: Symbolic Racism Reconsidered. *Journal of Social Issues* 41(3): 117–38.

Zong, Li. 1994. Structural and Psychological Dimensions of Racism. *Canadian Ethnic Studies* 26(3): 122–34.

——. 1997. New Racism, Cultural Diversity, and the Search for A National Identity. In A. Cardoza and L. Musto, eds., *The Battle over Multiculturalism: Does It Help or Hinder Canadian Unity?* Ottawa: Pearson-Shoyama Institute.

——. 1998. Chinese Immigration to Vancouver and New Racism in Multicultural Canada. In G. Zhuang, ed., *Ethnic Chinese at the Turn of the Centuries*. Fujian: Fujian People Press.

——. 2003. Language, Education, and Occupational Attainment of Foreign-Trained Chinese and Polish Professional Immigrants in Toronto, Canada. In Michael W. Charney, Brenda S.A. Yeoh, and Tong Chee Kiong, eds., *Chinese Migrants Abroad: Cultural, Educational and Social Dimensions of the Chinese Diaspora*. Singapore: Singapore University Press.

——. 2004. International Transference of Human Capital and Occupational Attainment of Recent Chinese Professional Immigrants in Canada. *American Journal of China Studies* 5(1/2): 81–89.

7 | INCORPORATION OF ABORIGINAL LABOUR

Terry Wotherspoon

INTRODUCTION

As Canadian officials seek to improve the country's position in a globally competitive economy, the labour market participation of Aboriginal people has become an important public policy issue. Federal, provincial, and First Nations governments, along with numerous public sector, private sector, and community organizations and agencies, have introduced a diverse array of policy initiatives and active interventions aimed at integrating Aboriginal people more fully into the labour market. There is a powerful sense of urgency for Aboriginal people to gain increasing levels of education, training, skill development, and aptitudes for work at a time when an aging Canadian labour force, combined with intensified global competition, is creating demands for new workers. While such general imagery is widely accepted, it is important to examine in greater detail the diverse places that Aboriginal people occupy in and out of the workforce. This chapter highlights Aboriginal people's incorporation into capitalist labour markets in terms of processes that are relatively complex and dynamic, as they are shaped through interactions among key social, economic, and political structures and relationships.

THE DYNAMICS OF INCORPORATION

Incorporation is commonly understood in two general ways: individual and structural. The first emphasizes the extent to which individuals or aggregates, categorized on the basis of particular attributes or features such as age, ethnicity, gender, or place of birth, come to be integrated into labour markets. Human capital theory, for example, analyzes the cultivation of credentials, skills, and capacities as economic assets that benefit both the individual and society. Consequently, public systems of education, training, and labour market development are viewed within this orientation as important complements to individual and family initiatives to provide potential workers with a strong foundation of marketable skills that will enhance individual and social well-being. Human capital theory and related orientations to labour market incorporation have gained ascendancy among policy-makers and economic analysts who consider it crucial for individuals and nations to enhance education and skill development to remain competitive in global knowledge-driven economic development. Public and personal anxieties over employability and uncertain job prospects are heightening concerns to strengthen linkages among labour market incorporation and individual or social investment in education, training, and other forms of capacity development. Nonetheless, human capital approaches are limited in several ways, including the relatively narrow and uncritical conceptions of skills they adopt; their failure to take into account divergent economic and social policy contexts; and their lack of attention to substantial disparities in education, skills, and marketable credentials (Brown 2001: 14–15; Livingstone 2004: 169–70).

The second set of structural orientations offers an alternative, more critical understanding of relations among education, labour markets, and social position-ing. Structural orientations also understand incorporation as part of a complex process that varies through changing socio-economic and political conditions. Marxist analysis, for instance, emphasizes inequalities related to the differential incorporation of social participants into capitalism or other dominant systems of production. Employment opportunities and work, rather than being posed in terms of abstract processes (or economic "goods" to which everyone should be entitled), are understood with reference to particular social relationships and historical activities. Whereas both individual and structural approaches make comparisons among groups, communities, or societies in terms of rates of employ-ment, occupational sectors, income, and other important factors, structural orien-tations are concerned with the social processes and structures that cause observed changes and variations, as well as with the outcomes of those processes.

Recent analysis of immigration and international migration has advanced this understanding by examining how key forms of social differentiation, including class, race, and gender inequalities, are shaped by the development of capitalist enterprises across global, national, and regional sectors. A fundamental char-acteristic of capitalist economies is the continual struggle for profitable invest-ment and production. This is strongly interconnected with ongoing changes in the ways in which workers, as sources of labour power, are produced and utilized. Workplaces, skills, and jobs, along with the characteristics and capacities of the people who perform the work, are continually renewed, transformed, or rendered redundant as production, markets, and investment priorities shift. Variations in the patterns and extent to which different groups are integrated into, or excluded from, labour markets and other social venues are understood in these terms as modes of incorporation (Portes and Rumbaut 1990: 83–84; Satzewich 1991). The concept of modes of incorporation shifts the focus of analysis beyond relatively abstract or general comparisons between individuals or groups in order to take into account variations in economic relations, government policies, and social and cultural factors. The mode of incorporation moreover, might be particular to specific regional or national contexts even when shaped by international forces.

These insights have considerable relevance for understanding the changing labour market experiences of Aboriginal people in Canada. Canada's Aboriginal population is highly differentiated, both internally and in relation to other groups, as a consequence of interactions among distinct historical, cultural, and legal experiences (which, in turn, affect access to particular forms of rights, recognition, and regulation over time). Gender, age, geography, residential location, and class also matter. The next section draws attention to major dimensions and variations in historical patterns of Aboriginal people's incorporation into capitalist production and labour markets. This is followed by a more detailed discussion of the varying positions occupied by different segments of the Aboriginal population within the contemporary workforce and labour markets.

ABORIGINAL PEOPLE'S LABOUR FORCE ACTIVITY IN CANADA: HISTORICAL DIMENSIONS

Indigenous societies and the economic activity performed within them were transformed through European colonization. The striking contrast between self-sufficient and thriving communities that prevailed in many First Nations as late as the 19th century (and well into the 20th in the case of populations in some of the most remote and northern regions), and massive desolation over the course of a few decades in the post-fur trade era, has been well documented (e.g., Royal Commission on Aboriginal Peoples 1996a). The combined impact of settlement, trading patterns, large-scale agriculture, urbanization, industrialization, massive transportation, resource and infrastructural projects, and state control over Indians and Indian lands relegated Aboriginal people to the margins of the historical narrative of the Canadian nation-building project. However, the growing body of literature that has accompanied Aboriginal claims for cultural renewal and self-determination demonstrates that their employment relations and economic activity have been much more varied and diverse than commonly assumed. The expansion of capitalist relations across Canada occurred as an extended period of transformation marked by an uneven pace and scale of economic development and state consolidation. In the process, at least three different forms of relationships were evident in Aboriginal people's experiences with capitalist labour markets: continuous exclusion, discontinuity, and standard or regular employment.

The first pattern, continuous exclusion, lies at the heart of concerns over employment-related problems in Aboriginal communities. There are two major forms of non-participation in, or exclusion from, capitalist labour markets. First, wage labour is not essential for people who can support themselves outside the sphere of capitalist relations (e.g., informal and subsistence economic activities). Second, non-wage support through state or charitable organizations becomes a more likely option for those who have lost their autonomous means of subsistence or have limited employment options in a wage economy. The latter form of exclusion, posed especially as a problem of welfare dependency, has received the most public and policy-related attention (see Flanagan 2000; Royal Commission on Aboriginal Peoples 1996b; Neu and Therrien 2003). The issue is particularly acute among the First Nations population living on reserves, where reliance on government assistance, precipitated by a combination of restricted work options, barriers to employment, and government policies, has persisted. In some instances, reliance on government assistance has lasted for several generations.

Since the early 1970s, social assistance has been the major source of income for about 40% to 45% of the on-reserve population in Canada (ranging from between about one-quarter of the reserve population in Ontario to three-quarters in the Atlantic region). These rates are about four to five times the average for the general population and double that of non-status First Nations, Métis, and Inuit populations (Department of Indian and Northern Affairs Canada 1997: 37; Moscovitch and Webster 1995: 218–19). Reliance on social assistance tends to exacerbate individual and family poverty, and it is often compounded by serious social, personal, community, and health-related concerns. It is also exacerbated by difficulties in gaining access to crucial resources like transportation, credentials, work experience, and social (employment) networks.

Welfare dependency and exclusion from the labour market are serious problems, but they are also highly complex, taking on different forms and meanings in diverse contexts. They are conceptualized, experienced, and responded to in varying ways, reflecting interactions among such factors as destruction of traditional forms of economic support, shifting patterns of employment, changing government policies, and federal-provincial jurisdictional boundaries and disputes (Moscovitch and Webster 1995). Recent research and analysis demonstrates that even in areas such as the far north, where stable employment is highly limited, most social assistance recipients do not receive welfare on a continuous basis, with long-term dependence on welfare concentrated mostly among older age cohorts or persons whose employability is limited due to health, disability, or care of dependants (HRDC 1995: 9–10).

The general emphasis on welfare in their communities tends to obscure the fact that Aboriginal people, whether living on or off reserve, are more likely to derive income from wages than from social assistance. The significance of wage labour has often been overlooked, in part because Aboriginal people's labour market involvement throughout much of the 20th century has been marked by labour market discontinuities or transitions—the second type of Aboriginal-capitalist labour market relationship (High 1996). One of the first documents to draw public attention to the uneven and highly regional nature of Aboriginal employment and income was the Hawthorn Report on social and economic conditions for Indians in Canada in the mid-1960s (Hawthorn 1966: 51–52, 65–66). Aboriginal employment patterns reveal the combined impact of several factors, including economic development strategies, geographic locale, and state policies (including those related to residential schools, reserve location, and band relocation). Reserves and Aboriginal communities, for instance, are typically concentrated in rural areas and regions where employment prospects tend to be associated with primary and resource-based industries. Among these industries, which are often seasonal or volatile, are logging, fishing, trapping and hunting, mining, and agriculture (Knight 1996; Wien 1986). Subsistence and informal economic activity, maintained as long as people could support themselves and family or community members through trapping, harvesting, fishing, and other pursuits, were often interrupted or terminated by economic crises, state restrictions, or external developments.

Moreover, employment prospects for Aboriginal people were often regulated by government policies and hiring practices in particular industries or sectors. The terms and administration of the Indian Act placed heavy constraints on the economic activity and prospects for First Nations people in critical domains, including access to resources, travel, mobility, and ability to secure effective education and training. In the private sector, discriminatory hiring and workplace practices, combined with less overt racism and exclusionary practices, served to limit or disrupt Aboriginal employment in many industries (Buckley 1992: 74–75). The federal government frequently cooperated with, or acted on behalf of, non-Aboriginal farmers, businesses, and employers, serving variously to curtail Aboriginal economic activity or to create temporary work programs and arrangements for reserve-based band members to travel to other locales as migrant seasonal workers (Carter 1990; Laliberte and Satzewich 1999). Aboriginal people have also relied on wage labour as a temporary or interim measure where options existed to engage in independent production and informal activities in order to maintain community relations and cultural traditions (High 1996). Some workers, such as those with in-demand trade skills or employment in lucrative resource sectors, may be able to generate high incomes even while working only part of the year. More generally, though, prospects for part-time, seasonal, or temporary workers in sectors where Aboriginal people are concentrated tend to be less promising and often associated with economic vulnerability.

The third type of relationship is continuous work, typically on a full-time, full-year basis with a single employer. This model is often termed the standard employment relation, reflecting prevailing norms and assumptions that place ongoing job tenure and progressive career development at the heart of much work-related policy and analysis in highly industrialized nations (Vosko 2000: 21–22). Despite notable examples (e.g., Hill 1987), the absence of continuous employment by Aboriginal people received more attention than has its presence. This unbalanced focus reflects legitimate concerns about limited employment prospects, but a preoccupation with Aboriginal people's discontinuous employment or non-participation in labour markets also conceals important ideological and cultural assumptions about work, as well as variations in the extent to which people may be able to attain standard employment. Gender, race, ethnicity, age, physical status, and other factors influence people's desire and ability to perform wage labour, reflecting in part differences in access to education and community services, qualifications, personal circumstances, and domestic and caregiving responsibilities. All these factors intersect with opportunities and imperatives to engage in public service, independent production, or economic activities beyond the sphere of capitalist production. These mechanisms often reinforce one another as well. Discriminatory practices or policies, for instance, may both contribute to and reflect negative stereotypes and damaging cultural representations such as images that suggest an incompatibility between Aboriginal people and work.

Aboriginal men and women have participated extensively as long-term workers within diverse industries, professions, and economic sectors, although their employment has been influenced by broader patterns of colonization, trade, and economic development mediated by specific restrictions and forms of regulation (Satzewich and Wotherspoon 2000: 43ff; Ray 1974: 46–48; Knight 1996; Wien 1986). Employment patterns in the second quarter of the 20th century illustrate clearly the contradictory dynamics associated with Aboriginal employment. Aboriginal people were especially hard hit by the economic crisis of the 1930s, which entailed massive unemployment and displacement along with discriminatory and exclusionary practices that accompanied intensified competition for jobs and resources. In the early 1940s, Aboriginal workers were recruited, along with women and other groups which had been on the margins or outside of standard labour market activities, to replace the largely male working population engaged in the armed forces and to fuel rising industrial productivity induced by the wartime economy. Aboriginal people were also actively involved in the war effort as volunteers and through conscription into military service. These activities created opportunities for recognition, skill development, and social integration, but some Aboriginal workers and veterans were confronted at the same time with discrimination and loss of formal status and entitlements under the Indian Act. While demands for wage labour remained high after the war, much of the temporary workforce was displaced in the immediate postwar period by returning non-Aboriginal war veterans. The latter were assisted by government programs to promote training and employment, as well as some entitlements to agricultural land, some of which had been expropriated from Indian reserve lands (Moses 2000). Overall, the wartime experience exposed and solidified awareness of the shifting and often uncertain place of Aboriginal people in Canadian social and economic life. This led simultaneously to a deterioration of conditions among large segments of the Aboriginal population and to a basis for new forms of solidarity and consciousness which produced demands for action to improve conditions in many Aboriginal communities (Stevenson 1996).

By the end of the 20th century, paradoxically, widespread expectations that Aboriginal people should become more centrally engaged in labour market-related activities were emerging in a context where employment norms and the economic capacity to sustain full-time continuous work throughout the labour force were being reshaped. Intense global economic competition, rapid technological innovation, shifting skill demands, and more extended processes of transition between education and working life are altering both the nature of work and the conditions by which people enter into and engage with labour markets. The next section highlights the mixed implications these changes have in contributing to new opportunities, as well as additional barriers, to labour market options for Aboriginal people.

SOCIAL INEQUALITIES AND ECONOMIC RESTRUCTURING

This section examines patterns of labour market participation and employment among Aboriginal people to understand the place of and implications for them in the context of contemporary economic transformations. Aboriginal people are represented across a wide range of occupations and industries in Canada. Table 7.1 provides an overview of the labour market positioning among people reporting Aboriginal identity in comparison with the total Canadian labour force. The data reveal the significance that wage labour, or the capacity to engage in waged employment, holds for most of the Aboriginal population. They are active participants in the labour market, with about four out of five men and more than two out of three women deriving income from employment in 2000. Self-employment, reported by more than 27,000 Aboriginal people in the 2001 census, is increasing more rapidly among the Aboriginal population than in the overall Canadian population (Treasury Board of Canada 2005). Levels of self-employment and the ratio of wage-workers or paid employees to self-employed persons, however, are consistently lower than national averages for all Aboriginal identity categories.

The general pattern of distribution of workers is broadly comparable across population groups, although distinct variations become evident along some indicators and categories when more detailed comparisons are explored. Rates of labour market participation by Aboriginal people overall—about two-thirds for men and slightly more than half (56.5%) for women—are slightly lower than the national average. Participation rates by both men and women declaring Métis identity are higher than the national average, and they are lowest for those indicating North American Indian identity. More significant gaps are evident with respect to unemployment rates and employment patterns. Within the Aboriginal population, unemployment rates vary between about 1.7 times higher than the national average for women indicating Métis identity to over three times the average for Inuit and North American Indian men. The incidence of those who did not work in 2000, or who worked part-time or on a partial year basis, is also higher than the national averages for both men and women in nearly all Aboriginal identity categories (the exceptions are the lower than national proportions of Métis and Inuit men and women who did not work).

TABLE 7.1 | EXPERIENCED LABOUR FORCE, BY MAJOR INDUSTRY GROUPS AND SELECTED LABOUR MARKET INDICATORS, GENDER, AND ABORIGINAL STATUS.[1]

			CANADA 2001: MALE LABOUR FORCE				
INDUSTRY	TOTAL MALE POPULATION	TOTAL MALE ABORIGINAL IDENTITY	NORTH AMERICAN INDIAN (TOTAL)	ON RESERVE	OFF RESERVE	MÉTIS	INUIT
Goods-Producing Sector	**35.4**	**40.1**	**39.3**	**39.5**	**39.1**	**42.6**	**27.6**
Agriculture, forestry, fishing, and hunting	4.9	8.1	9.2	13.6	6.3	6.9	3.1
Mining, oil and gas extraction	1.7	3.8	3.0	2.6	3.3	5.0	4.2
Utilities	1.1	1.4	1.2	1.6	1.0	1.3	3.6
Construction	9.3	14.2	14.2	15.6	13.2	14.6	12.2
Manufacturing	18.5	12.6	11.6	6.1	15.4	14.7	4.6
Services-Producing Sector	**64.6**	**59.9**	**60.8**	**60.5**	**60.9**	**57.4**	**72.3**
Wholesale/retail trade	15.2	10.7	8.9	5.4	11.3	13.2	11.7
Transportation/ warehousing	7.0	7.2	6.5	4.7	7.7	8.3	7.4
Information/ cultural industries	2.6	1.3	1.1	0.6	1.5	1.6	1.8
Finance, insurance, real estate, and leasing	4.5	2.0	1.6	0.7	2.2	2.2	3.6
Professional, scientific, and technical services	6.6	2.3	2.3	1.2	3.0	2.4	1.8
Management of companies and enterprises	0.1	~	~	0	~	~	0.1
Administrative/ support, waste management, and remediation services	4.0	5.0	5.2	4.0	5.9	4.9	3.6
Educational services	4.2	3.7	4.2	6.3	2.8	2.8	5.2
Health care/social assistance	3.3	3.8	4.2	5.4	3.5	3.1	4.8
Arts, entertainment, and recreation	1.9	2.6	2.9	2.7	2.9	2.1	3.9
Accommodation and food services	5.1	5.2	5.1	2.7	6.8	5.5	3.2
Public administration	5.8	12.4	15.5	24.5	9.4	6.9	22.0
Other services	4.4	3.8	3.3	2.3	4.0	4.6	3.1

INDUSTRY	TOTAL MALE POPULATION	TOTAL MALE ABORIGINAL IDENTITY	NORTH AMERICAN INDIAN (TOTAL)	ON RESERVE	OFF RESERVE	MÉTIS	INUIT
TOTAL CLASSIFIED INDUSTRIES (%²)	100	100	100	100	100	100	100
n	8,311,130	196,985	108,790	44,115	64,680	74,075	8,380
Number of paid employees	7,062,685	179,390	100,645	41,525	59,120	65,790	7,795
Number self-employed	1,230,755	17,275	7,990	2,530	5,465	8,125	580
Participation rate	72.7	66.8	62.7	56.0	68.6	74.5	65.4
Employment rate	67.2	52.5	47.0	37.7	55.2	63.0	49.2
Unemployment rate	7.6	21.4	25.0	32.7	19.5	15.4	24.7
% with employment income	80.6	80.8	78.5	71.5	82.1	84.0	81.1
% who did not work in 2000	25.1	31.7	36.1	42.0	31.6	23.8	29.2
% who worked full year, full time	44.6	28.7	25.1	18.7	29.3	35.8	24.8
% who worked part year or part-time	30.2	39.6	38.8	39.3	39.2	40.4	46.0

CANADA 2001: FEMALE LABOUR FORCE							
INDUSTRY	TOTAL FEMALE POPULATION	TOTAL FEMALE ABORIGINAL IDENTITY	NORTH AMERICAN INDIAN (TOTAL)	ON RESERVE	OFF RESERVE	MÉTIS	INUIT
Goods-Producing Sector	13.3	9.4	8.7	6.4	10.0	10.9	6.4
Agriculture, forestry, fishing, and hunting	2.3	2.1	2.0	2.4	1.8	2.3	0.9
Mining, oil and gas extraction	0.4	0.7	0.5	0.4	0.5	1.0	1.0
Utilities	0.4	0.4	0.3	0.2	0.3	0.5	0.6
Construction	1.4	1.6	1.4	1.5	1.4	1.8	1.5
Manufacturing	8.8	4.8	4.5	1.9	6.0	5.3	2.4
Services-Producing Sector	86.7	90.6	91.3	93.6	90.0	89.1	93.7
Wholesale/retail trade	16.2	12.9	11.3	8.0	13.1	15.0	14.9
Transportation/ warehousing	2.7	2.8	2.6	2.0	3.0	3.1	3.1
Information/cultural industries	2.7	1.7	1.5	0.7	2.0	1.9	2.1

INDUSTRY	TOTAL FEMALE POPULATION	TOTAL FEMALE ABORIGINAL IDENTITY	NORTH AMERICAN INDIAN (TOTAL)	ON RESERVE	OFF RESERVE	MÉTIS	INUIT
Finance, insurance, real estate, and leasing	7.2	3.6	2.9	1.1	4.0	4.7	2.9
Professional, scientific, and technical services	6.0	2.8	2.2	0.8	3.0	3.6	1.9
Management of companies and enterprises	0.1	~	~	~	~	0	0.1
Administrative/support, waste management, and remediation services	3.8	4.3	4.5	3.0	5.3	4.2	1.9
Educational services	9.3	9.9	10.9	16.4	7.7	7.7	15.5
Health care/social assistance	17.0	19.6	20.4	23.7	18.6	18.2	20.7
Arts, entertainment, and recreation	2.0	2.7	3.1	2.2	3.6	2.3	1.2
Accommodation and food services	8.6	11.5	9.9	5.7	12.0	14.2	7.5
Public administration	5.8	13.8	17.2	27.3	11.5	8.3	17.1
Other services	5.3	5.2	4.7	2.7	5.9	5.9	5.0
TOTAL CLASSIFIED INDUSTRIES (%²)	100	100	100	100	100	100	100
n	7,265,430	181,160	102,140	36,780	65,365	64,470	7,795
Number of paid employees	6,591,760	170,555	97,230	35,645	61,585	59,545	7,550
Number self-employed	630,445	9,935	4,635	1,090	3,540	4,575	235
Participation Rate (%)	60.5	56.5	52.6	47.2	56.2	63.8	59.7
Employment Rate (%)	56.1	47.1	42.5	37.0	46.2	55.9	48.0
Unemployment Rate (%)	7.2	16.7	19.2	21.8	17.7	12.4	19.4
% with employment income	71.6	68.2	64.8	59.5	66.2	73.5	71.4
% who did not work in 2000	37.0	41.4	45.6	50.6	43.8	33.6	35.9
% who worked full year, full time	29.9	22.8	20.9	18.8	21.3	26.6	21.6
% who worked part year or part-time	33.2	35.8	33.5	30.6	34.9	39.7	42.5

Notes: 1. Figures for North American Indian, Métis, and Inuit include only those who report a single ethnic identity; 2. Totals do not always add to 100 due to rounding; ~ Figure is less than 0.1

Source: Calculated and compiled from data in Statistics Canada 2005b and 2005c.

The data in Table 7.1 reveal that the Aboriginal labour force, like the Canadian labour force in general, is concentrated in the service sector much more fully than in goods-producing industries. This pattern applies to men and women. As with labour market status, however, both gender and identity comparisons yield important variations. Aboriginal women are mostly concentrated in industries classified as services producing, which encompasses nearly nine out of ten participants in the total female labour force. Although the service sector is also prevalent for the male labour force, men—especially those with relatively high proportions of work in primary industries and construction—are much more likely than women to be engaged in goods-producing industries. Aboriginal men and women tend to be under-represented, relative to the populations as a whole, in manufacturing, trade, and financial industries; professional, technical, and managerial enterprise; and information and cultural industries. The reverse is true in public administration. About half of the Aboriginal labour force is concentrated in four main industry groups—government services; wholesale and retail trade; manufacturing; and accommodation, food, and beverage services (see also Department of Indian and Northern Affairs Canada 2004).

These data provide some indication of the diverse locations of Aboriginal people in, or in relation to, the Canadian labour force. They reveal, at the same time, significant concentrations or clustering of positions in ways that both reflect and influence important differences in life chances more generally. The industrial distributions outlined in Table 7.1 reveal that Aboriginal men and women are more likely than the general population to be clustered either outside the labour market or in occupations and positions (such as those in sales and services) that are characterized, to a large extent, by relatively low wages along with limited job security, benefits, and opportunities for advancement. Those in the weakest labour market positions, in turn, tend to be concentrated within specific subgroups, constituting a matter of particular concern with respect to the registered Indian population living on reserves. The gap in levels of unemployment and labour market participation rates experienced by Aboriginal people relative to the general population is more highly marked in western Canada (especially in Manitoba and Saskatchewan) than in the eastern provinces, to such an extent that some commentators suggest there are at least two distinct Aboriginal labour markets (Mendelson and Battle 1999: 13, 17). Uneven interactions among state policies and economic development have had an especially strong impact on this observed segmentation. In the Prairie region, and later in the far North, federal government policies and actions played an active role in fostering conditions to promote the consolidation of territories and an economy largely dependent on agriculture and resource industries. Government control over Indian lands and people took several forms, including the residential schooling system and administrative discretion through the Indian Act and reserve system, which affected access to labour markets and farming enterprises for many status Indians. While state constraints were not limited to the West, they were less significant in core regions of central Canada and coastal areas in which prior, more extensive development of industrial enterprises and urbanization had already either displaced or integrated Aboriginal populations into markets for wage labour.

The shifting but interdependent relationship between public and private sectors continues to play a significant part in Aboriginal affairs. State agencies maintain a central role in defining, regulating, establishing, and responding to conditions for Aboriginal people and their activities This is done directly through legislation such as the Indian Act and the Constitution Act, through the maintenance of structures like the Department of Indian and Northern Affairs, and through mechanisms associated with such functions as social assistance or promotion of Aboriginal employment and economic development. It is done indirectly through numerous branches, bureaucratic organizations, legal and judicial procedures, and activities undertaken by federal, provincial, and First Nations governments. Through these regulations and activities, Aboriginal people are constituted as subjects of the state, but increasingly they are also actors within the state, as revealed, for instance, in the relatively high concentrations of work activity among all Aboriginal groups in public services, education, health care, and social services (which, combined, represent over two-thirds of First Nations women and one-third of First Nations men living on reserve and over half of Inuit women).

The strong presence of state activities with respect to Aboriginal people and their communities has contradictory significance. In addition to providing employment prospects at entry and more senior and managerial levels, governments, augmented by the strong recent development of First Nations and Aboriginal state sectors, have been crucial in ensuring that Aboriginal people have access to a wide range of social, labour market, and community development supports and services. Government programs, services, and options, in turn, tend to be contested, highly regulated, and susceptible to changing policy and economic climates. The role of the state in Canada and other advanced industrial nations is being reassessed and modified in conjunction with challenges posed by social and political realignment and intense economic competition associated with globalization. At least some segments of the Aboriginal population may benefit from emerging policy directions, such as those that enable First Nations and Aboriginal people to improve prospects for self-determination, integration into the labour force, control over resources, or partnerships with other groups. Much of the Aboriginal population, nonetheless, is not well positioned to benefit from these initiatives, and others may be excluded from opportunities and benefits as state activities are reframed to promote economic investment, market opportunities, and technological innovation. As government policies and actions come to be guided increasingly by narrow economic conceptions of people as consumers or entrepreneurs rather than in terms of broader notions of citizenship understood as widespread entitlement across populations to social rights and economic security, the relatively close relationships that have emerged between Aboriginal people and governments become a matter of particular concern. These policy shifts, signified in several recent trends such as measures to reduce the size of public sector workforces, privatize services, and change eligibility criteria for access to social programs, along with rising costs and funding restrictions associated with state-supported activities in fields like health, welfare, job training, and education, tend to be most detrimental to members of communities with the fewest resources or options to fulfill their capacities (Vosko 2000; Slowey 1999).

FIGURE 7.1 | HIGHEST LEVEL OF SCHOOLING, POPULATION 25-44 YEARS

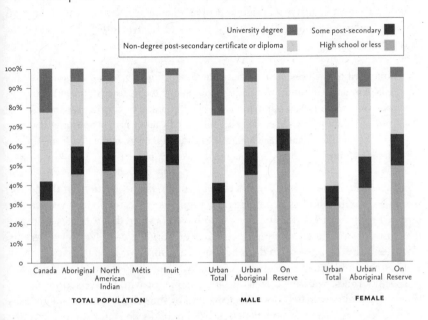

Source: Compiled from data in Statistics Canada 2005a.

   Education has special significance for labour market prospects, providing credentials, knowledge, and aptitudes widely associated with employment and income opportunities. Consistent with labour market participation trends, Aboriginal people in general have lower levels of educational attainment and participation than the population as a whole. Figure 7.1 illustrates the discrepant patterns of educational attainment within the Aboriginal population and between Aboriginal people and the general population in an age cohort representing a phase in which people are likely to have completed their basic education and entered the labour market (25 to 44 years of age). The two columns on the left, highlighting overall population comparisons, reveal that nearly half of the Aboriginal population, compared to just under one-third of the Canadian population as a whole, has no formal education beyond high school. About 6% of the Aboriginal population, compared to about 20% of Canadians, have a university degree. Within the Aboriginal population, as the next three columns to the right indicate, those with a North American Indian and Inuit identity are least likely to have completed formal education beyond high school. Those reporting Métis identity are most likely to have post-secondary and university credentials, although these are still well below the rate for the population as a whole. The six columns on the right side of the figure, illustrating the importance of gender and area of residence, reveal that Aboriginal people, particularly men, living on reserve have the lowest levels of educational attainment. Those living in urban centres, where educational options, employment prospects, and services are likely to be concentrated, tend to have the highest levels of education, especially among women, although the formal educational attainment of urban Aboriginal people remains well below that of the total urban population. Hull (2005: 30) also points to further differentiation evident in regional variations:

> Compared to the Canadian averages, the proportions of the population with post-secondary education are relatively low among the Registered Indian, Métis and Non-Status Indian populations of Manitoba and Saskatchewan and the Inuit population of Quebec. Post-secondary education proportions are relatively high in the Atlantic region among Registered Indians, in the North among Métis, and among Inuit in Ontario and the western provinces.

Differences across groups are less evident among the proportions of the respective populations who have completed non-university post-secondary education, referred to in Figure 7.1 as persons who have completed certificates or diplomas in trades training, community colleges, or non-degree university programs. Vocational and trades-related credentials can improve labour market entry, employment and income prospects, especially when they are required for access to specific trades, vocations, or workplaces (some of which have serious labour shortages), and they may be less expensive and of shorter duration than university degree programs. There is, nonetheless, a risk in rapidly changing job markets that such credentials cannot be directly translated into jobs or facilitate transfer into other, more generally recognized, credentials.

The data presented above represent a single cohort or point in time. They do not show the extent to which educational attainment is increasing among the Aboriginal population. Whereas those in younger cohorts typically attend school for longer periods than older generations, Aboriginal people in adult cohorts also have higher than average levels of educational participation, encompassing many people who had previously left school or had their schooling delayed for various reasons. This is especially evident among Aboriginal women, whose participation rate of 10.2% in full-time educational studies is double the national average for women aged 25 to 44 years.

Despite promising trends, there is strong evidence that substantial education gaps between Aboriginal and general populations will be prolonged for at least one generation. The proportion of the Aboriginal population who have less than high school (about 48%) is over ten times the corresponding proportion of those with a university degree (about 4.4%) and remains high (about six times higher) even within younger (i.e., 25- to 44-year) age cohorts. The 2001 census reports that, in the 15- to 24-year age cohort (the stage at which important transition processes through secondary and post-secondary studies normally occur), about two-thirds of the population overall attended school (57% on a full-time basis and another 6% on a part-time basis), compared to about half of those with Aboriginal identity (calculated from Statistics Canada 2005a). The relative youth of the Aboriginal population (with one-third below the age of 15 in 2001 compared to 19% of the non-Aboriginal population) means that higher numbers and concentrations of people of Aboriginal ancestry are moving through the education system and will be seeking integration into labour markets over the next several years (Statistics Canada 2003: 7–8). Some estimates suggest that, at the current rate of change, it will take nearly three decades before high school graduation levels in First Nations communities approach the national average (Auditor General of Canada 2004).

Differential educational qualifications are strongly interconnected with labour market participation, employment, and income prospects. Hull (2005: 136–38) shows both that the proportion of the population who derive their major source of income from employment rises with education levels for all Aboriginal identity groups and that the gaps between groups are lowest among those with the highest levels of schooling. Similarly, substantial differences in unemployment rates among Aboriginal identity groups and between Aboriginal and non-Aboriginal populations for those with lowest levels of education tend to disappear when only those with post-secondary education are compared (Hull 2005: 84).

FIGURE 7.2 | AVERAGE EMPLOYMENT INCOME BY ABORIGINAL STATUS AND HIGHEST LEVEL OF SCHOOLING, 2001 CENSUS

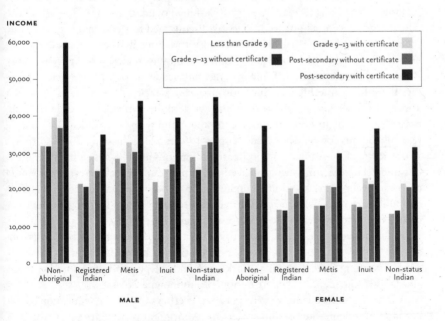

Source: Compiled from data in Hull 2005: 116, 118.

Figure 7.2 illustrates the relationship between education level and income. The figures point to the staged and, for nearly all groups, steady progression as incomes rise from the lowest levels for those with less than high school, to slightly higher totals among those with at least high school graduation, and to more notable increases for those with post-secondary credentials. As with labour market participation rates, income levels for all Aboriginal status categories are well below those of the non-Aboriginal population, with registered Indians (except among males with less than high school) having the lowest incomes in all education categories.

The strong association between higher education and improved social and economic opportunities lies at the centre of much of the policy interest in Aboriginal conditions, accompanied by numerous proposals and initiatives to enhance education, training and workforce integration for Aboriginal people and their communities. These developments signify the considerable promise that education holds for advancing Aboriginal people's position within Canadian society. Educational success is enabling increasing numbers of Aboriginal people to gain credentials and experiences that open doors to employment in numerous professional, technical, and managerial fields for individuals, while contributing at the same time to social and institutional environments that may be more generally conducive to Aboriginal community interests. Nonetheless, several factors stand in the way of the achievement of full equity. Returns from education in the form of occupational placement and earnings tend to be lower for Aboriginal people than for other Canadians (Canadian Race Relations Foundation 2001: 20–24). Those who complete high school are frequently discouraged from or unable to continue their schooling or convert their education into labour market success due to an absence of suitable education and training programs in close proximity to many Aboriginal communities, difficulties in meeting academic or work-related requirements within some higher education programs, lack of workplaces in which apprenticeships can be undertaken and work skills applied, inflexible training programs and institutional requirements, and inability to secure adequate funding (Royal Commission on Aboriginal Peoples 1996c: 523; Schissel and Wotherspoon 2003: 108ff). Educational and occupational options are also restricted by numerous interrelated factors, such as placement in programs or fields of study oriented to lower level positions within an organization or occupational category; domestic and childcare responsibilities that affect disproportionately a younger, predominantly female demographic cohort; differences in social resources and networks that mediate entry into jobs and workplaces; and barriers posed by "a disconnect ... between the potential skills contribution to be made by an increasingly educated and mobile Aboriginal workforce, and the perception of some business and labour leaders on this contribution" (Lamontagne 2004: 6).

A more significant concern arises insofar as efforts to improve education, training, and labour market qualifications for Aboriginal people are occurring in a context in which, confronted with rapidly changing and uncertain job markets, various groups seek to position themselves strategically for competitive advantage. The escalation of educational qualifications, training, and numerous alternative forms of learning throughout the population, combined with policies emphasizing high level skill development for a knowledge-based economy, has enhanced educational possibilities for many groups, but it also poses dangers that the most disadvantaged groups will be further marginalized (Wotherspoon 2005: 196). Aboriginal organizations have drawn attention to dilemmas imposed by priorities to expand capacities among the most highly educated and productive workers in the knowledge sectors insofar as resources may be diverted from initiatives to meet more fundamental community needs. The National Aboriginal Educational Development Board (2003), for instance, points to the federal government's Innovation Strategy, which is oriented to increase Canada's economic competitiveness in part by investing more heavily in research and development and immigration of highly qualified workers, as potentially "insulting" and irrelevant to the concerns of the majority of the Indigenous population, stressing that, "Without a focused Aboriginal component that deals with the fact that Aboriginal people suffer from Canada's worst socio-economic conditions and until their issues are addressed, the Strategy is unacceptable to Aboriginal Canadians." This observation echoes assessments based on evidence from several national contexts that policies to promote a high skills economy, in the absence of appropriate consideration for the cultivation and application of talent among all social groups, is likely to produce increasing economic polarization (Brown 2001).

CONCLUSION

This chapter has explored Aboriginal people's changing labour market positions and work conditions in relation to an extended process of transformation from participation in diverse, relatively autonomous First Nations economies to absorption into capitalist economic relations. Subsequently high levels of economic displacement and marginalization for much of the Aboriginal population have eventually prompted widespread demands in and outside of indigenous communities to implement active strategies to advance social and economic development for Aboriginal people. Various organizations, representing governments, community agencies, and private sector groups, have in response introduced a broad array of programs to promote education and skill upgrading, enhance job creation on and off reserve, and facilitate employment placement and career development. The success of specific initiatives or policies is likely to be a critical factor in determining the likelihood that objectives to replace dependency with workforce integration can be achieved.

It is crucial, more generally, to understand particular initiatives and employment-related options in conjunction with broader, contradictory transformations in social, economic, and political structures. Aboriginal people have occupied diverse, though typically subordinate, positions in relation to varying modes of incorporation into and within labour markets. Their entry into, or exclusion from, participation in wage labour, as well as their occupational prospects and working relationships, have been shaped by intersections among changing economic and social conditions, particular legal and policy frameworks, and varied responses by Aboriginal people to those circumstances. Within the Aboriginal population, contradictions and tensions may be intensified as global competition for resources and profits, government reorganization, and social realignment produce new options for some people while restricting and excluding others. Indigenous organizations in Canada and internationally are strengthening global connections with one another, while an increasing number of Aboriginal-controlled enterprises and governments have gained significance and created strong potential for investment, employment opportunities, and wider social and economic returns within many Aboriginal communities. Nonetheless, these communities, the people they represent, and the interests with which they are linked are highly diverse. Decisions concerning such crucial matters as community development strategies, resource allocation, education and training alternatives, and meanings and entitlements associated with Indigenous identities, for instance, tend to be contested by groups representing varied interests and political alignments. Emerging socio-economic conditions and the policies and initiatives that accompany them, in other words, have considerable potential to affect Aboriginal people in a highly uneven manner as class dynamics associated with global capitalism intersect with race and legal status, gender, age, geographical locale, and other major forms of social differentiation.

REFERENCES AND FURTHER READINGS

Auditor General of Canada. 2004. Chapter 5: Indian and Northern Affairs Canada: Education Program and Post-Secondary Student Support. *2004 Report of the Auditor General of Canada*. Ottawa: Office of the Auditor General of Canada.

Brown, Phillip. 2001. Skill Formation in the Twenty-First Century. In Phillip Brown, Andy Green, and Hugh Lauder, eds., *High Skills: Globalization, Competitiveness, and Skill Formation*. Oxford: Oxford University Press. 1–55.

Buckley, Helen. 1992. *From Wooden Ploughs to Welfare: Why Indian Policy Failed in the Prairie Provinces*. Montreal and Kingston: McGill-Queen's University Press.

Canadian Race Relations Foundation. 2001. *Unequal Access: A Canadian Profile of Racial Differences in Education, Employment and Income*. A Report Prepared by the Canadian Council for Social Development. Ottawa: Canadian Race Relations Foundation.

Carter, Sarah. 1990. *Lost Harvests: Prairie Indian Reserve Farmers and Government Policy*. Montreal and Kingston: McGill-Queen's University Press.

Department of Indian and Northern Affairs Canada. 1997. *Socio-Economic Indicators in Indian Reserves and Comparable Communities 1971–1991*. Information Quality and Research Directorate (Summer), Catalogue No. R32-181/1991E. Ottawa: Minister of Public Works and Government Services Canada.

——. 2004. Economic Development. Fact sheet prepared for Canada's Aboriginal Action Plan. Ottawa: Indian and Northern Affairs Canada, updated November 4. <http://www.ainc-inac.gc.ca/gs/ecdv_e.html>.

Flanagan, Tom. 2000. *First Nations, Second Thoughts*. Montreal and Kingston: McGill-Queen's University Press.

Hawthorn, H.B. (ed.). 1966. *A Survey of the Contemporary Indians of Canada: A Report on Economic, Political, Educational Needs and Policies*. Vol. 1. Ottawa: Indian Affairs Branch.

High, Steven. 1996. Native Wage Labour and Independent Production During the "Era of Irrelevance." *Labour/Le Travail* 37 (Spring): 243–64.

Hill, Richard. 1987. *Skywalkers: A History of Indian Ironworkers*. Brantford, ON: Woodland Indian Cultural Education Centre.

Hull, Jeremy. 2005. *Post-Secondary Education and Labour Market Outcomes Canada 2001*. Minister of Indian Affairs and Northern Development. Ottawa: Minister of Public Works and Government Services Canada.

Human Resources Development Canada [HRDC]. 1995. Paying Dividends: An Evaluation of the Northwest Territories' Investing in People Strategic Research Initiatives—Year One Final Report. Ottawa: Human Resources Development Canada, November.

Knight, Rolf. 1996. *Indians at Work: An Informal History of Native Labour in British Columbia 1858–1930*. Vancouver: New Star Books.

Laliberte, Ron, and Vic Satzewich. 1999. Native Migrant Labour and the Alberta Sugar Beet Industry. *Canadian Review of Sociology and Anthropology* 36,1 (February): 65–86.

Lamontagne, François. 2004. *The Aboriginal Workforce: What Lies Ahead: CLBC Commentary*. Ottawa: Canadian Labour and Business Centre.

Livingstone, D.W. 2004. *The Education-Jobs Gap: Underemployment or Economic Democracy*. Aurora, ON: Garamond.

Mendelson, Michael, and Ken Battle. 1999. *Aboriginal People and Canada's Labour Market*. Ottawa: Caledon Institute of Social Policy.

Minister of Indian Affairs and Northern Development. 1997. *Gathering Strength: Canada's Aboriginal Action Plan*. Ottawa: Minister of Public Works and Government Services Canada.

Moscovitch, Alan, and Andrew Webster. 1995. Aboriginal Social Assistance Expenditures. In Susan D. Phillips, ed., *How Ottawa Spends, 1995–96*. Ottawa: Carleton University Press. 209–35.

Moses, John. 2000. Aboriginal Participation in Canadian Military Service: Historic and Contemporary Contexts. *The Army Doctrine and Training Bulletin: Canada's Professional Journal on Army Issues* 3,3 (Fall): 14–18.

National Aboriginal Economic Development Board. 2003. *Submission to Government of Canada: Innovation in Canada*. 16 November. <http://www.innovation.gc.ca/gol/innovation/site.nsf/en/in02361.html>.

Neu, Dean, and Richard Therrien. 2003. *Accounting for Genocide: Canada's Bureaucratic Assault on Aboriginal People*. Black Point, NS: Garamond and Zed Books.

Portes, Alejandro, and Rubén G. Rumbaut. 1990. *Immigrant America: A Portrait*. Berkeley, CA: University of California Press.

Ray, Arthur J. 1974. *Indians in the Fur Trade: Their Roles as Hunters, Trappers and Middlemen in the Lands Southwest of Hudson Bay 1660–1970*. Toronto: University of Toronto Press.

Royal Commission on Aboriginal Peoples. 1996a. *Report of the Royal Commission on Aboriginal Peoples, Volume 1: Looking Forward, Looking Back*. Ottawa: Minister of Supply and Services Canada.

——. 1996b. *Report of the Royal Commission on Aboriginal Peoples, Volume 2: Restructuring the Relationship*. Ottawa: Minister of Supply and Services Canada.

——. 1996c. *Report of the Royal Commission on Aboriginal Peoples, Volume 3: Gathering Strength*. Ottawa: Minister of Supply and Services Canada.

Satzewich, Vic. 1991. *Racism and the Incorporation of Foreign Labour: Farm Labour Migration to Canada since 1945*. London: Routledge.

Satzewich, Vic, and Terry Wotherspoon. 2000. *First Nations: Race, Class and Gender Relations*. Regina: Canadian Plains Research Centre.

Schissel, Bernard, and Terry Wotherspoon. 2003. *The Legacy of School for Aboriginal People: Education, Oppression, and Emancipation*. Don Mills, ON: Oxford.

Shewell, Hugh. 2004. *"Enough To Keep Them Alive": Indian Welfare in Canada, 1873–1965*. Toronto: University of Toronto Press.

Slowey, Gabrielle Ann. 1999. Neo-Liberalism and the Project of Self-Government. In Dave Broad and Wayne Antony, eds., *Citizens or Consumers: Social Policy in a Market Society*. Halifax: Fernwood. 116–28.

Statistics Canada. 2003. *Aboriginal Peoples of Canada: A Demographic Profile*. 2001 Census Analysis Series. Ottawa: Minister of Industry. Catalogue #96F0030XIE2001007.

———. 2005a. Selected Educational Characteristics, Aboriginal Identity, Age Groups and Sex for Population 15 Years and Over, for Canada, Provinces, Territories and Census Metropolitan Areas, 2001 Census—20% Sample Data. Ottawa: Statistics Canada, 27 October. Catalogue #97F0011XCB2001043. <http://www12.statcan.ca/english/census01/products/standard/themes/>.

———. 2005b. Selected Income Characteristics, Registered Indian Status, Age Groups, Sex and Area of Residence for Population, for Canada, Provinces and Territories, 2001 Census—20% Sample Data. Ottawa: Statistics Canada, 27 October. Catalogue #97F0011XCB2001062. <http://www12.statcan.ca/english/census01/products/standard/themes/>.

———. 2005c. Selected Labour Force Characteristics, Aboriginal Identity, Age Groups and Sex for Population 15 Years and Over, for Canada, Provinces, Territories and Census Metropolitan Areas, 2001 Census—20% Sample Data. Ottawa: Statistics Canada, 27 October. Catalogue #97F0011XCB2001045. <http://www12.statcan.ca/english/census01/products/standard/themes/>.

Stevenson, Michael D. 1996. The Mobilisation of Native Canadians During the Second World War. *Journal of the Canadian Historical Association* (New Series) 7: 205–26.

Treasury Board of Canada Secretariat. 2005. *Canada's Performance Report 2005—Annex 3—Indicators and Additional Information*. Ottawa: Government of Canada. <http://www.tbs-sct.gc.ca/report/govrev/05/amn304_e.asp>.

Treaty 7 Elders and Tribal Council. 1996. *The True Spirit and Original Intent of Treaty 7*. Montreal and Kingston: McGill-Queen's University Press.

Vosko, Leah. 2000. *Temporary Work: The Gendered Rise of a Precarious Employment Relationship*. Toronto: University of Toronto Press.

Wien, Fred. 1986. *Rebuilding the Economic Base of Indian Communities: The Micmac in Nova Scotia*. Montreal: The Institute for Research on Public Policy.

Wotherspoon, Terry. 2005. The Boundaries of Public Education in the Knowledge-Based Economy. In Bruce Ravelli, ed., *Exploring Canadian Sociology: A Reader*. Toronto: Pearson Prentice-Hall. 187–98.

8 CANADA'S GUEST WORKERS
Racialized, Gendered, and Flexible

Ricardo Trumper and Lloyd L. Wong

INTRODUCTION

This chapter examines the incorporation of guest workers that come to Canada under the auspices of the Immigration and Refugee Protection Act, specifically the Temporary Foreign Worker Program (TFWP). We focus on unfree modes of incorporation in the Canadian labour market (see Satzewich 1990). Unfree labour market incorporation means that workers are unable to circulate in a labour market due to legal constraints. Canada's TFWP deals with "unfree" migration populations, a mode of incorporation that has also been described as a bonded forced-rotational system (Wong 1984: 87) and as highly exploitative (Bolaria and Bolaria 1997: 200).

Global political economy provides an explanation for guest workers in the context of global capitalism (see Wallerstein 1974; Froebel, Heinrichs, and Kreye 1980; Castles 1984; Castles and Kosack 1985), and it is congruent with Marx's reserve army thesis regarding flexible sources of labour (Satzewich and Wong 2003: 365). Guest workers in Canada are flexible; they provide "just-in-time" labour to meet what are perceived to be shortages of workers in the labour market. While this labour is flexible from the point of view of the employer, it is "precarious" from the point of view of the worker. Although global political economy is a good starting point for framing unfree migrant labour in Canada, it is not sufficient. As Sharma (1997: 11, 31) points out, it is important to pay direct attention to the relationship between labour mobility and the investment strategies of capital—in other words, to the integral relationship between the international movement of both capital and labour. To this end, Sharma points to the importance of a state-centred approach that examines state immigration policy, its development and evolution, and its relation to the interests of capital.

Historically, many forms of stratification have organized labour forces and markets via processes such as slavery, indentured labour, unpaid labour, contract labour, and seasonal labour. Segmented labour market theorists, in their critique of neo-classical human capital theory, have argued that social factors such as "race," ethnicity, and gender are important for one's opportunity and allocation in the labour market (see Rumberger and Carnoy 1980; Petras 1981; Gordon, Edwards, and Reich 1982; Piore 1983). As Portes (1981: 284–86) notes, secondary labour market immigrant workers have tenuous juridical status; they are hired not primarily on the basis of their ability but rather on their ethnicity; and they are destined to work in jobs with low remuneration, poor working conditions, and restricted mobility opportunities.

It can be argued that global capitalism does not purposely create barriers based on "race" and gender because consumers and capitalists come from all "races" and both genders. Nevertheless, the past occurrence of colonialism and slavery under patriarchical structures means that "race" and gender remain salient in terms of work and labour. "Race" and gender are important factors in the social organization of guest workers in Canada (Sharma 2000), and there is a racialization process behind the TFWP (Trumper and Wong 1997). De facto, the TFWP legitimizes differential treatment once these workers are inside Canada (Sharma 2002).

This chapter begins with an examination of Canada's TFWP and considers the extent of its flexibility, racialization, and genderization. Then, specific cases of Canadian guest workers will be examined. These include seasonal agricultural labour (farm workers), live-in caregivers (domestic workers), and highly skilled high-tech workers.

CANADA'S GUEST WORKERS: THE TEMPORARY FOREIGN WORKER PROGRAM

Since Confederation, Canada has always had some type of guest worker program. The ideal of creating a British settler community was Canada's original nation-building goal, but the reality was that the Canadian capitalist class preferred non-white or less-white guest workers for agricultural and industrial work, infrastructure and railway construction, and domestic work. Asian and Southern and Eastern European males filled many of these positions because "foreign" workers assigned to manual work were preferred over "white" British or Scandinavian labourers. Thus, "foreigner" was a racialized label of "non-whiteness" that connoted ready but highly controlled mobility, while "white" implied settler's capability. In railway construction and mining, for example, this resulted in a racialized labour force with distinct groups of workers: "whites" in higher paid and "safe" occupations and "foreigners" who were in lower paid and dangerous jobs (Vosko 2000: 49). The latter group were often hired as guest workers. An example is Chinese migrant labour in the 19th and early 20th centuries. Work programs, such as Chinese coolie railway labour, were designed to bring men without their families with the express goal that they would leave Canada when their labour was no longer required. Chinese men also worked as "houseboys" and domestic servants for genteel British and American settlers in British Columbia and Alberta at the turn of the last century (Kupferschmid-Moy 2005; Middleton 1986). Lady Aberdeen, the wife of the Governor General, commented on the fact that she could not see how British Columbia "folk" could get by without Chinese men as domestic help and that they were much better than "girls" whom she thought were not always "sensible" (Middleton 1986: 35).

There is a long history in Canada of unfree foreign domestic workers serving middle- and upper-class families, dating back to the late 1800s and early 1900s. In the early 1900s black women from Guadeloupe worked as domestic servants in Montreal and Quebec City (Mackenzie 1988). Thus, while domestic work was gendered historically, it was also racialized. In the immediate aftermath of World War II, the Canadian government devised domestic worker schemes to recruit European female displaced persons (Harzig 2003). Women were subsequently recruited from the Caribbean and the Philippines. The evolution of the Foreign Domestic Movement Program into the Live-in Caregiver Program (LCP) in the 1990s has resulted in the continuation of the racialized and gendered nature of domestic labour in Canada into the 21st century.

World War II reversed the ten years of economic crisis after the worldwide capitalist crash of 1929. Women and prisoners of war filled the jobs created by the war economy. After the war, Canada experienced a shortage of labour to maintain the Fordist industrialization that had burst forth. These urban and industrial jobs were particularly attractive for workers and dwarfed agricultural employment. As Satzewich (1991) has shown, the solution to the scarcity of labour in general was immigration. Of these immigrants, about 11% were destined to the agricultural sector. However, fruit, vegetable, and tobacco growers in Ontario were faced with the unwillingness of immigrants and Canadian workers to apply for these jobs and to stay in them. Thus, displaced persons and veterans of war, who did not want to return to their nations of origin, were recruited.

The Polish war veterans of the 2nd Polish Corps, who had fought in the Italian campaign, were among these groups. While the UK absorbed more than 100,000 of them, it encouraged other countries to admit others. The Canadian state seized the opportunity to let in more than 4,000 male veterans as temporarily unfree workers. They were on probation, granted temporary visas for two years to work in specific locations, and they could not quit or change jobs without permission. A second group of people who were placed on probation were a large proportion of the 165,000 displaced persons who were admitted in Canada between the end of the war and 1954. These people were assigned to a specific employer for one year, received a set wage, and were unable to change jobs. If they did not remain in their employment, they were subject to deportation and/or prosecution under provincial civil law. Both Polish veterans and displaced people earned considerably less than Canadian farm labourers and were unable to move, spatially or socially, for a set period of time.

In the postwar period, immigration fed the labour market, keeping an unsteady balance between racism and the pressures of the capitalist economy. Until the 1960s immigrants to Canada were mainly from Europe. Other than racist barriers, immigration rules were relatively loose, and immigrants arrived in Canada to work on numbing assembly lines where they eventually received salaries commensurate with the Fordist economy that fostered their employment. As Europe recovered from the war, however, the pool of immigration from white countries began to dry up. The beginning of the reversal of the historical movement of immigrants from Europe to the rest of the world had already begun. Instead of Europeans moving to the rest of the world, people from the Caribbean moved to the UK, Turks to Germany, Northern Africans to France, Spaniards and Portuguese to Switzerland. Many would never be able to become full citizens in industrialized Europe. Canada was no exception to the shift in the skin colour of workers, as factories, infrastructure, and the growing service sector required immigrants to be drawn from all over the world. Discourse and legislation adjusted to this shift, at least partially. The discourse of Canada as a white settler society changed, and a discourse of multiculturalism became hegemonic. New immigration laws appeared to be objective in the transformation into a "point system" in the late 1960s, measuring seemingly non-racialized characteristics in people. This meritocratic method to draw immigrants has made permanent immigration to Canada more difficult for the poor and less educated whose language is neither English nor French (Cook 2004: 1.7). The legal barriers to permanent immigration for poor uneducated workers from countries in the global south became insurmountable.

From the immediate postwar period up to the early 1970s, the Canadian state had an accommodating system of regulating temporary foreign workers as the Canadian economy was undergoing expansion. They were admitted and counted in the same category as "visitors." For a few select industries, such as mining, logging, and lumbering, Canada set up a contract labour program in 1947, and this program expanded to include other specialized industries such as sugar beet production and seasonal agricultural workers in western Canada (Knowles 2000: 70–71). In the early 1970s, although the Fordist Canadian economy entered a period of crisis, temporary foreign workers continued to be needed, but their entry and movement were placed under stricter legal control and management. The Non-Immigrant Employment Authorization Program was instituted by the Canadian government in 1973 and subsequently became the Temporary Foreign Worker Program (TFWP) in the 1990s.

On the whole, unfree workers who enter Canada under the TFWP have lower levels of human capital than those who enter as free immigrant workers. Since Canada's immigration policy is one of selecting immigrants with high amounts of human or financial capital, it is logical to expect that the TFWP would be skewed to selection of workers with lower skill levels.

There has been a major shift in the source countries of temporary workers over the past 25 years. In 1982, the US was the country of origin for 48% of all temporary work permits issued; by 2005 this figure had dropped to 16.4%. Moreover, the absolute numbers for the US have also been dropping (see Table 8.1). Over this same time period, the proportion from Europe has remained the same at approximately 20% while the proportion from Asia and Pacific, Africa and the Middle East, and the Americas (excluding the US) has increased substantially. In the case of Asia and Pacific, the proportion has doubled from 1982 to 2005, while for Africa and the Middle East it has increased five-fold. The proportion for the Americas has increased one and a half-fold. It is clear from these data that the shift of temporary workers has been from the developed northern nations of the world to the developing southern nations. In 1982, two out of three temporary workers were from Europe and the US. By 2005, only one out of three were from these areas.[1] Yet, as we emphasize below, more than two-thirds of the temporary migrants in the managerial, professional, and skilled categories still originate in Europe and the US.

TABLE 8.1 | SOURCE AREA OF FOREIGN TEMPORARY WORKERS* FOR SELECTED YEARS, 1982, 1995, AND 2005

	1982		1995		2005	
SOURCE AREA	NUMBER	%	NUMBER	%	NUMBER	%
Asia & Pacific	20,013	16.1	48,775	28.7	85,504	34.8
Africa & Middle East	2,468	2.0	19,029	11.2	23,543	9.6
Americas	15,663	12.6	24,871	14.7	45,337	18.5
Europe	25,917	20.9	29,991	17.7	46,434	18.9
US	59,805	48.2	46,295	27.3	40,253	16.4
Unknown/Not Stated	248	0.2	780	0.5	4,355	1.8
TOTAL	124,114	100.0	169,741	100.1	245,426	100.0

*Based on temporary work permits issued data.

Note: In terms of racialization there needs to be a caution in assuming that all temporary workers from Europe and the US are white.

Source: Citizenship and Immigration 2006.

The flexibility of temporary workers is illustrated in Table 8.2. From 1995 to 2005 the number of unfree temporary workers has increased 45%—more rapidly than the number of free immigrant workers who increased by 30%. By 2005, the number of unfree temporary worker entries (245,426) was almost double the number of free immigrant workers (128,727) who entered Canada. While the actual ratio of unfree to free workers has fluctuated over this ten-year period, the overall trend is an increase from 1.7:1 in 1995 to 1.9:1 in 2005, which represents an 11% increase.

Moreover, as the unemployment rate in Canada dropped over this time period, along with the drop in the absolute number of unemployed persons, the number of temporary workers has correspondingly increased. These data indicate that for-eign temporary workers fulfill a "flexible" function in meeting labour force needs more so than free immigrant workers whose numbers are smaller but also whose presence in Canada is not contingent on being active in the labour force. When gender is analyzed, the data indicate that there has been a feminization of unfree temporary workers, although gender-specific unemployment has dropped approxi-mately the same for both males and females. Unfree temporary male workers increased only 29% from 1995 to 2005 compared to unfree temporary female workers who increased 76% (Citizenship and Immigration 2006). The unfree to free ratio for males remained essentially the same over this period, whereas for females there was a large increase of 43%, demonstrating the feminization of unfree temporary female workers relative to free immigrant female workers.

TABLE 8.2 | LABOUR MIGRATION TO CANADA AND CANADIAN
UNEMPLOYMENT, 1995 TO 2005

	LABOUR MIGRATION TO CANADA			CANADIAN UNEMPLOYMENT	
YEAR	IMMIGRANT WORKERS*	TEMPORARY WORKERS**	TEMPORARY TO IMMIGRANT RATIO	NUMBER OF UNEMPLOYED (X 1,000)	UNEMPLOYMENT RATE
1995	98,823	169,741	1.72	1,402.1	9.6
1996	107,349	168,768	1.57	1,442.9	9.7
1997	102,172	163,911	1.60	1,382.0	9.2
1998	83,748	173,023	2.07	1,277.6	8.4
1999	93,817	186,492	1.99	1,185.2	7.6
2000	113,744	200,465	1.76	1,083.5	6.8
2001	123,853	209,675	1.69	1,164.1	7.2
2002	112,239	211,590	1.89	1,272.2	7.7
2003	111,672	213,160	1.91	1,288.9	7.6
2004	117,515	238,287	2.02	1,233.7	7.2
2005	128,727	245,426	1.91	1,172.8	6.8
% CHANGE 1995–2005					
+30%	+45%	+11%	-16%	-29%	

* Based on permanent residents data with live-in caregivers and business immigrants excluded. Persons entering Canada under the Live-in Caregiver Program are counted along with other immigrants because they can apply for permanent residence after two years; however, they are not "free." Rather, they are contractually bound to a specific employer as a condition of their stay in Canada. Business immigrants are either self-employed, entrepreneurs, or investors, and thus are not workers.

**Based on temporary work permits issued data.

Sources: Citizenship and Immigration 2006. Labour Force Survey 2006: Table 282-0002: Annual estimates (LFS), by sex and detailed age group (age group: 15 years and over), Geography: Canada. Statistics Canada, CANSIM, Table: Labour force characteristics by age and sex (for fee). 282-0002. Statistics Canada: Labour Force, Employed and Unemployed, Numbers and Rates, by Province, <http://www40.statcan.ca/101/cst01/labour07a.htm>.

A further comparison by source area reveals that for Asia and Pacific, Americas, and Europe, the percentage increase in unfree temporary workers far outstrips the percentage increases in free immigrant workers from 1995 to 2005 (see Table 8.3). In the case of Asia and Pacific, free immigrant workers increased 29%, while unfree temporary workers increased 75%; in the Americas the increases were 52% and 82% respectively; and in Europe it was 4% and 55%. The figures for the US show a reverse trend from 56% to minus 13%, although the absolute numbers of free immigrant workers from the US are very small. In contrast, the absolute number of unfree temporary workers from the US is very large due to the large number of border crossings by management consultants, musicians, and artists, many of whom have very short stays in Canada. Thus, the contiguous border and extensive economic integration of the Canada-US economy account for the large number of temporary workers from the US.

When the source area data are broken down by gender, they show that the feminization of unfree temporary workers mentioned earlier comes primarily from Asia and Pacific, the Americas, and Europe. Overall, the percentage increase from 1995 to 2005 in the number of female unfree temporary workers from Asia and Pacific was 110%; for the Americas it was 84%; and for Europe it was 71%. The overall increase of female unfree temporary workers from all source areas was 76% (Citizenship and Immigration 2006).

It was noted earlier that unfree temporary workers generally have lower skills than those who enter as free immigrant workers. A significant percentage of the workers from the US, Europe, and Africa and the Middle East[2] are skilled and highly skilled. For example, for workers coming from the US, 64% have managerial or professional skill levels; from Europe 53%; and from Africa and the Middle East 61%. Workers from Asia and Pacific, by contrast, represent only 29%, and workers from the Americas only 10%. Added to which, 59% of workers from Asia and Pacific and 85% from the Americas have low skill levels, whereas only 23% from Africa and the Middle East, 15% from Europe, and only 5% from the US have low skill levels. Most of the temporary workers at the managerial, professional, and highly skilled levels come from Europe and the US. Most of the workers at the lower skilled levels come from Asia and Pacific, and the Americas (Citizenship and Immigration 2006).

Thus, some overall generalizations can be made about the TFWP:

» There is a racialization of temporary workers by skill level in that skilled and highly skilled workers tend to come from the US and Europe and lower skilled workers tend to come from Asia and Pacific and the Americas.

» There is a gendered occupational pattern, with men more likely to be in highly skilled or skilled occupations (with the exception being farm workers from the Americas) and women of colour to be in lower skilled occupations (with the exception being nurses who come as live-in caregivers from the Philippines).

To some extent, the feminization and racialization of Canada's TFWP can be attributed to Canada's solicitation not only of low skilled labour but also of some highly skilled, flexible labour throughout the world. Three labour market segments where this occurs are agricultural labour, domestic labour, and high-tech labour. The remainder of the chapter examines these in further detail.

TABLE 8.3 | FLOW OF ALL WORKERS TO CANADA BY MIGRATION STATUS AND SOURCE AREA, 1995 AND 2005

| SOURCE AREA | IMMIGRANT WORKERS* | | |
	1995	2005	% CHANGE 1995–2005
Asia & Pacific	47,415 (48%)	61,008 (47%)	+ 29%
Africa & Middle East	14,916 (15%)	23,928 (19%)	+ 60%
Americas	9,841 (10%)	14,959 (12%)	+ 52%
Europe	23,271 (24%)	24,217 (19%)	+ 4%
US	2,898 (03%)	4,513 (04%)	+ 56%
Unknown/Not Stated	482 (00%)	102 (00%)	–
TOTAL	98,823 (100%)	128,727 (101%)	+ 30%

| SOURCE AREA | TEMPORARY WORKERS** | | |
	1995	2005	% CHANGE 1995–2005
Asia & Pacific	48,775 (29%)	85,504 (35%)	+75%
Africa & Middle East	19,029 (11%)	23,543 (10%)	+24%
Americas	24,871 (15%)	45,337 (18%)	+82%
Europe	29,991 (18%)	46,434 (19%)	+55%
US	46,295 (27%)	40,253 (16%)	-13%
Unknown/Not Stated	780 (00%)	4,355 (02%)	–
TOTAL	169,741 (100%)	245,426 (100%)	+45%

* Based on permanent residents data.

** Based on temporary work permits issued data.

Source: Citizenship and Immigration 2006.

AGRICULTURAL WORKERS

Despite the desperate need for workers in the agricultural sector, and the lack of Canadian residents to do these jobs, agricultural workers come to Canada under temporary migration arrangements. The arrangements satisfy the interests of the agricultural producers of cash crops whose demands for a disciplined and low-paid labour force could only be satisfied by an unfree, immobile labour force. The control of the Mexican, Caribbean, or Guatemalan labourers' movement reflects the view that many, mostly non-white, labourers are needed to perform certain jobs. They do not qualify, however, for permanent residence and free mobility within Canada, and they are expelled every year.

The recruitment of agricultural workers started in 1966 when Caribbean workers were hired to work seasonally in Ontario to grow tobacco, vegetables, and fruit in an agreement between the Jamaican and Canadian governments under Canada's Seasonal Agricultural Workers Program (SWAP) (Satzewich 1991: 110).

These migrants were mostly male, travelling without families and under definite state-administered contracts with employers to whom they were bound for the time of their stay in Canada. Early seasonal workers were from Jamaica, but workers from other islands like Trinidad and Tobago, Dominica, and Barbados were hired in the following years. The contract could last from six weeks to eight months, but the workers had to leave Canada at its end. Their families had to stay in the countries of origin, thus placing the cost of the reproduction of the labour force outside Canada. This was also a means of discipline to ensure that the workers understood their tenuous position in Canada and was a means to pressure them to go back to their home countries.

The program was "successful" from the beginning. As Basok (2002) and Satzewich (1991) have pointed out, agriculture in Ontario in the last decades could not have been profitable without these workers who assured capitalists a steady, hardworking, cheap, disciplined, and immobile labour force. The number of workers increased rapidly to more than 1,000 in the first year the program and continued to grow, reaching about 5,000 mostly non-white males by 1974. In that year, a new source of workers was found. Mexican male workers began to migrate to Canada to work in farms under an agreement between the Mexican and Canadian government. Their number climbed steadily, eventually surpassing the number of Caribbean workers whose numbers stagnated (Cook 2004). It should be noted that up to 1983 this program explicitly required participants to be married men. While in 1974 there were 203 Mexican workers employed in the SWAP, the numbers increased dramatically in the next 30 years. According to the organization Justicia for Migrant Workers, in 2002 there were 10,779 Mexican workers and 7,756 workers from the Caribbean. In total, 18,535 workers were hired that year for the farms and greenhouses of Canada. More recent figures from Citizenship and Immigration Canada for 2005 indicate that there were 8,139 Caribbean workers and 12,009 Mexican workers (see Table 8.4).

Although most of the agricultural workers go to Ontario, there are temporary agricultural workers from coast to coast. This ethnic shift from the Caribbean to Mexico, and more recently Central America, points out how deep seated are the racialized views of these workers. Binford (2005) points out that in the US a similar process has taken place. Certification for temporary or seasonal agricultural work (called H-2A) provides temporary visas to workers from Mexico and the Caribbean to work in tobacco, cucumber, and onion production. Mexican workers have become a majority among this group. She argues that both in the US and in Canada, "at different times and places employers' stereotypes about the endurance and abilities of particular ethnic or racial groups, their perceptions of Mexicans' docility and exploitability, the changing fortunes of ethnically based linked crop regimes have all played [a] role" (Binford 2005: 35). Mexican temporary workers are the vast majority in the Ontario flower industry and in hothouse tomato and cucumber production—the key sectors that have expanded most rapidly under the North American Free Trade Agreement (NAFTA). Caribbean labourers are highly valued by apple orchardists and tobacco farmers, because they are seen as culturally conditioned to be efficient. They are also valued, as Basok (2002) has persuasively argued, because they are immobile, work under poor conditions, cannot refuse dangerous or unhealthy jobs, and can live by themselves for many months unencumbered by family or social obligations. In all Canadian provinces, save for British Columbia, they are not permitted to organize.

TABLE 8.4 | CARIBBEAN AND MEXICAN SEASONAL AGRICULTURAL WORK PERMITS ISSUED BY GENDER,* 1995–2005

	CARIBBEAN			MEXICO			
YEAR	MALE	FEMALE	TOTAL	MALE	FEMALE	TOTAL	OVERALL TOTAL
1995	6,154	29	6,183	4,845	57	4,902	11,085
1996	5,993	28	6,021	5,190	57	5,247	11,268
1997	6,476	24	6,500	5,634	66	5,700	12,200
1998	6,703	24	6,727	6,352	142	6,494	13,221
1999	6,881	44	6,925	7,359	160	7,519	14,444
2000	6,919	33	6,952	9,024	232	9,256	16,208
2001	7,434	78	7,512	10,154	362	10,516	18,028
2002	7,351	96	7,447	10,487	346	10,833	18,280
2003	7,580	80	7,660	10,284	302	10,586	18,246
2004	7,802	63	7,865	10,553	378	10,931	18,796
2005	8,061	78	8,139	11,653	356	12,009	20,148
% INCREASE 1995–2005							
	31%	169%	32%	141%	524%	145%	82%

Source: Citizenship and Immigration 2006.

Mexican guest workers are usually extremely poor and immobile in their own country; they are peasants who have little job mobility in Mexico and who have little money to move in search of employment. It is often the case that their only chance is to illegally migrate to the US—a dangerous, uncertain, and potentially more expensive option. The comparison makes migrating temporarily to Canada look attractive. The spread of neo-liberalism worldwide has resulted in more than 100 million annual migrants, and the Mexican neo-liberal experiment is one that can survive only by exporting a growing surplus population. Ironically, the free market dogma of neo-liberalism has squeezed Mexican peasants out of their lands and crops, pushing them into the production of tomatoes and cucumbers that move far more easily than the workers. In this case, the more successful Canadian enterprises that can grow these products competitively at a global scale for supermarkets that stock food from around the world are subsidized by Mexican labour. The red fetish that is the tomato masks the fact that it may be produced in foreign-controlled operations in Mexico, or by Mexican workers toiling for agro-industrial complexes in California, or by Mexican workers on farms in Leamington, Ontario.

Indeed, many of the most successful operations in Leamington (the tomato capital of Canada) have skilfully adjusted to the use of these labourers. Cheap labour is central for competitiveness in the global economy, but as Basok (2002) reaffirms, the immobility of these labourers is crucial too, as they have to accept any condition of work. The discipline to which they are subjected is overwhelming. In addition to the threat of deportation and blacklisting, they are bound by a government-to-government arrangement that screens them and keeps them in check. Conditions of employment are negotiated between the Canadian and Mexican governments, and, as depicted in the film *El Contrato*, the role of the Mexican general consulates is to keep the workers subordinate even when faced with the worst abuses. The Mexican government searches for workers and screens them, making sure that they are poor enough to accept the conditions imposed on them, that they have families that depend on their acquiescence to the Canadian conditions, and, crucially, that they understand that their families will stay in Mexico. In addition, the Mexican government insures that the workers spend what amounts to a significant investment of their finances to put them in debt so that they need to stay on the job to pay this debt (Basok 2003).

In Canada, the program is regulated by an established set of institutions. Human Resource Centres of Canada serves as the conduit between farmers' needs and workers' recruitment, administering the Caribbean/Mexican SWAP on behalf of the Government of Canada. Since 1987, a strategic alliance has been forged between Human Resources and Social Development Canada (HRSDC) and industry representatives, and in 1997 HRSDC and horticulturalists formed the Ontario Horticultural Advisory Committee so that government and industry work cooperatively, setting policy for this program. As HRSDC (2006) points out, "representatives work closely with the employer representatives on the FARMS [Foreign Agricultural Resource Management Services] Board of Directors and with the Ontario Horticultural Advisory Committee towards a shared vision of a reliable agricultural workforce, thereby enabling the agriculture industry to continue to grow and remain a vital and important force in the Ontario economy" and thus maximizing benefit for Canada. This formidable array of institutions, in addition to the employers and the designated supervisors, has the object of keeping the labour force subservient and making sure both that these people will not stay in Canada and that these are precarious forms of employment subject to short contracts. Thus, those who want to return as seasonal workers to Canada, as happens often, need to be rehired. In this sense, the key idea of "flexibility" of the labour force is directly reinforced by the state as representative of a segment of the capitalist class.

There have been some instances of resistance. For example, British Columbia started to import Mexican workers for greenhouses throughout the province in 2004. When some workers faced conditions of employment that did not match what was offered to them in Mexico, they resorted to work stoppages and demonstrations during the Mexican president's recent visit to Canada (Fuchs 2006).

Overall, the use of temporary workers in agriculture has been a feature of Canadian society for several decades. Canada has moved from a Fordist society with a relatively strong welfare state and protectionist policies to a neo-liberal society firmly ingrained in a global capitalist system. Throughout, the use of temporary workers has remained a characteristic of the agricultural sector.

DOMESTIC WORKERS

The Canadian literature on post-1940 foreign domestic labour, state regulation, and working conditions is extensive (e.g., Daenzer 1993; Schecter 1998; Harzig 1999, 2003). The vulnerable, tenuous, and exploitive status of foreign domestic workers in Canada has been well-documented (Silvera 1989; Calliste 1991; Arat-Koc 1989, 1992; Macklin 1994). Much study has focused on the actual processes of racialization and the placement of foreign domestics (Bakan and Stasiulis 1995; Arat-Koc 1997; Stasiulis and Bakan 2003: Ch. 4), on issues of non-citizenship and resistance (Stasiulis and Bakan 1997a, 1997b, 2003: 5; Fudge 1997), and on the legalistic framework (Langevin and Belleau 2000). In the case of Filipina domestic workers, participatory and policy-oriented research has emerged with proposed short- and long-term policies and recommendations dealing with the dilemmas of this form of labour migration (Grandea 1996; Spitzer and Bitar 2002; Oxman-Martinez et al. 2004).

The contemporary movement of unfree domestic labour is linked to an international political economy, where factors such as the structural adjustment programs of the World Bank and the International Monetary Fund in underdeveloped nations (Stasiulis and Bakan, 2003: Ch. 3) intersect with social reproduction[3] and the crisis in the Canadian domestic sphere as a result of women's greater participation in the labour force (Arat-Koc 1989). Thus, the conditions of poverty and underdevelopment in the Philippines have produced a flexible group of women, many of whom are professional nurses, for work in private households in Canada. In an earlier period, from the 1960s to the mid-1980s, unfree domestic labour came primarily from the underdeveloped Caribbean and the countries of Jamaica and Barbados before shifting to the Philippines in the 1980s. In 1992 the Canadian government replaced the Foreign Domestic Movement Program (in effect from 1981) with the Live-in Caregiver Program (LCP).[4] This government policy and program link international migration with Canadian ideological positions of familialism and maternalism to produce flexible unfree temporary labour consisting primarily of women of colour.

Over the past decade, the number of foreign domestic workers who entered Canada under the LCP has increased substantially (see Table 8.5). In 1995, there were 6,805 permits issued; this number grew to 22,870 in 2005, a three-fold increase.

As noted earlier, Canada's unemployment rate has decreased over this same time, and this fact, combined with a growing labour force and an aging population, has produced a high demand for domestic help, which has been met by temporary unfree labour. While the data in Table 8.5 demonstrate the gendered nature of the LCP, it is interesting to note that in 2005 there were approximately

1,100 male entries into Canada under this program. Although males only constituted 5% of the total, this was proportionately much larger than in 1995. Further,
this program has also had a greater concentration of source countries over this
time period. In 1995, the top source country for work permits was the Philippines
(68%) and the top five countries constituted 80% of all work permits issued. By
2005, the Philippines rose to 86%, and the top five countries constituted 93% of
all work permits (Citizenship and Immigration 2006). Filipina domestic female
workers are found worldwide. In Canada, the concentration of Filipina women
in the LCP, combined with the fact that there are no longer any European source
countries in the top five, means that almost all domestic workers who come under
the LCP are women of colour. Thus the "visibleness" of nannies and care-givers in
Canada has increased substantially over the past decade as part of the racialization of women's household work (Bakan and Stasiulus 1995).

TABLE 8.5 | LIVE-IN CAREGIVER WORK PERMITS ISSUED BY GENDER,
1995–2005

	GENDER		
YEAR	FEMALE	MALE	TOTAL
1995	6,700	105	6,805
1996	7,455	148	7,603
1997	7,864	188	8,053
1998	8,150	211	8,361
1999	8,316	244	8,560
2000	8,583	270	8,853
2001	10,857	333	11,190
2002	12,977	431	13,408
2003	14,719	558	15,277
2004	18,908	865	19,773
2005	21,755	1,115	22,870
	% INCREASE 1995–2005		
	31%	169%	32%

Source: Citizenship and Immigration 2006.

The material conditions of privatized household work are separated from a
public work sphere, and this creates working conditions that include isolation,
loneliness, and invisibility (Arat-Koc 2005: 367). In the 1980s, a landmark study
by Silvera (1989) chronicled the exploitation, vulnerability, harassment, and racism experienced by West Indian domestic workers. A recent report by Spitzer and
Bitar (2002: 14) reports that working conditions have not changed much since
Silvera's study. While the number of hours of work performed by these domestic workers is subject to provincial legislation, the live-in aspect of the program
allows exploitative employers to abuse these workers' labour rights (Walia 2006:

2). Further, this live-in aspect and the privatized nature of domestic work facilitate the possibility of panoptical power in terms of discipline and surveillance. Macklin (1994: 32) has described the role of the foreign domestic worker as being "anomalous" and "anachronistic," and both Schecter (1998: 1) and Daenzer (1993: 7) have described it as "mistress-servant," while Arat-Koc (2005: 368) has described it as "neither a wife nor a worker."

Given the predominance of Filipina women in the LCP over the past two decades, some non-governmental organizations have become involved in community-based action-oriented research in order to further reveal their working conditions and to suggest strategies for ensuring their security, labour rights, and human rights (Grandea 1996; Oxman-Martinez et al. 2004).

HIGH-TECH WORKERS

It was pointed out earlier that permanent immigrant workers tend to be more highly skilled than those unfree temporary workers who enter under the TFWP. Over the past decade, high-tech workers who have come to Canada as permanent immigrant workers have been near or at the top of all occupational categories. For example, in the period from 1996 to 2000 high-tech computer programmers and computer systems analysts were the top two most common intended occupation of all skilled workers; most of them came from China, India, and Pakistan (Citizenship and Immigration Canada 2003: 4). Even after the decline in the high-tech sector in the early 2000s, high-tech computer programmers and technologists were still within the top five occupations of immigrant workers. Under a fast-track program called the Information Technology Professionals Software Program, approximately 1,200 workers, the majority of whom were from India, entered Canada in 2004 (Citizenship and Immigration Canada 2005).

Thus, by 2004, computer programmers and technologists were ranked second, right behind engineers (many of whom are also in high tech) and above nurses and welders (Volpe 2005). Despite these significant numbers in the flow of immigrant high-tech workers, in 1997 the Canadian government, in partnership with the Software Human Resource Council, attempted to also attract temporary migrants to fill the shortage of high-tech workers crucial for the post-Fordist economy. Departing sharply from the practice of bringing only bachelor men or women to work in the agricultural sector or in domestic labour, it promoted programs that accentuated the right of high-tech workers to bring their families. Accordingly, it instituted a fast-track pilot project to facilitate spousal employment of high-tech workers under the TFWP. In the year 2000, HRSDC also became involved in this project. The program was expanded to include systems software designers, software products developers, MIS software designers, senior animation effects editors, and the like. Currently this program is called the Spouses and Common-Law Partners of Skilled Temporary Workers.

TABLE 8.6 | HI-TECH* WORK PERMITS ISSUED BY SOURCE AREA, 1995–2005

| | | | SOURCE AREA | | | | |
YEAR	ASIA & PACIFIC	AFRICA & MIDDLE EAST	AMERICAS	EUROPE	US	UNKNOWN/ NOT STATED	TOTAL
1995	1,793	289	226	2,350	4,577	16	9,251
1996	2,138	312	313	2,592	4,933	15	10,303
1997	2,695	382	371	3,728	6,773	142	14,091
1998	3,821	553	459	4,946	7,794	371	17,944
1999	3,752	660	576	6,019	7,378	451	18,836
2000	4,511	845	722	7,084	8,096	462	21,720
2001	4,520	861	763	6,841	7,456	492	20,933
2002	4,127	699	646	5,680	7,013	427	18,592
2003	3,625	495	625	4,377	6,242	383	15,746
2004	3,981	618	831	4,678	5,996	401	16,505
2005	4,880	731	804	5,054	5,783	543	17,795
			% CHANGE 1995–2005				
	172%	153%	256%	115%	26%	–	92%

*Hi-Tech occupations were established by the authors using National Occupational Classification (NOC) codes provided by Citizenship and Immigration Canada in conjunction with the following documents and personal assessments: 1. BC Stats (1999). High technology occupations in British Columbia; 2. BC Work Futures (2006). Information technology occupations.

Source: Citizenship and Immigration 2006.

In 2005, 17,795 high-tech workers, comprising approximately 7.3% of all foreign temporary workers, entered Canada under the TFWP (see Table 8.6). The largest percentage increases in high-tech foreign workers are from the Asia and Pacific, the Americas, and Africa and Middle East, although the absolute numbers from the Americas and Africa and Middle East are very small. In contrast, the number of high-tech workers from Asia and Pacific in 2005 is approaching the levels of those from Europe and the US where the percentage increases have been more modest. Indeed, the US has also experienced a dearth of high-tech workers; its H1-B Visa program recruits heavily in India and China, competing with the Canadian effort. Further, labour in this group is still very gendered. Approximately 85% of high-tech workers in 2005 were male and only 15% were female, although the percentage increase in female workers (152%) has been much higher than males (92%) over the past decade. This is also true for all source areas except the US.

In the US, there is much controversy about foreign high-tech workers who enter under the H1-B Visa program. The largest source countries of H1-B Visas in 2003 were India (35%), China (9%), Philippines (5%), and Canada (5%) (Miano 2005). In 1998, the American Congress was lobbied by the high-tech industry to increase the quota on high-tech foreign workers under H1-B. They argued that the

US faced an extreme shortage of high-tech workers. Opponents and critics of this increase argued that there was no such shortage and that the motive for increasing the number of foreign high-tech workers was an industry strategy for depressing wages. Congress agreed to double the annual quotas for workers from 65,000 to 130,000,[5] but also commissioned an investigation into the opponents' criticisms. This investigation was conducted by the National Research Council (2001), which is industry funded, and found that use of large numbers of H1-Bs by American high-tech firms was warranted as the demand for labour was outstripping the supply and essentially there was no wage exploitation of H1-Bs. Since the release of the National Research Council report, opponents have highly criticized it, stating that it was biased toward the high-tech industry and, in particular, that it ignored research findings that demonstrated exploitation of high-tech workers' wages and work conditions (Matloff 2001). Over the past few years, the controversy has not abated. Miano (2005), for instance, has recently concluded that H-1B workers' wages are significantly lower than American workers and that the average (mean and median) differences were in the neighbourhood of $12,000 to $15,000 annually. This situation approaches that of a split labour market wherein foreign high-tech workers, who tend to be primarily Asian, are paid less for comparable work.

The empirical question that arises from these data is whether or not the same issues of the supply of domestic high-tech workers and wages are similar in Canada but only on a smaller scale. As indicated above, the proportion of high-tech workers from Asia and Pacific, Africa and Middle East, and the Americas has increased dramatically over the past decade compared to much smaller increases from Europe and the US. However, there has been no research on these issues of domestic supply and a split labour market in Canada. A second issue remains to be studied. Is it possible to place the high-tech workers of colour in the same group with Mexican, Caribbeans, and Filipinas, or are these workers temporarily enjoying greater degrees of freedom?

CONCLUSION

Canada has a long history of racialized, gendered, and classed immigration. The import of a temporary labour force to take positions that could not be filled by tapping into the native labour pool has been central to this development. This situation has remained basically unchanged. Neither the post-Fordist shift of the Canadian economy nor the loosening of openly racist categories and the usage of a "meritocratic" point system of immigration have changed this situation. On the contrary, the point system that attempts to attract highly educated permanent immigrants to fill the needs of a post-industrial society has served as a barrier to agricultural workers, live-in caregivers, and others who labour in occupations that do not require high skill levels and formal training. Neo-liberalism in Canada and abroad has forced Canadian capitalists to compete in the global market. A "principled" rejection of subsidies has forced agricultural businesses to hire poorly paid and immobile Mexican or Caribbean workers.

The neo-liberal shift has been accompanied by reliance on a two-wage family due to the demise of a family wage earned by a single person, thus the care for children has increasingly shifted to Filipino and other women of colour. Moreover, as the population ages and the neo-liberal state refuses to take charge of the aging population, domestic workers are also imported to look after the elderly. This is the core of programs that in 2005 brought in more than 20,000 live-in caregivers and more than 20,000 agricultural workers. The former have a long period of probation in which they are unfree, while the latter can spend no more than eight months each year in Canada. Moreover, these workers must forfeit many of the rights of citizenship that Canadians take for granted, including the right of having their families with them.

However, there are other guest workers who also come under the TFWP. Indeed, there are categories of workers who do not need work permits to work in Canada at all, such as journalists, performers, and the like. There are also computer programmers and other high-tech workers for whom the exact same rules do not apply. The spousal programs for hi-tech workers point in that direction. There are others for whom the length of employment or the family restrictions or the threat of deportation do not apply. Foreign managers of the transnational corporations that dominate the Canadian economy and medical personnel also enter Canada to work on a temporary basis. All of these latter groups are highly mobile people, part of a transnational labour force capable of moving seamlessly around the world. In contrast to the mostly non-white, unfree, immobile black and Mexican agricultural labourers and Asian domestics, the highly skilled and those of a transnational capitalist class are allowed to bring their families, send their children to Canadian schools, and have the possibility of job mobility in the rest of the world. Thus, an analysis of guest workers in Canada must proceed cautiously in order to unmask the dichotomization of labour markets under global neo-liberalism.

NOTES

1   Caution must be used in assuming that *all* temporary workers from Europe and the US are white given patterns of international migration over the past 30 years. However, it is a safe assumption to assume that almost all temporary workers from Asia, Africa, and the Americas are people of colour.

2   Unfortunately, the data do not allow for a differentiation between Africa and the Middle East, and thus they are treated as one source area.

3   Social reproduction is conceptualized here as "… the social processes and labour that goes into the daily and generational maintenance of the working population" (Fudge and Vosko 2003: 185).

4   Under the former program, foreign domestics were truly "unfree temporary" labour. Under the present LCP, foreign domestics are still very much unfree as they can work only in the home of the employer whose name is stated on their work permit. However, after working in Canada for two years, they are allowed to apply for permanent residence status, a process that takes about a year to a year-and a-half. Thus, after this initial time period of approximately three years, they have the potential to change their "temporary" status and if successful they also become "free."

5   This level eventually tripled to 195,000 between the years 2001 and 2003 before reverting back to the pre-1998 level 65,000 as a result of the decline in high tech in the early 2000s. Even at current levels of 65,000, opponents are arguing that this level is too high and still depresses wages.

REFERENCES AND FURTHER READINGS

Arat-Koc, S. 1989. In the Privacy of Our Own Home: Foreign Domestic Workers as Solution to the Crisis in the Domestic Sphere in Canada. *Studies in Political Economy* 28: 33–58.

——. 1992. Immigration Policies, Migrant Domestic Workers and the Definition of Citizenship in Canada. In V. Satzewich, ed., *Deconstructing a Nation: Immigration, Multiculturalism and Racism in the '90s Canada.* Halifax: Fernwood. 229–42.

——. 1997. From "Mothers of the Nation" to Migrant Workers. In A. Bakan and D. Stasiulis, eds., *Not One of the Family: Foreign Domestic Workers in Canada.* Toronto: University of Toronto Press. 53–79.

——. 2005. The Politics of Family and Immigration in the Subordination of Domestic Workers in Canada. In V. Zawilski and C. Levine-Rasky, eds., *Inequality in Canada: A Reader on the Intersections of Gender, Race, and Class.* Toronto: Oxford University Press. 363–409.

Bakan, A., and D. Stasiulis. 1995. Making the Match: Domestic Placement Agencies and the Racialization of Women's Household Work. *Signs: Journal of Women in Culture and Society* 20(2): 303–35.

——. 1997. Foreign Domestic Worker Policy in Canada and the Social Boundaries of Modern Citizenship. In A. Bakan and D. Stasiulis, eds., *Not One of the Family: Foreign Domestic Workers in Canada.* Toronto: University of Toronto Press. 29–52.

Basok, T. 2002. *Tortillas and Tomatoes: Transmigrant Mexican Harvesters in Canada.* Montreal and Kingston: McGill-Queen's University Press.

——. 2003. Mexican Seasonal Migration to Canada and Development: A Community-Based Comparison. *International Migration* 41(2): 3–25.

Binford, L. 2005. A Generation of Migrants. Why They Leave, Where They End Up. *Nacla Report on the Americas* (July): 31–37.

Bolaria, B.S., and R.V.E. Bolaria. 1997. Immigrants, Migrants, and Labour Market Opportunities. In B.S. Bolaria and R.V.E. Bolaria, eds., *International Labour Migrations.* Delhi: Oxford University Press. 192–209.

Calliste, A. 1991. Canada's Immigration Policy and Domestics from the Caribbean: The Second Domestic Scheme. In J. Vorst, ed., *Race, Class, Gender: Bonds and Barriers.* Toronto: Garamond. 136–68.

Castles, S. 1984. *Here for Good.* London: Pluto Press.

Castles, S., and G. Kosack. 1985. *Immigrant Workers and Class Structure in Western Europe.* Oxford: Oxford University Press.

Citizenship and Immigration Canada. 2003. *Immigrant Occupations: Recent Trends and Issues.* <http://www.cic.gc.ca/english/research/papers/occupations/occupations%2Dtoc.html>.

——. 2005. *2004 Foreign Worker Overview.* The Monitor, Summer 2005. <http://www.cic.gc.ca/english/monitor/issue10/05-overview.html>.

——. 2006. Special tabulations run specifically for authors by Citizenship and Immigration Canada.

Cook, V. 2004. Workers of Colour Within a Global Economy. CLC Research Paper on Migrant Workers. December. <http://canadianlabour.ca/updir/research.pdf>.

Daenzer, P. 1993. *Regulating Class Privilege.* Toronto: Canadian Scholars' Press.

Froebel, F., J. Heinrichs, and O. Kreye. 1980. *The New International Division of Labour: Structural Unemployment in Industrialized Countries and Industrialization in Developing Countries.* Cambridge: Cambridge University Press.

Fuchs, Erika del Carmen. 2006. Mexican Migrant Farm Workers in BC Say "Enough!" *Conexión Latina* 6(4),Winter/Invierno: 1 and 8.

Fudge, J. 1997. Little Victories and Big Defeats: The Rise and Fall of Collective Bargaining Rights for Domestic Workers in Ontario. In A. Bakan and D. Stasiulis, eds., *Not One of the Family: Foreign Domestic Workers in Canada.* Toronto: University of Toronto Press. 119–45.

Fudge, J., and L. Vosko. 2003. Gender Paradoxes and the Rise of Contingent Work: Towards a Transformative Political Economy of the Labour Market. In W. Clement and L. Vosko, eds., *Changing Canada: Political Economy as Transformation.* Montreal and Kingston: McGill-Queen's University Press. 183–209.

Gordon, D., R. Edwards, and M. Reich. 1982. *Segmented Work, Divided Workers.* Cambridge: Cambridge University Press.

Grandea, N. 1996. *Uneven Gains.* Ottawa: North-South Institute and the Philippines-Canada Human Resource Development Program.

Harzig, C. 1999. The Movement of 100 Girls: 1950s Canadian Immigration Policy and the Market for Domestic Labour. *Zeitschrift fur Kanadastudien* 19: 131–46.

——. 2003. MacNamara's DP Domestics: Immigration Policy Makers Negotiate Class, Race, and Gender in the Aftermath of World War II. *Social Politics* (Spring): 23–48.

HRSDC. 2006. Agricultural Programs and Services: Overview. <http://www.hrsdc.gc.ca/en/on/epb/agri/overview.shtml>.

Knowles, V. 2000. *Forging Our Legacy: Canadian Citizenship and Immigration, 1900–1977.* Ottawa: Public Works and Government Services Canada.

Kupferschmid-Moy, D. 2005. *Across the Generations: A History of the Chinese in Canada.* Government of Canada, Canada's Digital Collections. <http://collections.ic.gc.ca/generations.index2.html>.

Labour Force Survey. 2006. Table 282-0002: Annual Estimates (LFS) by Sex and Detailed Age Group, Geography Canada.

Langevin, L., and M. Belleau. 2000. *Trafficking in Women in Canada: A Critical Analysis of the Legal Framework Governing Immigrant Live-in Caregivers and Mail-order Brides.* Ottawa: Status of Women Canada.

Mackenzie, I.R. 1988. Early Movements of Domestics From the Caribbean and Canadian Immigration Policy: A Research Note. *Alternate Routes* 8: 123–43.

Macklin, A. 1994. On the Inside Looking In: Foreign Domestic Workers in Canada. In W. Giles and S. Arat-Koc, eds., *Maid in the Market.* Halifax: Fernwood. 13–39

Matloff, N. 2001. *A Missed Opportunity.* Washington, DC: Center for Immigration Studies.

Miano, J. 2005. *The Bottom of the Pay Scale.* Washington, DC: Center for Immigration Studies.

Middleton, R. 1986. *The Journal of Lady Aberdeen: The Okanagan Valley in the Nineties.* Victoria: Morriss Publishing.

National Research Council. 2001. *Building a Workforce for the Information Economy.* Washington, DC: National Academic Press.

Oxman-Martinez, J., J. Hanley, and L. Cheung. 2004. *Another Look at the Live-in Caregivers Program.* Montreal: Immigration and Metropolis, no 24, <http://im.metropolis.net/research-policy/research_content/doc/oxman-marinez%20LCP.pdf>.

Petras, E. 1981. The Global Labor Market in the Modern World-Economy. In M. Kritz, C. Keeley, and S. Tomasi, eds., *Global Trends in Migration.* New York: Center for Migration Studies. 44–63.

Piore, M. 1983. Labour Market Segmentation: To What Paradigm Does It Belong? *American Economic Review* 73: 249–53.

Portes, A. 1981. Modes of Structural Incorporation and Present Theories of Labor Immigration. In M. Kritz, C. Keeley, and S. Tomasi, eds., *Global Trends in Migration*. New York: Center for Migration Studies. 279–97.

Rumberger, R., and M. Carnoy. 1980. Segmentation in the US Labour Market: Its Effects on the Mobility and Earnings of Whites and Blacks. *Cambridge Journal of Economics* 4: 117–32.

Satzewich, V. 1990. Rethinking Post-1945 Migration to Canada: Towards a Political Economy of Labour Migration. *International Migration* 28(3): 327–46.

——. 1991. *Racism and the Incorporation of Foreign Labour: Farm Labour Migration to Canada since 1945*. London: Routledge.

Satzewich, V., and L. Wong. 2003. Immigration, Ethnicity, and Race: The Transformation of Transnationalism, Localism, and Identities. In W. Clement and L. Vosko, eds., *Changing Canada: Political Economy as Transformation*. Montreal and Kingston: McGill-Queen's University Press. 363–90.

Schecter, T. 1998. *Race, Class, Women and the State*. Montreal: Black Rose Books.

Sharma, N. 1997. Birds of Prey and Birds of Passage: The Movement of Capital and the Migration of Labour. *Labour, Capital and Society*, 30(1): 8–38.

——. 2000. Race, Class, Gender and the Making of Difference: The Social Organization of "Migrant Workers" in Canada. *Atlantis* 24(2): 5–15.

——. 2002. Immigrant and Migrant Workers in Canada. *Canadian Woman Studies* 21/22(4/1): 18–25.

Silvera, M. 1989. *Silenced*. 2nd ed. Toronto: Sister Vision.

Spitzer, D. and S. Bitar. 2002. *In the Shadows: Live-in Caregivers in Alberta*. Edmonton: Changing Together ... A Centre for Immigrant Women.

Stasiulis, D. and A. Bakan. 1997a. Regulation and Resistance: Strategies of Migrant Domestic Workers in Canada and Internationally. *Asian and Pacific Migration Journal* 6(1): 31–57.

——. 1997b. Negotiating Citizenship: The Case of Foreign Domestic Workers in Canada. *Feminist Review* 7: 112–39.

——. 2003. *Negotiating Citizenship: Migrant Women in Canada and the Global System*. New York: Palgrave Macmillan.

Trumper, R. and L. Wong. 1997. Racialization and Genderization: The Canadian State, Immigration, and Temporary Workers. In B.S. Bolaria and R. Bolaria, eds., *International Labour Migrations*. Delhi: Oxford University Press. 153–91.

Volpe, J. 2005. Notes for an Address by the Honourable Joe Volpe, Minister of Citizenship and Immigration. New Brunswick Policy Forum on Immigration. Fredericton, NB. 17 June. <http://cic.gc.ca/english/press/speedh-volpe/nb-forum.html>.

Vosko, L. 2000. *Temporary Work: The Gendered Rise of Precarious Employment*. Toronto: University of Toronto Press.

Walia, H. 2006. Colonialism, Capitalism and the Making of the Apartheid System of Migration in Canada: Part II. *Seven Oaks*, 27 March. <http://sevenoaksmag.com/features/100_feat1.html>.

Wallerstein, I. 1974. *The Modern World-System: Capitalist Agriculture and the Origins of the European World-Economy in the Sixteenth Century*. New York: Academic Press.

Wong, L. 1984. Canada's Guestworkers: Some Comparisons of Temporary Workers in Europe and North America. *International Migration Review* 18(1): 85–98.

PART THREE
Articulations of Race and Gender

INTRODUCTION

In different and unique ways, each chapter in this section is guided by the general principles of anti-racist feminism. Anti-racist feminist/scholars generally adopt some form of intersectional approach to assess how social systems are structured by racism and sexism. They are keenly interested in developments emerging from second- and third-wave feminism, particularly the different experiences and social positions among women from different socio-cultural backgrounds. By bringing together anti-racism and feminism, anti-racist feminists engage the historical complexities of race and gender constructions and seek to eradicate racist and sexist hierarchies by interrogating race and sex. More recently, anti-racist feminists have also developed alternative ways of knowing about, and inquiring into, social inequality.

Enakshi Dua introduces the section by exploring the intersections of race and gender with other important social indicators. She begins by situating contemporary relations of race, gender, and sexuality in the context of colonialism, Orientalism, and Canadian nation-building. For at least 200 years, Dua maintains, European discourses of otherness have marginalized non-European men and women, and they have constructed "the other" as sexually deviant. She links the history of European colonialism to the ways in which racially oppressed women experience systemic relations in the contemporary Canadian labour force, social policy, and education. Examining secondary data, she illustrates how race and gender intersect to limit the lives and life chances of women who are racialized as minorities. With this understanding of the intersection of race and gender, Dua argues that too often studies focus on a single category and fail to understand variation among racially oppressed women. She examines variation among racially oppressed women in the realm of immigration, religious affiliation, ableism, and sexual orientation. With a comprehensive review of the literature on multiple intersecting forms of inequality, Dua considers alternative modes of inquiry to better enable understanding of the complexity of inequality. She concludes by interrogating locational and Foucauldian approaches to find a new space to theorize the complexity of relations involved in the production of inequality today.

In the following chapter, Patricia Monture examines the relationship among race, class, gender, and the law in white settler societies. Situating the formation of law historically, she argues that law needs to be conceptualized as a component of a wider social-structural system that links personal biography to history. In a manner similar to Dua, she warns against prioritizing particular forms of oppression, and she encourages researchers to understand how inequality is embedded in equality and rights discourses that exist in Canadian legal structures. While law requires evidence of racism in judicial process, Monture maintains that this colour blindness fails to understand either lived reality or history. A more vibrant and reflective sociology emerges when the sociological analysis of race and gender is shifted beyond demography to a place that permits socially and economically vulnerable groups to articulate the experiences and meanings of their own lives.

In the third chapter of this section, Cheryl Suzack addresses the extent to which Aboriginal women's assertions of collective rights to Aboriginal identity reflect claims to citizenship rights through property interests (see also Chapter 16). Against the backdrop of the Barry case, she assesses the significance of Bill C-31 on discrimination faced by Aboriginal women, particularly new categories of gender blindness and historical erasure. Suzack compellingly demonstrates how enfranchised women's struggles for legal recognition and citizenship position them at the intersections of history, law, and political-legal discourse through the court system. She maintains that Aboriginal women assert their property interests through identity attachments in a number of social domains, and she concludes with a number of recommendations to legal scholars for expanding property law and band citizenship where Aboriginal women are concerned.

Finally, taking up Dua's argument about the paucity of research on how women who are racialized as minorities currently experience economic and political institutions, Guida Man examines the experiences of skilled Chinese transnational women. She begins by briefly situating her analysis in relation to anti-racist feminist thought. For Man, however, it is also important to address the literature on transnationalism to fully understand the factors influencing Chinese immigrant women's experiences. She conceptualizes transnationalism as a process through which immigrants forge social relations, linking their societies of origin and settlement, but she warns against emphasizing agency too much. She emphasizes instead the importance of skilled immigrants in the transnational process and the intersections of racialization, gender, and transnational migration. Following an historical overview of Chinese transnationalism and the barriers facing Chinese women entering Canada (and the effects on the Chinese-Canadian community), Man analyzes recent immigrants' experiences. Informed by the methodological strategy of institutional ethnography, she compares the experiences of women immigrants from Mainland China and Hong Kong through focus groups and in-depth interviews. Her data demonstrate how the women in her sample experienced difficulties finding employment on the basis of labour market conditions and requirements and how new immigrants adopt various transnational migration practices to negotiate paid work and household work in a racialized and gendered environment in the new country.

Collectively, the chapters in Part III address the significance of anti-racist feminist thought and the dangers of reducing inequality to a single factor or variable. Each author is attuned to the importance of history, and each prioritizes contemporary lived realities. The chapters address the complexity of racism in Canada, and they shed light on avenues of resistance, advancement, and perseverance.

9 | EXPLORING ARTICULATIONS OF "RACE" AND GENDER
Going Beyond Singular Categories

Enakshi Dua

INTRODUCING GENDER, PROBLEMATIZING "WOMEN"

Second wave feminist theory explicitly and implicitly assumed that there was a singular experience with gender. However, in the mid-1980s, these assumptions were shattered when anti-racist feminists asked how "race" intersects with gender. They began by demonstrating the ways in which middle-class women's standpoint(s) historically came to configure the contours of liberal, radical, and socialist-feminist theory (Dua 1992). They pointed out that racially oppressed women's experiences with all aspects of gender—for example, femininity, sexuality, marriage, family, and work—varied substantially from the experiences of middle-class white women. Such differences raised the question of whether a universal experience with gender existed, and this led others to argue that by marginalizing the study of race in feminist analyses, mainstream feminists continued to marginalize racially oppressed women in feminist organizations (Bannerji 1995).

In this chapter, I explore the ways that race and gender intersect. I begin by examining how processes of Orientalism, colonialism, and nationalism have racialized and gendered women. Second, I examine how women are positioned as racialized minorities in contemporary society, particularly in the labour market, educational institutions, and state policies. As we shall see, there is a paucity of research on the ways in which women racialized as minorities currently experience economic and political institutions. Third, as racially oppressed women are a heterogeneous group, I look at how gender and race intersect with other forms of oppression. Finally, I discuss recent feminist methodologies for the study of intersectionality. Despite important gaps in our understandings, what emerges is a stunning picture of the way in which racism and sexism shapes the life chances of racially oppressed women in Canadian society.

THE HISTORICAL CONSTRUCTION OF RACE, GENDER, AND SEXUALITY

Recently, a number of anti-racist feminist researchers have been examining the influences of Orientalism, colonialism, modernity, and nationalism on racially oppressed women, gender identity, and sexuality. These scholars have illustrated that gender and sexuality have been important sites through which racialized difference was constructed. Orientalist ideas were constructed by making connections between lands and "deviant" forms of sexuality, femininity, and masculinity. With colonialism, colonized women's bodies were inscribed in terms that reflected further differentiation and conquest. Montrose (1991) has illustrated that in the early stages of European contact with the Americas, Aboriginal women were masculinized and Aboriginal men were femininized (see also Stevenson 1999). Such racialized constructions of gender were tied to racist ideas of Aboriginal peoples as "closer to nature," childlike, and uncivilized. European art often represented the Americas through feminized and sexualized tropes through which sexuality and gender were deployed to suggest that colonized spaces were available for plunder, possession, discovery, and conquest (Hall 1999). Racialized constructions of gender and sexuality also legitimated colonialism, as they allowed colonizers to suggest that women in the colonies would benefit from colonialism.

Colonizers differed in their modes of constructing difference, and, as a result, racial discourses vary according to place and period (Loomba 1998). Because slavery defined those who were of African descent as "not human," people of African descent were defined as devoid of the right to control their own labour, reproduction, sexuality, and bodies. Throughout the history of slavery, a number of racialized images of black women have been produced (hooks 1981; Hill-Collins 1991). For women in the Middle East, South Asia, and Asia, the discourse of Orientalism collided with colonialism. As Said (1978) illustrates, Europeans had constructed Muslim men as ruthless and greedy tyrants who were religious fanatics, excessively patriarchal and oppressive to women, and beyond the pale of rationality and civilized values because of their belief in Islam. As Middle Eastern, South Asian, and East Asian men were constructed as excessively patriarchal, women from these cultures have been socially constructed as veiled, backward, unable to break the bounds of the past, and thus needing to be saved and taught modern gender relations (Grewal 1996). Notably, these discourses of the deviant sexuality of colonized, "Oriental," and enslaved women were also deployed to consolidate practices of "white" bourgeois femininity (Gilman 1985; McClintock 1998; Stoler 1995).

Thus, by the 18th century, skin colour, gender, and sexual practices had come together to establish a cultural hierarchy with Europe at the top and black Africa at the bottom (Gilman 1985). The colonized subject was constructed as the antithesis to the European bourgeois male subject. However, as Loomba (1998) has noted, these representations are ambivalent and contradictory: while they encode barbarism and backwardness, at the same time they also include colonial fantasies about perfect feminine behaviour, that is, devotion, passiveness, and sexual availability.

Ideologies of racial difference were intensified during the periods in which European and other nations emerged. By the 18th century, the word "race" became synonymous with nation, and nations became the expression of biological or racial attributes. Nations were imagined to exclude those who were deemed to be not of the same racial group (see Balibar 1991; Yuval-Davis and Anthias, 1997). In the Canadian context, John A. MacDonald articulated the vision of the Canadian nation-building project when, in a speech to Parliament, he proclaimed that Canada was a white man's country. Constructing a white settler nation was an inherently racialized activity, marginalizing Indigenous peoples from the emerging nation-state, continuing to recruit white settlers to occupy lands appropriated from them, and implementing immigration and citizenship policies that excluded those racialized as non-white (Dua 2000).

Constructing racialized nations was also inherently gendered and sexualized, since racialized nations need to be physically and culturally reproduced (Yuval-Davis and Anthias 1997. The racial politics of nation-building reorganized ideas of femininity, so that in the 19th century white bourgeois women came to be seen as exalted breeders of a virile race of nation- and empire-builders, as "mothers of the nation." In contrast to the exalted fertility of white middle-class women, Aboriginal women and women racialized as not white were gendered as dangerous to the nation-state (Dua 2000). Thus, with the emergence of nation, women racialized as minorities have continued to be portrayed as the antithesis of progressive and liberated Canadian mainstream women (Dua 2000).

The legacy of colonialism and nationalism continues to shape postwar processes of inclusion and exclusion. Paul Gilroy (1987) has suggested that as nations have become associated with forms of national culture, national culture becomes the site where race is constructed. In the context of nation and culture, skin colour becomes reinscribed, not as a marker of biological difference but rather as a marker of who is seen as a "real Canadian." Ng (1986) points out that such markers make those who are white (including those who are not Canadian-born) appear native, while racially oppressed women (including Aboriginal women) appear as outsiders. In this context, it is not surprising that people of colour, no matter how many generations their ancestors may have resided in Canada, are often asked "where did you come from?"

SYSTEMIC DISCRIMINATION

Processes of racialization and gendering have had a tremendous impact on the lives of racially oppressed women. Major institutions in Canada directly or indirectly work to systemically discriminate against them. However, in the past decade, very few researchers have examined how this is experienced. Rather, much of the work has employed either the categories of race or of gender. In the following sections, I explore the ways in which racially oppressed women experience systemic discrimination, resulting in unequal access to rights and to incomplete citizenship.

The Paid Labour Force

Much of the research on employment, income, and poverty does not systemati-cally examine the ways in which racially oppressed women experience the labour force. However, it does provide important insights into the ways in which systemic discrimination works. Importantly, it challenges one of the most pervasive myths that there is no widespread discrimination in the labour force. It also points to the ways that women racialized as minorities experience discrimination.

More than two decades of statistical analysis of labour market patterns has shown how the colour of one's skin translates into advantages or discrimina-tion (e.g., Li 1998a; Pendakur and Mata 1998). Despite having higher rates of labour force participation, working more hours, and having higher levels of educational attainment, racially oppressed men and women earn less than their white counterparts. Li, employing 1991 census data, reported that foreign-born racially oppressed people earned $2,710, Aboriginal peoples earned $1,122, and Canadian-born racially oppressed people earned $1,096 below the national mean income (Li 1998a: 22). Li also found significant differences among racially oppressed people, as those of Latin American origin had average incomes $5,894 below the Canadian average. These figures were followed by income returns for Chinese, Filipino, or Vietnamese, which stood at over $3,000 less than the national average, and black/Caribbean at $2,682 below the national average. Li concluded that the Canadian economy places a market value on skin colour, such that racially oppressed people suffer an income penalty in the labour market.

Few studies examine the intersections of race and gender, the exception being Boyd (1992). Employing 1986 data, Boyd compared the experiences of racially oppressed women in the labour market to the experiences of racially oppressed men and white women. She illustrated that the effects of being foreign-born, a member of a visible minority group, or a female are cumulative. Compared to white women, she found that racially oppressed women were more likely to have higher educational attainments, be employed in the paid labour force, and work more hours per week. However, these characteristics did not translate into higher earnings: Canadian-born and foreign-born racially oppressed women earned the lowest salaries and wages of all groups. Boyd also reported significant differences in income among racially oppressed women. Foreign-born racially oppressed women had the lowest average earnings.

Explaining these patterns of discrimination, researchers point to a number of dynamics. First, they argue that the Canadian labour market is organized into two segments: first, a well-paying market with a wide range of occupations, rela-tively high rates of unionization, and reasonable working conditions; and, sec-ond, a market characterized by less favourable rates of pay, working conditions, and little job security. Location in these two labour markets is structured by race and gender, as white women and workers from racialized groups are over-rep-resented in low-paying jobs. While clearly there are strong forces that lead to racially oppressed women's over-representation in the secondary labour market, it is important to recognize the "split" character of their participation—racially oppressed women also occupy some of the better jobs in Canadian society as well. As we shall see, being located in the primary labour market does not mean that one escapes discrimination.

Secondly, researchers also point to racist hiring and employment practices. Henry and Ginzberg's (1985) classic study found that white applicants received three times more job offers than racially oppressed people. More recent studies suggest that such hiring practices persist. In 1992, the Ontario Ministry of Citizenship released a report on the ways designated groups experience the labour force in Ontario (Office of the Employment Equity Commissioner 1992: 9). It documented extensive barriers in employment, including invisible barriers such as assessments of candidates qualifications based on biases, stereotypes, and skin colour. Saloojee (2003: 8) succinctly summarized the racist hiring and employment practices when he stated that "the prevalence of prejudice and discrimination in society at large guarantees that many members of racialized minority groups encounter the 'steel door' before the glass ceiling."

Third, researchers point out that, once hired, racially oppressed people often face the glass ceiling. Some have reported that those racialized as minorities encounter barriers to advancement, including a hostile or poisoned work environment caused by racial jokes, abusive slurs, being assigned unpleasant tasks, being excluded from the inner circle of their workplace, being passed over for promotion, and, on occasions, physical abuse (Canadian Race Relations Foundation 2000). This not only leads to a poisoned work environment but also to occupational ghettoization and underemployment. These researchers report that such discrimination increases higher up in the organizational ladder. The Canadian Race Relations Foundation has argued that such racism is tied to normative whiteness in the workplace, as dominant notions of who belongs are deployed to evaluate performance. As the authors state "a world of normative whiteness is not a colour blind world but it is a world in which the pressures to deny, to ignore, to refuse to know, and to be complicit in everyday racism are tremendously strong" (Canadian Race Relations Foundation 2000: 14–15).

Social Policy

A number of writers have argued that racially oppressed women are in a position of marginalization and disadvantage in a range of mutually reinforcing social policies, from immigration to the provision of social services. First, racially oppressed women are prone to becoming dependent on social policies, such as employment equity polices, welfare programs, income supplements, housing subsidies, and educational and training programs to address the outcomes of inequality. Second, dependence leaves them more vulnerable to changes and/or cutbacks in services and programs. And finally, because of the multiple forms of discrimination they face, racially oppressed women require programs that deal with the intersections of gender and race; however, such programs are often unavailable.

Beginning in the 1960s, feminist scholars developed a sustained critique of and proposals to remedy the ways in which Canadian social policy is gendered (see Bakker 1994; Brodie 1996). Surprisingly, there is little work on the connections between race and social policies, let alone on the intersections of race and gender. In part, this reflects the lack of initiatives by governments to deal with the ways in which social policies are racialized. Campling, in a review of social policy in Europe and North America, found that while governments have been active and effective in making changes in the area of gender, in the area of race they have been much less proactive. As she states, "in fact, the lack or even negative activity in the area of 'race' is shown to be in stark contrast to the area of gender" (Campling 1997: 3).

This suggests that it is important to examine not only how social policies are gendered but also how they are racialized. In Canada, in the 19th century and early 20th century, Aboriginal peoples, African-Canadians, and Asian-Canadians were denied access to education and health care programs. In a number of ways, the legacy of such racism is reflected in current policies. First, programs designed to address inequities often fail to address racism. For example, in 1988 the federal government implemented the Federal Contractors Program, an employment equity policy aimed at increasing the numbers of equity group members in workplaces. However, an examination of the history of employment equity policies illustrates that while these policies have been tied to increasing the number of women in non-traditional workplaces, it has been less successful in increasing the number of racially oppressed women and men. Agocs and Harish (2001: 3) reported that between 1987 and 1996 in the federal jurisdiction, the proportion of visible minorities within upper levels of management did not increase, and at the same time the salary gap between visible minorities and all other workers widened. Second, racially oppressed people may be informally excluded from social programs, especially the right to make claims for certain social benefits. Under current immigration rules, immigrants are formally limited in their ability to draw on public funds.

While these examples illustrate how social policy has failed to address racialized inequities, there is very little research in Canada that has analyzed the way in which race shapes social policy. Recently in the US and the UK, a small number of scholars have started to illustrate that social programs are based on a white male model. Their research suggests that racially oppressed people under-use social services. Contrary to the common stereotype that they are more likely to claim welfare, a study by Law (1994) found evidence of substantial under-claiming and delays in claiming among racially oppressed people because, fearing a racist reaction to their claims, they are more reluctant to claim social benefits. Similarly, a study by Gohil (1987) found that Asian claimants fearing racism often failed to submit claims. In addition, Gohil reported that Asian residents relied more on family members, community resources, and temporary work to get through periods of unemployment.

In addition, studies have begun to illustrate that racially oppressed people often receive a poorer quality of service. Campling found that racially oppressed people receive a "qualitatively and a quantitatively worse service from social services" (1997: 15). In part, these writers attribute the poor quality of service to the inappropriateness of social provisions. Several have illustrated that social services are often based on the white cultural model, which fails to address the needs of racially oppressed people. They have suggested that providers of services need to recognize and acknowledge that appropriate services cannot be provided on a "race and gender" blind approach (in Canada, see Agnew, 1998). However, Campling (1997) has warned against over emphasizing a cultural sensitivity approach, as it does not address the way in which racism has shaped the use of social services.

Education

In a labour market where formal-institutional credentials are important criteria for success, the ability of racially oppressed women to gain such credentials is crucial. Yet, racially oppressed women are often unable to gain access to educational criteria or to translate criteria into labour market success. Given the importance of the educational system in structuring life chances, there is a large body of work that focuses on the ways in which the processes of education reinforce racism and sexism (see Dei 1997, 2003). Three processes in particular work to marginalize racially oppressed female students: the imposition of Eurocentric curriculum, the teachers' attitudes and expectations, and streaming.

An important process through which racism is manifested in the educational system is through the curriculum and pedagogy. Several writers have illustrated that school curriculum contains both overt and implicit racist material. Texts, stories, narratives, and photographs often reflect racialized images of racially oppressed people. For example, Rezai-Rashti (1995) has reported that Toronto's school curriculum often deploys stereotypes of racially oppressed women as from "other cultures," which are more oppressive and characterized by greater sexism within the family. Moreover, school curriculum contains not only overt racist curriculum but also often is constructed through Eurocentric views. Klein (1985), in a comprehensive analysis of textbooks, found that the history of racially oppressed people was represented to begin when Europeans discovered them. Human civilization was represented as the linear evolution of Europe and the West's history; thus, Western legal systems, government, and economy become positioned as superior. Notably, it is the understanding of Western gender relations as normative that allows for the constructing of other cultures as more sexist and patriarchal.

Finally, racism works through the curriculum through the erasure of the history of racially oppressed women and men. Written and visual materials that include some groups and exclude others, are the basis on which whiteness is asserted, as Canadians are represented as only those who have migrated from parts of Europe.

A second barrier for female students of colour within the educational system is the kind of assumptions that teachers have. Brah (1992), Mirza (1999), and

Rezai-Rashti (1995) have illustrated that teachers often have stereotypical notions of Asian and Muslim female students as "passive" and of black and Caribbean female students as having little motivation in school and as disruptive and less academically able. They also report that teachers in Toronto schools defined those who were Muslim and female as being submissive, obedient, oppressed, and even mutilated individuals incapable of experiencing any sort of sexual pleasure.

Such stereotypes also lead to female students of colour receiving less attention from teachers. Brah (1992) reported that Asian and Muslim girls received less attention than white female students, who in turn receive less attention than white male students. Similarly, the stereotypes of black and Caribbean female students listed above means that they are often overlooked (Mirza 1999). These stereotypes influence the assumptions of teachers and guidance counsellors as to what programs are most appropriate for these students. For example, Mirza reported that teachers and guidance counsellors often directed female students of colour into non-university streams because they assumed that their families would not allow them to continue their education and enter universities (Mirza 1999). Such stereotypes also lead white students to stereotype female students of colour. Rezai-Rashti (1995) reported that Muslim female students in Toronto reported that stereotypical class discussions contributed to an environment in which it was easier for them to be harassed (see also Danzear 1992).

As Brah (1992) points out, given that curriculums make racially oppressed girls feel inferior and undervalued, it is not surprising that they underachieve in the educational system. As a result, anti-racist writers and advocates have recommended a review of curriculum and pedagogical practices in schools. However, as Rezai-Rashti (1995) cautions, education practitioners and theorists continue to see race and gender as separate issues. As a result, each becomes compartmentalized, and a systemic analysis of the intersections of race, gender, and class is lost. As a result, Rezai-Rashti has recommended that there is a need to bring together anti-racist and gender-equity practitioners in order to construct anti-racist feminist pedagogies that look at the integration of race and gender issues.

VARIATION AMONG RACIALLY OPPRESSED WOMEN

The lives of racially oppressed women are clearly shaped by the ways in which race and gender intersect in Canadian society. At the same time, their lives and experiences are also shaped by many other factors. Unfortunately, since researchers often employ singular categories such as gender, race, ability, or sexual orientation to analyze questions of inequality, experiences, and identity, there is a paucity of research on the ways in which race and gender intersect with other forms of oppression. While there is little information on the ways in which multiple intersections work, in this next section I will document how immigration status, religious affiliation, ableism, and sexual orientation intersect with race and gender in shaping the life chances of racially oppressed women.

Immigration Status

While the term "immigrant women" is often used to refer to racially oppressed women, the two are not synonymous. Immigrant women include those who are racialized as white, and racially oppressed women include Canadian-born and migrant women. The category of racially oppressed immigrant women also is heterogeneous, and in this section I explore the specific barriers faced by documented immigrant racially oppressed women.

The intersections of race and gender begin with immigration policies. The first point of contact with Canadian society is with the application for immigration. In 1967, Canadian regulations changed to prioritize education, age, and training in selecting immigrants on a point system. While the immigration policy may appear to be more objective and inclusive, several scholars have illustrated that the point system continues to encode racial and gender biases (Arat-Koc 1992; Satzewich 1992; Thobani 1999).

Such biases in immigration policies mean that most racially oppressed immigrant women enter Canada as either dependants or through specific programs, such as the Live-in Caregivers Program (LCP). Entry through either of these policies is associated with differential immigration status and conditions. Until 1981, those who entered under the LCP were classified as temporary migrants and thus were not able to gain landed status (see Arat-Koc 1992). Those who enter as dependants are defined as part of the "family package" that men are allowed to bring in. As a result, these women do not have access to programs and services designed to assist in settlement, language training, and employment integration (Boyd 1990; Ng 1988). As a number of studies have documented, such differential treatment has serious consequences for women. First, these policies support patriarchal relations since they make both paid domestic workers and immigrant women financially and legally dependent on, respectively, their employers or their husbands, even in cases of abusive relationships (Arat-Koc 1992: Giles 1988). Secondly, they make both of these groups more vulnerable to poverty and underemployment. For those who enter as paid domestic workers, LCP requires that they work for their employer for at least two years, work with low remuneration, long hours, and no benefits (Arat-Koc 1992). Similarly, to those who enter as dependants, not having access to language-training programs has implications for participation in the labour force. Bauder (2000) reported that immigrant women who were not fluent in either official language earned 20% less than other immigrant women.

In addition to the way in which the state has structured gender and racial inequality, the labour market also works to marginalize these women. In explaining how such differentiation occurs, researchers have pointed to two interrelated processes: first, immigrant women are more vulnerable to racism; and second, foreign credentials are undervalued. Questions such as "where do you come from" lead to greater hostility towards immigrant women as they are seen as taking jobs away from "Canadians" (see, for example, Saloojee 2003). For many immigrant women, their accents or deviation from the language standard of the dominant groups is another marker that leads to discrimination. For example, respondents in a study by the Canadian Race Relations Foundation (2000) reported that they had been denied access to employment because they were identified as having an accent.

A second process through which immigrants face discrimination is by the undervaluing of foreign degrees. An employment counsellor expressed the dominant view of foreign degrees when he stated: "foreign degrees are not recognized. Whatever degrees they have in their country, it is not compatible, and they don't equate. Like a degree from UBC is not equivalent to the degree from India, Pakistan, or UK" (cited in Bauder and Cameron 2002: 12). The Conference Board of Canada has reported that "key among the barriers to appropriate labour market participation is the non recognition of international credentials and experiences by Canadian employers, regulators, and educational institutions" (2001: 1). Rajagopal (1990) argued that the lack of recognition of foreign credentials directly leads to lower incomes for immigrants. Saloojee (2003) reported that for those who immigrated to Canada between 1991 and 1996, the poverty rate was 52%. In the past decade, many feminist and other organizations have made recommendations that the federal government facilitate the recognition of foreign credentials (see National Organization of Immigrant and Visible Minority Women of Canada 1999; Conference Board of Canada 2001; The Maytree Foundation 2000). However, as the Canadian Race Relations Foundation (2000: 11) recently noted, "these have largely fallen by the way-side."

Religion

There are very few studies that examine how religion shapes racially oppressed women's experiences with race and gender. Much of the work focuses on a particular group—Muslim women. It is important to note that women who have migrated from the Middle East, and their descendants are a diverse group, including Muslims, Christians, Bahais, Jews, and those who are secular. They also include lesbian women and disabled women. However, due to the prevailing stereotypes of women and Islam, women who migrate from Middle Eastern countries and their descendants often get homogenized as "Islamic." We have seen that the image of the passive and traditional Islamic woman is a powerful one that has been constructed as the antithesis of Canadian society. We have also seen that such gendered stereotypes have impacted on young women in schools. In the deployment of stereotypes, the hijab, in particular, works as a marker for discrimination. Those who wear the hijab are considered dangerous, with the potential to destroy everything in society or civilization (Jiwani 1992). Thus, racialized stereotypes of Islam are tied to patterns of hostility and discrimination towards Muslim women.

In addition, studies suggest that after 9/11, women racialized as Islamic face increasing violence, hostility, and discrimination in housing and employment. These studies also suggest that women who practise Islam may be subject to the most intense discrimination. In 2001, over 200 hate crimes against Muslims and those perceived as Muslim were reported in Canada (*Toronto Star* 5 March 2003).

A recent community-based action study by Persad and Lukas (2002) conducted a survey and carried out focus groups with Muslim women to examine their experiences in the workplace. They report that, since 9/11, women identified as Muslim have had greater difficulty securing employment, housing, and services, as well as experiencing increased levels of violence and hostility. Moreover, anti-terrorist legislation has targeted Islamic groups for increased surveillance. As one respondent reported, "After Sept 11th, I've experienced lots of problems. One guy would follow me in his car yelling racist words. He followed me to the bus station to my job.... he followed me for 2 weeks" (quoted in Persad and Lukas 2002: 5).

Persad and Lukas report that women who wear a hijab experience greater harassment and discrimination as they are often denied jobs, told that they must remove the hijab, harassed in the workplace, and even fired. Of the women who participated in the study, 78.1% reported that they had been denied employment because they were wearing the hijab, 90.6% of women reported having an employer make reference about their hijab while applying for work, and 40.6% reported that they had been told by employers that they must take off the hijab if they wanted to keep their jobs.

Such discrimination is tied to experiences of being made unwelcome in the workplace and of overt hostility. One Muslim described her supervisors' and co-workers' hostility to Muslim colleagues: "It is clear that they did not want us, because of our hijab and wanted to get rid of us. They accorded us the worse treatment, always openly making smearing comments about our religion and culture. They said we were dirty and odd people" (quoted in Persad and Lucas 2002: 36). As Persad and Lukas concluded, "It is important to recognize and understand the negative impact that this treatment can have on these women's self-esteem" (2002: 40). As result of such discrimination, some women have resorted to changing their names or appearance as a way of surviving. However, as Persad and Lukas (2002) point out, discrimination cannot be accommodated but needs to be eliminated. They call on governments and institutions to develop strategies and programs to educate and ensure that discrimination is not encouraged and does not continue.

Ableism

While there is very little research in Canada that examines the ways in which experiences with disability intersect with race, sexuality, and gender, there is an emerging acknowledgement that disability cannot be studied in isolation. According to Statistics Canada, currently 17% of all Canadians have some kind of disability. As Warner (2002) has noted, given the continuing social stigma associated with declaring a disability, this number is likely to underestimate the actual persons with disabilities.

People who are differently abled experience significant legal, social, and physical barriers. As Helen Healy of the Bloorview MacMillan Centre, a community organization for people with disabilities, noted, "Most of the reasons people with disabilities are not employed or don't hold their jobs are more related to social factors than they are to physical accommodation.... The social factors mean disability awareness and discomfort with those with disabilities" (*Toronto Star* 4 July 2000). As a result of such barriers, people with disabilities face reduced chances for employment, have lower earnings, and are more vulnerable to poverty. They also experience inadequate transportation services, inadequate housing, and inaccessible buildings. And they face barriers in their ability to participate in decision-making and in civil, social, and cultural life. Canadian immigration procedures screen out applicants with disabilities and/or with disabled family members.

Given the degree to which people with disabilities experience discrimination, it is important to understand the intersections of disability with race, gender, immigration status, sexual, and gender orientation. While there is little data available in Canada, data from the US suggest that disability rates vary by gender, race, and ethnicity. Aboriginal peoples and blacks have higher rates of disability than the national average, while Hispanics and Asian-Americans have lower rates (McNeil 2000). Disabled racially oppressed people are far more likely to face discrimination in the labour market. According to the US Census Bureau's 1994–95 data, approximately 72.2% of African Americans with disabilities and 51.9% of Hispanics with disabilities were unemployed. Further, 85.5% of African Americans and 75.4% of Hispanics with severe disabilities were unemployed. The employment opportunities facing minorities with disabilities are bleak (Office of Disability Employment Policy's Cultural Diversity Initiative 1998).

In explaining the higher rates of unemployment for those racially oppressed people with disabilities, researchers point to the ways in which ableism intersects with racism. As a York University student who is disabled and black states, "being disabled and black are two separate issues with different implications.... My life has been mixed. Race is one thing, but having a disability is another thing because people see your race then they also witness your physical condition" (quoted in Young Peoples Press 2001). As one report in the US argued, since racially oppressed disabled people on average have lower incomes than others, they are less able to afford the kinds of educational programs that would allow their children to succeed (Office of Disability Employment Policy's Cultural Diversity Initiative 1998).

Another element that shapes the way in which racism intersects with disability is the underutilization of services. In Canada and the US, a number of studies have documented that racially oppressed people under-use prevention, treatment, rehabilitation, and counselling services (for example, see Bau 1999; Choi 2001; Fricke 1998; Office of Disability Employment Policy's Cultural Diversity Initiative 1998). These writers point out that service providers have been unable to design programs that support racially oppressed people with disabilities. These patterns have led a number of researchers to claim that disabled racially oppressed people experience three strikes against them from the beginning (Block, Balcazar, and Keys 2002).

For disabled racially oppressed women, the situation is also complicated by gender. While they have not been studied specifically in Canada, research on "women" illustrates that the consequences of being differentially abled are particularly serious for women. Until not so long ago, it was not uncommon to hear of forced sterilization of disabled women, the denial of a family life, low employment levels, and high levels of poverty (Garland-Thomson, 1997). Women with disabilities have less access to essential services such as health care, education, and vocational rehabilitation. In addition, they are also vulnerable to sexual and domestic violence. Institutional and other settings frequently expose women with disabilities to abusive individuals (Disabled Women's Network of Canada 2000).

Clearly, for disabled racially oppressed women, disability, race, and gender intersect. It will take the efforts of many organizations and employers to reverse the negative employment picture for racialized women with disabilities. Researchers and advocates have argued that laws, such as the Ontario Disabilities Act, are a vital component in addressing the systemic inequalities and discrimination that people with disabilities face. However, I would suggest that there is a need to review legislation governing accessibility with regard to the intersections of race and gender. In the US, attention to the needs of racially oppressed people with disabilities has become a priority. In response to their high unemployment statistics, the Office of Disability Employment Policy has been working with the National Association for the Advancement of Colored People, the National Urban League and other minority organizations in an effort to meet this challenge.

Sexual and Gender Orientation

Many racially oppressed women are lesbian, bisexual, or transgendered. As such, they experience the intersections of race, gender, and sexual orientation. Lesbian and bisexual women face homophobia in their communities of colour as well as in mainstream communities. They also experience racism and sexism in society as well as in queer communities. Transgendered people not only experience transphobia in their communities of colour, in queer communities, feminist communities, and mainstream communities, but they also experience the racism.

In the past two decades, a large body of work has emerged, mostly from community and advocacy groups, documenting the experiences of queer racially oppressed people. In addition, academic researchers have also begun recently to address the intersections of race, gender, and sexuality (see, for example, Kumashiro 2001).

The choice of sexual partners fundamentally affects how a person is perceived. As Judith Butler has suggested, sexuality is tied to gender, so that a woman who is involved with another woman is often seen "as not truly a woman" (Butler 1997). Heterosexuality is also regulated by the judicial, medical, and educational systems (Weir and O'Brien 1999). For example, in some jurisdictions it is still not possible for same-sex couples to be legally married. Another way in which discrimination takes place is through heteronormativity—the taken-for-granted assumption that everyone is heterosexual and, if not, should be. Such assumptions have excluded lesbian and bisexual women from accessing many social programs in Canada, as these organize benefits according to a heterosexual model of relationship.

Similarly, immigration policies restrict same-sex couples from claiming sponsorship. And refugee policies do not allow for claims on the basis of homophobia and/or transphobia.

Discrimination faced by lesbian and bisexual women is compounded by race, religion, class, ability, and immigration status. Several writers have suggested that such intersections rarely get addressed. As Kumashiro (2001) notes, the efforts to challenge heterosexism rarely take into account the intersections of race. As a result, efforts to challenge one form of oppression often unintentionally contribute to other forms, and efforts to embrace one form of difference often exclude and silence others. Kumashiro has illustrated that being queer often highlights race in contradictory ways: in queer communities and communities of colour, queer identity is defined as a "white thing" (2001: 4). Not only does this reinforce binaries of us/them, it excludes queer racially oppressed people from both communities. The result is that the needs of queer racially oppressed women are often overlooked.

Indeed, for queer racially oppressed people, dealing with issues of sexual and gender orientation intersects with topics such as familial relations, religion, educational attainment, racism, sexism, immigration, and sexuality. For queer racially oppressed people, the everyday experience of dealing with racism often locates them within larger community and family structures and gives them racialized identities (Kumashiro 2001; Varney 2001). Due to racism, queer racially oppressed women value relationships within communities of colour, where, similar to mainstream communities, heterosexism is reinforced. This has contradictory effects. On the one hand, it makes the fear of losing familial relationships play a central role in the experience of coming out. In addition, since being queer in these communities is often defined as "a white thing," being queer becomes associated with being a race traitor. As a result, queer racially oppressed people have much inner conflict as they fear the loss of their racialized communities (Misa 2001). On the other hand, Russell and Troung (2001) have noted that the experience of dealing with racism may allow queer youth of colour the ability to negotiate the minority status associated with being queer. Through a national survey of queer youth, they found that racially oppressed students were more likely to come out in school environments, and were more able to deal with a minority status associated with sexuality; in fact, for "most white queer youth, being a minority is a new status.... the realization of a sexual minority status may feel particularly threatening" (Russell and Troung 2001: 116).

The awareness of the importance of communities of colour to queer racially oppressed women has led to initiatives to make anti-racism sensitive to queer issues and to anti-homophobic and anti-transphobic work within communities of colour. As Varney (2001) notes, Asian communities are beginning to change. For example, queer members are being accepted as participants in "ethnic" festivals. Community initiatives to create safe spaces for queer racially oppressed people focus on creating spaces where they can develop alternative communities. Notably, the vast majority of these initiatives takes place in large metropolitan centres. As a result, those located outside of these areas may experience the harshest intersections of race, gender, and sexual orientations.

THEORIZING INTERSECTIONS

While we have been able to gain insights into the ways in which racially oppressed women experience the intersections of gender, race, immigration, sexuality, and ability, we have also seen how much of the literature has not systematically examined these intersections. Can this gap in research be filled by more informed studies? Or does this gap itself reflect more fundamentally the theories that inform methodologies?

The past two decades have witnessed efforts to develop frameworks that theorize the connections between race and gender. Those who have undertaken such projects have done so with very different intentions. For some theorizing interconnections comes out of the desire to make racism as central as gender inequality to feminist theory (Carby 1986; hooks 1981, 1984, 1989; Parmar and Amos 1984; Hill-Collins 1991). For others, the task is to 'combine' racism with gender and class in analyzing oppression (Ramazanoglu 1989; Stasiulis 1990).

This body of literature, labelled anti-racist feminist thought, provides interesting insights on how to begin theorizing intersections. Many anti-racist feminist writers begin by pointing out that conventional theoretical models do not allow for a study of the intersection of gender, race, and class (see Bannerji 1995; Monture-Angus 1995; Stasiulis 1990; Kobayashi and Peake 1994; Creese and Stasiulis 1996). In particular, they argue that feminist political economy and race relations approaches focus on one form of oppression—gender, class, or race. As a result, they assume a universal experience: not only are other forms of oppression subsumed under one analytical category, each of these theoretical paradigms also privileges one form of oppression. As a result, racism is erased. As Stasiulis (1990), Kobayashi and Peake (1994), and Creese and Stasiulis (1996) conclude, these paradigms are marred by theoretical limitations that make the interconnections between racism and sexism invisible (see also Bannerji 1995; Monture-Angus 1995).

From this critique, anti-racist feminist writers discuss how to develop new methodologies to answer their concerns. For example, Bannerji asks, "Where are we to find interpretive frameworks and methods that are more than alternative and would go beyond inclusion? How can we gain insight into the social relations and culture of advanced capitalism?" (1995: 63). The recognition that theoretical paradigms have worked to obscure the interconnections between race, class, and gender have led anti-racist writers to offer two distinct approaches to theorizing these intersections: a "locational" model (Stasiulis 1995; Creese and Stasiulis 1996) and a Foucauldian model (for example, see Brah, 2001).

For some, studying intersectionality involves examining the way in which women experience different forms of oppression in their lives. Creese and Stasiulis have argued that "understanding the multiple and contradictory intersections of race, class, gender and sexuality in local and international contexts, is central to developing a more adequate political economy" (1996: 5). The clearest exposition of this approach has been put forward by Stasiulis, who advocates an epistemology that focuses on "the structural *location* of particular groups of women in concrete and historically specific social relations and to the accompanying discourses that aid in the processes of denigration, subordination, and exploitation" (1990: 290). Through this, anti-racist feminism is better able to produce "a more complex mapping of oppression, inequality and resistance" (Stasiulis 1995: 6). The advantage of beginning with an individual's location is that it allows for an epistemology that focuses on how "the boundaries of race, gender, class, and sexuality intersect to make visible the various nuances of each category" (Khayatt 1994: 10).

However, a number of writers have pointed to limitations in a locational model. First, as Satzewich (1988) points out, a locational model does not resolve the issue of what to prioritize in the study of interconnections. He notes that there are considerable differences among writers about how to study the interrelationship between race, class, and gender: "there are class approaches to race and gender, gender approaches to race and class, and race approaches to class and gender" (Satzewich 1988: 41). Second, a locational model is seen as "adding" up the many structures of oppression that intersect in shaping lives (Briskin 1990). As Elizabeth Spellman has stated, "One's gender identity is not related to one's racial and class identity as the parts of pop-bead necklaces are related, separable and insertable in other 'strands' with different racial and class 'parts'" (1990: 15). In other words, different forms of oppression are inseparable. Third, writers point out that the focus on "mapping women within systems of multiple oppression" leaves the systems of oppression unexplained, thus raising the danger of taking them for granted. As Bannerji states: "But why is racism still at the level of being named rather than an integral part of the economic analysis? ... How fundamental a role 'ethnicity' and 'race' have played as organizational and administrative categories of both the economy and the state" (1995: 77).

For Bannerji (1995), Dua (2000), Brah (1992), and Kaplan and Grewal (2001), studying intersectionality involves developing new paradigms. Bannerji states: "Concepts such as capital, class, imperialism etc. are thus considered totalizing, abstract 'master narratives,' an untenable basis for political subjectivity since they are beyond the concreteness of immediate experience" (1995: 73). Many who called for new paradigms have turned to a Foucauldian epistemology (Dua 2000; Brah 1992), which, they believe, allows for a more sophisticated understanding of the ways in which the discourse of race shapes the contingent character of colonialism, imperialism, and capitalism. They begin by conceptualizing race as a discourse, constituted in multiple ways through knowledge, culture, and power, as well as influenced by the imperatives of imperialism and capitalism. They then analyze institutional mechanisms that locate women in differential positions and social relations, since it is through discursive operations that racialized structures are created. As Bannerji states, acknowledging these regimes "allows us to create a knowledge which shows how the social relations and forms come into being in and through each other, to show how a mode of production is an historically and socially concrete formation" (Bannerji 1995: 84).

A Foucauldian methodology also allows researchers to conceptualize race, gender, class, sexuality, and ability as interconstituted, in other words, constructed through each other. As we have seen, the concepts of discourse, knowledge, culture, and power have been employed in the study of gender, sexuality, and ability. Discourse, knowledge, and power are constituted in multiple ways and also through each other, allowing researchers to map out intersections in integrative ways. However, despite these arguments, very little work has made these linkages (for exceptions, see Brah 1992; Kaplan and Grewal 2001; and Stoler 1995).

The locational and Foucauldian approaches offer two very different epistemological frameworks for how to study intersectionality. First, they differ on what should constitute the subject of study or on what is the central question that needs to be investigated. For those who employ a Foucauldian methodology, the central question is how differences are created and maintained in relation to each other. For those who work within the locational model, it is how individuals come into and experience multiple locations and identities. These are two different but not contradictory questions. Second, the two approaches also adopt very different implicit epistemological assumptions on how to theorize racism. Foucauldian theorists see race as a discourse, and racism as the form of discrimination that results from racist knowledge; they feel that it is important not to conflate racism with social location. Conversely, those employing a locational model posit racism as a phenomenon that differs according to one's structural location; they see racism as having multiple meanings and expressions.

CONCLUSION

In this chapter, we have seen how women racialized as minorities experience the intersection of race and gender. Historically, race was constructed through ideas of gender and sexuality, such that skin colour, gender, and sexual practices came together to establish a hierarchy among women, men, and space. I have also illustrated that such racialization and gendering continues to have significant impact, as it makes racially oppressed women one of the most vulnerable groups in Canadian society. Racially oppressed women are more likely to confront racism and employment-related discrimination; increased vulnerability to poverty, domestic violence, and sexual assault; and decreased access to social and community services. In addition, we have seen that there is no singular experience with race and gender. Rather than fitting neatly into a new category, racially oppressed women fit into multiple and fluid overlapping categories. Finally, we have explored two new methodological approaches for the study of intersectionality.

While it is possible to glean insights from the current scholarship, it is also clear that there are important gaps in our understanding. There is a paucity of research that examines how race and gender intersect to shape experiences with employment, income, poverty, and social programs or that considers the intersections of gender and race with other forms of oppression such as class, sexuality, immigration status, ableism, and language. Notably, there is no single study that addresses all of these categories.

These gaps have two important implications. First, more research needs to be undertaken before we can adequately assess the range and complexities of the ways in which racially oppressed women experience society. Second, since researchers continue to employ singular categories such as gender, race, ability, or sexual orientation to analyze questions of inequality, experiences, and identity, our current ways of conceptualizing questions of inequality, lived experience, and identity are significantly limited.

REFERENCES AND FURTHER READINGS

Agnew, V. 1998. *In Search of a Safe Place: Abused Women and Culturally Sensitive Services.* Toronto: University of Toronto Press.

Agocs, C., and J. Harish. 2001. *Systemic Racism in Employment in Canada: Diagnosing Systemic Racism in Organizational Culture.* Toronto: Canadian Race Relations Foundation.

Arat-Koc. S. 1992. Immigration Policies, Migrant Workers, and the Definition of Citizenship. In V. Satzewich, ed., *Deconstructing a Nation: Immigration, Multiculturalism, and Racism in '90s Canada.* Saskatoon: University of Saskatchewan Press.

Bakker, I. 1994. *The Strategic Silence: Gender and Economic Policy.* London: Zed Books.

Balibar, E. 1991. The Nation Form: History and Ideology. In E. Balibar and I. Wallerstein, eds., *Race, Nation, Class.* London: Verso.

Bannerji, H. 1995. *Thinking Through: Essays on Feminism, Marxism, and Anti-Racism.* Toronto: Women's Press.

Bau, A.M. 1999. Providing Culturally Competent Services to Visually Impaired Persons. *Journal of Visual Impairment and Blindness* 93(5): 291–98.

Bauder, Harold. 2000. Reflections on the Spacial Mismatch Debate. *Journal of Education and PLanning Research* 19(3): 316–20.

Bauder, Harold, and Emilie Cameron. 2002. Cultural Barriers to Labour Market Integration: Immigrants from South Asia and the former Yugoslavia. *RIIM/Metropolis* (February).

Block, P., F. Balcazar, and C. Keys. 2002. Race, Poverty, and Disability: Three Strikes and You're Out! Or Are You? *Social Policy* 33(1): 34–38.

Boyd, M. 1990. At a Disadvantage: Occupational Attainments of Canadian Immigrant Women. *International Migration Review* 18 (Winter):1091–1119.

———. 1992. Gender, Visible Minority and Immigrant Earnings Inequality: Reassessing an Employment Equity Premise. In V. Satzewich, ed., *Deconstructing a Nation: Immigration, Multiculturalism, and Racism in '90s Canada.* Saskatoon: University of Saskatchewan Press.

Brah, A. 1992. Women of South Asian Origin in Britain: Issues and Concerns. In P. Braham, A. Rattansi, and R. Skellington, eds., *Racism and Antiracist: Inequalities, Opportunities, and Policies.* London: The Open University/Sage.

Brah, A., M.J. Hickman, and M. Mac an Ghaill. 2001. Thinking Identities: Ethnicity, Racism, and Culture. *Contemporary Sociology* 30(2): 129–30.

Briskin, L. 1990. Hierarchy of Oppressions. *Feminist Review* 35: 343–51.

Brodie, Janine. 1996. Canadian Women, Changing State Forms, and Public Policy. In J. Brodie, ed., *Women and Canadian Public Policy.* Toronto: Harcourt Brace. 1–28.

Butler, J. 1997. Against Proper Objects. In E. Weed and N. Schor, eds., *Feminism Meets Queer Theory.* Bloomington, IN: Indiana University Press.

Campling, J. 1997. *Women and Social Policy.* London: Macmillan Press.

Canadian Race Relations Foundation. 2000. *Unequal Access: A Canadian Profile of Racial Differences in Education, Employment, and Income.* Canada: Canadian Race Relations Foundation.

Carby, Hazel. 1986. White Women Listen! Black Feminism and the Boundaries of Sisterhood. In *The Empire Strikes Back.* London: Centre for Contemporary Culture Studies.

Choi, N.G. (ed.). 2001. *Psychosocial Aspects of the Asian American Experience: Diversity Within Diversity.* Binghamton, NY: Haworth.

Conference Board of Canada. 2001. One-Third of Labour Force Contribution to GDP Growth Provided by Visible Minorities, Despite Gap in Wages. In *Making a Visible Difference: The Contribution of Visible Minorities to Canadian Economic Growth.* Toronto: Conference Board of Canada.

Creese, G., and D. Stasiulis. 1996. Introduction: Intersections of Gender, Race, Class, and Sexuality. *Studies in Political Economy* 51 (Fall): 5–14.

Daenzer, P. 1992. Black Youth and Elementary and Secondary Education in Metropolitan Toronto. In *Towards a New Beginning: Report of the Four-Level Government/African Canadian Community Working Group.* Toronto: Neighbourhoods Committee of the City of Toronto.

Dei, G.J.S. 1997. *Reconstructing "Drop-out": A Critical Ethnography of the Dynamics of Black Students' Disengagement from School.* Toronto: University of Toronto Press.

———. 2003. Anti-Racism and Inclusive Schooling Practices. Special Issue *Orbit* 33(3).

Disabled Women's Network of Canada. 2000. *Strengthening the Links, Stopping the Violence: A Guide to the Issue of Violence Against Women with Disabilities.* Toronto: DAWN.

Dua, E. 1992. Introduction. *Scratching the Surface.* Toronto: Women's Press.

———. 2000. The Hindu Woman's Question: Canadian Nation-Building and the Social Construction of Gender for South Asian-Canadian Women. In G. Dei and A. Calliste, eds., *Anti-Racist Feminism.* Halifax: Fernwood.

Fricke, Y. 1998. *Disability and Development.* World Bank.

Garland-Thomson, Rosemarie. 1997. The Body and the Disabled Figure. In Bonnie G. Smith and Beth Hutchison, eds., *Gender and Disability Studies.* Chapel Hill, NC: Rutgers University Press.

Giles, W. 1988. Language Rights Are Women's Rights: Discrimination Against Immigrant Women in Canadian Language Training Policies. *Resources for Feminist Research* 17(3): 129–32.

Gilman, S.L. 1985. *Difference and Pathology: Stereotypes of Sexuality, Race, and Madness.* Ithaca, NY: Cornell University Press.

Gilroy, Paul. 1987. *There Ain't No Black in the Union Jack.* Chicago: University of Chicago Press.

Gohil, V. 1987. DHSS Service Delivery to Ethnic Minority Clients. *Leicester Rights Bulletin* 32.

Grewal, I. 1996. *Home and Harem: Nation, Gender, Empire and Cultures of Travel.* London: Duke University Press.

Hall, S. 1999. The West and the Rest. In S. Hall *et al.*, eds., *Modernity: An Introduction to Modern Societies.* London: Blackwell.

Henry, F., and E.J. Ginzberg. 1985. *Who Gets the Work? A Test of Racial Discrimination in Employment.* Toronto: Social Planning Council of Metropolitan Toronto and the Urban Alliance on Race Relations.

Hill-Collins, P. 1991. *Black Feminist Thought: Knowledge, Consciousness, and the Politics of Empowerment.* New York and London: Routledge.

hooks, bell. 1981. *Ain't I A Woman: Black Women And Feminism*. Boston: South End Press.

——. 1984. *From Margins to Centre*. Boston: South End Press.

——. 1989. *Talking Back: Thinking Feminist, Thinking Black*. Boston: South End Press.

Jiwani, Y. 1992. The Exotic, the Erotic, and the Dangerous: South Asian Women in Popular Film. *Canadian Woman Studies* 13(1): 42-46.

Kaplan, Caren, and Inderpal Grewal. 2001. Configuring Feminist Cultural Studies: The Undergraduate Introductory Course. In R. Wiegman, ed., *Locating Feminism: The Politics of Women's Studies*. Durham, NC: Duke University Press.

Khayatt, Didi. 1994. The Boundaries of Identity at the Intersections of Race and Gender. *Canadian Woman Studies* 14(2): 6–14.

Klein, G. 1985. *Reading in Racism: Bias in Children's Literature*. London and New York: Routledge and Kegan Paul.

Kobayashi, A., and L. Peake. 1994. Unnatural Discourse: "Race" and Gender in Geography. *Gender, Place and Culture* 1(2): 225–43.

Kumashiro, Kevin (ed.). 2001. *Troubling Intersections of Race and Sexuality: Queer Students of Color and Anti-Oppressive Education*. New York: Rowman and Littlefield.

Law, G. 1994. Making Sense of Social Citizenship: Some User Views on Welfare Rights and Responsibilities. *Critical Social Policy* 14(40): 273–99.

Li, P. 1998a. The Colour of Money: Wage Differentials Across Ethnic Groups. *Canadian Journal of Economics* 31(3): 518–48.

Li, P. 1998b. The Market Value and Social Value of Race. In V. Satzewich, ed., *Racism and Social Inequality in Canada: Concepts, Controversies and Strategies of Resistance*. Toronto: Thompson Educational Publishing.

Loomba, A. 1998. *Colonialism/Post-colonialism*. London: Routledge.

The Maytree Foundation. 2000. *Brain Drain, Brain Gain*. Session Proceedings. Toronto: Caledon Institute of Social Policy.

McClintock, A. 1998. *Imperial Leather*. London: Routledge.

McNeil, J. 2000. *The Disability Report*. Washington, DC: US Census Bureau.

Mirza, H. 1999. *Black British Feminism*. London and New York: Routledge.

Misa, Christina. 2001. Where Have All the Queer Students of Color Gone? Negotiated Identity of Queer Chicana/o Students. In Kevin K. Kumashiro, ed., *Troubling Intersections of Race and Sexuality: Queer Students of Color and Anti-oppressive Education*. New York: Rowman and Littlefield.

Montrose, Louis. 1991. The Work of Gender in the Discourse of Discovery. *Representations* 33 (Winter): 1–34.

Monture-Angus, P. 1995. *Thunder in My Soul: A Mohawk Woman Speaks*. Halifax: Fernwood.

National Organization of Immigrant and Visible Minority Women in Canada. 1999. *Recognition and Accreditation of Foreign Qualifications; Case Studies of the Nursing, Teaching and Social Work Professions*. Ottawa.

Ng, R. 1986. Immigrant Women In Canada: A Socially Constructed Category. *Resources for Feminist Research* 15(1): 13–14.

——. 1988. Immigrant Women and Institutionalised Racism. In S. Burt, L. Code, and L. Dorney, eds., *Changing Patterns: Women in Canada*. Toronto: McCelland and Stewart.

Office of Disability Policy. 1998. *Cultural Diversity Initiative Survey*. Ottawa: Human Resources and Social Development Canada.

Office of the Employment Equity Commissioner. 1992. *Working Towards Equality: The Discussion Paper on Employment Equity Legislation.* Toronto: Ontario Ministry of Citizenship.

Parmar, Pratibha, and Valerie Amos. 1984. Challenging Imperial Feminism. *Feminist Review* 17 (Autumn): 3–19.

Pendakur, Ravi, and Fernando Mata. 1998. The Colour of Money: Wage Differentials Across Ethnic Groups. *Canadian Journal of Economics* 31(3): 518–48.

Persad, J., and S. Lukas. 2002. *No Hijab Is Permitted Here.* Toronto: Women Working With Immigrant Women.

Rajagopal, I. 1990. The Glass Ceiling in the Vertical Mosaic: Indian Immigrants to Canada. *Canadian Ethnic Studies* 22: 96–105.

Ramazanoglu, Caroline. 1989. *Feminism and the Contradictions of Oppression.* London: Routledge.

Rezai-Rashti, G. 1995. Multicultural Education, Anti-racist Education, and Critical Pedagogy: Reflections on Everyday Practice. In R. Ng, P. Staton, and J. Scane, eds., *Anti-Racism, Feminism and Critical Approaches to Education.* Westport, CT: Greenwood.

Russell, Stephen T., and Nhan Truong. 2001. Adolescent Sexual Orientation, Race and Ethnicity, and School Environments: A National Study of Sexual Minority Youth of Color. In Kevin Kumashiro, ed., *Troubling Intersections of Race and Sexuality.* New York: Rowman and Littlefield. 113-30.

Said, E. 1978. *Orientalism.* London: Chatto and Windus.

Saloojee, A. 2003. *Social Inclusion, Anti-racism and Democratic Citizenship.* Laidlaw Foundation in Canada. <http://www.laidlawfdn.org/programmes/children/agenda-discuss-wp.html.>

Satzewich, V. 1988. The Canadian State and the Racialization of Caribbean Migrant Farm Labour, 1947-1966. *Ethnic and Racial Studies* 11(3): 282–304.

——. 1992. Introduction. In V. Satzewich, ed., *Deconstructing a Nation.* Saskatoon: Social Research Unit, University of Saskatchewan.

Spellman, Elizabeth, 1988. *Gender and Race: The Ampersand Problem of Exclusion in Feminist Thought.* Boston: Beacon Press.

Stasiulis, D. 1990. Theorizing Connections: Gender, Race, Ethnicity, and Class. In P. Li., ed., *Race and Ethnic Relations in Canada.* Toronto: Oxford University Press.

——. 1995. The Fractious Politics of a Settler State. In D. Stasiulus and N. Yuval-Davis, eds., *Unsettling Settler Societies.* London: Sage.

Stevenson, W. 1999. Colonialism and First Nations Women in Canada. In E. Dua and A. Robertson, eds., *Scratching the Surface: Canadian Anti-Racist Feminist Thought.* Toronto: Women's Press. 49–75.

Stoler, L. 1995. *Race and the Education of Desire.* Durham, NC: Duke University Press.

Thobani, S. 1999. Sponsoring Immigrant Women's Inequalities. *Canadian Woman Studies* 19(3): 11–16.

Toronto Star. 2000. Overcoming Stereotypes. 4 July: 1.

——. 2003. Hate Crimes Increase. 5 Mar: 1.

United States Labour Department. 1998. Cultural Diversity Initiative. <http://www.dol.gov/odep/archives/programs/cultural.htm>.

Varney, Joan. 2001. Undressing the Normal: Community Efforts for Queer Asian and Asian-American Youth. In Kevin Kumashiro, ed., *Troubling Intersections of Race and Sexuality.* New York: Rowman and Littlefield.

Warner, Jody. 2002. Report on Disability and Accommodation. *York University Faculty Association Reports.* Toronto: York University.

Weir, Lorna, and Carole-Anne O'Brien. 1999. Lesbians and Gay Men: Inside and Out. In Nancy Mandell, ed., *Feminist Issues: Race, Class, and Sexuality*. Toronto: Prentice-Hall.

Young Peoples Press. 2001. *Living With A Disability*. Toronto: York University.

Yuval-Davis, N., and F. Anthias. 1997. *Theorizing Gender and Nation*. London: Sage.

10 | RACING AND ERASING
Law and Gender in White Settler Societies

Patricia A. Monture

THE MEANING OF LAW

Law is a core structure in Canadian society, commonly viewed as essential to keeping order. The relationship between law and social order is most often "accepted as an unquestioned truism" (Tamanaha 2001: 2–3). Law and order are not neutral concepts, however, and they benefit some segments of society more than others (Tanovich 2006: 2). The origins of law trace to a sphere of male activity, and racial biases created multiple patterns of exclusion. But before we can address the relationships among race, gender, class, and the law, it is necessary to consider the meaning of law.

Law is part of a much larger system that is what we think of as society. Legal scholar Gerald Gall explains:

> Our society functions through the interaction of a complex matrix of highly interrelated processes. Our society can be looked at in terms of our economic system and the economic processes inherent within that system, or it can be examined in terms of our political system, including the political processes which define the nature of our political system. Even our individual interactions, according to the conventional wisdom espoused in the disciplines of psychology and sociology, are also part of this overall complex matrix we call our society. In short, the legal process is but one of the many ongoing processes that make society function. (Gall 2004: 4)

Law, then, cannot be seen as a simple construct; it should be explained, rather, as part of a much larger legal process. It is about enforcement and the manner in which various officials, ranging from police officers to judges, interpret it (Mosher 1998: 33). Nonetheless, law is most often considered "the vehicle by which we resolve disputes in a just, orderly, and peaceful fashion" (Mosher 1998: 4).

The degree to which law in modern, Western, industrial society operates justly is the broad subject examined in this chapter. Critical legal theorists continue to assert that law is a system of privilege and that, as a result, certain individuals have impaired access to equality, benefit of, and protection by law (Valdes *et al.* 2002). The law has historically created racialized subjects; certain persons were considered as the property of whites or as indentured servants, and Indigenous peoples were exploited for their land and resources (St. Lewis 2002: 295). Canadian legal scholar Joanne St. Lewis explains:

> The inequitable history of the law, which facilitated the acquisition of power by an elite few, is not discussed by courts and is rarely a part of legal argument. Instead, the law and the legal system have been used to reinforce oppression and social inequality. This inequality has sometimes been built on specific policies of discrimination or exclusion, such as those used to foster the expansion of the colonial empire. Inequality has also resulted from the operation of seemingly non-discriminatory concepts and practices such as precedent (in the common law system) and adherence to liberal notions of individual rights. These practices have been assumed to be neutral in spite of their disparate impact on vulnerable equality-seeking groups. (St. Lewis 2002: 299)

Two concerns are foremost in St. Lewis's analysis: precedent and the individual nature of rights. First, precedent is the process that forces law to look backward. It is argued that rules of the past need to be brought into the present to maintain consistency in decision-making. As precedent is rooted in a history of decision-making in which women "were not legal persons, when chattel slavery was enforced by the courts, when rape within marriage was a legal impossibility, and Indigenous peoples' cultural practices were outlawed and their lands confiscated..." (St. Lewis 2002: 301), law can be viewed as a means by which the inequalities established in earlier time periods persist in the present.

Second, it is widely held that rights belong to individuals, and that they protect property, insure safety, and guarantee equality. Sherene Razack concisely expresses the first problem with rights:

> Rights thinking on the whole, a way of looking at the world that begins from the position that human beings operate as autonomous and isolated individuals, is a profoundly limiting and masculinist perspective. It is a way of thinking that, through the dualisms of reason and desire, public and private, and individual and community, denies the realities of women's lives and, most critically, represses the domination of women by men. (Razack 1991: 127).

Rights are a central structure in Canadian legal systems, a trait shared with other Western legal systems. The problem, as feminist scholars see it, is the way rights operate to reinforce gendered inequalities, largely because litigation in any matter, including rights, is a costly endeavour. Rights, as legal structures, are more accessible to those citizens who have wealth. Thus, class exclusion is built into the Canadian legal system's structure.

As critical legal theorists have demonstrated, there are patterns to the exclusions of persons who do not receive equal access to, benefit from, and protection of the law. In this chapter, the race-class-gender trinity (Stasiulis 2005: 38) forms the basis of the analysis of legal relations as a source and a site of the reproduction of oppression. Legal scholars who analyzed the first cases to be heard in Canadian courts found that for women it was "one step forward and two back" (Brodsky and Day 1989). The Charter of Rights and Freedoms proved disappointing as a tool to challenge inequality, subordination, and oppression. To diagram this oppression, a particular focus in this analysis is placed on the relationship between Aboriginal peoples and the state, including the Canadian legal system.

INTERSECTIONALITY AND THE SOCIOLOGICAL IMAGINATION

There is an implicit danger in focusing solely on the race-class-gender trinity, namely, the tendency to understand power in terms of hierarchies of exclusion, where some forms of oppression are explained as more damaging than others. And it appears that legal remedy often attaches only to those cases that are viewed as the most intolerable or the least unsettling for decision-makers who are still, overwhelmingly, white. Decision-makers have a desire to be seen as innocent of racial misdoings; they strive to present themselves as individuals without history, in a country without history, living lives of merit rather than privilege. The result of the need to be an "innocent, white subject" (Razack 1999: 282) is that there can be no general right to humanity for all individuals. The race-class-gender trinity is not introduced in a limiting way in this discussion but rather as the place to start considering issues of multiple condition oppression.

Two decades ago, Kirkness (1987–88: 413) concluded that the experiences of Aboriginal women were not accurately described as double discrimination, as they had been previously labeled by scholars, but were "discrimination within discrimination." This phrase reflects the complexity of the experience of multiple source discrimination. The meaning of intersectionality is *not* that a combination of grounds of discrimination operates on an individual simultaneously to make sex discrimination worse. It, in fact, makes the intersection a "unique and distinct" experience of racialized women (Eaton 1994: 230–31).

Carol Aylward traces the origins of intersectionality as such:

> The first analysis of "intersectionality" in the context of race/sex and class oppression was put forward by American Critical Race theorist Kimberle Crenshaw. Crenshaw examined how sex, race and class combine to oppress Black women and other women of colour in a social order based on race and sex oppression. Mary Eaton, crediting Crenshaw with the "coining" of the phrase intersectionality, defines it as "intersectional oppression [that] arises out of the combination of various oppressions which, together, produce something unique and distinct from any one form of discrimination standing alone..." (Aylward 1999: 7)

Racialized women, therefore, can and often do experience life differently than men of the same race and other women. This is precisely the point of the discourse around rights called intersectionality. It means that equality considerations must look to the specific experiences of the relevant comparator group and take into account the points of intersection of race, class, and gender. Essentializing women or race is an ineffective activity if the goal is to truly include and respect all persons.

Canadian legal structures can and often do operate to deny structural and systemic patterns of legal subordination by maintaining a tight focus on the individual and single incidents of violation rather than on systemic and historical patterns of exclusion. This is a contradiction embedded in the structure and operation of Canadian systems of law and criminal justice. Feminist efforts at legal reform have not always accomplished changes that benefit all women, and this in part can be attributed to the individual nature and incident-based construction of discrimination. It can also be traced to the failure to acknowledge multiple source oppression.

The kinds of knowledge sociologists acquire can form the basis for considering the relationship between law and conditions of oppression such as gender, class, and race. As Dorothy E. Smith (1987: 2) suggests, "sociology is a systemically developed consciousness of society and of social relationships." The problem is that many people do not see the impact that law has in their daily lives. It only becomes an apparent influence during crisis such as divorce, death, or arrest. Contemporary sociologists, however, can make visible what, how, and who has been erased. In the last few decades, the study of race, class, and gender has become a definite focus in feminist literature as well as within sociology (Bannerji 1999; Dua 1999: 13). However, as Carol Smart (1989) concluded, racialized voices have flourished in literary works more so than in law and the social sciences.

In 1959, C. Wright Mills wrote, "The sociological imagination enables us to grasp history and biography and the relations between the two within society. That is its task and its promise. To recognize this task and this promise is the mark of the classic social analyst" (Mills 1959: 6). He recognized "the present as history" (Mills 1959: 146). Indigenous knowledge traditions—traditions that have existed on what is now called Canadian territory since time immemorial—also acknowledge the importance of understanding tradition and oral history. People are trained in skills of self-reflection and often hear the Elders say that you must understand where you have come from to know where you are going. Thus, biography and history are two commonalities shared by Indigenous and academic systems. It is a significant demonstration that sociological understanding can accommodate Aboriginal worldviews and knowledges when we, as sociologists, consciously make attempts to respect both ways of learning and knowing.

Indeed, as other feminist scholars have noted, Mills's sociological imagination could have been better informed by an understanding of gender (as discussed in Knuttila 2005: 1; Tepperman and Rosenberg 1998: 230). Equally, his sociology, as representative of his time, lacks a sophisticated analysis of the diversity of *men*, including the impact of race. This is especially important to developing under-standings of Indigenous peoples who represent many diverse nations. Since Mills's introduction of the sociological imagination, and more specifically in the last two decades, many scholars have contributed to developing imaginations that are reflective of diversity, power, and oppression. Both race and gender intersect with biography and history. That a scholar is white and male (or Mohawk and female) informs his or her standpoint and hence, understanding of both the world and its history. Some sociologists advocate an absolute form of objectivity that demands colour, class, and gender blindness. This epistemology, however, closes our view of the world in unnecessary ways, and it denies us a full understanding of human relations, social institutions, and social structures. Colour and gender blindness leaves incomplete our understanding of class since poverty is both raced and gen-dered. Colour, class, and gender blindness also creates the circumstance wherein only white, middle-class, heterosexual men are seen as the norm. This dismisses race and gender to the space of personal trouble rather than public issue. In this way, whiteness, maleness, and so on become invisible rather than being seen as the social conditions and social constructs they are. The various forms of blindness to race, class, and gender makes them invisible sources of privilege and power while their invisibility guarantees the privilege will not be available to challenge.

Power, Privilege, Whiteness, and Law

Writing about race and gender in the courtroom, Sherene Razack identifies the problem of colour blindness as resting on the tenets of formal equality. Equality, from the formalist perspective, is reached by ensuring that each individual is treated the same. Formal equality dismisses the differences in people's lives. By treating individuals who are unequal in their social circumstances in the same way, equality is often denied (McIntyre explains this in the *Andrews* decision). Colour blindness is assumed in written laws and by many legal decision-makers, such as judges. The presumption is that racism is not a factor, unless there are specific indi-cators that it is present (Razack 1999). To acknowledge the impact of race without specific evidence is seen by the court as a violation of the legal process. Consider that Canadian law owes its origins to a system of law by, for, and about white men. Law neither takes into account nor accurately reflects the lived experiences of the "Other" until those conditions are demonstrated to the court. This turns the lived and self-evident experiences of racialized persons who *know* that race matters inside out. In Mills's terms, it turns the acknowledgement of racialized persons that race is a public issue and forces it into an inaccurate characterization of personal and private trouble.

Scholarship has increasingly focused on the racial experience of so-called minorities, and until recently the experience of whiteness has escaped the scholarly gaze. As noted by Constance Backhouse (1999: 9), "the transparency of 'white-ness' is misleading and contributes to an erasure of the privileges that attach to membership in the dominant race." That means the study of race is about oppression and subordination and only indirectly about the power held over people who are racialized, including racialized women. But racism is principally a relationship of power that requires the submission of whiteness to critical sociological rigour in order to provide a full understanding of the privileged/oppressed dichotomy. The study of racism must be about both the disadvantage of racism and the advantage it confers (Moreton-Robinson 2005: 63).

Discrimination, as a legal concept, casts the focus on those who are oppressed, who are denied rights and/or services, or who are excluded from social life in other ways. It does not consider the privileges conferred on those who have the social, economic, or political power to discriminate. The "victim" must bear the burden of proof of discrimination and must also shape representations of what their life experiences are. This helps to conceal the power and privilege of whiteness, which thus operates to deny the opportunity to ensure that equality is shared across social collectivities. In fact, race is a social construct from which law constructs a racial hierarchy (Chang 2002: 87–91; Comack 1999: 57) in which whiteness is both invisible and powerful.

As Razack notes, court cases tell the official story—they are a public truth (Razack 1999: 287). A brief discussion of two recent court cases, both heard before the Supreme Court of Canada, demonstrates not only the complexity of dealing with intersectionality and the problems with individual rights, but also with the official story that is told about race. In *R. v R.D.S.*, Judge Corrine Sparks, a black woman, considered issues of witness credibility in the context of the witness's race. A black 15-year-old was charged with interfering with the arrest of another young man and with assaulting the police officer who was making the arrest. His story and that of the police officer did not mesh.

> The Judge weighed the evidence and determined that the accused should be acquitted. While delivering her oral reasons, the Judge remarked, in response to a rhetorical question by the Crown, that police officers had been known to overreact particularly to non-white groups, and that such behaviour would indicate a questionable state of mind. She also stated that her comments were not tied to the police officer testifying before the court. The Crown challenged these comments as raising a reasonable apprehension of bias. (Razack 1999: 281)

The three charges laid are the first indication that the officer was exercising vigorously his power to arrest. All three stem from a single incident and are very similar in nature, so similar that one must wonder why one charge would not suffice. This phenomenon, known as over-charging, is not limited to the experience of black people; it has also been identified in a comparison made between the number of charges laid against Aboriginal and non-Aboriginal peoples in Manitoba (Hamilton and Sinclair 1991a: 102). Evidence of over-charging suggests that the insights of Judge Sparks were well grounded in the facts of the case, as well as in her own experiences of race.

The problem for Judge Sparks arose because she dared to challenge the official story. She dared to say in a courtroom that race matters (Razack 1999: 283). Her comments were not merely her own personal opinions but were substantiated by "numerous federal and provincial reports including the Nova Scotia Royal Commission regarding the wrongful conviction of Donald Marshall Jr." (St. Lewis 2002: 304). Both of the Nova Scotia appeal courts in this case supported the Crown's view that there was a reasonable apprehension of bias at trial on the part of the judge. This demonstrates that the expertise of a racialized person can easily be devalued.

Three of the justices of the Supreme Court of Canada agreed with the lower courts that the evidence did not show that the police officer's actions were racist (Razack 1999: 385). Richard Devlin, in his analysis of *R.D.S* (1995: 436), concludes that a formal definition of equality was honoured. Formal equality emphasizes the individual, either police officer or judge, and denies the context and systemic nature of the question before the court.

The satisfied response of racialized persons to the allegation of reasonable apprehension of bias, which is not softened by the victory in the Supreme Court, where six of the nine justices did not believe Judge Sparks had crossed the line, is no consolation. What was the case doing in the high court in the first place? As April Burie, representing the Congress of Black Women who intervened in the appeal, explained about the mere utterance of the term, racism:

> ... has the power to bring down the full wrath of the justice system, to define who is reasonable and who is not, who is a good judge and who is not, and who belongs and who does not. Conversely, when it is acknowledged, the word "racism" has the power to make Canada home. It has the power to heal. (Razack 1999: 283)

If racism is not part of the official story in Canada, then it still "separates the citizens from the non-citizens" (Razack 1999: 284) re-entrenching informally the denial of civil rights. Therefore, racialized persons are left no opportunity to seek justice.

In the case of *Conway v. The Queen*, a male prisoner complained that his right to privacy was denied by the presence of female guards in the cellblock. The Women's Legal Education and Action Fund (LEAF) intervened in the case and argued for the right of women to work for the Correctional Service of Canada as prison guards in male prisons. The conflict this litigation presented is between the rights of women and the rights of prisoners. Joanne St. Lewis, a black woman and a member of LEAF's legal committee at the time the factum was being drafted, uses narrative to analyze the consequences of a legal system that structures rights in a competing paradigm:

> The prisoner's privacy right claim was viewed as suspect by many women's rights advocates ... I suggested in the initial legal committee meeting that as between the rights of a female correctional officer and a prisoner, the prisoner was the most vulnerable given his social location and lack of rights. Furthermore, I noted the impact of systemic racism meant that a disproportion-

ate number of prisoners being spoken about were men from racialized communities and that the women being spoken of were largely of Euro-Canadian decent. (St. Lewis 2002: 315)

As is the case with many feminist groups, the majority of LEAF's legal committee has always been comprised of white women (see also the discussion in Razack 1991). In an adversarial system—a system that produces winners and losers—the pressure is to simplify the complexity of social experiences in situations like *Conway*. The question that was obscured was how law and lawyers balance the rights of male prisoners (many of whom are racialized men) against the rights of women to be employed as guards (many of whom are white women). How can both sets of interests be accommodated? But this should not be the end of the consideration of competing interests in the case; women prisoners (many of whom are racialized women) are impacted differently by the presence of male guards on the ranges because many of these women have survived violence.

Law as a social contract suggests that each citizen receives the benefit of believing that they live in a just, safe, and peaceful society. However, decisions such as *R.D.S.* and *Conway*, which are only two of many decisions that could be offered for consideration, send a different message to racialized persons and especially to racialized women. In both of the cases considered here, where the participants were men, race is ignored in the official rendering of law. And although there have been feminist successes in Canadian courts both before and after the *Charter*, these successes have most often been secured by white, middle-class and able-bodied women. This leaves racialized women little hope that courts can or will understand how "race structures a woman's experience of oppression as well as her responses to it" (Razack 1991: 292). In a society where violence against women is also racialized, the victims of such violence often have little faith that the law will protect them. Not only is there vulnerability to racialized violence in our daily lives, but the hope to engage law to protect ourselves is suspect, and a further form of vulnerability is exposed.

FEMINISM, INEQUALITY, AND LAW

Critical race scholars have established new boundaries that are inclusive of the voices and experiences that were marginalized or erased from stories about the origins of feminism and sociology. In telling their stories of race and gender, they exercise the personal power of biography. Margaret E. Montoya says that narratives often express the "emotion of marginality," providing the writer several opportunities for purging their pain:

... narratives invoke the right of the subordinated person to narrate—to interpret events in opposition to the dominant narratives, and to reinvent one's self by bringing coherence to one's life stories. These counter stories constitute social practices that reconstruct the storyteller's individual identities while expanding

> the possible life scripts available to Others. For this reason, narratives are also
> cultural tools: They are tools for teaching Others not only how to be and how
> to behave, but also how it is possible to be and behave. (Montoya 2002: 245)

As Montoya explains, by choosing to narrate, critical race scholars claim power—
the power to tell our own stories in our own ways. This is the first step in challenging the pain of racialized encounters, and it re-creates a sense of self, of strength
and self-respect.

Narratives also address the shortcomings of a history told from the monolithic
perspective of the white man who held the pen (Dickason 2000: 11–12). History
is not only told in books but also in the Indigenous story traditions shared orally
across generations and which some Indigenous scholars now choose to share in
written form. In Canada, feminist scholars have examined the exclusionary nature
of Western legal history and brought both narrative and biography to their works
(Backhouse 1991, 1999; Chunn 1988; Monture 1995, 2002b). The acceptance of
narration as an academic form provides the opportunity for Aboriginal people to
choose to share their oral traditions in new contexts.[1]

Examining the history of feminism, and tracing the exclusions within it, brings
forward the appropriate context for understanding the courts' failure to grapple
with racialized experience. Canadian feminist scholars understand the history of
feminism as occurring in three waves. In the first (approximately 1880–1950),
the aspiration was to end the civil subordination of women (Chunn, 1999: 238).
These early feminists did not challenge the structure of the bourgeois family but
rather concentrated on securing rights for women on the dissolution of marriage,
to hold public office, to become lawyers, and to vote. Women were no longer
to be disenfranchised from civil society but were to be citizens because of the
contributions they must be able to make to public life. The first-wave feminists
were mostly middle-class white women who lived in urban areas and followed
the Protestant faith. They pressed for "measures to eradicate the drunkenness,
gambling, lewd public entertainments, adultery, bigamy, desertion, child abuse,
prostitution, white slavery and opium dens" (Chunn 1988: 93). All of these activities were seen to threaten the family as well as social order; thus, social order and
family stability were their goals, not equality. Because of this focus on family, the
beneficiaries of this era of the movement were white, middle-class, heterosexual
women (Dua 1999: 10).

This glimpse of feminist history demonstrates that the way in which goals and
objectives are set out within a myriad of social actions likely determines how
inclusive the movement or research is. To this day, Canadian family law does
not operate inclusively of all women. Women living on "Indian" reserves are still
unable to access a matrimonial property law regime. This leaves some racialized
women with unequal access to the legal redress of family law since the 1986
decision of the Supreme Court of Canada in the *Derrickson* case (Canada 2005;
Jacobs and Eberts 2004; Turpel, 1991; Turpel-Lafond 1997). Two decades later,
there are still no uniform matrimonial property laws that apply to all persons living on lands designated as Indian reserves.

In part a response to the unequal benefit of first-wave feminist reforms, a more liberal kind of feminism emerged in the 1960s. These women struggled to understand why legal equality, defined as achieving such civil rights as the right to vote or hold public office, had not ended women's subordinate status (Chunn 1999: 245). They also continued to see the family as the norm and struggled to ensure women's equality in the home. Liberal feminists believed that the state would not "treat their interests differently from men's" (Chunn 1999: 246) once women gained the same access to and respect in the public sphere as men. Women achieved some successes during this time, including the equal division of property on the dissolution of marriage. Sex-specific clauses in family law regimes were removed although some research demonstrates this has benefited fathers more than mothers (Chunn 1999: 250). It is the more affluent sectors of society that have benefited from these reforms. Poor women, racialized women including Aboriginal women, lesbians, and women with disabilities have not equally benefited (Chunn 1999: 254).

It was during the second wave of feminism (the early 1980s) when issues of racialized understanding, analysis, and inclusion gained momentum in feminist circles and women's organizations. Studies demonstrated that women of colour had higher rates of labour force participation but were employed in the most poorly paid jobs (Das Gupta 1987). As Arat-Koc demonstrated, an irony in the lives of domestic workers, many of whom are racialized women employed to care for children of well-to-do families, is that they are often forced to leave their own children in their home countries (cited in Dua 1999: 15). The *Symes* case (1993)—in which a lawyer claimed child care costs as an expense for a professional woman doing business—made invisible the severe discrimination child-care workers experienced (St. Lewis, 2002: 309). Thus, middle-class gender discrimination and not the rights of all women workers was the focus for the second wave.

Legal reform was a characteristic of both of the first two waves of feminism. The tension created by the realization that such reforms were not bringing women much closer to equality (Chunn 1999: 246) was one of the factors that contributed to a more complex theoretical and social analysis by feminist scholars, who recognized how race matters influenced the social activism of the 1960s. The civil rights movement in the US introduced the idea that "Black was beautiful," and many other racialized persons felt inspired by the knowledge that they too were beautiful. By the end of the second wave of feminist scholarship and action, race, class, and other conditions of oppression were remapping feminist analysis, and race was a consideration many asserted must be at the forefront.

One of the defining characteristics of the third wave of feminism (1990 and onward) was anti-racist feminist theorizing. Feminist writers continue to challenge both theory and praxis when they are presented in such a way that they perpetuate racial exclusions. It is an energizing scholarship, as it presents new ways of thinking about the connections between race and gender as well as other sources of oppression (Dua 1999: 16). Scholars who work in the area have demonstrated that racialized women experience "femininity, sexuality, marriage, family and work differently" (Dua 1999: 16). More recent work has shown that racialized women experience violence differently and have higher rates of involvement with the criminal justice system (Monture, 2002a). However, the debate over the utility of legal reforms still exists. What is clear is that:

> ... structured inequality cannot be rectified by piecemeal reform and (re)socialization. Women's oppression can only be eradicated through systemic change that will not only challenge patriarchal ideologies and discourses but transform the bourgeois family form that sustains them. (Chunn, 1999: 256)

Thus, racialized women challenged the lack of representation of their experiences and concerns in the thinking and action of the feminist movement, and the knowledge that "woman" was not a homogenous category came to be accepted.

BIOGRAPHY, COLONIALISM, AND ABORIGINAL WOMEN

As has been briefly demonstrated above, feminist history was (and remains) both raced and erased and unnecessarily so. Similar patterns of racing and erasing can be observed in the structure of the discipline of sociology and its relationship with Aboriginal peoples.

It is important to understand race and gender in the Canadian context in terms of the relationship between newcomers and First Nations, as this is the foundation of present interracial relationships in this nation-state. In Canada, early relations between both colonial powers, the British and the French, and Aboriginal peoples were based on a mutual respect often determined by the needs of the colonizers, who, for example, sometimes needed the knowledge of Indigenous peoples about the land in order to survive and later required their military strength to help win colonial battles. But colonialism must never be viewed as a simple relationship or single historical period. It has nuances and complexities. Eventually, colonial relations required that First Nations were characterized as inferior (Monture-Angus 1999: 44–45) as this idea justified not only the taking of Aboriginal land but also child welfare and educational policies that resulted in the taking of Aboriginal children from their homes and placing them in residential schools where they were forbidden from speaking their languages or following their cultural practices. This idea of inferiority is still embedded in many stereotypes about Aboriginal peoples. And stereotypes are the process by which oppression is delivered. Colonialism must be seen as a living phenomenon, not an historical fact. The past impacts on the present, and today's place of Aboriginal peoples in Canadian society cannot be understood without a well-developed historical understanding of colonialism and the present-day trajectories of those old relationships.

Demographic study of Aboriginal peoples' social and economic situation in Canada has long demonstrated that they occupy the lowest rung of socio-economic status (Frideres 2000, Frideres and Gadacz 2001). Often, sociologists did not attempt to explain the social and economic ostracism of Indigenous populations, and the various forms of marginalization apparently were accepted as self-evident (Wotherspoon and Satzewich 1993). In some cases, sociologists viewed the socio-economic status of Aboriginal peoples as resulting from "personal deficiency." Particularly in the early period where the work of sociologists focused on social stability and social harmony, the impact of structural inequality including colonization was frequently viewed as a matter of individual failure or the inferiority of Aboriginal societies. This had significant consequences for any individual or collectivity that experienced marginalization, since sociological research and analysis provided no opportunity for transformative change.

The study of social problems has shifted from the "deficiency and disorder" model to a more critical one in which the focus is on "social, political, and economic conditions, and institutional arrangements, that produce social problems" (Bolaria 2000: 2). Colonialism is one of those arrangements that has produced multiple social problems for both Aboriginal peoples and Canadians. But even within this framework of critical sociology, vigilance is necessary to ensure that the sociological gaze remains inclusive. The positioning of contemporary critical social analysis should challenge rather than embed stereotypes, such as Indigenous inferiority, which sustain colonialism and other hierarchies of power.

When the analysis of race and gender is shifted beyond a demographic analysis to a place that gives space for the experience and meaning of socially and economically vulnerable groups, a more vibrant and reflective sociology emerges. This can be demonstrated through an examination of the life experiences, biographies, and narratives of Aboriginal women. One of the documented social problems within Aboriginal lives and Aboriginal communities is violence. Violence, here, is given the broadest definition beyond the outrage of physical assaults against women to include issues such as the failure to provide equal access to law and justice. As Freire (1970: 37) wrote: "With the establishment of a relationship of oppression, violence has *already* begun." The failure of Canadian law and justice systems to acknowledge the life circumstances of Aboriginal women provides a factual reference for sociologists and feminists to theorize more fully about issues of equal access to the protection and benefit of the law. More scholarly work has considered the experience of Aboriginal women who are accused of criminal acts and those who have been convicted and imprisoned (see Comack and Balfour 2004; Faith 1995; Hayman 2000; Monture 2002a) than those who have experienced victimization.

The brunt of the violence in communities is often borne by women and children. But when the definition of violence includes more than physical assaults—that is, the violence of oppression Freire noted—then it is clear that violence can be a general condition of life for an Aboriginal person and/or in Aboriginal communities. Despite the efforts of an individual to obtain an income and to secure employment and a violence-free home, she still experiences both physical and sexual violence immediately but indirectly through the lives of sisters and daughters and the suicides or loss of loved ones through addictions, violent deaths, and other disappearances (such as those occasioned by the criminal justice system and child welfare authorities).[2] The experience of violence, thus, has an inescapable quality that leaves Aboriginal women feeling traumatized and powerless.

In 2004, the Native Women's Association of Canada estimated that 500 Aboriginal women were missing or have been murdered in the last two decades in this country (Jacobs 2005).That same year, Amnesty International released their report, "Stolen Sisters," which documented ten of these cases of missing or murdered women. The researchers heard from relatives that police often responded with indifference to the missing persons reports that families filed. As a result, many of the murders have gone unsolved, and many of the missing women have not been found (Amnesty International 2004: 11, 24, 25). This is but one example of the lived experience of gender and racial disadvantage in Canada. It extends beyond the immediate experience of the families and leaves many Aboriginal women feeling both unsafe and not valued.

The violent deaths of Aboriginal women in Canada are not a recent phenomenon and should not be viewed as an emerging problem. In November 1971, Helen Betty Osborne was murdered in The Pas, Manitoba. Like many prairie towns, it was described by the Aboriginal Justice Inquiry of Manitoba as a town divided. There were separate spaces for whites and "Indians" (Hamilton and Sinclair 1991b: 2-3). Osborne was a high school student who was forced to move from her First Nation, Norway House, to continue her education, as the upper grades were not offered on the reserve. She wanted to be a teacher and was described to the Inquiry as "shy," "very kind," and a "good friend" (Hamilton and Sinclair 1991b: 5, 6). Eva Simpson, a classmate and close friend, described Osborne and their experience of moving to The Pas as follows:

> (S)he was hard working in school and she liked to have a good laugh I guess, and we tried to cover up our feelings because we were lonesome to go home and yet we knew we had no way to survive if we were in Norway House so we kind of hung around together ... We were very lonesome. (Hamilton and Sinclair 1991b: 6)

Osborne's murder went unsolved for almost 16 years; it was one of the incidents of police misconduct and inaction that lead to the establishment of the provincial justice inquiry in Manitoba (Hamilton and Sinclair 1991b: 2–3).

Reporting in 1991, 13 years before the estimate of missing and murdered women provided by the Native Women's Association of Canada, the Aboriginal Justice Inquiry of Manitoba concluded that the police were aware that white men were sexually preying on Aboriginal women and girls in The Pas but apparently concluded they "did not feel the practice necessitated any particular vigilance" (Amnesty International 2004: 1). The Commissioners wrote:

> It is clear that Betty Osborne would not have been killed if she had not been Aboriginal. The four men who took her to her death from the streets of The Pas that night had gone looking for an Aboriginal girl with whom to "party." They found Betty Osborne. When she refused to party she was driven out of town and murdered. Those who abducted her showed a total lack of regard for her person or her rights as an individual. Those who stood by while the

physical assault took place, while sexual advances were made and while she was being beaten to death showed their own racism, sexism and indifference. Those who knew the story and remained silent must share their guilt. (Hamilton and Sinclair 1991b: 98)

An examination of the death of Helen Betty Osborne leads to the recognition that racism can also regularly be a gendered experience. It demonstrates that racialized sexism and misogyny creates a unique and distinct experience for Aboriginal women.

Acknowledging this history and recognizing the damning conclusions of the Aboriginal Justice Inquiry of Manitoba, the logical question is: why is further action required for Aboriginal women to access the protection of both the law and police services? One answer is that the lives of Aboriginal women, which represent just one example of racialized experience in this country, are not valued in a way that engages active and respectful legal and police response.[3] This conclusion indicates one way in which the Canadian justice system does not provide equal access to the right to live safely.[4]

Within the Canadian criminal justice system, racialized sexual violence against Aboriginal women is not a phenomenon that is limited to the experience of policing. Razack analyzed the trial transcripts in the prosecution of the two white men, Steven Tyler Kummerfield (then 20 years old) and Alexander Dennis Ternowetsky (then 19) who murdered Pamela George in Regina in 1995. The charge laid was manslaughter and not murder. They received six-and-a-half-year sentences from Justice Ted Malone. Vice-Chief Lawrence Joseph of the Federation of Saskatchewan Indian Nations called the sentence "a gross miscarriage of justice" (Jacobs 2002: 6). On the night of her murder, Ternowetsky hid in the trunk of the car, and George was not aware that there were two men in it. When she found out about the deception—which could have been characterized as a lack of consent so that her death would have occurred during a criminal assault and the proper charge would have been first degree murder—she fought with the two men. They beat her so badly that the casket had to remain closed at the funeral (Jacobs 2002: 6). As the vice-chief indicated, the decision to charge with manslaughter and not murder, as well as the sentence, sent a clear message about the official version of the value of Aboriginal women's lives on the prairies.

A key conceptual framework in Razack's work is the manner in which "race is place" (Razack 2002: 1). Space is also connected to the way privilege is reproduced and affirmed by and for white men in the colonial context of Canada's history and present. From time to time, George did frequent marginalized space. She sometimes supported herself and her children through prostitution and frequented "the stroll" in Regina. This part of her social circumstances is a reflection of race, class, and gender conditions resulting from the dispossession of Saulteaux people from their land and resources.

Land and dispossession—Aboriginal nations only have the right to occupy marginal space, space the white settlers found undesirable—is a repetitive theme running through Canada's colonial history. This is often the unacknowledged backdrop to the story of land claims in this country.[5] Aboriginal peoples see clearly the connection between "race and space." The dispossession from land results in social and economic isolation, and this is causally connected to the violent deaths of Aboriginal women. Not as frequently acknowledged is how this dynamic of "race and place" bestows privilege. Razack explains:

> Moving from respectable space to degenerate space and back again is an adventure that confirms that they are indeed white men in control of who can survive a dangerous encounter with the racial Other and who have an unquestioned right to go anywhere and do anything. (Razack 2002: 127)

Acknowledging the relationship between race and space is a framework that allows scholars to examine beyond simple issues of dispossession and illuminate the ways in which white privilege continues to operate. This privilege is as much a consequence of colonialism as are the more well-known effects of socio-economic status, dispossession, and the trauma resulting from multiple experiences of violence that Aboriginal peoples carry.

CONCLUSION

Much of my writing has followed the tradition of my people, the Mohawk, and I have written using the first person. When I sat down to write this paper, I struggled with the subject position (Razack 1999: 290) I should take. Having recently come back to sociology after a 20-year hiatus, it was important for me to write in its academic style. This hiatus involved journeys through law school, law teaching, and the discipline of Native Studies. Sociology is a space where I have most often been able to bring my Indigenous self to my studies. As I contemplated this paper, I wanted to honour the fact that sociology was the academic place and the only academic place where I could feel at home.

But writing about something so personal at the distance the style of sociological writing demands was a very unsettling experience that at times was painful as I was forced to negotiate my anger and my fears repeatedly. I have walked with my children for the murdered and missing women. I helped to console the family and child of one of them. As Daleen was our neighbour, I had to explain to my children—the two younger ones were 9 and 11 at the time of her disappearance—what had happened to Faith's mommy. They struggled with the idea that a mother could vanish. I realized that they did not understand racial hatred but have learned it over the last two years. As I conclude this article, which really will never have a conclusion until Aboriginal women in this country are not being murdered and are not disappearing, it was important for me to put the pain and frustration, the hurt and the loss, and the lived experience of powerlessness and frustration back into the text. Razack (1999) has taken a similar approach.

Aboriginal youth are confronted with racialized experiences in Saskatchewan in the hockey rink, in school, in stores, and at the hands of police. I feel for the mothers and other family members of all the Aboriginal persons I have written about in this paper and cannot understand how they can come to terms with their losses and move forward with their lives. The way I have been touched is minimal compared to theirs. But, mostly, it is the self-silencing that academia demands that causes my concern that my work is devalued, a constant reality for an Indigenous scholar and a woman.

NOTES

1   It should be carefully noted that some stories are never written. These are the sacred stories of Indigenous nations, and they exist within an Indigenous system of "copyright." Care should be taken to understand the protocols involved. For a fuller discussion, please see Monture 2006.

2   As I completed the last edit on this paper, another body was found on the outskirts of Saskatoon. I wondered if it was my former neighbour and student Daleen Muskego Bosse who has been missing since May 2004. A few days later I learned it was the remains of another Aboriginal woman, Victoria Nashacappo, who had been missing since September 2002.

3   In the wealth of literature on policing and Aboriginal persons, little mention is made of the specific issues women confront. See, for example, Cummins and Steckley 1995. Although they discuss the deaths of a number of Aboriginal women, the importance of gender analysis is only briefly raised.

4   Knowledge and action should go hand-in-hand. For information on what you can do or how to support the Sisters in Spirit campaign, please go to: <http://www.sistersinspirit.ca/enghome.htm>.

5   The author is a citizen of the Mohawk Nation, Grand River Territory. Recently, a number of community members have taken back the land just beyond the reserve where a subdivision was being developed.

REFERENCES AND FURTHER READINGS

Amnesty International (Canada). 2004. Stolen Sisters: A Human Rights Response to Discrimination and Violence Against Aboriginal Women in Canada Ottawa: Amnesty International. <http://www.amnesty.ca/campaigns/sisters_overview.php>.

Aylward, Carol A. 1999. Intersectionality: Crossing the Theoretical and Praxis Divide. Paper presented at the Women's Legal Education and Action Fund (LEAF) Conference, Vancouver, BC, 2000.

Backhouse, Constance. 1991. *Petticoats and Prejudice: Women and Law in 19th Century Canada*. Toronto: Osgoode Society and Women's Press.

——. 1999. *Colour-Coded: A Legal History of Racism in Canada, 1900–1950*. Toronto: The Osgoode Society by University of Toronto Press.

Bannerji, Himani. 1999. A Question of Silence: Reflections on Violence Against Women in Communities of Colour. In Enakshi Dua and Angela Robertson, eds., *Scratching the Surface: Canadian Anti-Racist Feminist Thought*. Toronto: Women's Press. 261–77.

Bolaria, B. Singh (ed.). 2000. *Social Issues and Contradictions in Canadian Society*. Toronto: Thomson-Nelson.

Brodsky, Gwen, and Shelagh Day. 1989. *Canadian Charter Equality Rights for Women: One Step Forward or Two Steps Back?* Ottawa: Canadian Advisory Council on the Status of Women.

Canada, Standing Committee on Aboriginal Affairs and Northern Development. 2005. *Walking Arm-In-Arm to Resolve the Issue of On-Reserve Matrimonial Real Property.* Ottawa: Communications Canada.

Chang, Robert S. 2002. Critiquing "Race" and Its Uses: Critical Race Theory's Uncompleted Argument. In Francisco Valdes *et al.*, eds., *Crossroads, Directions, and a New Critical Race Theory.* Philadelphia: Temple University Press. 87–96.

Chilly Editorial Collective. 1995. *Breaking Anonymity: The Chilly Climate for Faculty Women.* Waterloo: Wilfrid Laurier Press.

Chunn, Dorothy E. 1988. Maternal Feminism, Legal Professionalism and Political Pragmatism: The Rise and Fall of Magistrate Margaret Patterson, 1922–1934. In R. Wesley Pue and Barry Wright, eds., *Canadian Perspectives on Law and Society: Issues in Legal History.* Ottawa: Carleton University Press. 91–117.

———. 1999. Feminism, Law, and "the Family": Assessing the Reform Legacy. In Elizabeth Comack, ed., *Locating Law: Race/Class: Gender Connections.* Halifax: Fernwood. 236–59.

Comack, Elizabeth, ed. 1999. *Locating Law: Race/Class/Gender Connections.* Halifax: Fernwood Publishing.

Comack, Elizabeth, and Gillian Balfour. 2004. *The Power to Criminalize: Violence, Inequality, and the Law.* Halifax: Fernwood.

Cummins, Bryan D., and John L. Steckley. 1995. *Aboriginal Policing: A Canadian Perspective.* Toronto: Prentice Hall.

Das Gupta, Tania. 1987. Unraveling the Web of History. *Resources for Feminine Research* 16(1): 13–15.

Devlin, Richard F. 1995. We Can't Go on Together with Suspicious Minds: Judicial Bias and Racialized Perspectives. *R.D.S. Dalhousie Law Journal* 18: 408–446.

Dickason, Olive Patricia. 2000. Toward a Larger View of Canada's History: The Native Factor. In David Long and Olive Patricia Dickason, eds., *Visions of the Heart: Canadian Aboriginal Issues.* Toronto: Harcourt Brace. 11–29.

Dua, Enakshi. 1999. Canadian Anti-Racist Feminist Thought: Scratching the Surface of Racism. In Enakshi Dua and Angela Robertson, eds., *Scratching the Surface: Canadian Anti-Racist Feminist Thought.* Toronto: Women's Press. 7–31.

Dua, Enakshi, and Angela Robertson (eds.). 1999. *Scratching the Surface: Canadian Anti-Racist Feminist Thought.* Toronto: Women's Press.

Eaton, Mary. 1994. Patently Confused: Complex Inequality and *Canada* v. *Mossop. Review of Constitutional Studies* 1: 203–245.

Faith, Karlene. 1995. Aboriginal Women's Healing Lodge: Challenge to Penal Correctionalism. *The Journal of Human Justice* 6(2): 79–104.

Freire, Paulo. 1970. *Pedagogy of the Oppressed.* New York: Continuum.

Frideres, James S. 2000. First Nations: Walking the Path of Social Change. In B. Singh Bolaria, ed., *Social Issues and Contradictions in Canadian Society.* Toronto: Thomson-Nelson. 195–227.

Frideres, James S., and Rene R. Gadacz. 2001. *Aboriginal Peoples in Canada: Contemporary Conflicts.* Toronto: Prentice Hall.

Gall, Gerald L. 2004. *The Canadian Legal System.* 5th ed. Toronto: Carswell.

Hamilton, A.C., and Murray Sinclair. 1991a. *The Report of the Aboriginal Justice Inquiry of Manitoba.* Vol. 1. Winnipeg: Queen's Printer.

—. 1991b. *The Report of the Aboriginal Justice Inquiry of Manitoba.* Vol. 2. Winnipeg: Queen's Printer.

Hannah-Moffat, Kelly, and Margaret Shaw (eds.). 2000. *Ideal Prisons: Critical Essays on Women's Imprisonment in Canada.* Halifax: Fernwood.

Hayman, Stephanie. 2000. Prison Reform and Incorporation: Lessons from Britain and Canada. In Kelly Hannah-Moffat and Margaret Shaw, eds., *Ideal Prisons: Critical Essays on Women's Imprisonment in Canada.* Halifax: Fernwood. 61–70.

Hocking, Barbara A. (ed.). 2005. *Unfinished Constitutional Business: Rethinking Indigenous Self-Determination.* Canberra, Australia: Aboriginal Studies Press.

Jacobs, Beverley. 2002. *Native Women's Association of Canada Submission to the Special Rapporteur Investigating the Violations of Indigenous Human Rights.* Ottawa: NWAC.

—. 2005. President's Address to the Annual General Meeting of the Native Women's Association of Canada. Yellowknife, NWT, September.

Jacobs, Beverley, and Mary Eberts. 2004. Matrimonial Property on Reserve. In MacDonald and Owen, eds., *On Building solutions for Women's Equality: Matrimonial Real Property on Reserve, Community Development and Advisory Councils.* Ottawa: CRIAW.

Jhappan, Rhada (ed.). 2002. *Women's Legal Strategies in Canada.* Toronto: University of Toronto Press.

Kirkness, Verna. 1987–88. Emerging Native Women. *Canadian Journal of Women and the Law* 2(2): 408–15.

Knuttila, Murray. 2005. *Introducing Sociology: A Critical Approach.* 3rd ed. Toronto: Oxford University Press.

Long, David, and Olive Patricia Dickason. 2000. *Visions of the Heart: Canadian Aboriginal Issues.* Toronto: Harcourt Brace.

Mills, C. Wright. 1977 [1959]. *The Sociological Imagination.* London: Oxford University Press.

Montoya, Margaret E. 2002. Celebrating Racialized Legal Narratives. In Francisco Valdes *et al.*, eds., *Crossroads, Directions, and a New Critical Race Theory.* Philadelphia: Temple University Press. 243–50.

Monture, Patricia. 1995. Introduction: Surviving the Contradictions: Personal Notes on Academia. In Chilly Editorial Collective, eds., *Breaking Anonymity: The Chilly Climate for Faculty Women.* Waterloo: Wilfrid Laurier Press. 11–27.

—. 2002a. The Lived Experience of Discrimination: Aboriginal Women Who Are Federally Sentenced. Paper prepared for CAEFS submission to the Canadian Human Rights Commission.

—. 2002b. On Being Homeless: One Aboriginal Woman's "Conquest" of Canadian Universities, 1989-98. In Francisco Valdes *et al.*, eds., *Crossroads, Directions, and a New Critical Race Theory.* Philadelphia: Temple University Press. 274–87.

—. 2006. Indigenous Legal Traditions: The Rights, Roles and Responsibilities of Indigenous Women. Paper produced for the Law Commission of Canada.

Monture-Angus, Patricia. 1999. *Journeying Forward: Dreaming First Nations Independence.* Halifax: Fernwood.

—. 1995. *Thunder in My Soul: A Mohawk Woman Speaks.* Halifax: Fernwood.

Moreton-Robinson, Aileen. 2005. Patriarchal Whiteness, Self-Determination and Indigenous Women: The Invisibility of Structural Privilege and the Visibility of Oppression. In Barbara A. Hocking, ed., *Unfinished Constitutional Business: Rethinking Indigenous Self-Determination.* Canberra, Australia: Aboriginal Studies Press. 61–73.

Mosher, Clayton James. 1998. *Discrimination and Denial: Systemic Racism in Ontario's Legal and Criminal Justice Systems, 1892-1961.* Toronto: University of Toronto Press.

Native Women's Association of Canada. 2004. Welcome to the Official Site of the Sisters in Spirit Campaign. <http://www.sistersinspirit.ca/enghome.htm>.

Pue, R. Wesley, and Barry Wright (eds.). 1988. *Canadian Perspectives on Law and Society: Issues in Legal History.* Ottawa: Carleton University Press.

Razack, Sherene. 1991. *Canadian Feminism and the Law: The Women's Legal Education and Action Fund and the Pursuit of Equality.* Toronto: Second Story Press.

——. 1999. R.D.S. v Her Majesty: A Case About Home. In Enakshi Dua and Angela Robertson, eds., *Scratching the Surface: Canadian Anti-Racist Feminist Thought.* Toronto: Women's Press. 281–94.

——. (ed.). 2002. *Race, Space and the Law: Unmapping a White Settler Society.* Toronto: Between the Lines.

Reber, Susanne, and Robert Renaud. 2005. *Starlight Tour: The Last, Lonely Night of Neil Stonechild.* Toronto: Random House Canada.

Smart, Carol. 1989. *Feminism and the Power of Law.* London and New York: Routledge.

Smith, Dorothy E. 1987. *The Everyday World as Problematic: A Feminist Sociology.* Boston: Northeastern University Press.

St. Lewis, Joanne. 2002. Beyond the Confinement of Gender: Locating the Space of Legal Existence for Racialized Women. In Rhada Jhappan, ed., *Women's Legal Strategies in Canada.* Toronto: University of Toronto Press. 295–332.

Stasiulis, Davia K. 2005. Feminist Intersectional Theorizing. In Valerie Zawilski and Cynthia Levine-Rasky, eds., *Inequality in Canada: A Reader on the Intersections of Gender, Race and Class.* Toronto: Oxford University Press. 36–62.

Tamanaha, Brian Z. 2001. *A General Jurisprudence of Law and Society.* New York: Oxford University Press.

Tanovich, David M. 2006. *The Colour of Justice: Policing Race in Canada.* Toronto: Irwin Law.

Tepperman, Lorne, and Michael Rosenberg. 1998. *Macro/Micro: A Brief Introduction to Sociology.* 3rd ed. Scarborough: Prentice Hall Allyn and Bacon Canada.

Turpel, Mary Ellen. 1991. Home/Land. *Canadian Journal of Family Law* 10(1): 17–40.

Turpel-Lafond, Mary Ellen. 1997. Patriarchy and Paternalism: The Legacy of the Canadian State for First Nations Women. In Caroline Andrew and Sandra Rodgers, eds., *Women and the Canadian State.* Montreal and Kingston: McGill-Queen's University Press. 64–78.

Valdes, Francisco, Jerome McCristal Culp, and Angela P. Harris (eds.). 2002. *Crossroads, Directions, and a New Critical Race Theory.* Philadelphia: Temple University Press.

Wotherspoon, Terry, and Vic Satzewich. 1993. *First Nations: Race, Class, and Gender Relations.* Toronto: Nelson Canada.

Wright, The Honourable Mr. Justice David H. 2004. *Report of the Inquiry into Matters Relating to the Death of Neil Stonechild.* Regina: Saskatchewan Justice.

Zawilski, Valerie, and Cynthia Levine-Rasky (eds.). 2005. *Inequality in Canada: A Reader on the Intersections of Gender, Race and Class.* Toronto: Oxford University Press.

CASES CITED

Andrews v. Law Society of British Columbia, [1989] 2 W.W.R. 289 (S.C.C.).

Derrickson v. Derrickson, [1986] 1 S.C.R. 285.

R. v. Conway, [1989] 1 S.C.R. 1659.

R. v. Kummerfield, [1998] 9 W.W.R. 619.

R. v. Kummerfield and Ternowetsky, [1998] 163 Saskatchewan Reports. 257.

R. v. R.D.S., [1997] 3 S.C.R. 484.

R. v. Williams, [1988] 1 S.C.R. 1128.

Symes v. Canada (1993), 110 D.L.R. (4th) 470.

11

NOTES TOWARDS ESTABLISHING A PROPERTY INTEREST IN ABORIGINAL CULTURE

Cheryl Suzack

In May 1997, six women from the Garden River Band of Ojibway First Nations appeared as plaintiffs before the Ontario Court of Appeal in a class action suit to recover an equal *per capita* distributive share of land claim monies from the settlement of the band's outstanding claim against the Canadian government for the unauthorized sale of land on Squirrel Island. The six women each sued on behalf of themselves and all women reinstated, and entitled to be reinstated, to band membership. Their claim included their minor-age children and all lawful wards of the women who might eventually become band members. The women argued that the chief and council erred in withholding settlement trust monies from them by reducing their settlement sums by amounts that they had received previously when they were deemed to have left the band and become "enfranchised" by reason of their marriage to non-status Indians (*Barry v. Garden River Ojibway Nation #14* [*Barry*] 1997: para. 2). They sought an injunction against the band restraining them from distributing any part of or the whole balance of $1 million that band members had voted to divide equally among themselves (para. 8). They contended that the band's decision to reduce their settlement sums by amounts already received, and its resolve to deny their children shares in the disbursement by reason of non-membership, violated section 15 of the Canadian Charter of Rights and Freedoms and constituted discrimination against them on the basis of sex, due to the failure of their right to equal treatment. They insisted that the band account for all distributions of settlement monies and, in the event that there was an insufficient balance to satisfy their claims, that the court order the band to trace the money and declare the band in violation of the Charter's equity principles (para. 3).

The Ontario Court of Appeal upheld the women's claim and set aside the lower court judgement. It found that the band breached its trusteeship duty of "fairness" and "standard of care" by imposing an arbitrary indebtedness against which it withheld the women's share of the financial settlement (*Barry* 1997: para. 47–48).[1] It also maintained the entitlement claims of the women's minor-age children by determining that the refusal of their membership was a consequence of their mothers' "lost status" and thus a violation of the "non-discriminatory clause in the Band's membership rules" (para. 26). It ordered the appellants and all those they represented entitled to an equal distributive part of the settlement monies, without deduction of any kind,[2] and permitted them to pre- and post-judgement interest until payment of their claim. The court chose not to address the issue of the women's insistence of violation of the equity principles under section 15 of the Charter.[3]

The *Barry* case, in its lower court ruling[4] and subsequent appeal, raises a number of complex questions concerning the nature of reinstated Aboriginal women's equality claims, their citizenship rights through band membership and the rights of their minor-age children, and the dilemma of ongoing sexual discrimination in the post-Bill C-31 legal and social climate in Canada. This essay begins with an overview of the issues raised by the case because I wish to claim it as an exemplary illustration of the problem of recognition that formerly enfranchised Aboriginal women face in attempting to transform their status as "reinstated members" into citizenship rights to band membership through colonial legal means. If, on the one hand, the reasoning of the trial judge and appellate court register an inexorable process of effacement that Jennifer Nedelsky (1997: 97) describes as the "infinite regress of specificity" through which "a hierarchy of power" is transposed into "a hierarchy of [social] values,"[5] then, on the other, the case discloses the salient problem of contemporary courts assessing and failing to validate the equality claims of reinstated Aboriginal women.[6] As the appellate case indicates, these women asserted a tangible interest in the distribution of monies that established the sovereign and fiduciary rights of the government towards First Nations communities, and they insisted that the band acknowledge their status as legitimate and entitled members to this claim. They thus expressed what might be considered a possessory interest in band membership that could be understood as a claim to title. This paper sets out to ask to what extent Aboriginal women's legal assertions of collective rights to Aboriginal cultural identity may be understood more generally as attempts to secure a claim to citizenship through property interests; that is, to what extent might Aboriginal women, through their reinstatement claims, be asserting a property interest in Aboriginal culture?

The *Barry* case represents one of several attempts by Aboriginal women to challenge the discriminatory provisions that have arisen through amendments to Indian Act legislation. Canadian case law records a series of decisions dating from the mid-1970s to the present in which Aboriginal women, who were disenfranchised from their Indian status for "marrying out," sued for reinstatement to Indian band membership under the terms of this act. According to the membership codes of the legislation,[7] Aboriginal women who married non-Aboriginal men were subject to the entitlement provisions of section 12(1)(b) which stated that "a woman who married a person who was not an Indian" was not entitled to be registered (Native Women's Association of Canada [NWAC] 1986: 7). This amendment had far-reaching implications for Aboriginal women, both historically and in the present, due to the enormity of losses they suffered as a consequence of their failure to retain band membership through colonial legal means. As Kathleen Jamieson notes in *Indian Women and the Law in Canada: Citizens Minus*, the loss of Aboriginal women's rights traversed the social, political, economic, and civil sphere, to stretch literally from "marriage to the grave":

> [t]he consequences for the Indian woman of the application of section 12(1)(b) of the Indian Act extend from marriage to the grave—and even beyond that. The woman, on marriage, must leave her parents' home and must dispose of any property she does hold. She may be prevented from inheriting property left to her by her parents. She cannot take any further part in band business. Her children are not recognized as Indian and are therefore denied access to [the] cultural and social amenities of the Indian community. And, most punitive of all, she may be prevented from returning to live with her family on the reserve, even if she is in dire need, very ill, a widow, divorced or separated. Finally, her body may not be buried on the reserve with those of her forebears. (Jamieson 1978: 1)

Although the membership provisions in section 12(1)(b) were amended in 1985 with the passage of "Bill C-31—An Act to Amend the Indian Act, R.S.C. 1985, c. 32 (1st Supp.)—which restored status to persons "who had previously lost status through sexual discrimination and enfranchisement," allowed for the "first-time registration of children whose parents lost status," and eliminated the sections of Indian Act legislation that subjected women to "gain or lose status through marriage" (NWAC 1986: 8), the cultural and political implications of section 12(1)(b) continue to determine the legal standing of Aboriginal women in relation to Indian status, the legal implications of which prompted Justice Hargrave of the Federal Court of Canada to remark in *Moses v. R.*, "the apparent heavy hand of the 1970 *Indian Act* is still very much with us" (*Moses* 2002: para. 5).

The passage of Bill C-31 has not only complicated a system for determining band membership already fraught with race and sex discriminations, a system premised on an earlier colonial government's attribution of distinct legal status for Aboriginal peoples, it has also ushered in a new social and political climate for Aboriginal/non-Aboriginal relations in Canada, especially for Aboriginal women. In the wake of Bill C-31, the question of Aboriginal women's historical and cultural disadvantages has been widely debated,[8] with important contributions to this discussion provided by Aboriginal legal scholars Sharon McIvor and Val Napoleon who focus on the implications of these changes for Aboriginal women. McIvor has been especially strategic in politicizing the language and normative assumptions of self-government claims by asserting that "the human rights of Aboriginal women—including their civil and political rights—[are] part of the inherent right to Aboriginal self–government under the terms of the Constitution Act, 1982," and in emphasizing "the rights of women" as "[cultural] rights which [they] have exercised since the formation of their indigenous societies" (McIvor 1995: 35). Val Napoleon has drawn attention to the divisive effects that Bill C-31 amendments have had for First Nations communities through "ongoing litigation over membership and status, and serious internal conflicts and divisions among First Nations over the meaning and implementation of Bill C-31" (Napoleon 2001: 119). She notes the proliferation of "divisive classes of Indians" that have come into effect to replace former categories, such as "status and non-status," with terms that signal the incongruities of these new designations of "'real' Indians and 'half' Indians, or simply, 'C-31s'" (119). She observes, with irony, the "success" of Bill C-31 "[in] shift[ing] the burden of discrimination from the Indian woman to her children and grandchildren." She also emphasizes the need for remedial efforts by First Nations communities to "identify the guiding principles of their own societies and begin rebuilding inclusive civic societies based on nations rather than bands." These strategies of reconstruction include "reclaiming geographically and culturally dislocated members and developing strategies for their constructive participation as citizens within their nations" (144).

The arguments raised by McIvor and Napoleon interrupt the gender-blindness of colonial legislation by illustrating how it creates new categories of gender inequalities. Yet, these scholars also suggest the problem of historical erasure that Aboriginal women confront in trying to account for their political exclusions. Without recourse to evidence of Aboriginal women expressing their rights historically, they have the challenging task of determining the legal grounds on which to argue for their civil and political rights. Moreover, scholars who look to the judiciary to advocate on behalf of historical injustice issues risk omitting recognition of the law's contradictory social effects.[9] For example, in *Moses v. R*, argued before the Federal Court of Canada, Yvelaine Moses contended that the provisions of Bill C-31, which allow her to be reinstated as an Indian but do not allow her children to be registered as Indians, discriminate against her on the basis of sex because of the continuing legal implications of section 12(1)(b), which guarantee that her brother's children may "enjoy Indian status" by benefit of his reinstatement (*Moses* 2002: para. 5). In that judgement, the court recognized that Moses sought to test the "specific provisions of the 1970 Indian Act, which, depending on sex, set a different test and outcome for who may and may not be registered as an Indian" (*Moses* 2002: para. 2). Although the court determined that the 1970 Indian Act continued to have legal implications under the revised amendments, it refused in its subsequent hearing in 2003 to grant standing to Moses's constitutional challenge to "the entire Indian registration scheme and the changes to that scheme brought about by what was Bill C-31, an act to amend the Indian Act" (*Moses* 2003: para. 18). The court "struck out" the application "as moot," stating that because Moses obtained "the status and rights she sought," it saw no reason to review further the registrar's decision with regard to her reinstatement (*Moses* 2003: para. 27).[10] It is also important to note here the foundational case brought by Sandra Lovelace before the United Nations Human Rights Committee in 1981, in which Lovelace challenged the "Indian Act provisions wherein a woman lost Indian registration upon 'marrying'" (Mann 2005: 17). As Michelle Mann notes, the Canadian "government responded to this international criticism with Bill C-31, restoring registration to these women" (Mann 2005: 17).

I would argue that these women's legal claims to Indian status and band membership not only signify both assertions of "existing Aboriginal and treaty rights," and "efforts to preserve their traditional culture and way of life" (McIvor 1995:

37), they also represent strategic "acts of communication" that give "notice" in order to create a "public record" before an interpretive community constituted by law (Rose 1985: 81). These claims may be understood as expressing a property interest in Aboriginal culture. As Carol M. Rose explains, in theorizing the relationships between "voice," "authority," and "possession": "Possession begins to look even more like something that requires a kind of communication, and the original claim to property looks like a kind of speech before an audience composed of all others who might be interested in claiming the object in question" (Rose 1985: 79).

Aboriginal women's challenges before a powerful judicial audience illuminate a range of strategies of voicing their attachments to Aboriginal culture in order to secure legal recognition of their rights; these include protests on behalf of "illegitimate children" deleted from band lists because illegitimacy precluded direct descent,[11] challenges under the Canadian Bill of Rights for unequal treatment before the law,[12] appeals in the interest of under-age children barred from admission to band schools,[13] and complaints against band administrators for removing reinstated family members and evicting them from the reserve.[14] These women assert their rights to affirmative sites of cultural identity represented by their reserve communities in order to secure access to a cultural homeland that provides cultural education, language retention, security through extended family relations, and social well-being by means of community membership. Mary Ellen Turpel explains the gender dimensions that attach Aboriginal women to these cultural rights which signify, through property, less in terms of the "commodity character of property" and more of conferring security through "economic, cultural and linguistic factors" (1991: 31, 32). In arguing for their rights to matrimonial property, she states:

> The significance of matrimonial property for aboriginal women must be understood in the context of what the reserve represents: it is the home of a distinct cultural and linguistic people. It is a community of extended families, tightly connected by history, language and culture. It is often the place where children can be educated in their language and with culturally-appropriate pedagogies. The reserve home is generally not that of a nuclear family—parents, grandparents, brothers, sisters and others in need will all share the home. The home may be the only access a woman and her children have to their culture, language and family. (Turpel 1991: 32)

The distinctive "rights as relationship" (Nedelsky 1993: 1) paradigm for Aboriginal women that Turpel defines as access to the reserve homeland has also been theorized more abstractly as "*sui generis* citizenship rights" by legal scholar Sákéj Youngblood Henderson. Henderson explains the "ecological order" of these rights through the "vision of belonging to the land, a people, and a family" in which "everyone and everything is part of a whole" (Henderson 2002: 425).[15] For Henderson, these rights are expressed through "kinship," a foundation of "Aboriginal sovereignty and order" that conveys each person's "right to a personal identity as a member of a community, but also [that person's] responsibilities to other life forms and the ecology of the whole" (425).

The horizontal configuration of Aboriginal rights that Henderson proposes through the "ecology of the whole" advances broader claims for the distinctiveness of Aboriginal constitutional and legal orders, yet the problem presented by reinstated Aboriginal women litigants whose rights to equality are determined through the paradox of part-for-whole differentiated citizenship troubles abstract theorizations premised on universalist claims. Feminist scholars have examined Indian Act legislation for positioning Aboriginal women's interests in conflict with those of band councils and the federal government[16] and have suggested that not only are Indian women the "most unequal in Canada" (Dingman 1973: 38) but also that their demands for Indian status stage the problem of "individual rights vs. cultural rights" (Miner 1974: 28). Their claims to equality and retention of Indian status are interpreted as attempts to extend their individual autonomy by retaining their rights to Indian status even after they have "married out." Their individual autonomy and purported social mobility, in this view, are perceived to undermine the political sovereignty of reserve communities (Miner 1974: 30).

However much Aboriginal women's legal assertions of their autonomy as rights-bearing citizens may be said to occur at the expense of their reserve communities, the patterns of effacement and misrecognition represented by these cases demonstrate the need for an expanded conceptualization of their social and legal agency and the more urgent concern for advocating politically on their behalf. This is especially so given what might be characterized as a "backlash" climate that undermines their claims to Aboriginal culture and identity by attributing social power and cultural autonomy to them when they pursue such claims through colonial legal means. These women are often accused by their communities of securing their individual rights at the expense of the collective cultural rights of the community. The contours of this discourse, in which the least powerful members of society are attributed with the most social mobility, have been theorized as articulating a turn in late capitalist social culture to a philosophy of rights that has precipitated a corresponding dependence on the ideal of autonomy. Lorraine Code explains this shift through the emergence of a controlling, even dystopian ideal in which the "confluence of autonomy with individualism" has produced a series of regulative principles, positive and negative, visible and invisible in effect. Code states, "the [perversion of autonomy] has generated a social-political-epistemic imaginary visibly peopled by the self-reliant rational maximizer, the autonomous moral agent, the disinterested abstract knower, and the rational economic man … [It has conversely generated] an invisible social imaginary peopled by less consequential, because less perfectly autonomous, Others" (Code 2000: 184). The tensions between these positions, Code contends, have facilitated a further opposition between "stark autonomy" and "a cluster of moral practices 'known as advocacy' in which representing, arguing for, recommending, acting, and engaging in projects of inquiry and support … become a denigratory slogan with which to dismiss research that appears to serve 'special' as opposed to universal interests" (185). For Code, the label of "special interest," understood more generally as "speaking for," conditions an individualistic discourse in which "the mythologized 'individual' achievements of autonomous man produce as their foil and negative counterexample a reinstituted subjection of women." "Women," Code contends, "come to be judged as unreliable knowers, women on welfare as failing to meet a standard of civic self-sufficiency, women seeking child support care ... [these women are considered] inadequately autonomous in assuming responsibility for their 'own' choices, all represented as 'entirely up to them'" (185).[17]

Writing from a similar standpoint of the concrete social other, Sophia Moreau contends that "analytic philosophers" concerned with the "valuing of equality" have constructed the social terrain within which to undertake ameliorative tasks by producing a discourse concerned with the "just distribution of resources" without correspondingly "broaching questions about the just distribution of political and social power" (Moreau 2004: 292). For Moreau, the dilemma of failing to conceptualize an analogous distribution of "social or political power" leaves unexamined "the wrong that is done by institutional structures and policies that stigmatize individuals, marginalize them, or perpetuate their domination by others" (292). Both Code and Moreau articulate the need for social justice work that attends to the vertical distribution of power relations and advocacy action within the state formation, advocacy that supports women yet does so without also reproducing the effects of adverse conceptions of autonomy. Their calls for "special interest research" that facilitates the "just redistribution of social power" represent an important contribution to a broader debate by feminist scholars concerned with "[t]he inequality of citizenship in democracy" and the creation of "new *kinds* of gender inequalities" (Stepan 2000: 62). Nancy Leys Stepan theorizes the challenge posed to expansive citizenship rights for women posed by the "same/different/equality/inequality" problem which, despite the "opening up of spaces of civil and political society in the post-1989 years," continues to structure how women advocate on behalf of political and economic rights yet paradoxically also informs why they fail to achieve "full citizenship rights":

> Against the theoretical universality and neutrality of individual rights, affirmative actions (or positive discrimination) on behalf of (some) women somehow looks suspect, because they seem to privilege the "difference" of sex. On the other hand, to claim to be the same as men often backfires against women, because some women—not all, not all the time—are different from (some) men. (Stepan 2000: 61, 63)

Contesting the normative principle of the "*universal individual* who was the bearer of equal political rights," Stepan argues for a conceptualization of gender difference as a "historically specific variable whose meaning and importance are recognized as potentially different in different historical contexts," and as a "biologically relevant" category that has significant consequences for women, because "gender exclusions" are "fundamentally political" (Stepan 2000: 63, 79). She situates "rights and citizenship" within the specificities of "individuals and groups" both to "avoid reducing complex populations to simple dichotomous groupings" and "to separate the argument about rights from any simple view of the natural." Her purpose is to engender a more complex understanding of historically situated gender identity that, on the one hand, provides a "deeper understanding of the significance of body differences to our political histories" and, on the other, "construct[s] a more adequate and inclusionary model of citizenship and rights" (80).

Stepan's exemplary argument about the uncertain political outcomes that follow from demands made on behalf of gender differences extends even further to contend that the dilemma of "same/different/equality/inequality" may not be understood simply as a "problem" within feminist theory, but may in fact emerge as a "tension within the heart of liberal theory itself"(Stepan 2000: 63). Her assertion resonates in important ways with the concern for liberal accommodation policies, "aimed at leveling the playing field between minority communities and the wider society," developed by Ayelet Shachar. Shachar conceptualizes the relationship between citizenship and rights in the multicultural state as engendering the "paradox of multicultural vulnerability," which arises when "well-meaning attempts to empower traditionally marginalized minority communities ultimately [...] reinforce power hierarchies within the accommodated community" (Shachar 2000: 386, 388). The adverse consequences of these policies are not reducible to what Shachar describes as "the prevailing yet misleading culture/rights dichotomy" (388), nor does the problem refer to "incidental rights violations" (393). Rather, what defines "multicultural vulnerability" are "systemic intragroup practices that adversely affect a particular category of group members" (393).

To situate the problematic within the terms raised by Stepan, "multicultural vulnerability" occurs when "respect for difference [...] become[s] a license for subordination" (Shachar 2000: 393). Shachar's examples of such disparities include struggles between the group and the state "to decide which entity, the state or the group, may control the terms and procedures validating marriage and divorce" (393). As she explains, "By punishing individuals who engage in 'illegitimate' marriage and childbirth, certain minority groups (as well as various states) use marriage and divorce regulations as a sociopolitical tool for policing a given collective's membership boundaries" (394). Addressing the disparities that arise from policies that support a "differentiated citizenship" model, Shachar proposes that differentiated citizenship policies begin with a "principle of jurisdictional autonomy" in order to establish that "neither the state nor the group can govern an arena of social life that matters greatly to both (such as education and family law) without the other entity's cooperation" (418). Her "joint governance" approach begins by recognizing that "group members can be attached to more than one membership community and subject to more than one legal authority," thus "prohibit[ing] the concentration of power in any one centre of authority." Such a model, Shachar argues, not only "enable[s] individuals to act as group members and as citizens simultaneously" but also "break[s] the vicious cycle of reactive culturalism whereby the group adopts an inflexible interpretation of its traditions precisely because of the perceived threat from the modern state" (418, 423).[18]

Shachar's analysis illustrates how "multicultural vulnerability" attaches to women through the problem of a "choice of penalties" scenario in which they must either "accept violation of their rights as citizens in intragroup situations as the precondition for retaining their group identities, or they must forfeit their group identities as the price of state protection of their basic rights" (Shachar 2000: 405). This either/or circumstance is an apt description of the dilemma facing formerly enfranchised Aboriginal women, especially in its assessment of the gendered social and political disadvantages provoked by their political struggle to act legally in order to secure citizenship rights and ethical relationships within Aboriginal communities. Law, as Shachar and others have shown, represents a crucial site not only for establishing categories of identity that are "necessary for both political theory and legal reasoning" (Nedelsky 1997: 97) but also for articulating the role legal interpretations play in creating meaning and deploying social power. As Vicki Schultz explains, "judicial decisions [...] simultaneously flow from and feed back into a larger stream of cultural understandings and practices" (Schultz 1992: 322). Legal decisions thus also influence the wider social reality they purport to describe. To combat assertions of unmitigated self-interest or victim status, which lead to a one-dimensional view of Aboriginal women's experience in the social sphere, feminist scholars need to embrace law's transformational capacity by understanding how they deploy legal statuses to "articulate and respond to rather than mask the systemic workings of gender subordination" (Mackinnon, cited in Brown 1995: 128).

The importance of this project to a politicized conception of Aboriginal women's identity has been argued by Sherene Razack who, in commenting on the relationship between law and gender analysis, observes pointedly that: "[I]n law, the issues that preoccupy women ... are all issues that emerge out of a male-defined version of female sexuality. Abortion, contraception, sexual harassment, pornography, prostitution, rape, and incest are 'struggles with our otherness,' that is, struggles born out of the condition of being other than male" (Razack 1990: 111, quoted in Monture-Okanee 1992: 241). To recover the experiences and legal claims of Aboriginal women in order to complicate the representation of their "otherness" in relation to dominant narratives of politics and government requires a more complex rationale of their legal rights and social identities. More importantly, a historical understanding of voice and agency in the texts of the colonial legal archive would complicate the work of recovering the motivations and presence of Aboriginal women, which has taken shape almost exclusively through an ethnographic focus on voice and experience.

Clara Sue Kidwell, in "Indian Women as Cultural Mediators," grapples with this problem of representation that expresses for her "the mythology of Indian women" stereotyped either "as the hot-blooded Indian princess" or "the stolid drudge plodding behind her man" (Kidwell 1992: 98). As she explains, "The[se] are not real people," but rather manifestations of "colonialism and manifest destiny" produced through their "associations with European men." Kidwell's ethnographic approach advocates that the cultural critic situate these women within their "own cultures" in order to "discover some clues to intention by examining the cultural context of women's lives" (98). This form of "indigenizing ethnography" (Findlay 2000: 310)[19] needs also to explain how to conceptualize these women's voices without configuring them either as autonomous agents, thus extracting them from their cultural context, or as abject objects, thus scripting them as powerless subjects. Moreover, without recourse to colonial legal texts that provide evidence of the distinct status Aboriginal women hold within the nation-state, the ethnographic approach remains dependant on "culturalis[t]" paradigms of social analysis (Hall 1980: 57).

What the colonial legal archive demonstrates is that under colonial law, given changing historical conditions of gender formation signaled by amendments to Indian Act legislation among other forms of legislation, Aboriginal women, by virtue of this colonial legal inheritance, occupy a different relation within the social formation from other communities of women constituted in part by differential identity narratives such as immigration, settler-colony status, and multiculturalism. Aboriginal women's historical identities thus need to be recognized as marking sites for the excavation of both presence and absence and for the recovery of social agency both raced and gendered in uneven ways.

I have been suggesting that colonial case law not only represents an important archive that illustrates Aboriginal women's struggles for legal recognition, but also that their "citizenship claims" tell a much more complicated story about their legal status, one that situates them both as objects of colonial policy through ongoing amendments to Indian Act legislation, and as subjects of political and legal discourses through the court system, in which their challenges to the legal definition of their social identities articulate a continuing attachment to Aboriginal cultural identity. In disclosing how Aboriginal women assert identity attachments across social factors such as family relations, property inheritance, and residency patterns, these judicial decisions show strategies of speaking for and claiming an interest in Aboriginal culture which might be interpreted as a *property interest*. As a remedial strategy that can account for claims to voice, status, and authority undertaken by Aboriginal women, property law may represent a legal category that both recognizes and legitimates their claims to culture. In the final pages of this essay, I will assess what principles within property law may be applied to claims on behalf of cultural identity and ask what may be the implications of claiming Aboriginal identity and culture as a property interest.[20]

The rationale for considering cultural identity as a property interest emerges in Cheryl Harris's ground-breaking critical race study "Whiteness as Property." Harris analyzes the relationship between concepts of race and property in order to consider "how rights in property are contingent, intertwined with, and conflated with race" (Harris 1993: 1714). Her purpose is to show how the normative distribution of social and political resources within the nation-state depends on "settled expectations" of tangible and intangible interests and property rights that express race hierarchies. She writes,

> Whiteness is not simply and solely a legally recognized property interest. It is simultaneously an aspect of self-identity and of personhood, and its relation to the law of property is complex. Whiteness has functioned as self-identity in the domain of the intrinsic, personal, and psychological; as reputation in the inter-

stices between internal and external identity; and, as property in the extrinsic, public, and legal realms. (1725)

Because "whiteness," according to Harris, "defined the legal standing of a person as slave or free," "whiteness" and the "right to white identity as embraced by the law" became synonymous with "a person's legal rights" (1726). The protection of these rights, Harris argues, shifted classical meanings of property from an understanding of things that are "valued" and to which a person has a "right," to "changing social relations" as the basis for "expectations":

> The relationship between expectations and property remains highly significant, as the law has recognized and protected even the expectation of rights as actual legal property. This theory does not suggest that all value or all expectations give rise to property, but those expectations in tangible or intangible things that are valued and protected by law are property. (1729)

Harris's purpose in theorizing the law's protection of "settled expectations to whiteness as a property interest" is to demonstrate that the American court system's hostility to "affirmative action" marks a historical continuation of existing inequality that naturalizes the "current distribution of power, property, and resources" (1778). Yet, in exposing the law's ability to express dominant conceptions of "rights," "equality," "property," "neutrality," and "power," Harris also suggests how property law may be reconfigured to advocate on behalf of subordinate groups' claims. She argues, "Rereading affirmative action to de-legitimate the property interest in whiteness suggests that if, historically, the law has legitimated and protected the settled expectations of whites in white privilege, de-legitimation should be accomplished not merely by implementing equal treatment, but by *equalizing* treatment among the groups that have been illegitimately privileged or unfairly subordinated by racial stratification." While Harris acknowledges that "equalizing treatment" varies according to the "extent of privilege and subordination," her ultimate goal is to shift practices of exclusion toward practices of redistribution: "[E]xposing the critical core of whiteness as property as the unconstrained right to exclude directs attention toward questions of redistribution and property that are crucial under both race and class analysis" (1780).

Property law, as Harris shows, represents one of the most complex arenas of common law that regulates tangible and intangible rights regarding use and access to things. In its determination of "ownership principles," that is, in establishing a system of social relationships in which "contested resources are to be regarded as separate objects each assigned to the decisional authority of some particular individual" and in reifying in law the rights and obligations of individuals to establish property interests in an object by "occupying, using, or modifying [an] object" and by withholding this liberty from other people (Waldron 1999: 6, 7), property law represents a powerful political medium that establishes both conscious and unconscious normative social practices and rights expectations. Its pervasive role in structuring interactions between people—"of power, responsibility, obligation, respect, and caretaking," not to mention "commodification, alienation, and exploitation" (Nedelsky 1993a: 345, 351)—promotes such widespread and authoritative appeal to forms of "power, autonomy, and liberty" that its unavoidable use in negotiations between colonial governments and indigenous peoples has prompted Paul Nadasdy, speaking of Aboriginal land claims in the Canadian subarctic, to conclude that:

> It comes down to a question of power. If, in the context of the modern nation-state, aboriginal people wish to claim some form of control over their lands, and they wish those claims to be seen as legitimate by others, they must [...] speak 'in a language that power understands.' ... And that language is, and has long been, the language of property. (Nadasdy 2002: 253)

Property law, however, not only provides a means to secure norms and objectives that we value as important through a constitutive legal category, it also raises crucial questions for scholars interested in issues of unequal or differential treatment. In adjudicating between claims to entitlement, "property," according to Nedelsky, "is both a source of power and an indicator of what counts as power. It is a marker of what is valuable, and a means of claiming what is valuable to the owner" (Nedelsky 1993a: 347). Moreover, it provides a delegation of "sovereign power, giving owners an ability, limited but real, to induce others to do what the owner wants"; thus, Joseph Singer explains, "defining an interest as a property right provides the owner some protection from having that interest confiscated by the state. The state therefore both defines property rights and defines limits on its ability to alter the definition and distribution of property rights. Property is derived from sovereignty, but also creates sovereignty" (Singer 1991: 51). By expanding the realm of property law to the sphere of Aboriginal women's citizenship claims, social justice advocates can achieve a two-fold method of intervention on their behalf: on the one hand, they could situate claims to identity within the framework of property law, thereby expanding the range of "purely" juridical solutions to legal disputes as they are presently resolved; and, on the other, they could deploy legal means to achieve socially just ends, not least of which would facilitate a positive view of Aboriginal women's historical and legal agency as rights-bearing citizens.

It is safe to argue that ideas about property law are shifting and that property rights remain key components of the underlying structure within which Aboriginal rights and Aboriginal title are adjudicated.[21] John Borrows has argued that property rights have long been an area of concern and transformation in negotiations between Aboriginal and non-Aboriginal communities. He writes, "[T]he allocation of property rights between Aboriginal and non-Aboriginal people [remains] an issue that has occupied the inhabitants of what is now Canada for over 300 years" (Borrows 1992: 180). He also contends that First Nations people have long held discernable interests in land "to preserve their culture and way of life" (206). By recognizing the relational attachments that Aboriginal women hold with regard to Aboriginal culture and identity, and by situating their citizenship claims to band membership under the rubric of property rights, where "property rights are understood as rights, privileges, powers, and immunities that govern the relative power of individuals over tangible and intangible things" (Underkuffler 2002: 16), we can expand property law to incorporate a remedial purpose that recognizes Aboriginal women's rights to cultural identity as particular objects that are "important for human flourishing or human personality" (28). More importantly, we can retain a notion of individual protection that is a paramount feature and purpose of property rights (32), but deploy this concept to support legal and ethically just ends.[22]

NOTES

1   The court noted the differential treatment of the women reflected in the band's decision to reduce the women's shares by sums received previously through enfranchisement payments. Because such indebtedness to the band did not also apply to members who owed sums for "water use charges"—these members were allowed to collect full shares—the court found that, "Since all beneficiaries received full shares, the Band should have advanced full shares to the adult appellants" (*Barry* 1997: para. 36).

2   "Enfranchisement payments" represent monies that were eligible to Aboriginal persons who became enfranchised or otherwise ceased to be members of a band. On leaving, these persons were "entitled to receive one *per capita* share of money held in the band's capital fund, one *per capita* share of money held in the revenue fund, and if they were in a treaty area, 20 years treaty annuity" (*Barry* 1997: para. 19). The case indicates that "Each of the adult appellants had received an aggregate sum of less than one thousand dollars at the time she lost status" (*Barry* 1997: para. 19).

3   Appellate court Judges Finlayson, Charron, and Rosenberg stated, "We are of the opinion that this case can be decided on the basis of well recognized principles relating to the fiduciary obligations of any person who undertakes to make a *per capita* distribution of a fund of money entrusted to that person's care. Accordingly, we find it unnecessary to address the appellants' submissions regarding s. 15 of the Charter of Rights and Freedoms" (*Barry* 1997: para. 49).

4   As the lower court decision illustrates, the women's entitlement to equal treatment depended on their status as reinstated members relative to the status of women who had not "married out" and who retained band membership at the time of the disbursement. Their "restored status" was thus held to be an advantage that the trial judge considered remedied through the band's decision to withhold their settlement sums. The trial judge argued, "In my opinion, what the Band Council did was fair and equitable and restored the financial interests of the restored C-31 Indian women to equal that of their Indian sisters who had not been deprived of their status and who had not received earlier distribution" (*Barry* 1997: para. 31). Similarly, because the "restored status" of the reinstated women also attached to the membership standing of their minor-age children, the trial judge determined that "[t]here was nothing sinister or deliberate in the sense of lacking fairness [n]or was there anything legally improper in the decision to make distribution on December 17 and 18, 1987 to those persons who were, at the that time, recorded in the records of the Garden River Band of Ojibways as members of the Band" (*Barry* 1997: para. 30). He thus found that the women's children, "could not claim membership based on any of the enumerated classes found within the Band's membership rules" (*Barry* 1997: para. 29) and therefore were not entitled to participate in the disbursement of funds.

5   Nedelsky is here citing the work of Carol Gilligan who demonstrates how the language of rights mediates between sites of social inequity through a process of legal abstraction and displacement. The specific example from Gilligan's *In a Different Voice* reads as follows, "Transposing a hierarchy of power into a hierarchy of values, he defuses a potentially explosive conflict between people by casting it as an impersonal conflict of claims" (Gilligan 1982: 32 cited in Nedelsky 1997: 97).

6   The women's failed Charter challenge represents one manifestation of this ambiguous outcome.

7   Indian Act, R.S.C. 1970, c-I-6.

8   Debate about the implications of Bill C-31 legislation for Aboriginal women is extensive. For useful background information, see NWAC 1986. Status of Women Canada also has an excellent report by Michelle M. Mann which examines the paternity implications of the revised status provisions (see Mann 2005). Val Napoleon (2001) provides an especially thoughtful consideration of how to rebuild Indigenous communities according to an inclusive civic model of nationhood that moves beyond establishing identity according to "blood" and "ethnicity."

9   Pierre Bourdieu reminds us that the social practices of law function like a "field" whose specific logic is determined by two factors: the "power relations which give it its structure and which order [its] competitive struggles" and "the internal logic of juridical functioning which constantly constrains the range of possible actions, and, thereby, limits the realm of specifically juridical solutions" (1987: 816). Bourdieu explains the process of "narrowing" the interpretative range of legal texts to the legal question at hand as arising from the "extraordinary elasticity of texts," which enables "jurists and judges ... to exploit the polysemy or the ambiguity of legal formulas by appealing to such rhetorical devices as *restrictio* (narrowing) ... [and] *extensio* (broadening) ... to maximize the law's elasticity" (Bourdieu 1987: 827). Given the court's dissimulation of Aboriginal women's rights in *Barry* 1997 that I have outlined above, dispensing with the uneven and unpredictable terrain of the historical risks participating in the law's tendency toward historical presentism, which narrows the juridical field to socially normative representations of Aboriginal women's agency, in spite of the doctrine of precedent. My point here is that we need access to the historical record to complicate our understandings of Aboriginal women's agency over time in order to demonstrate how these women have asserted their rights under changing social conditions and in order to understand what political strategies they have employed. Case law, as I hope to have shown, represents one site that records a historical presence in need of recovery.

10 The remedy provided by the court restored status to Moses under section 6(1)(f) of the Indian Act, R.S.C. 1985, c. I-5, which provided registration to "an individual where both parents were or could have been registered as Indians" (2003: para. 6). Moses had previously been registered under section 6(2), which "allows a person with one registered or registerable parent to be registered as an Indian" (2002: para. 2). Moses's claim of sex discrimination resulted from the differential categories of reinstatement under which her status and that of her brother were restored. As the illegitimate son of a registered Indian, Moses's brother's status was restored under provision 6(1)(a), a category of reinstatement that did not extend to "an illegitimate daughter of a registered Indian" (2002: para. 8). Moses claimed that "her registration as an Indian [was] in some way provisional or conditional" (2002: para. 14), but the court argued that "Ms. Moses could not gain more benefit were she [...] registered, for example, under section 6(1)(a)" (2002: para. 15).

11 *Two-Axe v. The Iroquois of Caughnawaga Band Council* [1978].

One of most significant amendments for Aboriginal women, known commonly as the "double mother" rule, stipulated that persons ineligible to be registered included the following: "(iv) a person born of a marriage entered into after the coming into force of this Act and [who] has attained the age of twenty-one years, whose mother and whose father's mother are not persons described in paragraph (a), (b), (d), or entitled to be registered by virtue of paragraph (e) of section eleven [of the Indian Act], unless, being a woman, that person is the wife or widow of a person described in section eleven" (Venne 1981: 319). Kathleen Jamieson illuminates both the gendered dimensions of these discriminatory provisions and their continuation of the historical erasure of Aboriginal women *as* Indians in history. She states, "What this means is that a child of a white or non-registered Indian mother and grandmother, who therefore has only one-quarter Indian Act 'blood,' is to be deprived of Indian status on reaching the age of 21. This section would apply to children whose maternal grandmothers were voluntarily or involuntarily enfranchised Indians, or Indians who were left off band lists or lived in the US for over five years, or Métis who might have three Indian grandparents, as much as the children of white women. This has in fact clearly nothing to do with biology or Indian 'blood' but everything to do with the *Indian Act*" (Jamieson 1978: 60).

12 *A.G. of Can. v. Lavell—Isaac v. Bédard* [1974].

13 *Courtois v. Canada (Department of Indian and Northern Affairs)* [1991].

14 *Ermineskin Band Council v. Registrar of Indian and Northern Affairs and Quinn et al.* [1987].

15 I would like to thank Diana Brydon for drawing this aspect of Henderson's argument to my attention.

16 See, for example, Green 1985 and Jamieson 1978.

17 For a sobering illustration of the social and economic disadvantages that follow for women who cannot acquire property or entitlements, see Rose 1992. In Rose's account, women's failure to act in their self-interest to protect their rights as citizens and to make "substantial investments in influencing either culture or politics" engenders reciprocal effects in the political arena that have ideological and material consequences for them. She writes, "The law, for example, may deny her the capacity to own her own property, to be employed outside the home, to contract on her own, to obtain an education, or to form associations outside her father's or her husband's family" (Rose 1992: 451). Her point, made through an analysis of analytical "games," is that the hard-won rights that women have come to expect through rights-based activism cannot be left to the impulses of legal culture for their protection and continuing validity.

18 I have not done justice to the complexity and vision of Shachar's argument which, in its engagement with citizenship and family law, shows unavoidably how women are the bearers of injury through remedial state policies that attempt to negotiate between the group, the state, and the individual, yet fail to take into account the difference that gender makes to intragroup dynamics. For an especially thoughtful engagement with this problem for indigenous women and a companion piece to the above cited article, see Shachar 1998.

19 For a complex analysis of the narrowing of the cultural field within which an Indigenous resistant presence could be marked given the confines of settler-colony colonialism, see Findlay 2006.

20 "Aboriginal culture" is an especially tricky term to decipher in judicial decision-making. Michael Asch demonstrates the "ethnocentric logic" that mediates assessments of Aboriginal culture through "scales of social organization" (2000: 127) which then become crucial to "test[s]" for determining "whether or not a culture had Aboriginal rights" (2000: 121). Peter W. Hutchins and Anjali Choksi argue against judicial conceptions of Aboriginal culture that entail "reconciling contemporary non-Aboriginal society with a museum diorama approach to Aboriginal societies" (2002: 248). Bearing in mind the aspects of reification that follow from elevating a "particularism to universal status" (Stepan 2000: 4), I have attempted to define Aboriginal culture according to the attachments expressed by Aboriginal women who assert their rights and those of their children to cultural education,

language retention, and extended family relations. I understand that there are setbacks to the reification of cultural identities as civil rights through law. For a persuasive discussion of the problem of advancing cultural rights as a "logical [...] extension of traditional civil rights protections for racial minorities" (Ford 2002: 41), see Ford 2002.

21 Michael Asch seems to me to argue this point when he states:

> In legal theory, the Supreme Court's decision in *Delgamuukw* is largely deriva-
> tive in that it builds on the logical frame already outlined in *Van der Peet*. The
> primary innovation is the incorporation of a property right into the constel-
> lation of features that may be asserted as rights by indigenous peoples. The
> property right is differentiated from other rights on the basis of a distinction
> made between Aboriginal title and Aboriginal rights. According to the Court, it
> is possible for a society to have an institution sufficiently similar to a property
> right, yet sufficiently distinct to be considered an Aboriginal right. If so, the
> Aboriginal society may make a claim to Aboriginal title. (Asch 2000: 132)

22 I would like to thank Len Findlay, Lily Cho, Lisa Surridge, members of the Department of English Faculty Colloquium (2005–06), and participants in the "Law, Culture, Humanities Symposium" (Carleton University 2005), especially Sheryl Hamilton and Logan Atkinson, for their essential feedback and helpful comments in the development of this paper.

REFERENCES AND FURTHER READINGS

Asch, Michael. 2000. The Judicial Conceptualization of Culture after *Delgamuukw* and *Van der Peet*. *Review of Constitutional Studies* 2: 119–37.

Borrows, John. 1992. Negotiating Treaties and Land Claims: The Impact of Diversity within First Nations Property Interests. *Windsor Yearbook of Access to Justice* 12: 179–234.

Bourdieu, Pierre. 1987. The Force of Law: Toward a Sociology of the Juridical Field. Trans. Richard Terdiman. *Hastings Law Journal* 38(July): 814–53.

Brown, Wendy. 1995. *States of Injury: Power and Freedom in Late Modernity*. Princeton, NJ: Princeton University Press.

Code, Lorraine. 2000. The Perversion of Autonomy and the Subjection of Women: Discourses of Social Advocacy at Century's End. In Catriona Mackenzie and Natalie Stoljar, eds., *Relational Autonomy: Feminist Perspectives on Autonomy, Agency, and the Social Self*. New York: Oxford University Press. 181–209.

Dingman, Elizabeth. 1973. Indian Women—Most Unequal in Canada. *Chatelaine* (February): 38, 39, 78–83.

Findlay, Len. 2000. *Always Indigenize!* The Radical Humanities in the Postcolonial Canadian University. *ARIEL* 31(1/2): 307–26.

——. 2006. Spectres of Canada: Image, Text, Aura, Nation. *University of Toronto Quarterly* 75(2): 656–72.

Ford, Richard T. 2002. Beyond "Difference": A Reluctant Critique of Legal Identity Politics. In Wendy Brown and Janet Halley, eds., *Left Legalism/Left Critique*. Durham and London: Duke University Press. 38–79.

Gilligan, Carol. 1982. *In a Different Voice: Psychological Theory and Women's Development*. Cambridge, MA: Harvard University Press.

Green, Joyce. 1985. Sexual Inequality and Indian Government: An Analysis of Bill C–31 Amendments to the *Indian Act*. *Native Studies Review* 1(2): 81–95.

Hall, Stuart. 1980. Cultural Studies: Two Paradigms. *Media, Culture and Society* 2(1): 57–72.

Harris, Cheryl I. 1993. Whiteness as Property. *Harvard Law Review* 106(8): 1707-91.

Henderson, James (Sákéj) Youngblood. 2002. *Sui Generis* and Treaty Citizenship. *Citizenship Studies* 6(4): 415–40.

Hutchins, Peter W., and Anjali Choksi. 2002. From *Calder* to *Mitchell*: Should the Courts Patrol Cultural Borders? *Supreme Court Law Review* 16 (2nd ed.): 241–83.

Jamieson, Kathleen. 1978. *Indian Women and the Law in Canada: Citizens Minus*. Canada: Minister of Supply and Services.

Kidwell, Clara Sue. 1992. Indian Women as Cultural Mediators. *Ethnohistory* 39(2): 97–107.

MacKinnon, Catharine A. 1989. *Toward a Feminist Theory of the State*. Cambridge and London: Harvard University Press.

Mann, Michelle M. 2005. Indian Registration: Unrecognized and Unstated Paternity. Ottawa: Status of Women Canada. <http://www.swc-cfc.gc.ca/pubs/pubspr/066240842X/200506_066240842X_e.pdf>.

McIvor, Sharon D. 1995. Aboriginal Women's Rights as "Existing Rights." *CanadianWoman Studies/Les Cahiers de la Femme* 15(4): 34–38.

Miner, Valerie. 1974. Indian Women and the Indian Act. *Saturday Night* 89 (April): 28–31.

Monture-Okanee, Patricia. 1992. The Roles and Responsibilities of Aboriginal Women: Reclaiming Justice. *Saskatchewan Law Review* 56: 237–66.

Moreau, Sophia Reibetanz. 2004. The Wrongs of Unequal Treatment. (May). University of Toronto, Public Law Research Paper No. 04-04. <http://ssrn.com/abstract=535622>.

Nadasdy, Paul. 2002. "Property" and Aboriginal Land Claims in the Canadian Subarctic: Some Theoretical Considerations. *American Anthropologist* 104(1): 247–61.

Napoleon, Val. 2001. Extinction by Number: Colonialism Made Easy. *Canadian Journal of Law and Society* 16(1): 113–45.

Native Women's Association of Canada [NWAC]. 1986. Guide to Bill C-31. 2–41. <http://www.nwac_hq.org/reports.htm>.

Nedelsky, Jennifer. 1993a. Property in Potential Life? A Relational Approach to Choosing Legal Categories. *Canadian Journal of Law and Jurisprudence* 6(2): 343–65.

——. 1993b. Reconceiving Rights as Relationship. *Review of Constitutional Studies* 1: 1–26.

——. 1997. Embodied Diversity and the Challenges to Law. *McGill Law Journal* 42(1): 91–117.

Razack, Sherene. 1990. Speaking for Ourselves: Feminist Jurisprudence and Minority Women. *Canadian Journal of Women and the Law* 4(2): 440–58.

Rose, Carol M. 1985. Possession as the Origin of Property. *University of Chicago Law Review* 52(1): 73–88.

——. 1992. Women and Property: Gaining and Losing Ground. *Virginia Law Review* 78(2): 421–59.

Schultz, Vicki. 1992. Women "Before" the Law: Judicial Stories about Women, Work, and Sex Segregation on the Job. In Judith Butler and Joan W. Scott, eds., *Feminists Theorize the Political*. New York and London: Routledge. 297–338.

Shachar, Ayelet. 1998. Group Identity and Women's Rights in Family Law: The Perils of Multicultural Accommodation. *Journal of Political Philosophy* 6(3): 285–305.

——. 2000. The Puzzle of Interlocking Power Hierarchies: Sharing the Pieces of Jurisdictional Authority. *Harvard Civil Rights-Civil Liberties Law Review* 35: 385–426.

Singer, Joseph. 1991. Sovereignty and Property. *Northwestern University Law Review* 86(1): 1–56.

Stepan, Nancy Leys. 2000. Race, Gender, Science, and Citizenship. In Catherine Hall, ed., *Cultures of Empire*. Manchester: Manchester University Press. 61–86.

Turpel, Mary Ellen. 1991. Home/Land. *Canadian Journal of Family Law* 10: 17–40.

Underkuffler, Laura S. 2002. *The Idea of Property: Its Meaning and Power*. London: Oxford University Press.

Venne, Sharon Helen. 1981. *Indian Acts and Amendments 1868–1975, An Indexed Collection*. Saskatoon: University of Saskatchewan Native Law Centre.

Waldron, Jeremy. 1999. Property Law. In Dennis Patterson, ed., *A Companion to Philosophy of Law and Legal Theory*. Malden, MA: Blackwell. 3–23.

CASES CITED

A.G. of Can. v. Lavell—Isaac v. Bédard [1974] 2 S.C.R. 1349. Supreme Ct. of Can. 27 August 1973.

Barry v. Garden River Ojibway Nation #14 [1997] 100 O.A.C. 201. 17 April 1997.

Canada. *Indian Act*, R.S.C. 1970, c-I-6.

Courtois v. Canada (Department of Indian and Northern Affairs) [1991] 1 C.N.L.R. 40.

Ermineskin Band Council v. Registrar of Indian and Northern Affairs and Quinn et al. [1987] 2 C.N.L.R. 70. Federal Ct. of Canada. 5 June 1986.

Lovelace v. Canada. 1981. Communication No. R.6/24, U.N. Doc. Supp. No. 40 (A/36/40) at 166.

Moses v. R. [2002] F.C. T. 1088. 15 October 2002.

Moses v. R. [2003] F.C. 1417. 26 November 2003.

Two-Axe v. The Iroquois of Caughnawaga Band Council [1978] 1 CNLB 9. Quebec Superior Ct. 9 December 1977.

12 | RACIALIZATION OF GENDER, WORK, AND TRANSNATIONAL MIGRATION

The Experience of Chinese Immigrant Women in Canada

Guida Man

INTRODUCTION

Canada is a country comprised of immigrants. The most recent statistics show that foreign-born Canadians now make up 18.4% of the population. Since 1987, the Chinese have constituted the largest immigrant group entering the country, exceeding one million people for the first time in Canadian history. Chinese immigrants come to Canada under a range of immigration designations, and almost three-quarters of the Chinese population in Canada lived in either Toronto or Vancouver in 2001 (Chui, Tran, and Flanders 2005: 26).

Since the 1980s, neo-liberal and neo-conservative strategies of restructuring, privatization, and deregulation have aggravated labour market conditions by lowering wages and fostering precarious employment, i.e., employment that is part-time, insecure, and contingent (Vosko 2006). This has a polarizing effect on the interaction of gender, race, ethnicity, and class. Previous studies have found that minority women and immigrant women of colour have a propensity to be channelled into "secondary" employment, and they tend to stay in it through their working career (Hiebert 1997). These studies also found that immigrant women have higher unemployment rates than Canadian-born women (Boyd 1992; Badets and Howatson-Lee 2000) and that Chinese immigrant women are susceptible to underemployment or unemployment (Man 2004a; Preston and Man 1998; Salaff 2000).

Recent studies on Chinese immigrant women have found an increasing prevalence of transnational practices amongst Chinese immigrant families (Man 1995a, 1997, 1998). A survey conducted in the Richmond area of Vancouver in the 1990s, for example, found that 40% of the Chinese from Hong Kong lived in transnational arrangements (SUCCESS, 1991). There is a growing literature that addresses globalization and the transnational migration of Chinese immigrants, and this literature focuses particularly on gender differences (Man 2000, 2002, 2006; Kobayashi, Preston, and Man 2006).

This chapter addresses the racialization of gender, work, and the transnational migration of Chinese immigrant women in Canada. It is divided into four sections. In the first, I discuss the theoretical underpinning of my research. In the second, I illustrate the historical development of transnational Chinese families in Canada, and in the third I describe Chinese communities and recent Chinese immigrant women in Canada. Finally, in the fourth section, I present empirical data to illustrate transnational migration and the experience of recent Chinese immigrant women in contemporary Canadian society. I conclude with recommendations.

THEORETICAL DEBATES

The theoretical underpinning of this chapter is informed by anti-racist feminist theories, as well as debates on transnational migration. In the last two decades, Canadian feminist scholars have been attempting to develop an inclusive feminist theory by examining the connections of racism, sexism, and classism in analyzing social inequality (e.g., Agnew 1996; Bannerji 1987; Creese and Stasiulis 1996; Calliste and Dei 2000; Das Gupta 1987; Dua 2000; Ng and Estable 1987; Razack 1998; Stasiulis 1990). These anti-racist feminist scholars challenge mainstream feminist theorizing about the common experience of women and the universal and essentialist notion of gender.

Anti-racist feminism is an attempt to theorize the interconnections between race, class, and gender (Stasiulis 1990). Ng (1993), for example, conceptualizes race, gender, and class as socially constructed relations that have to do with how people relate to each other through productive and reproductive activities. Jhappan argues that "the interaction of gender and race [and class] produces a distinct result not captured by analyzing race and gender [and class] separately" (Jhappan 1996, as quoted by Satzewich 1998: 42). Dua defines anti-racist feminist thought as "a body of writing that attempts to integrate the way race and gender function together in structuring social inequality" (Dua and Robertson 1999: 9). Other Canadian anti-racist feminist scholars have demonstrated how race and gender have to be located in the history of a colonial, white settler formation (e.g., Brand 1984; Monture-Okanee 1992; Stevenson 1999).

As well as anti-racism feminism, this chapter is also informed by literature on transnational migration. Migration has previously been conceptualized as immigrants transplanting themselves from their country of origin into the culture and society of another country (Handlin 1973; Takaki 1993). This has, however, been challenged. The intensification of globalization, and the rapid and mass movement of people, has transformed the meaning of migration. In recent years, the concepts of transnationalism, transnational processes, and transnational migration have emerged. Transnationalism implies the flow of capital, labour, and cultural knowledge production between nations and regions (Grewal and Kaplan 1994), and transnational processes are considered by some social scientists (e.g., Knight and Gappert 1989) as part of the globalization phenomenon, "marked by the demise of the nation-state and the growth of world cities that serve as key nodes of flexible capital accumulation, communication, and control" (Schiller et al. 1995: 49). Transnational migration is "the process by which immigrants forge and sustain simultaneous multi-stranded social relations that link together their societies of origin and settlement" (Schiller *et al.* 1995: 48). This conceptualization, however, has its limitations: it overemphasizes human agency without addressing the structural processes that enable—or disable—immigrants to hedge linkages across national boundaries. Hence, there is an absence of power relations in this configuration.

Speaking from a post/neo-colonial perspective, Spivak describes transnationalism as "Eurocentric migration, labour export both male and female, border crossings, the seeking of political asylum, and the haunting in-place uprooting of 'comfort women' in Asia and Africa" (Spivak 1996: 245). Other social scientists also posit that those immigrants who experience social exclusion in the host country are most likely to maintain strong ties to their home countries (Basch *et al.* 1994; Goldring 1998; Hanlon and Kobayashi 1998).

In the last decade, there has been a proliferation of literature written on transnationalism and transnational migration. Social science research increasingly addresses intersections of gender and transnational migration (e.g., Mahler 1999; Levitt 2001; Wong 2003), and a body of work by transnational feminist scholars has begun to explore borders and the linking of spaces and bodies, particularly in the realms of asylum seekers, prostitution, and refugees (Razack 2000). Little research, however, has paid attention to the transnational migration of skilled immigrants or has explored the intersections of racialization, gender, and transnational migration of these immigrants.

I adopt the conceptualization that transnationalism is not a new phenomenon but rather a new form of colonialism and that transnational migration is one form of globalization. I draw on anti-racist feminist theory by examining how race/racialization interact with gender and class in complex ways to define the position of majorities and minorities in society and to create separate yet interrelated hierarchies. Race/racialization, gender, and class are not fixed, distinct, unitary entities that operate separately. Rather, they have to be conceptualized as intersecting, fluid, dynamic, and subject to changes in time and space. As concrete social relations that can be discovered in the everyday world of experience, they converge, diverge, and change over time as people's relations to productive and reproductive activities change within a given society (Ng 1993).

In this chapter, I intend to accomplish the following:

» illustrate that "transnational migration" is not a recent phenomenon but rather one that is rooted in the historical processes of colonization and racialization in Canada; and

» elucidate that new immigrants adopt transnational familial arrangements/ practices in separate geographical spaces (such as China and Canada) in response to gendered and racialized institutional processes in the new country and as a strategy to negotiate paid work and household responsibilities in the context of globalization and neo-liberal/neo-conservative restructuring. I demonstrate how the latter has polarizing effects in the relations of gender, ethnicity, race, and class. I argue that Chinese immigrant women's productive and reproductive labour, and their contradictory nature, is paramount in the social construction of transnational families and communities.

COLONIALISM, RACISM, AND THE HISTORICAL DEVELOPMENT OF TRANSNATIONAL CHINESE FAMILIES IN CANADA

The historical development of transnational Chinese communities in Canada harkens back to the 19th century, when Western imperial powers such as the UK and France were seeking international hinterlands for exporting their finished products and for extracting raw materials and cheap labour to be used for capitalist production. The invasion of China by Western powers determined to open that country for trade through gunboat policy resulted in unequal treaties that infringed on its territorial and economic integrity. These European powers were successful in securing trading and other concessions from the Chinese government (Chan 1983).

The defeat of China by the British in the Opium Wars, followed by the British bombardment of China with opium grown in its colonies and cheap cotton goods made with machines, aggravated opium addiction in China. It also ruined the local cotton industry, turning China into the "sick man[sic] of the east." By the mid 19th century, economic instability, internal strife, and natural disasters had devastated the Chinese peasantry. Impoverished peasants joined the bandits who roamed the countryside. A large number fled China for Southeast Asia, Africa, Latin America, and North America, and a significant number of Chinese were sold as coolies or labourers on plantations and mines (Chan 1983).

Canada's nation-building project in the 19th century was based on a white settler society construct (Stasiulis and Jhappan 1995) which imposed racialized and gendered discriminatory policies on the Indigenous peoples and other "undesirable groups" belonging to "inferior races" such as the Chinese, South Asians, and African blacks. The demand for cheap labour to fulfill the country's expansionist projects, however, allowed some restricted immigration from Asia.

The discourse of racial purity and the fear of miscegenation regulated relationships between white women and racialized men through strict policies (Valverde 1991, 1992). At the same time, the Canadian state's racist, sexist, and class discriminatory immigration policies toward racialized groups hampered the entrance of Asian women (Dua 2000). The presence of these racially "inferior" women was defined as "polluting" the nation, and their ability to reproduce future generations of "non-preferred races" was taken as a threat to the whiteness of the nation (Thobani 1999). This overt racialization of immigrants was maintained into the 1960s and 1970s.

In 1886, soon after the Canadian Pacific Railway was completed and cheap Chinese labour was no longer needed, a head tax[1] of $10 was levied on Chinese labourers wishing to enter Canada. This tax was increased to $500 in 1904.[2] This exorbitant amount was intended to deter poor labourers from coming, since many could not afford it. However, some managed to secure a loan from relatives by promising to repay the money from their earnings.

The racist and sexist climate offered few opportunities for Chinese female workers at that time. Without the promise of a job, most Chinese women could neither afford to pay the head tax nor were they able to secure a loan. As a result, the head tax was effective in preventing many Chinese women from entering the country. The few who managed to come to Canada laboured as indentured workers under contract in order to repay their head tax and travel expenses, with a high rate of interest. Some women worked for more than ten years before they could pay off their loans (Adilman 1984a: 47). Furthermore, with an average wage of $25 a month (Chan 1983: 129), most Chinese labourers could not afford to bring their wives and children to Canada. Predictably, when the head tax was increased to $500, the number of Chinese immigrants, and Chinese women in particular, was significantly reduced.

The imposition of the head tax demonstrated the institutionalization of the interaction of race, class, and gender in state policies. It was not uniformly imposed on all Chinese. Prior to 1900, certain classes, such as merchants, diplomats, and university students, were allowed to enter Canada without paying it. And by 1900, the government included under the class of exempt Chinese the wives and children of clergymen and merchants (Con *et al.* 1982). Wealthy merchants, whose businesses were favoured by the Canadian government, were allowed to come into Canada with their wives and children exempt of the head tax, while poor labourers had to pay a heavy tax for themselves and their family members. Many could not afford to pay for their wives and children. Hence, many labourers' wives had to endure a lonely widow-like existence in China while their husbands lived in a bachelor society in Canada.

The opportunity for Chinese wives to unite with their husbands in Canada depended on the wealth and status of their husbands. It has been reported that between 1911 and 1923, a larger number of Chinese merchant wives entered Canada (Sedgewick 1973: 129; Con *et al.* 1982: 94).[3] Most of these women were middle-class wives of Chinese merchants who operated small businesses such as laundries, restaurants, tailor shops, and grocery stores.

The racist exclusion of Chinese immigrants culminated in 1923 with the passing of the Chinese Exclusionary Act,[4] which excluded all Chinese from entering Canada. This act was not repealed until 1947. As we have seen, due to gendered and racialized regulations, there were few Chinese women in Canada. Prior to the imposition of the Chinese Exclusion Act, those Chinese labourers who could afford it, returned to China to take a wife. However, due to the exorbitant head tax, many could not afford to bring their wives and children to Canada. Some labourers were able to visit their families in China when they had saved up enough money. After 1923, however, such visits were not possible. At the same time, during the exclusionary period between 1923 and 1947, special privileges to enter Canada were given to wealthy Chinese merchants and their wives, who would otherwise have been prevented due to their race. They were useful in procuring trade for Canada and therefore were accorded preferential treatment *vis-à-vis* their poor counterparts. However, the number of qualified merchants was small, and the number of wives who belonged to this elite class was minuscule.

The Chinese Exclusionary Act effectively stopped Chinese women and men from coming into Canada. Thus, the ratio of immigrant Chinese women to immigrant Chinese men remained disproportionate; for example, it was approximately 1:28 in 1911, 1:15 in 1921, and 1:12 in 1931. Even as late as 1951, the ratio was 1:3.7 (see Li 1988: 61, Table 4.2). With few Chinese women around, families could not be formed or settled permanently in Canada, and the Chinese population was effectively kept low. This has had a tremendous effect on Chinese family structure and community development. By 1925, there were only 1,000 families out of an adult Chinese population of approximately 40,000 in the whole of Canada, most of which were families of merchants (Adilman 1984b: 67). In 1941, there were 20,141 "separated" or "transnational" families in the Chinese community in which the husbands resided in Canada while the wives remained in their home country. In the same year, there were only 1,177 "intact" Chinese families in Canada in which both the husbands and wives resided here (see Li 1988: 67, Table 4.4). The number of "transnational" Chinese families remained high even as late as 1951.[5] Chinese women and their children from China were not able to join their husbands in Canada until the 1970s. Some women were in their sixties when they were finally allowed to immigrate, and they had been separated from their husbands for over 40 years (Li 1988; Chinese Canadian National Council 1992).

For many families of Chinese labourers, transnational networks among family members started in the early periods of Chinese immigration. A transnational separate sphere of production and reproduction was created. Chinese wives stayed in China with their children, while their labourer husbands worked in Canada. These male Chinese labourers typically sent letters and remittances to China to support their wives and children. Money was also sent for the construction of the family home or for rebuilding the village (see, for example, Li 1988; Chinese Canadian National Council 1992).

CHINESE COMMUNITIES AND RECENT CHINESE IMMIGRANT WOMEN IN CANADA

Members of ethnicized and racialized communities have typically been regarded by social scientists as a single homogenous entity to whom little differences have been accorded. Within racialized communities, there is also a tendency to ignore gender and class issues in order to promote greater group solidarity in response to racism in the larger society.

Recent Chinese immigrants come mainly from three geographical areas: Mainland China, Hong Kong, and Taiwan. From 1981 to 2001, an average of 35,400 immigrants arrived from these three sources yearly (Chui, Tran, and Flanders 2005). However, Chinese immigrants also come from Vietnam, India, Mauritius, South Africa, and many other places in the world. Hence, they have diverse social, cultural, economic, and political locations; they have different sexual orientations; and they speak various dialects. Chinese women are also different from Chinese men in their experiences. Thus, the Chinese in Canada are fragmented into different communities, with divergent gender and sexual politics; geo-political affiliations; national allegiances; and linguistic, religious, and cultural practices. As a result, they struggle against each other for limited resources and recognition, but they do come together as a group in their struggle against racism and other forms of oppression, most notably, in petitioning the Canadian government to redress the historical racist imposition of the head tax and the Chinese Exclusionary Act on Chinese immigrants.

Today, the Chinese in Canada are highly educated. Nearly one-third, whether foreign-born or Canadian-born, have a university education. The latter is in comparison to 18% among the general population. Despite their high level of education, however, the employment rate of Chinese Canadians lags behind the general population (71% versus 80%, respectively). The most recent immigrants are also the most vulnerable to unemployment. Although the employment rate of Canadian-born Chinese men and women is comparable to all Canadian-born men and women, prime working-age Chinese who immigrated in the 1990s had an employment rate of 61% as compared to 80% for the total population (Chui, Tran, and Flanders 2005: 29).

Recent Chinese immigrants entered under the highly selective Canadian immigration policy that targets highly educated and skilled professionals and wealthy entrepreneurs and investors. The state assumption behind the new immigration initiatives is to bolster Canada's competitiveness in the global market place with a skilled, fluid, and flexible labour force that would provide Canada with a "competitive advantage" (Brecher and Costello 1994; and see Chapter 8 of this volume) in this post-industrial era of globalization. Inevitably, most of those allowed to enter the country are skilled professionals or entrepreneurs, regardless of where they come from. Once in Canada, these immigrants experience difficulties in finding employment that is commensurate with their qualifications and experience. Employers' requirements of Canadian experience and the lack of recognition of international degrees render immigrants' previous experiences in their home countries obsolete. The costly and laborious process of recertification of internationally trained professionals also deters many from re-entering their professions.

RACIALIZATION OF GENDER AND THE RECENT INVOLVEMENT OF TRANSNATIONAL MIGRATION

As outlined previously, transnational migration is neither a new phenomenon nor the purview of rich business migrants, as asserted by such scholars as Aiwa Ong (1999). Poor and racialized men and women have always had to adopt transnational familial practices historically, and they continue to do so in contemporary Canadian society. For example, women from the Philippines and the Caribbean who work as domestics in Canada have had to leave their families behind in their home country in order to care for the families of their employers (Arat-Koc

1990; Cohen 1999; Bakan and Stasiulus 1997). More recently, Chinese immigrant women have resorted to transnational migration as a strategy to cope with the contradictory demands of their work in the labour market and in the home.

In this section, I present empirical data from my research to illustrate Chinese immigrant women's experience of transnational migration. The methodology I use for this research is called institutional ethnography. It is also known as the "standpoint of women" developed by Dorothy Smith (2006, 1987). Rather than treating Chinese immigrant women as objects of the study, I place them as the subject of the research and start from their actual, everyday world. But an ordinary daily scene has "an implicit organization tying each particular local setting to a larger generalized complex of social relations" (Smith 1987: 153). The researcher's task is to explore and explicate the social relations and social organization that have an impact on the subjects' world, but which are organized extra-locally in the historical, social, political, cultural, and economic spheres, and which are not necessarily visible to the subjects.[6]

The Sample

This study focuses on two groups of Chinese immigrant women in Canada: those from Hong Kong and those from Mainland China (People's Republic of China). The two groups lived in different social, political, and economic systems. While Hong Kong immigrants were recent post-colonial subjects who lived in a capitalist system under British rule for 99 years, immigrants from Mainland China lived under a fast-changing communist regime. In general, the Hong Kong immigrants tend to be more affluent, and the Mainland immigrants tend to be more highly educated.

The data are derived from focus group interviews and individual in-depth interviews of two groups of Chinese immigrant women: four from Hong Kong and eight from Mainland China. In addition, in-depth interviews with women who were engaged in precarious employment in Toronto—both from Mainland China and from Hong Kong—have been included.

All the women are married and have at least one child. Those from Mainland China all have either a BA or MA, while only half of the Hong Kong women have a BA. Two have tertiary education. Those from Hong Kong are older, ranging from 29 to 53, while those from China range in age from 25 to 36.

I use a purposive sampling method. Chinese women from Hong Kong and Mainland China who immigrated to Canada with their families since 1998 were selected with the assistance of a community agency that services these immigrants, the Centre for Information and Community Services. The interviews were taped, translated, and transcribed, and the data analyzed.

Analysis

While transnational families developed in the early period of Chinese immigration were comprised of poor labourers and their families, many more recent transnational families include skilled professionals in their home country.

It has been demonstrated that immigrant women's employment opportunities in the new country are contingent on labour market conditions and gendered and racialized institutional processes, as well as the demands on their reproductive labour in the home (Man 2002, 2004a, 2004b). Similarly, the women in my study encountered considerable difficulties in finding employment commensurate with their qualifications. Like other immigrant women, their entry into Canada as dependants of their husbands labelled them officially as non-participants in the labour market. Since female education and skills are generally undervalued due to gender biases (Arat-Koc 1999), Chinese immigrant men are typically the principal applicants as they are able to garner more points under the highly selective point system of the immigration policy. Hence, the immigration process reproduces and structures inequality within the family by rendering one spouse (typically the wife) legally dependent on the other (Ng 1993).

This gender differentiation in immigration status (principal applicant versus dependants) indicates the structural difference between male and female immigrants with regard to their occupation and status in their home country as well as in Canada. Despite being labelled as "dependants," recent Chinese immigrant women are highly educated and skilled, and have worked in professional or administrative positions in Hong Kong or in Mainland China. There are some women who are the principal applicants, particularly if their skills fit the labour market demands in Canada at the time of their application (e.g., computer programmers in the 1990s). However, these women are few and far between.

In the last 20 years, a series of gender equality policies have elevated the labour market position of women in Hong Kong. As well, labour shortages mean that women with higher education or possessing professional skills have a very good opportunity to participate in productive processes. Many of the Hong Kong women in the study have benefited from the booming economy and the shortage of skilled professionals such as teachers, nurses, computer programmers, and administrators in the 1970s and 1980s, and therefore they were able to enjoy successful professional careers with good benefits.

In China, women participation in the work force was enforced through various social policies and legislation, which led to China having one of the highest rates of women participation (Da 2003). In fact, dual-earner families appeared in China earlier than in the West. Mainland Chinese women, particularly those who were new university graduates during the Cultural Revolution, became the "new blood" of China and were able to enjoy tremendous opportunities with very promising career paths in their homeland.

In Canada, while 20% of husbands were the sole earners in families in the 1990s, during the 1970s almost 50% of families depended on the husbands' income alone (Baker 2001). Although the second-wave feminist movement helped to improve women's educational and employment opportunities, in recent years globalization and the effect of restructuring, privatization, and deregulation has aggravated labour market conditions, which has had a polarizing effect in the relations of race, ethnicity, gender, and class. Many skilled immigrants are not able to reinsert themselves in the Canadian labour market due to the devaluation of international credentials and experience. Skilled immigrant women, in particular, often have to take on menial positions, with low pay and no job security. This process is variously called "proletarianization," "deprofessionalization" (Flynn 1999) or "deskilling" (Man 2004a; Mojab 1999), and it is considered by some scholars to be rooted in the nature of capitalism (see, for example, Mojab 1999; Shields 1996). Despite immigrant women's high education and prior experience, they are treated as a source of cheap labour and relegated to precarious employment.

Here is how one woman from China talked about her labour market experience. She was a medical doctor in China, but her qualifications and previous work experience were not recognized in Canada. As a result, she was being channelled into part-time, menial, and insecure positions:

> I was a doctor [in China] for 8 years. During the first days after I came here I worked 4 days at a garment factory... The salary was paid by piece, about 10 cents per piece. The first day I only made 200 pcs ... Later I got a telemarketing job in a friend's company and was paid $7.50 per hour. Now during the weekends I'm still working for this company, although I got another part-time job in a physiotherapy clinic as an assistant, $10 per hour. My job is to prepare medical material and do some cleaning. (MLFG:N3)

Hong Kong women also experienced similar difficulties in their job search. A woman in the Hong Kong focus group who was a financial analyst in Hong Kong found that her less than perfect English language fluency, coupled with institutionalized processes which did not recognize her credentials and her previous experience, made it very difficult for her to find a job in the same field as the one she was in prior to emigration.

> ... I have tried very hard to find a job in bank after I immigrated to Canada. But it was so difficult. I remember once I was interviewed for a position in a bank. I believe I performed quite well at the interview. I thought I would be successful. But it turned out that the bank didn't take me. They said that my qualifications and everything else were a good fit for the job. The only thing was I didn't have relevant Canadian experience ... my experience in Hong Kong was not recognized at all. (HKFG:N2)

Immigrant professionals whose labour market skills are not desired in Canada at a particular period of time have to declare at the point of entry to Canada that she or he will not practice her/his profession in Canada. Since female skills (e.g., elementary teaching) are typically not as desirable as male skills (e.g., engineering) in patriarchal societies such as Canada, immigrant women's employability in the new country is doubly jeopardized. The cumulative effects of gendered and racialized institutional processes in the form of state policies and practices, professional accreditation systems, employers' requirement for "Canadian experience," and racism and sexism in the labour market marginalize immigrant women's participation in the paid labour force. As a result, they are being channelled into menial, part-time, insecure positions or becoming unemployed. Increasingly, immigrant men whose skills are not in demand are also subjected to unemployment and underemployment. The channelling of immigrants into deskilled and precarious positions has tremendous impact on their familial relationships and household arrangements.

Furthermore, there is a dire shortage of regulated affordable childcare facilities for working mothers in Canada. Despite the efforts of feminist activists and childcare advocates, successive neo-liberal and neo-conservative governments have ignored women's needs and have pushed childcare back to the private sphere to be dealt with by individual parents, usually the mothers (Luxton and Reiter 1997; Waring 1999; Luxton 1990; Michaelson 1988; Lero 2003).

Like other women, Chinese immigrant women are responsible for bearing the bulk of the day-to-day housework and caring responsibilities. As a result, they are constantly juggling the contradictory demands of paid work and domestic labour. Some women, particularly those from China, find that the lack of subsidized daycare for their children makes it impossible for them to cope with the competing demands of paid work and childcare and prevents them from obtaining full-time work.

Because Chinese immigrant women are often limited to precarious work with low wages and no job security, both partners in many immigrant households have to engage in paid work in order to make ends meet. Some immigrant women from Mainland China, who have to negotiate the contradictory demands of childcare and paid work and who have had difficulties obtaining subsidized childcare, have resolved to send their children back to China to be taken care of by their grandmothers or other family members. This is what a Mainland woman in her early thirties, who was a medical doctor in China and whose husband was an engineer, told me when she made her decision:

> When we first came, I was pregnant with my daughter ... We were unemployed. Then my husband's friend took us to the factory where he worked, and we both got jobs in the factory. After my daughter was born, I couldn't work because I couldn't get subsidized childcare. So we decided to send my daughter back to China to be taken care of by her grandma.... (MLI:N6)

The gendered and racialized labour market has made it difficult for immigrant women to obtain positions that enable them to utilize their prior knowledge and experience. In order to pursue better job opportunities, this woman resorted to transnational mothering:

> I worked as an investment analyst during the first four years in a state-owned company, and then as a financial analyst in the China office of a foreign-invested

Fortune 500 company. I already got the CGA license when I was in China. The most recent year after I came here I had my first baby, so I didn't start to look for a job. Two months ago, I sent my child back to China and began my job search. It took me one and a half month to get a job as a bookkeeper and receptionist ... (MLFG:N7)

While occurrences of transnational mothering are prevalent among Mainland Chinese immigrants, the Hong Kong Chinese experience a transnational familial arrangement popularly called "astronaut families." Astronaut families are ones in which one spouse (typically the husband) returns to the home country for paid employment, leaving the other spouse (typically the wife) in Canada to obtain citizenship and to care for the children. The astronaut flies back to Canada periodically to visit the family, and, sometimes, the family returns to Hong Kong for a visit (see Man 1995a, 1995b). However, tales of isolation and loneliness leading to marriage breakdown are not infrequent.

One astronaut wife told of how the lack of employment opportunities, social capital, and social networks in Canada has prompted her spouse to return to Hong Kong:

You need connections to get an interview. But he doesn't have any business contact here. He was getting really desperate ... One day, he got a phone call from his former colleague who found him a very good job with good salary... So he went back, leaving me here alone with the children. (HKI:N2)

Some women from Hong Kong who were discouraged by their underemployment and unemployment in Canada have resolved to return to Hong Kong to find work, along with their husbands, leaving their children alone in Canada. These children are popularly known as "parachute children" or "satellite children" as they are literally being dropped off in a faraway place.

One couple planned their transnational family arrangement before immigration as a response to the uncertainty of finding a secure and permanent position in Canada. They travelled back and forth between Canada and Hong Kong to accommodate their work and household circumstances, leaving their children in Toronto to be taken care of by their grandmother. However, the separation eventually took its toll, and the couple eventually decided to curtail their transnational arrangements. Here is what the wife told me:

... So, after we had landed, we left behind our two kids [with my mother in Toronto] ... We flew back to Hong Kong to continue our career. In those days, every six months, we would fly back to Canada to stay for a while and then went back to Hong Kong to work. We had led this kind of life for sometime ... After long-time struggle, we decided to have my husband stay behind in Hong Kong to continue his work and I came to Canada by myself ... My husband eventually came back to Canada for good. (HKFG:N4)

Another couple was torn by having to care for two sets of aging parents in different geographical spaces. Their struggle is not unlike that of the "sandwich generation" in Canada, who are looking after children while their aging parents live in a different city or province.

> ... Besides, my mother-in-law and father-in-law are very old. We live with them. We don't feel comfortable leaving them behind if we go back to Hong Kong ... Well, if I do decide to go back to Hong Kong, it would be because I want to take care of my parents. You know, as a Christian, I always regret that I can't physically be with them all these years after I have immigrated to Canada. (HKFG:N3)

For many Hong Kong and Mainland Chinese women, the deterioration of their employment opportunities and material conditions in the new country prompted them to adopt transnational migration practices as a way to continue their productive and reproductive processes, that is, maintaining employment and the raising of children in separate geographical spaces through transnational familial networks and linkages.

My study has demonstrated that transnational migration practices of Chinese immigrants in Canada are gendered and racialized processes, complicated by the contradictory demands of immigrant women's paid work and household responsibilities in the context of globalization and economic restructuring, as well as racialized and gendered institutionalized and organizational processes, cultural practices, and immigrant women's own agencies. Transnational familial arrangements can have serious and adverse consequences. The long-term effect of the prolonged separation of children from their parents, and husbands from wife and children, are not known and certainly warrants investigation.

CONCLUSION

It is evident that, for the Chinese community, the transnational separate sphere of work and family is not a recent phenomenon. My study demonstrates that new immigrants, like their predecessors at the turn of the century, adopt various transnational migration practices, such as familial and child-rearing arrangements, as a strategy to negotiate paid work and household work in a racialized and gendered environment in the new country.

Over a century ago, Chinese immigrants conducted transnational familial arrangements as a response to racist and sexist institutional policies and practices. More recently, gendered and racialized institutional processes in the form of state policies and practices, professional accreditation systems, employers' requirement for "Canadian experience," and labour market conditions have channelled recent immigrant women into precarious employment or to becoming unemployed. This transforms their household arrangements, prompting family members to adopt transnational separate spheres of productive and reproductive activities.

Although the women were unemployed and underemployed in Canada, and experienced difficulties in their household arrangements, they refused to be portrayed as merely passive victims of the social, economic, and political processes of Canadian society. Despite the inhospitable reception, the Chinese immigrant women in my study consider themselves active participants of Canadian society. Many of the highly educated professional Mainland Chinese women participated in the paid labour force in precarious and menial employment in the new country in order to make ends meet. Others declined jobs that were exploitative. They are also vocal in their criticism of racism and sexism in the labour market. In light of the difficulties they confront, they have articulated several program and policy recommendations: the provision of flexible and affordable subsidized childcare programs to accommodate women's needs; the development of profession-specific English language courses, e.g., in medicine and engineering; the creation of job programs to provide on-the-job training and placement; and the requirement for regulatory bodies to liaise with other international bodies in their development of policies and practices in the area of access to professions and trades. However, it is uncertain that the implementation of these programs and recommendations would be effective in solving the Chinese immigrant women's problems in the labour market and in the home. Without an integrative anti-racist and anti-sexist approach, with concomitant structural changes, transnational migration practices in the Chinese immigrant communities will undoubtedly continue unabated.

NOTES

1   After much effort by advocacy groups to petition the Canadian government to redress the implementation of the Chinese Exclusion Act and the Head Tax and to compensate families whose members had paid the head tax, Prime Minister Stephen Harper, on behalf of the Canadian government, offered a formal apology on 22 June 2006. However, he restricted symbolic individual payments of $20,000 to only the very few living Chinese Head Tax payers (about 20) and spouses of deceased payers (about 250). The proposal did not mention the claims of another 4,000 deceased Head Tax payers, now represented by the elderly sons and daughters of the immediate family (email message from monsoon@yahoogroups.com).

2   According to "An Act Respecting and Restricting Chinese Immigration" (Colonial Office to Foreign Office, London, FO 371/8003, 16 June 1922), "every person of Chinese origin, irrespective of allegiance, shall pay into the Consolidated Revenue Fund of Canada, on entering Canada, at the port or place of entry, a tax of five hundred dollars except i) diplomatic corps or other government representatives, their suites, servants, consuls, and consular agents, ii) children born in Canada of parents of Chinese origins and who have left Canada for educational purposes or other purposes, and iii) merchants, their wives, and children, wives and children of clergymen, tourists, men of science and students. As well, no vessel carrying Chinese immigrants to any port in Canada shall carry more than one such immigrant for every 50 tonnes of its tonnage."

3   In 1921, merchants and store-owners comprised a mere 4.6% of the employed Chinese (Li 1988: 59, Table 3.2).

4   The Chinese Immigration Act of 1923 contained the following provisions: abolition of the head tax, students below university age were no longer admitted, only four classes of immigrants could enter Canada, all were categorized as temporary settlers. They were (i) university students; (ii) merchants—defined as "one who devotes his undivided attention to

mercantile pursuits, dealing exclusively in Chinese manufactures or produce or in exporting to China goods of Canadian produce or manufacture, who has been in such business for at least three years, and who has not less than $2,500 invested in it. It does not include any merchant's clerk, tailor, mechanic, huckster, peddler, drier or curer of fish, or anyone having any connection with a restaurant, laundry or rooming-house"; (iii) native-borns returning from several years of education in China; and (iv) diplomatic personnel.

5   By 1951, the situation only improved slightly, and the discrepancy still remains very high: 12,882 "transnational" or "separated" families versus 2,842 "intact" families (see Li 1988: 67, Table 4.4).

6   This part of the presentation is based on a preliminary analysis of my research project entitled "Chinese Immigrant Women in Toronto: Precarious Work, Precarious Lives," funded by an Atkinson Minor Research Grant (2004–05) at York University and a SSHRC Small Grant (2004–05). In the following, I will present some of the analysis of the data.

REFERENCES AND FURTHER READINGS

Adilman, T. 1984a. *Chinese Women and Work in British Columbia*. BA thesis, University of Victoria, April.

——. 1984b. A Preliminary Sketch of Chinese Women and Work in British Columbia 1858–1950. In B.K. Latham and R.J. Pazdro, eds., *Not Just Pin Money*. Victoria: Camosun College. 53–78.

Agnew, V. 1996. *Resisting Discrimination: Women from Asia, Africa, and the Caribbean and the Women's Movement in Canada*. Toronto: University of Toronto Press.

Arat-Koc, S. 1990. Importing Housewives: Non-Citizen Domestic Workers and the Crisis of the Domestic Sphere in Canada. In M. Luxton, H. Rosenberg, and S. Arat-Koc, eds., *Through the Kitchen Window: The Politics of Home and Family*. Toronto: Garamond. 81–104.

——. 1999. NAC's Response to the Immigration Legislative Review Report: Not Just Numbers: A Canadian Framework for Future Immigration. *Canadian Woman Studies* 19(3): 18–23.

Badets, J., and Howatson-Leo, L. 2000. Recent Immigrants in the Workforce. *Canadian Social Trends* 3. Toronto: Thompson Educational Publishing.

Bakan, A., and D. Stasiulis. 1997. *Not One of the Family: Foreign Domestic Workers in Canada*. Toronto: University of Toronto Press.

Baker, M. 2001. Paid and Unpaid Work: How Do Families Divide Their Labour? In M. Baker, ed., *Families: Changing Trends in Canada*. Toronto, ON: McGraw-Hill Ryerson. 96–115.

Bannerji, H. 1987. Introducing Racism: Notes Towards an Anti-Racist Feminism. *Resources for Feminist Research/Documentation sur la recherche féministe* 16(1): 10–13.

Basch, L., N. Glick Schiller, and C. Szanton-Blanc. 1994. *Nations Unbound: Transnational Projects and the Deterritorialized Nation-State*. New York: Gordon and Breach.

Boyd, M. 1992. Gender, Visible Minority, and Immigrant Earnings Inequality: Assessing an Employment Equity Premise. In Vic Satzewich, ed., *Deconstructing a Nation: Immigration, Multiculturalism, and Racism in 1990s Canada*. Halifax: Fernwood. 279–321.

Brand, D. 1984. Black Women in Toronto: Gender, Race, and Class. *Fireweed* (Summer/Fall): 26–43.

Brecher, J., and T. Costello. 1994. *Global Village or Global Pillage: Economic Reconstruction from the Bottom Up*. Boston: South End Press.

Calliste, A., and G.J. Dei (eds.). 2000. *Anti-Racist Feminism: Critical Race and Gender Studies*. Halifax: Fernwood.

Chan, A.B. 1983. *Gold Mountain: The Chinese in the New World*. Vancouver: New Star Books.

Chinese Canadian National Council (CCNC). 1992. *Jin Guo: Voices of Chinese Canadian Women*. Toronto: Women's Press.

Chui, T., K. Tran, and J. Flanders. 2005. Chinese Canadians: Enriching the Cultural Mosaic. *Canadian Social Trends* (Spring). Catalogue No. 11-008. Ottawa: Statistics Canada.

Cohen, R. 1999. Servants of Colour. In N. Amin *et al.*, eds., *Canadian Woman Studies: An Introductory Reader.* Toronto: Ianna Publications and Education Inc. 134–40.

Con, H., R.J. Con, G. Johnson, E. Wickberg, and W.E. Willmott. 1982. *From China to Canada: A History of the Chinese Communities in Canada.* Toronto: McClelland and Stewart.

Creese, G., and D. Stasiulis. 1996. Introduction: Intersections of Gender, Race, Class, and Sexuality. *Studies in Political Economy* 51 (Fall): 15–64.

Da, W. 2003. Gender Relations in Recent Chinese Migration to Australia. *Asia and Pacific Migration Journal* 12(3): 361–84.

Das Gupta, T. 1987. Unraveling the Web of History. *Resources for Feminist Research/ Documentation sur la recherche féministe* 16(1): 13–15.

Dua, E. 2000. The Hindu Women's Question: Canadian Nation Building and the Social Construction of Gender for South Asian-Canadian Women. In A. Calliste and G.J. Dei, eds., *Anti-Racist Feminism: Critical Race and Gender Studies.* Halifax: Fernwood. 55–72.

Dua, E., and A. Robertson (eds.). 1999. *Scratching the Surface: Canadian Anti-Racist Feminist Thought.* Toronto: Women's Press.

Flynn, K. 1999. Proletarianization, Professionalization, and Caribbean Immigrant Nurses. In N. Amin *et al.*, eds., *Canadian Woman Studies: An Introductory Reader.* Toronto: Ianna Publications and Education. 243–52.

Goldring, L. 1998. The Power of Status in Transnational Social Fields. In M.P. Smith and L. Guarnizo, eds., *Transnationalism from Below.* New Brunswick, NJ: Transaction Publishers. 165–95.

Grewal, I., and C. Kaplan. 1994. *Scattered Hegemonies: Postmodernity and Transnational Feminist Practices.* London and Minneapolis: University of Minnesota Press.

Handlin, Oscar. 1973 [1951]. *The Uprooted.* 2nd ed. Boston, MA: Little Brown.

Hanlon, N., and A. Kobayashi. 1998. *Rewriting Canada: Transnationalsim as a Challenge to Canadian Public Policy.* Paper presented at the Annual Meeting of the Canadian Association of Geographers, Ottawa, 1–5 June.

Hiebert, D. 1997. The Colour of Work: Labour Market Segmentation in Montreal, Toronto, and Vancouver, 1991. *Research on Immigration and Integration in the Metropolis,* Working Paper Series, No. 97–02.

Jhappan, R. 1996. Post-Modern Race and Gender Essentialism or a Post-Mortem of Scholarship. *Studies in Political Economy* 51: 15–64.

Knight, R.V., and G. Gappert (eds.). 1989. *Cities of Global Society.* Urban Affairs Annual Reviews Vol. 35. Thousand Oaks, CA: Sage.

Kobayashi, A., V. Preston, and G. Man. 2006. Transnationalism, Gender, and Civic Participation: Canadian Case Studies of Hong Kong Immigrants. *Environment and Planning.* Special Issue. (Forthcoming).

Lero, D. 2003. Dual Career Families. In Marion Lynn, ed., *Voices: Essays on Canadian Families.* 2nd ed. Toronto: Nelson Canada. 6–31.

Levitt, P. 2001. *The Transnational Villagers.* Berkeley, CA: University of California Press.

Li, Peter S. 1988. *The Chinese in Canada.* Toronto: Oxford University Press.

Luxton, M. 1990. Two Hands for the Clock: Changing Patterns in the Gendered Division of Labour in the Home. In M. Luxton, H. Rosenberg, and S. Arat-Koc, eds., *Through the Kitchen Window: The Politics of Home and Family.* Toronto: Garamond. 39–55.

Luxton, M., and E. Reiter. 1997. Double, Double, Toil and Trouble ... Women's Experience of Work and Family in Canada 1980–1995. In P.M. Evans and G.R. Wekerle, eds., *Women and the Canadian Welfare State.* Toronto: University of Toronto Press. 197–221.

Mahler, S. 1999. Engendering Transnational Migration: A Case Study of Salvadorans. *American Behavioral Scientist* 42: 690–719.

Mahler, S., and P. Pessar. 2001. Gendered Geographies of Power: Analyzing Gender Across Transnational Spaces. *Identities* 7: 441–59.

Man, G. 1995a. The Astronaut Phenomenon: Examining Consequences of the Diaspora of the Hong Kong Chinese. In J. DeBernardi *et al.*, eds., *Managing Change in Southeast Asia: Local Identities, Global Connections: Proceedings of the 21st Meeting of the Canadian Council for Southeast Asian Studies, October 15–17, 1993*. Alberta: University of Alberta Press. 269–81.

———. 1995b. The Experience of Women in Recent Hong Kong Chinese Immigrant Families in Canada. In M. Lynn, ed., *Voices: Essays on Canadian Families*. Toronto: Nelson. 271–300.

———. 1997. Women's Work is Never Done: Social Organization of Work and the Experience of Women in Middle-Class Hong Kong Chinese Immigrant Families in Canada. In V. Demos and M. Texler Segal, eds., *Advances in Gender Research*, Vol. 2. Greenwich: JAI Press Inc. 183–226.

———. 1998. Effects of Canadian Immigration Policies on Chinese Immigrant Women (1858–1986). In Noboru Watanabe *et al.*, eds., *Asia-Pacific and Canada: Images and Perspectives*. Tokyo: The Japanese Association for Canadian Studies. 118–33.

———. 2000. Racism, Sexism, and the Experience of Chinese Immigrant Women. Paper presented at *Era 21 Against Racism Conference*, Vancouver, 17–19 November. <http://geog.queensu.ca/era21/papers/man.htm>.

———. 2002. Globalization and the Erosion of the Welfare State: Effects on Chinese Immigrant Women. Special Issue: Women, Globalization, and International Trade. *Canadian Woman Studies/Les cahiers de la femme* 21/22(4/1): 26–32.

———. 2004a. Gender, Work, and Migration: Deskilling Chinese Immigrant Women in Canada. In P. Raghuram and E. Kofman, eds., Special Issue: Out of Asia: Skilling, Re-skilling and Deskilling of Female Migrants. *Women Studies International Forum* 27(2): 135–48.

———. 2004b. Chinese Immigrant Women in Canada: Examining Local and Transnational Networks. In K.E. Kuah-Pearce, ed., *Chinese Women and their Network Capital*. Asian Women and Society Series. London: Marshall Cavendish International. 44–69.

———. 2006. Globalization and the Racialization of Gender: Exploring the Experience of Precarious Employment of Skilled Chinese Immigrant Women in Toronto. In *Migration between East and West: Normalizing the Periphery, Manual of Symposium*, 2–5 April. Xiamen: Research School for Southeast Asian Studies (CSEAS), Xiamen University.

Michaelson, W. 1988. The Daily Routines of Employed Spouses as a Public Affairs Agenda. In L. Tepperman and J. Curtis, eds., *Readings in Sociology: An Introduction*. Toronto: McGraw-Hill Ryerson, 400–09.

Mojab, S. 1999. De-skilling Immigrant Women. *Canadian Woman Studies/Les cahiers de la femme* 19(3): 110–14.

Ng, R. 1993. Racism, Sexism, and Nation Building in Canada. In C. McCarthy and W. Crichlow, eds., *Race, Identity, and Representation in Education*. New York: Routledge. 50–59.

Ng, R., and A. Estable. 1987. Immigrant Women in the Labour Force: An Overview of Present Knowledge and Research Gaps. *Resources for Feminist Research/Documentation sur la recherche féministe* 16(1): 29–34.

Ong, A. 1999. *Flexible Citizenship: The Cultural Logics of Transnationality*. Durham, NC: Duke University Press.

Preston, V., and G. Man. 1999. Employment Experiences of Chinese Immigrant Women: An Exploration of Diversity. *Canadian Woman Studies/Les cahiers de la femme* 19(3): 115–22.

Razack, S. 1998. *Looking White People in the Eye*. Toronto: University of Toronto Press.

——. 2000. Your Place or Mine?: Transnational Feminist Collaboration. In A. Calliste and G.J. Dei., eds., *Anti-Racist Feminism: Critical Race and Gender Studies*. Halifax: Fernwood. 39–54.

Salaff, J.W. 2000. Women's Work in International Migration. In E. Chow, ed., *Transforming Gender and Development in East Asia*. London: Routledge. 217–38.

Satzewich, V. 1998. Race, Racism, and Racialization: Contested Concepts. In V. Satzewich, ed., *Racism and Social Inequality in Canada*. Toronto: Thompson Educational. 25–46.

Schiller, N.G., L. Basch, and C. Szanton Blanc. 1995. From Immigrant to Transmigrant: Theorizing Transnational Migration. *Anthropological Quarterly* 68(1): 48–63.

Sedgewick, C.P. 1973. *The Context of Economic Change: Continuity in an Urban Overseas Chinese Community*. Master's Thesis, Department of Sociology, University of Victoria.

Shields, J. 1996. Flexible work, Labour Market Polarization and the Politics of Skills Training and Enhancement. In T. Dunk, S. McBride, and R.W. Nelsen, eds., *The Training Trap: Ideology, Training, and the Labour Market*. Winnipeg: Fernwood. 53–72.

Smith, D. 1987. *The Everyday World as Problematic: A Feminist Sociology*. Toronto: University of Toronto Press.

——. 2006. *Institutional Ethnography: A Sociology for People*. Toronto: Altamira Press.

Spivak, G. 1996. Diasporas Old and New: Women in the Transnational World. *Textual Practices* 10(2): 245-69.

Stasiulis, D. 1990. Theorizing Connections: Gender, Race, Ethnicity, and Class. In P. Li, ed., *Race and Ethnic Relations in Canada*. Toronto: Oxford University Press. 269–305.

Stasiulis, D., and R. Jhappan. 1995. The Fractious Politics of a Settler Society. In D. Stasiulis and N. Yuval-Davis, eds., *Unsettling Settler Societies: Articulations of Gender, Race, Ethnicity, and Class*. London: Sage Publications.

Stevenson, W. 1999. Colonialism and First Nations Women in Canada. In E. Dua and A. Robertson, eds., *Scratching the Surface: Canadian Anti-Racist Feminist Thought*. Toronto: Women's Press. 49–82.

SUCCESS [Women's Committee Research Group]. 1991. *Chinese Immigrant Women's Needs Survey in Richmond*. Vancouver: SUCCESS.

Takaki, R. 1993. *A Different Mirror: A History of Multicultural America*. Boston, MA: Little Brown.

Thobani, S. 1999. Sponsoring Immigrant Women's Inequalities. *Canadian Woman Studies/Les cahiers de la femme* 19(3): 11–16.

Valverde, M. 1991. *The Age of Light, Soap, and Water: Moral Reform in English Canada, 1885–1925*. Toronto: McClelland and Stewart.

——. 1992. "When the Mother of the Race is Free": Race, Reproduction, and Sexuality in First-Wave Feminism. In F. Iacovetta and M. Valverde, eds., *Gender Conflicts*. Toronto: University of Toronto Press.

Vosko, L. (ed.). 2006. *Precarious Employment: Understanding Labour Market Insecurity in Canada*. Montreal and Kingston: McGill-Queen's University Press.

Waring, M. 1999. *Counting for Nothing*. Toronto: University of Toronto Press.

Wong, M. 2003. *Borders That Separate, Blood That Binds: Transnational Activities of Ghanaian Women in Toronto*. PhD dissertation, Department of Geography, York University, Toronto.

PART FOUR
Multiculturalism, Anti-Racism, and Public Policy

INTRODUCTION

Canada's multicultural policy is a major policy area that has received considerable attention over the past two decades. Introduced in 1971, the policy intended, among other goals, to break down discriminatory attitudes and barriers in the country. Various programs were established to achieve these goals, including a federal ministry responsible for multiculturalism, a multiculturalism sector in the department of the Secretary of State, a national strategy on race relations to develop and implement programs to eliminate racial discrimination in Canadian institutions, and the proclamation of an act in 1988 for the Preservation and Enhancement of Multiculturalism in Canada.

Whether levels of racial discrimination and prejudice are less prevalent today than in the past remains a topic of sociological debate, as the preceding three sections demonstrate. In the early 1990s, Charles Ungerleider (1992) argued that multiculturalism, as well as the development of policies and practices pertaining to immigration, citizenship, language, and human rights, gave rise to a social justice infrastructure ensuring equality in schooling, employment, income, and occupational attainment, but that this policy resulted in mixed successes. More recently, Rhoda E. Howard-Hassmann (1999) has argued that "Canadian" is an ethnic identity. While multiculturalism encourages Canadians to retain their ancestral ethnic heritage, she explains, most Canadians—foreign- and Canadian-born—

become ethnic Canadians. She argues that multiculturalism, far from promoting fragmentation and divisions among Canada's multiple cultural groups, tends to promote integration and unity. Not all observers agree, of course, and while some contributors to this final section are cautiously optimistic about the power of multiculturalism and related public policies, others advocate for a new or altered social justice framework.

Dhiru Patel opens the section with a chapter on racism and public policy in Canada. Patel is strategically positioned to comment on public policy formation, having worked in the public sector for over two decades. He begins with an important, yet often taken-for-granted observation that the shift from overt to covert racism in Canada over the past several decades has resulted from public policy formation. Offering a broad critical assessment of Canadian public policy on racism, Patel links historical and contemporary manifestations of racism to related myths, realities, and challenges of policy development in the 21st century. He argues that there have been significant changes in patterns of racism over the last few decades and that there have been significant changes in public policies designed to challenge it. He cautions, however, that the current realities of racism in Canada necessitate a reconfiguration of policy efforts to address forms of racism more appropriate to contemporary Canada.

In the next chapter, Rennie Warburton applies some of the general lessons of critical realism to Canada's multicultural policy. Using Archer's "morphogenetic model," he demonstrates how it is useful to conceptualize 35 years of multiculturalism in Canada as an emergent process of social change that began with particular structural and cultural conditions. He outlines how existing structural and cultural conditions in Canada stimulated the elaboration of a new set of structural and/or cultural conditions. He then turns his attention to criticisms of multicultural policy and concludes by advocating an integrated approach to multiculturalism.

Sarita Srivastava shifts attention away from multiculturalism towards anti-racism in the third chapter of this section. She examines the ways in which community and social movement organizations confront racism, and she argues that their efforts have often been constrained by the framework of "liberal multiculturalism." Srivastava begins by showing how organizing in the feminist movement is shaped by multiculturalism and how this poses certain limitations on feminist activism. Presenting data on anti-racist workshops, she contends that the techniques used in anti-racist workshops are more akin to liberal multiculturalism and that this actually reinforces racialized identities and relations of power. Srivastava concludes that alternative modes of activism offer the promise of transcending both problems with multiculturalism and with nationally based activism.

In the final chapter, Jennifer Dalton contends that the Canadian polis must be expanded in order to include international legal conceptions of Indigenous self-determination. Differentiating self-government from self-determiniation, she first provides an historical overview of Indigenous self-determination in international law. This is followed by an analysis of the applicability of international law to Canadian Aboriginal groups' self-determination. Dalton highlights several problems in defining Canadian Aboriginals as "peoples" with accompanying rights to self-determination, and she concludes that the Canadian polis must fully embrace developments in international law.

Collectively, the chapters in this section address the positive gains made through multicultural policy in Canada, as well as the continuing struggles that confront Canadian policy-makers, advocacy groups, and citizens.

REFERENCES

Howard-Hassman, R. 1999. "Canadian" as an Ethnic Category: Implications for Multiculturalism and National Unity. *Canadian Public Policy* 15(4): 523–33.

Ungerleider, C. 1992. Immigration, Multiculturalism, and Citizenship: The Development of the Canadian Social Justice Infrastructure. *Canadian Ethnic Studies* 24(3): 7–22.

13 PUBLIC POLICY AND RACISM
Myths, Realities, and Challenges

Dhiru Patel

> There are few topics more important for the well-being of our nation than public policy issues around racism, and its antidote, equality. (Fontaine 1998)

INTRODUCTION

In this chapter, I offer a broad critical assessment of Canadian public policy on racism. Considering historical and contemporary manifestations of racism, I examine related myths, realities, and challenges of policy development. I argue that there have been significant changes both in patterns of racism over the last few decades and in public policies designed to challenge racism. Nevertheless, current realities require that Canadian policy-makers continue to address racism, but their efforts must come in forms more appropriate to the predominant manifestations of racism at the beginning of the 21st century. In other words, public policies capable of eliminating racism from Canadian society are still a work in progress. Although quasi- or para-public institutions (or non-governmental organizations) play an important role in the public policy arena, the focus of this chapter is primarily on the federal government that, in the final analysis, drives public policy.

As Hier and Walby argue, there are competing analytical paradigms in the sociological study of racism that produce inconsistent and, at times, conflicting knowledge about racism in Canada. The latter, they say, necessitates "a critically reflexive research agenda that is able to account for the multidimensional realities of racism in Canada" (Hier and Walby 2006: 2).[1] Similarly, Satzewich, in his review of the academic literature, shows that there is little consensus regarding the meanings and uses of basic terms such as "race," "racism," and "racialization." His notion of "a range of *racism*" that encompasses the idea that "the expressions of racism need to be analyzed in their historical and social specificity, which takes into account variables such as class, ethnicity, and political interests" (Satzewich 1998: 22) is a useful one; it helps us understand the historical and contemporary reality of Canadian racism.[2] It is also useful from the standpoint of public policy, which emerges from a complex interplay of various social forces and conditions and which evolves with changing conditions.

To fully appreciate Canadian public policies regarding racism, one must appreciate the various interrelated factors that enter into the policy development process. Among these are an understanding of the complexity of the issues involved; specific material and ideological interests and power relationships—the relative "political weight" of individuals/groups; the public mood or opinion and political realities and priorities; the international context; the governing principles, ideals, and vision; the type leadership at the time; and the historical legacy of racism and anti-racism. The relative strength of these factors, and the complex interplay among them, determines the shape of policy. Thus, understanding racism as an aberration or as an isolated "bad apples" occurrence limited to some misguided individuals will engender a different set of responses than an understanding of it as either a result of impersonal social forces/conditions (e.g., poverty, unemployment) or a systemic or institutional/structural phenomenon (e.g., rules governing the operation of institutions). Whereas the explanation based on impersonal social forces calls for remedies that enlighten, reform, or remove "bad apples," an explanation based on institutional barriers addresses much wider and more costly fundamental changes in institutions/structures (see Patel 1980).

It is, therefore, important to consider the principal, multidimensional social bases (including class, ethnicity, etc.) of public policies regarding racism and to trace their evolution to the present. I do this briefly in the next two sections. I note in the first section that significant strides have been made since the 1960s to address racism in Canadian society and public policies. This is true to the extent that many (white) Canadians now apparently believe that racism is not a major problem (although survey results are not always consistent on this). The openly espoused racist ideology and formal legislative systems of the past have been replaced by non-racist policies and an aura of equality. However, policy has yet to address covert, subtle, or unpremeditated forms of racism that have persisted after the decline of explicit racist policies and procedures. The last part of the chapter encourages further work to determine what steps are required to address racism in its many forms and to develop a racism-free society.

THE EVOLUTION OF RACISM AND PUBLIC POLICY IN CANADA

To understand contemporary policies concerning racism, it is instructive to briefly put them in a historical perspective and to appreciate the contexts in which they arose. Broadly speaking, Canada is a child of European colonialism, which rationalized the domination, enslavement, and exploitation of other, overwhelmingly non-white peoples with the ideology of racial superiority. Racism was, therefore, an integral part of Canadian society from the beginning. It functioned to exclude non-Europeans (initially Aboriginal peoples and later others) or treat them as inferiors. Aboriginal peoples bore the brunt of racism, and they continue to do so today (see, for example, Satzewich 1998; Galabuzi 2004).[3] Other groups—blacks, Jews, Chinese, Japanese, East Indians—also suffered racist treatment (Winks 1971; Li 1988; Ferguson 1975; Adachi 1976), and various economic, political, and social interests benefited directly or indirectly from racism in Canada's past. Racism affected virtually every aspect of the lives of non-whites, as it became embedded in the political, economic, social, and cultural institutions of Canadian society. It also implicated *all* segments of white society and reached beyond governmental authorities—a fact that is often overlooked or insufficiently appreciated in understanding or analyzing racism today.

Major events—the Holocaust in Europe, World War II, the rise of Japan, the Universal Declaration of Human Rights, freedom movements in colonies—undermined the explicit ideology of racism and the formal societal structures associated with it. Asian-Canadians, for example, were re-enfranchised after the war, and the ban on Asian immigration lifted, albeit barely.[4] Formal institutional changes were introduced with the adoption of the declaratory Canadian Bill of Rights in 1960, superseded in 1982 by the much more powerful, constitutionally entrenched Charter of Rights and Freedoms (the Charter). And provincial human rights legislation that outlawed discrimination in varying degrees and areas (Hill 1977)[5] heralded the age of at least formal "equality" and tolerance. Similarly, a formal non-racist points system for admitting immigrants was introduced in 1967. The points system contributed significantly to new immigration patterns, and it led to a major, historically unparalleled expansion of racial and ethnic diversity in Canadian society. While these changes were significant, particularly in signalling an historical reversal of public policies regarding *overt* racism, they fell short in addressing the deeper causes of racism against non-whites (for a brief overview, see Patel 1980).

Most of the anti-racist measures adopted in the postwar era were either weak or inadequate, as were the mechanisms to enforce them, as evidenced by the manifestations of racist attacks throughout the country (Pitman 1977; Ubale 1977; Canada 1982). More fundamentally, however, the underlying approach on which these measures were based limited their effectiveness because it assumed that racism stemmed only from individual prejudice, ignorance, and misunderstanding that was manifested in overt, conscious racist behaviour. It overlooked systemic racism, namely, racism that was covertly embedded in societal institutional structures and that shaped basic beliefs, attitudes, and behaviour (see Patel 1980 for details). This was partly rectified in the 1980s when the focus of anti-racist policies was expanded to address systemic racism through such measures as affirmative action or employment equity, some of which were already in place for francophones, women, people with disabilities, and Aboriginal peoples. Again, however, policy scope and application varied in different jurisdictions, and there were serious rollbacks across the country in the 1990s (in Ontario, for example).

Anti-racist policy measures often emerged from (or with) the policy of multiculturalism, which was originally aimed at accommodating the demands of ethno-cultural minorities for recognition. The federal government was the first to adopt such a policy in 1971 in response to demands by non-British/French minority groups (of mostly European origin). This was done to complement the government's 1969 adoption of official bilingualism. The government's attention first expanded in the 1980s beyond ethnocultural issues (of primary concern to mostly those of European origins) to include "race relations" issues; it subsequently shifted to its current, almost exclusive, focus on racism (affecting mostly non-whites). A mounting number of often-violent racist incidents across the country (Patel 1980; Canada 1982) prompted the government to develop various initiatives to address institutional change. One of these was the National Strategy on Race Relations (Canada 1983). The government also created an all-party Parliamentary Special Committee on Participation of Visible Minorities in Canadian Society. The committee's report, *Equality Now!*, called for significant changes to eliminate racism in Canadian society (Canada 1984).[6] Other measures, such as the 1986 Employment Equity Act, 1988 Canadian Multiculturalism Act, and 1996 Canadian Race Relations Foundation, were undertaken as well. The provinces and many of the larger cities adopted various types and levels of multiculturalism policies and anti-racism measures, the latter generally under the rubric of broader human rights legislation (HRREC 2005). And, most recently, the federal government has moved to resolve the Aboriginal residential schools issue and to provide redress for several groups including Chinese- and Ukrainian-Canadians.

From an historical perspective, then, Canadian ideologies and public policies have shifted from explicit racism to an ostensibly non-racist position. The speed of change—less than 40 years—is indeed remarkable, and this can easily lead to the impression that Canadian society is now generally free of racism. Despite these changes, and despite differences within and among non-white groups discussed below, significant numbers of people continue to claim that they face racism in Canadian society. As Reitz and Breton (1998) note, although most Canadians deny harbouring racist views, they express social distance from minorities whose own experiences confirm the existence of racism (also noted below).

COMPLEXITIES OF RACISM AND SOCIAL CHANGE

Given Canada's history of overt and covert racism, it is not surprising that most policy-makers reflect attitudes of the variety that Simmons (1998) conceptualizes as explicitly non-racist but whose underlying processes are neo-racist.[7] These attitudes, moreover, translate into general public policy frameworks. Thus, the ethnic or racial hierarchy of desirability within the Canadian vertical mosaic, identified by Porter (1965), that places non-whites at the bottom, has not disappeared (Beck *et al.* 2002). As Galabuzi (2004) maintains, "racism remains intractable and racial hierarchies have replaced the ethnic vertical mosaic in giving form to the social order in Canada." Non-whites also continue to experience what Hughes and Kallen (1974) dubbed "polite racism"—racism that is not overt or explicit as in the past and that is, as a result, often difficult to assess and address.[8] The latter entails behaviours such as lower levels of cooperation with members of minority groups, treating fellow-whites more favourably, consistently not sitting next to non-whites on the bus, and maintaining social distance from non-whites. And the fact noted earlier that there is no agreement among analysts about the extent of racism or how to measure it leaves much room for inaction or piecemeal, long-drawn-out policy measures.

The frustrations experienced in trying to develop effective policy formation become clear in the context of the record of the last 50 years. Despite the fact that the continuing tragic situation of Aboriginal people persists, that claims to racial profiling of non-whites remain prominent, that the manner in which the 1985 Air India bombing tragedy involving the death of 329 mostly non-white people was handled outrages Canadians, and that reports of discriminatory treatment of non-whites continue,[9] scholars remain divided on racism in Canada.

Evidence pertaining to the extent of racism today appears to be somewhat unclear partially due to its covert and inadvertent nature. For example, in a major recent survey, a significant number of non-whites reported experiencing discrimination, primarily in the workplace, but also in banks, restaurants, streets, and the justice system (Canada 2003).[10] The fact that as many as 41% of second-generation non-white Canadians reported discrimination is even more troubling,[11] especially when compared to the view of Canadian youth in general who are overwhelmingly proud (83%) of Canada's fair treatment of minority groups (ISSP 2004). These perceptions of discrimination probably contribute to the sense of alienation from Canadian society expressed by non-white youth.[12] These results are similar to the Centre for Research and Information on Canada (CRIC) finding that three out of four Canadians believe that "there is still a lot of racism left in Canada" (CRIC 2003: 10),[13] a finding confirmed by human rights and other agencies (see, for example, CHRC 2005; OHRC 2005; and CRRF 2005). While the majority of Canadians *reject* the proposal that "nonwhites should not be allowed to immigrate to Canada," however, the same poll showed that 53% believe "Canada accepts too many immigrants from racial minority groups" (Reitz 2005). The critical point here is that, despite dismantling explicitly racist laws and policies over the last 50 years, racism is still a daily reality for many Canadians.

These apparently inconsistent, even contradictory and ambivalent positions are due to a combination of complex and dynamic factors: the relative decline of overt or explicit racism; policy changes since 1945; the entrenchment of the ideology and rhetoric of equality; most white Canadians' general self-image of a tolerant, fair-minded, non-racist, polite, and peace-loving people, especially compared to their American neighbours;[14] and Canadians' lack of experience with, and hence different sensitivities and perceptions about, the history of Canadian racism. Aboriginal leader Phil Fontaine observes (Fontaine 1998) that the cherished self-image Canada has as a tolerant country makes even the most liberal Canadians view racism only as overt acts by a few 'rotten apples,' not as something that is an integral part of the Canadian social system.

FIGURE 13.1 | EXPERIENCE OF DISCRIMINATION BY GROUP (%)

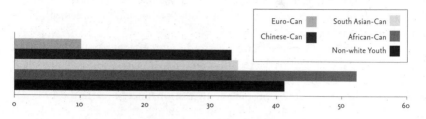

Source: Ethnic Diversity Survey (Reitz 2005).

Fontaine's observations about Aboriginal people's perceptions are also generally true of other non-whites (Reitz 2005). He analyzes modern racism in Canada, arguing that its "central and distinguishing characteristic" is the "vigour with which it is consistently denied" (Fontaine 1998: 3). He notes that euphemisms, stereotyping, and culturalization are other ways of sidestepping the issues of domination and discrimination. The differing perceptions and attitudes regarding the same event arise from different life experiences based on race. These different experiences of daily life—the abuse and taunts Aboriginal children are constantly subjected to, the obscenities Aboriginal women routinely have to suffer as they walk down the street, the disrespectful attitudes and condescending and racist behavior Aboriginals generally experience on a regular basis—treatment not usually experienced by most whites—leads to quite views of Canadian society.

He goes on to point out that non-whites, other than Aboriginal people, are also victims of racism such as what police have described as the racially motivated killing by five people of a 65 year old Sikh man in British Columbia, and that Aboriginal people (and, similarly, other non-whites) see linkages where whites do not. Their life experiences tell them that racial violence and harassment 'are widespread, common and life threatening' (Fontaine 1998: 8), although that is not the impression one gets from the media. For them, it is "*very* logical to link together several thousand real life stories into the interpretation" (emphasis in the original) they put on particular cases, such those of Connie Jacob, J.J. Harper, Dudley George, Donald Marshall, Betty Helen Osborne, and Kittynowdlok-Reynolds.

Others have made similar observations about non-whites in general (see, for example, Satzewich 1998; Reitz 2005). Small (1998: 84) argues, " ... ideologies of colour blindness create the appearance of equality and fairness, while hiding practices of discrimination." This has led to very different understandings (and experiences) among whites and non-whites regarding racism. Satzewich (1998) notes that many (white) Canadians have been generally reluctant to acknowledge their racism, while racial minorities' own accounts of their experiences, together with particular cases that come to light in the media and in surveys, clearly indicate that race and racism remain important aspects of reality in Canada.[15] The key point is that even if racism is not as extensive or serious as some analysts contend, the fact that so many non-whites, and in particular those born and/or raised in Canada, claim to experience racism regularly is sufficient grounds to see racism as an important public policy issue.

MYTHS, REALITIES, AND PUBLIC POLICY ON RACISM

Canadian public policies are usually influenced by the perceptions and attitudes of the majority (white) population. Policy-makers are usually members of the majority, and they generally share many of the dominant perceptions and attitudes. Although policy-makers, especially at the senior levels, usually have higher levels of education, they are not necessarily any more knowledgeable or enlightened than the general public about the subject of racism or its historical roots—such as awareness of the existence of slavery in Canada or of the historically unequal treatment of non-whites. Career advancement in the public service, at these senior levels, usually requires experience in handling different subject areas in which the government is involved, and a fundamental task involves *management* skills, not expertise in specific subjects.

Nevertheless, this does not stop most people from considering themselves as well informed as those who have acquired expertise about a given subject, and the readiness and certainty with which views about racism (or social issues in general) are held and expressed is indeed remarkable. Of course, such ignorance, accompanied by the certainty of opinion, helps sustain the myths of equality and to deny the pervasiveness of racism. The outcome is a troubling denial of contemporary racial oppression by, among others, policy-makers (Galabuzi 2004).

Related to this ignorance and lack of understanding of racism is the overzealous or patronizing mind-set of certain people who wish to be perceived as sensitive to minority concerns. This creates situations of unnecessary backlash and negative feelings against minorities. The recent trend of banning Christmas decorations and parties in the workplace, or Christmas pageants in schools, in the name of multiculturalism or inclusiveness are cases in point. Multiculturalism is about respecting other cultures and sharing one's own culture with others; it is certainly not about banning anyone's cultural festivities. Most members of minorities have generally little problem with diverse cultural festivities, since they realize that respect for their own cultural ways depends on respecting other cultural ways. Those who do have problems do not have to participate; they should be just as accommodating of others as they want others to be of them. Of course, even if policy-makers were knowledgeable or unpatronizing, the prevailing political dynamics can make it difficult or impossible to develop or implement the policies necessary to resolve the issue.

Since the popular media play such a vital role in modern society, significantly influencing if not forming people's images, ideas, and opinions, modes of presenting issues related to racism become critical to people's understanding. However, those who control and work in the media overwhelmingly share the perceptions and attitudes of the dominant white society. At a minimum, they frequently end up reinforcing the misperceptions, ignorance, and lack of understanding in Canadian society, including policy-makers (see, for example, Fontaine 1998; Henry and Tator 2002). These observations are applicable with variations to different aspects and institutional areas of life since, as Fontaine (1998) says, "racism in Canadian society continues to invade our lives institutionally, systematically, and individually."

Underlying all of this, however, is the issue of power relationships (between whites and others) that, as mentioned earlier, has long historical roots. Some argue that the institutional structures developed over time continue, wittingly or unwittingly, to reflect the fundamental inequality between whites and non-whites (Fontaine 1998; Li and Bolaria 1988; Satzewich 1998; Henry and Tator 2005; Reitz 2005). As Galabuzi (2004: 1) puts it: "Looking at access to key determinants of an individual's or a community's life chances, one realizes that the pronouncements of equality continue to come up against the legacy of the 'white settler colony.' It is this inequality and the resistance to rectifying it that is critical to the issue." As discussed earlier, while Canada has replaced the explicitly racist ideology and formal systems with non-racist ones, there is some way to go before Canadian society can be free of racism. It will require much more than the formal legal structures and rhetoric of equality or good intentions to overcome the built-in structural inequality of several centuries. Simmons's comment on immigration policy could probably be applied more broadly; while much of the evidence is ambiguous and subject to different interpretations:

> ... [w]hat is perhaps most clear from the analysis is that the policy framework—explicitly non racist but showing in fact many indicators of a neo-racist underlying process—has not incorporated a strong anti-racist stance. Rather it has tended to deflect and deny racist influences and outcomes by focusing on nation-building and national economic development discourses and associated imagined futures ... (Simmons 1998: 112)

NEW CHALLENGES FOR A NEW ERA

While initiatives promoting individual politico-legal equality and non-discrimination flourished in the post-1945 economic boom and led to the establishment of an ethos of equality, they were stalled or reversed with the budget-slashing, "reverse discrimination" backlash of the post-1990 era. As Galabuzi (2004: 1) noted with some alarm at the time: "Sadly, many of our governments are in retreat from social and economic engagement, leaving the rot to fester and many to speculate on the combustion down the road." By the mid-1990s, a majority of Canadians believed, contrary to evidence, that discrimination was not a major cause of inequality and government should not intervene to ensure equality (Reitz and Breton 1998). However, there appeared to be a change in public opinion once again in 2003: the CRIC survey cited earlier showed three in four Canadians believed there is a lot of racism in Canada, and two years later the federal government released Canada's Action Plan Against Racism (CAPAR) (Canada 2005a and 2005b).[16]

CAPAR, with its commitment of a five-year investment of $56 million, does not appear to be that different from earlier plans—which it does not mentioned anywhere (see, for example, Canada 1983 and Canada 1988). It does claim to represent "the first-ever horizontal, coordinated approach across the federal government to combat racism" and boasts of "solid achievements" such as the Charter and policies and programs "to enhance the multicultural nature of our society and to combat all forms of discrimination, and remove barriers to employment faced by minorities." It also asserts "we can count on the unwavering support of the majority of Canadians, who recognize that diversity enriches us, and who take a stand against racism in their daily lives, whether in the community or the workplace" (Canada 2005a: iii). As noted above, majority support on this subject is not always assured, despite the professed belief in equality.

Like its predecessors, CAPAR recognizes the need to go beyond legal solutions, and it is certainly quite ambitious in that over a five-year period it "seeks to eliminate racist behaviours and attitudes and to help close the gap in socio-economic outcomes for all Canadians" (Canada 2005a: 10). It details plans to eliminate systemic racism and to empower individuals and communities, although specifics on how this will be done are as unclear as how much of it will survive changes in the political environment. If the past is any guide, CAPAR may be completely changed, with the least threatening parts inching forward and the rest falling by the wayside. Dramatic events like the riots in France in late 2005 or those that occurred earlier in the UK could change that; the British and American experience is not encouraging, and there are significant differences between those and the Canadian situation.

Reitz (2005: 23) argues that "policies to address special needs of visible minorities and to promote racial equality have not been developed consistently in Canada" and "whatever the impact of policies such as multiculturalism [which generally include race relations] in paving the way toward the social integration of immigrants, it has not worked as well for non-whites as for white immigrant groups." This is not surprising if one considers the ignorance, denial, and minimization of racism that continues to occur in the mainstream and that shapes most policies. If CAPAR succeeds over its five-year lifetime in getting Canadians to acknowledge the existence of covert systemic racism and the need to take effective action to significantly reduce it, that will constitute real significant progress. At the most general level, "[T]he challenge, then, is to counter the dominant ideology, its related institutional practices and the blinders it imposes. Such an effort requires the promotion of new concerns and greater awareness of racist biases in current structures" (Simmons 1998: 112). This will not be an easy, smooth, or painless undertaking since it will involve abandoning long-established comfortable ways of thinking and replacing them with new, sometimes uncomfortable ways of sharing power and privilege. Fontaine comes to a similar conclusion, paraphrasing Mohawk legal scholar Patricia Monture:

> ... if the white society cannot bring itself to understand the pain that Aboriginal men, women and children go through, you are never going to understand anything. All the equality promises in the world will not get us anywhere because without that understanding, the theories do not reflect social reality, do not reflect peoples' experiences. To combat racism, we must give up on monolithic, ethnocentric reality and believe there is something to be learned and a better society to be achieved by listening to formerly silenced people. Listening to the

powerless may in turn, lead to the understanding that some groups and group members have enjoyed disproportionate privilege, including the power to define, appropriate, and control the realities of others. (Fontaine 1998: 9)

Similarly, Reitz concludes:

> It is time to recognize that the perceptions of significant discrimination among racial minorities are much more prevalent than many Canadians would like to believe, that these perceptions seriously erode commitments to Canadian society, and that a much more sympathetic response is centrally important to the future of Canadian society and identity." (Reitz 2005)

As I have argued elsewhere (Patel 1980), a wide range of policies touching on every major sector of society will have to be undertaken because racism is pervasive and affects virtually all aspects of life, requiring the long-term commitment and combined efforts of all the key sectors. More specifically, current realities require Canadian society to address the issue in forms more appropriate to its manifestations at the beginning of the 21st century. Thus, since covert and institutional racism are the main issues that need to be addressed, appropriate remedies will have to be developed, with effective incentives and sanctions. However, because "public understanding of systemic discrimination and employment equity remains rather poor" (Beck *et al.* 2002), it will make the task more difficult and long term. Similarly, the complex nature of racism and its differential impacts on different non-white groups and different sections *within* a group divided by, for example, class or gender, means the solutions will have to be tailored accordingly. For example, African-Canadian youth generally have lower than average university completion rates, while Chinese- and South Asian-Canadian youth are generally in the reverse situation but face a racial glass-ceiling in many areas. South Asian-Canadians get usually placed lower down on the social distance and acceptance scale than the other two groups, while Aboriginal peoples end up at the bottom of all the scales. The impact of terrorist attacks of the last few years in Western countries has had a negative impact principally on those who are of Arab or South Asian origins and their "look-alikes." Therefore, while all of these groups are victims of racism as non-whites and as such suffer some aspects of racism in common which require common remedies, only a specific group(s) experiences certain other aspects which then necessitate remedies particular to it and not the others. The challenge will be to balance these needs so that one does not end up with a complicated unmanageable patchwork and a bureaucratic nightmare.[17]

Given the generally low levels of elementary knowledge and understanding of some basic historical roots of modern racism, focused, serious, and effective efforts (*not* the kinds of slick public relations or superficial advertising campaigns undertaken in the past) to raise the levels of knowledge and understanding among the young as well as the adult population need to be undertaken. As Fontaine (1998: 9) says, "the truth of the present and past must be told"; without such truth-telling, little real progress will be possible.

A much more complex and difficult set of issues relates to the term "Canadian" as applied to all manner of things: individuals, identity, culture, history, heritage, etc. Although the term is not, in theory, directly part of the racism lexicon, it has acquired certain connotations or meanings that link it to racism. In many instances it has become a code word for "white"—for example, a Canadian-born and raised daughter of immigrants from Asia is not considered "Canadian," nor is a fifth-generation black Nova Scotian, simply because she is not white (i.e., of European origin). In this context, it will be interesting to see how Howard-Hassman's (1999) notion of an "ethnic Canadian" identity and "English-Canadian ethnicity" plays out as interpreted by and applied to different groups, especially many non-whites whose links to "ancestral homelands" are continually renewed by newcomers and modern technology (Patel 2006) and who cannot escape the impact on their psychological and emotional states of events elsewhere and how these are portrayed in the media in ways that may have hints of neo-colonialism or racial/cultural superiority.

Related to this, but much more complicated and problematic, are the closely intertwined notions of "Canadian identity" and "Canadian culture" (especially "high culture"), which currently still continue to be generally defined in ways that exclude identities and cultural elements that are not of European origin. Thus music, art, and literature *only* of European (particularly British) origin—which of course became dominant with the dominance and explicit racism of immigrants from Europe—is regarded as part of "Canadian culture," while the music, art, and literature of Canadians of other origins is not. "Canadian culture" continues to be largely defined from an exclusively white perspective despite four decades of major changes in the ethnocultural make-up of Canadian society and notwithstanding its much-touted claim to be multicultural.

This Eurocentric approach pervades other aspects of public life. Gagnon and Pagé (1999: 9) point out that "[t]he definition of national identity must, at the very outset, contain the coded elements which define the society as a whole and which have a universal value in that society." Many of Canadian society's "coded elements" embedded in its public culture and heritage, do not speak to the growing number of new citizens because they have evolved from and continue to be informed by a particular (i.e., Christian) perspective or worldview. New Canadians have different perspectives and worldviews and generally have few, if any, emotional ties to their new "nation." It is these coded elements that are being put to the test, creating a dilemma in increasingly ethnically diverse liberal democratic societies. As political philosopher Bhiku Parekh has argued, "full citizenship [includes] the right to shape the public culture; therefore, to ground the public culture in Christianity is to treat non-Christians as second-class citizens" (quoted in Gagnon and Pagé 1999, v.1: 86). Parekh makes a similar observation about schooling that is applicable to virtually every area of life:

> The general ethos pervading the educational system highlights the glory and uniqueness of European civilization and underplays or ignores the achievements and contributions of others' not only to human civilization in general but to European civilization itself. (Parekh 2000: 225)

Similarly, the portrayal or telling of Canadian history and of Canadian heritage has been equally problematic, since it is generally portrayed positively from the perspective(s) of the dominant group(s) (i.e., whites) and thus often excludes, devalues, or misrepresents the history and heritage of Canadians of non-European origins. However, historian Jack Granatstein (1999: B5) argues that "our teaching of the past.... focuses on victimology"; he basically dismisses the "tales of historical abuse" as accurate only sometimes and that "[n]ot everyone was or is a victim, despite the clamorous legal claims of the present."

From the perspectives of non-whites, many Canadian heroes, particularly those of the pre-1960s, were at best well-intentioned but patronizing individuals or, at worst, racists who often played pivotal or leading roles in the establishment or implementation of racist structures and policies. For example Canada's longest-serving prime minister, W.L.M. King, is not exempt from such an accusation: as Canada's first deputy minister of labour, he blamed the Asian victims for the 1907 anti-Asian riots by whites in Vancouver (Adachi 1976; Ferguson 1975), and as prime minister he passed the Chinese Exclusion Act in 1923 and refused to accept Jewish refugees fleeing Nazi Germany in the 1930s (Abella and Troper 1982). Canada's first female judge, Emily Murphy, one of the "Famous Five" who made history by securing the rights of women as persons and who is thus considered a hero by many, was a white supremacist (Murphy 1922). One cannot expect non-whites to join in the celebration of the work of such "heroes" nor have positive feelings about them; on the contrary, it would not be surprising if some of them considered such individuals as villains and if celebrations of them engendered feelings of apartness or even alienation.

While there has been some awareness of these issues among some Canadians, they have not been explored in any significant way. They need to be addressed, especially as they relate to Aboriginal peoples, but resolving the complex and contradictory needs or demands will not be easy in reality, as they will likely generate strong reactions. Explicitly acknowledging that heroes too are products of their times and not perfect, and rehabilitating or accepting as heroes those unfairly cast as villains or ignored, may help moderate such reactions. Relating a more accurate and balanced history, both within the educational system and more broadly—including an acknowledgement of the fundamental racism that runs through it—would also help create a better informed citizenry (including policy-makers). Obviously these steps are all medium-long term.

On a more tangible and immediate level, effective action needs to be taken to deal with more immediate, corrosive forms of covert and implicit racism, particularly in institutional settings (along the lines suggested in Patel 1980 and Satzewich 1998). Canadian society must tangibly and convincingly demonstrate, especially to its vulnerable members, its seriousness in eliminating racism by attacking it vigorously. Covert and institutional forms are more difficult to deal with than the earlier overt and explicit ones and will require different, even new, approaches based on innovative research (see, for example, Beck et al. 2002; Reitz 2005).

As stated earlier, it will not be easy to root out the multidimensional and pervasive racism that has been around for several centuries and that is embedded in the very foundations of Western societies. However, a promising a start has been made over the last half-century. Postwar policy reversals replaced earlier explicitly racist ideological principles and formal frameworks with those of equality that basically outlawed and virtually eliminated overt or explicit racism. Canadian society is therefore on the right track, especially compared to other Western countries, but it still has some way to go before it can claim to be truly racism-free. What are required now are the will and the dedication of resources to take the necessary difficult steps to get there. As has been argued elsewhere (Patel 2006), there may be little choice but to undertake such measures in this age of rapidly changing global dynamics that includes the emergence of Asian countries (China and India in particular, two of the largest contributors of immigrants to Canada) as important players in the international arena; instantaneous trans-border communications; the migration and establishment of significant ethnically and "racially" different communities in the West with their personal and family/group networks and professional mobility spanning the globe; and the advent of the ideology of equality and expectations of it by the Canadian-born and/or raised second-generation children of immigrants.

The fact that, despite the important strides in this area over the last 50 years and the ongoing debates about the extent of racism today, significant proportions of non-white Canadians (especially those born or raised here), who now constitute the fastest growing and relatively younger segment of the population, feel discriminated against and not at home in their own country is troubling. The fact that their peers, with whom they grew up, appear to be quite unaware of this (as noted above, they overwhelmingly believe that Canadian society treats different groups fairly) does not bode well for the future. How well these issues are addressed by Canadian society will be important in determining how successful a story Canada will be. Both scholars and policy-makers can play a vital role in this process by furnishing the tools required to understand the issues and effect the necessary changes. That is their challenge.

NOTES

1   This chapter is developed from the perspective that racism in Canada is not as manifestly pervasive as in many other Western countries, but neither is it insignificant based on the reported experiences of substantial numbers of non-whites. This alone makes it an important public policy issue.

2   While many European-origin groups also suffered discrimination historically (e.g., eastern and southern Europeans), the primary focus of this chapter is on current trends, which predominantly concern racism as it relates to "visible minorities" or non-whites (see Patel 1980). It should also be noted that there is little consensus about these labels, but the convenient term "non-whites" is used here because the principal distinctive characteristic relating to racism in Canada today is physiology, especially skin colour, even though there are different types, levels, or intensity of racism suffered by different groups of non-whites, some of which will be noted below. The term "whites," which obscures the enormous differences among the groups subsumed under that label, is similarly used.

3   The special situation of Aboriginal peoples requires separate treatment not possible in the limited space available here; it must be mentioned, nevertheless, because they are the first, the longest suffering, and the principal victims of racism in Canada.

4   Thus, for example, only 54 Indian and 1,036 Chinese immigrants were admitted in 1950, three years after the ban was lifted (Canada 1950).

5   The Canadian Human Rights Act was adopted in 1977.

6   Other levels of governments undertook similar inquiries, as in Ontario (Ubale 1977) and Toronto (Pitman 1977).

7   Simmons is referring here to immigration policy, but his observation has wider application (see Satzewich 1998).

8   On the issues relating to proving (especially systemic) discrimination, see Beck *et al.* 2002.

9   Perhaps the most famous, or infamous, example is the case of internationally renowned non-white scientist Dr. Chander Grover and his 20-year, ongoing, anti-racism battle with his federal agency employer, who refuses to accept findings of tribunals and courts in his favour (Pieters 2005).

10 These figures are similar to those of field tests done 20 years ago (Henry and Ginzberg, 1985). Racism even extends to leisure activities, including sports that idealize fairness (Tirone 2000).

11 Many of this group will likely play increasingly important leadership roles in the future, while others may form a racial underclass as in Europe and the US (Patel 2006; Reitz 2005; and Valpy 2005).

12 Ethnic Diversity Survey (EDS) data reveals much lower levels of trust, belonging to Canada, and Canadian identity among these youth (Reitz 2005).

13 This contradicts "a prevailing view ... that racism is marginal in Canada, and that discriminatory treatment of minorities is relatively rare" (Reitz 2005: 7).

14 Satzewich (1998: 11) notes that Canadians have this enduring national myth that there is less racism here than in the US, despite evidence suggesting they have nothing to feel superior about. Reitz and Breton (1998: 65) show, that despite historical differences, Canadians and Americans are roughly similar in their attitudes and behaviour toward racial minorities: a majority of both feel, despite evidence to the contrary, that "minorities are responsible for their own inequality and that discrimination is not a major cause of inequality and that government should not intervene to ensure equality."

15 Chander Grover's (Pieters 2005) and Shiv Chopra's (Beck *et al.* 2002) decades-long battles against racism are two classic examples that are not isolated or exceptional; see, for example, the annual reports of federal and provincial human rights commissions. For minorities' perceptions, see the unique Ethnic Diversity Survey (EDS), the largest one of its kind with a sample size of over 43,000 (Canada 2003).

16 This short chapter is limited by space and time to the federal area only. For a consideration at provincial/municipal levels see, for example, Reitz 2005 and Satzewich 1998. CAPAR consists of two related documents; the more detailed 50-page document includes a forward by the prime minister and an introduction by three federal ministers.

17 For a discussion of how complicated or unmanageable such issues can become, see Hum and Simpson 2003.

REFERENCES AND FURTHER READINGS

Abella, I., and H. Troper. 1982. *None Is Too Many*. Toronto: Lester and Dennys.

Adachi, K. 1976. *The Enemy that Never Was*. Toronto: McClelland and Stewart.

Beck, H., J. Reitz, and N. Weiner. 2002. Addressing Systemic Racial Discrimination in Employment: The Health Canada Case and Implications of Legislative Change. *Canadian Public Policy* 28(3): 373–94.

Canada. 1950. *Annual Report*. Ottawa: Department of Citizenship and Immigration for the Fiscal Year Ended March 31, 1950. Ottawa: Supply and Service Canada.

——. 1982. *A Series of Situation Reports on Race Relations in Several Cities*. Ottawa: Multiculturalism Directorate, Department of Secretary of State.

——. 1983. *National Strategy on Race Relations*. Ottawa: Multiculturalism Directorate, Department of Secretary of State.

——. 1984. *Equality Now! Report of the House of Commons Special Committee on Visible Minorities in Canadian Society*. Ottawa: Supply and Services Canada.

——. 1988. *Race Relations in Canada: A Background Paper*. Ottawa: Multiculturalism Sector, Department of the Secretary of State.

——. 2003. *Ethnic Diversity Survey: Portrait of a Multicultural Society*. Ottawa: Statistics Canada. <http://www.statcan.ca/english/freepub/89-593-XIE/89-593-XIE2003001.pdf>.

——. 2005a. *Canada's Action Plan Against Racism* (CAPAR). Ottawa: Department of Canadian Heritage. Minister of Public Works and Government Services Canada. <http://www.multi culturalism.pch.gc.ca>.

——. 2005b. *Overview: Canada's Action Plan Against Racism*. Ottawa: Department of Canadian Heritage. Minister of Public Works and Government Services Canada. <http://www. multiculturalism.pch.gc.ca>.

CDM (*Canadian Dimension Magazine*). 2004. Editorial: Racism in Canada. (January/February). <http://canadiandimension.com/articles/2004/01/01/155/>.

CHRC (Canadian Human Rights Commission). 2005. *Annual Report*. Ottawa. <http://www. chrc-ccdp.ca>.

CRIC (Centre for Research and Information on Canada). 2003. *A New Canada? The Evolution of Canadian Identity and Attitudes to Diversity*. <http://www.cric.ca/en_re/analys/index. html>.

CRRF (Canadian Race Relations Foundation). 2005. Various reports. Ottawa. <http://www. crr.ca>.

Ferguson, T. 1975. *The White Man's Country*. Toronto: Doubleday.

Fontaine, P. 1998. "Modern Racism in Canada." 1998 Donald Gow Lecture. Kingston, ON: Queen's University Policy Forum, 24 April. <http://www.queensu.ca/sps/working_papers/ files/gow98.pdf>.

Gagnon, F., and Pagé, M. 1999. Conceptual Framework for an Analysis of Citizenship in the Liberal Democracies. Vol. I: Conceptual Framework and Analysis. Ottawa: Department of Canadian Heritage.

Galabuzi, G-E. 2004. The Contemporary Struggle Against Racism in Canada. *Canadian Dimension Magazine* (January/February). <http://canadiandimension.com/ articles/2004/01/01/155/>.

Granatstein, J. 1999. A Politically Correct History Leads to a Distorted Past and a Bleak Future. *National Post* 28 August, B5. <http://www.conservativeforum.org/EssaysForm. asp?ID=6104>.

Henry, F., and E. Ginzberg. 1985. *Who Gets the Work? A Test of Racial Discrimination in Employment*. Toronto: Social Planning Council and Urban Alliance on Race Relations.

Henry, F., and C. Tator. 2002. *Discourses of Discrimination: Racial Bias in the Canadian English-Language Press*. Toronto: University of Toronto Press.

———. 2005. The *Colour of Democracy: Racism in Canadian Society.* Toronto: Thomson Nelson.

Hier, S., and K. Walby. 2006. Competing Analytical Paradigms in the Sociological Study of Racism in Canada. *Canadian Ethnic Studies* 26,1: 83–104.

Hill, D. 1977. *Human Rights in Canada.* Ottawa: Canadian Labour Congress.

Howard-Hassman, R. 1999. "Canadian" as an Ethnic Category: Implications for Multiculturalism and National Unity. *Canadian Public Policy* 25(4): 523–37.

HRREC (Human Rights Research and Education Centre). 2005. *Human Rights Protection Mechanisms, Legislation and Policy.* Ottawa. <http://www.uottawa.ca/hrrec/links/sitescan_e.html>.

Hughes, D., and E. Kallen. 1974. *The Anatomy of Racism.* Toronto: Harvest House.

Hum, D., and W. Simpson. 2003. Labour Market Training of New Canadians and Limitations to the Intersectionality Framework. *Canadian Ethnic Studies Journal* 35(3): 56–69.

ISSP (International Social Survey Program). 2004. *International Social Survey Program 2003 and 2004.* Ottawa: Carleton University Survey Centre and Department of Canadian Heritage.

Li, P. 1988. *The Chinese in Canada.* Toronto: Oxford University Press.

Li, P., and S. Bolaria. 1988. *Racial Oppression in Canada.* Toronto: Garamond.

Murphy, E. 1922. *The Black Candle.* Toronto: Thomas Allen.

OHRC (Ontario Human Rights Commission). 2005. News Release: New Human Rights Policy to Modernize Struggle Against Racism in Ontario, 28 June. <http://www.ohrc.on.ca/en_text/news/e_pr_racism-policy-launch.shtml>.

Parekh, B., 2000. *Rethinking Multiculturalism: Cultural Diversity and Political Theory.* London: Macmillan.

Patel, D. 1980. *Dealing with Interracial Conflict: Policy Alternatives.* Montreal: Institute for Research on Public Policy.

———. 2006. The Maple-Neem Nexus: Transnational Links of South Asian Canadians. In L. Wong and V. Satzewich, eds., *Transnational Identities and Practices in Canada.* Vancouver: University of British Columbia Press.

Pieters, S. 2005. *The Repulsive Face of Systemic Racism at the National Research Council of Canada.* Ottawa. <http://www.geocities.com/naboy.geo/Federalpublicservice/nrc/>.

Pitman, W. 1977. *Now Is Not Too Late.* Paper submitted to the Council of Metropolitan Toronto by the Task Force on Human Relations, November. Toronto.

Porter, J. 1965. *The Vertical Mosaic.* Toronto: University of Toronto Press.

Reitz, J. 2005. Canada's Growing Racial Divide: Perceptions of Bigotry Among Minorities Are More Widespread Than Canadians Believe. The Toronto Star, op. ed. piece October 20.

Reitz, J., and R. Bannerjee. 2005. Diversity, Inequality, and the Cohesion of Canadian Society: Research Findings and Policy Implications. Paper presented to Diversity and Canada's Future: Recognition, Accommodation, and Shared Citizenship. Institute for Research on Public Policy (IRPP). Montebello, Quebec, 13–15 October.

Reitz, J., and R. Breton. 1998. Prejudice and Discrimination in Canada and the United States: A Comparison. In V. Satzewich, ed., *Racism and Social Inequality in Canada.* Toronto: Thompson Educational. 47–68.

Satzewich, V., (ed.). 1998. *Racism and Social Inequality in Canada.* Toronto: Thompson Educational.

———. 2004. Racism in Canada: Change and Continuity. *Canadian Dimension Magazine* (January/February). <http://canadiandimension.com/articles/2004/01/01/155/CDM> .

Simmons, A. 1998. *Racism and Immigration Policy.* In V. Satzewich, ed., *Racism and Social Inequality in Canada.* Toronto: Thompson Educational. 87–114.

Small, S. 1998. The Contours of Racialization: Structures, Representation and Resistance in the United States. In V. Satzewich, ed., *Racism and Social Inequality in Canada.* Toronto: Thompson Educational. 69–86.

Tator, C. 2004. Advancing the Ontario Human Rights Commission's Policy and Education Function. Race Policy Dialogue Conference Paper. <http://www.ohrc. on.ca/english/consultations/race-policy-dialogue-paper-ct.shtml>.

Tirone, S. 2000. Racism, Indifference and the Leisure Experiences of South Asian Canadian Teens. *Leisure/Loisir: The Journal of the Canadian Association of Leisure Studies* 24(1): 89–114.

Ubale, B. 1977. *Equal Opportunity and Public Policy.* Toronto: Attorney General of Ontario.

Valpy, M. 2005. Could It Happen Here? *Globe and Mail* 12 November: A1.

Winks, R. 1971. *The Blacks in Canada.* New Haven, CT: Yale University Press.

Wong, L. and V. Satzewich (eds.). 2006. *Transnational Identities and Practices in Canada.* Vancouver: University of British Columbia Press.

14 CANADA'S MULTICULTURAL POLICY
A Critical Realist Narrative

Rennie Warburton

> This system of racial hegemony can present itself as color-blind and multicultural, not to mention meritocratic, egalitarian, and differentialist, all the while restricting immigration, exporting industry (and pollution) to the low-waged South and doing away with the welfare state in the North. (Winant 2001: 309)

INTRODUCTION

Although it is the individual and collective actions of human beings that make social life possible, we are nevertheless constrained and enabled by structural, cultural, and environmental conditions. These conditions are present in the various domains of reality that were discussed in Robert Carter's critical realist analysis of race and racism in this book (see Chapter 2). In order to explain the social world, realist social science asks what it is about a given situation or its context that triggers people to transform or reproduce existing states of affairs. To understand these processes, it is necessary to examine some of the factors that influence how people think about the contexts and settings in which they find themselves, especially about social positions where structural and/or cultural elements like social class or citizenship contain vested interests and situational logics. After reflecting on situations, people take or avoid certain actions, and they use whatever resources they have at their disposal (Archer *et al.* 1998; Sayer 1992, 2000; Bunge 1997; Merton, cited in Hedstroem and Swedberg 1998: 6; Carter 2000: 107; Carter and New 2004). The behaviours that result from this process of action exemplify the mechanisms described in the formula "context + mechanisms = outcome" (Pawson 2000). As manifested in social science's capacity to debunk illusions, this form of realism has a critical aspect for three major reasons: first, beliefs and assumptions that legitimate dominating structures may be false; second, reasons given by actors are not always real ones; and third, practices at one level of social organization may help to maintain underlying structures at another.

The following critical realist discussion takes an approach similar to Carter's (2000) narrative examination of the introduction of restrictive immigrant legislation in the UK between 1945 and 1981. Carter analyzes processes of immigration control as an example of what Archer (1995, 1998) calls "morphogenesis." Morphogenesis is an emergent process of social change that begins with a certain structural and cultural context. Within this context, people with vested interests, grievances, deprivations, or other reasons to change the situation use appropriate resources to complain, lobby, enter into alliances, or otherwise communicate with people who control, influence, or have significant involvement in the existing situation. As a result of these interactions, a new set of structural and/or cultural conditions is elaborated. The counterpart of morphogenesis, however, is morphostasis: the processes whereby social change is inhibited or where reproduction of an existing social order is accomplished (Archer 1995). For critical realists, understanding the multidimensional process of situational struggles is just as important as documenting their outcomes.

I begin by examining two morphogenetic cycles. The first deals with how Canada's multicultural policy emerged when certain structural and cultural conditions led spokespersons for non-anglophone and non-francophone groups to express grievances to the Royal Commission (the Bi-Bi Commission) on Bilingualism and Biculturalism, and to the federal government, about the lack of appreciation for their contributions to the formation of Canada. Next, I provide an examination of research and opinion on the impact of multicultural policy, including expressions of concern that the policy was not addressing racism and other forms of discrimination. The narrative continues by noting that those interactions led the federal government to elaborate the policy by introducing the Multiculturalism Act and Employment Equity Act, adopting explicit anti-racist programs, and establishing the Race Relations Foundation, thereby completing a second morphogenetic cycle. In the third section, I discuss several criticisms of multicultural policy, the most trenchant of which is offered by Bannerji (2000), who deems multiculturalism policy to be of little value in the struggle against racism and persistent colonialism. I contrast Bannerji's account with Kymlicka's (1998) positive appraisal of multiculturalism in Canada to address different domains of Canadian social reality, and I conclude that both Kymlicka's and Bannerji's accounts are not incompatible assessments of multicultural policy in Canada.

FIRST CYCLE: THE ORIGINS OF CANADA'S MULTICULTURAL POLICY

Several clearly identifiable structural and cultural conditions existed when Canada's multicultural policy was introduced; especially significant were the relationship between Quebec and the rest of Canada, ethnic inequalities (Porter 1965; Breton 1998: 32ff), and the class and gender structure of the country. One prominent cultural condition was Canada's weak conception of nationhood, which clung to the myth of a historical preserve of British traditions with emphasis on anglo-conformity, and various efforts to portray Canada as an essentially northern nation (Angus 1997: 141ff).

There were other contextual elements in the situation as well. The decade of the 1960s began with passage of the Canadian Bill of Rights. It was followed by several other policy amendments: the removal of overt racist elements from the Immigration Act, the creation of the Canadian Folk Arts Council, and the adoption of a new national flag. The Quiet Revolution in Quebec was accompanied by the growth of the separatist movement to which the federal government responded with the Bi-Bi Commission. And there was an increase in Canadian nationalism in response to growing American cultural domination and ownership of corporations. The decade ended with the flat rejection of the government's assimilationist White Paper (rejected by Aboriginal peoples), the passing of the Official Languages Act, and the ratification of the International Convention on Racial Discrimination (Pearson 2001: 108; Fleras and Elliott 1992: 75).

The changes noted above took place alongside significant economic growth, which enabled rapid increases in state expenditure on social and cultural institutions that constituted a further contextual element (Breton 1986: 32). It is important to remember, too, that structural and cultural developments in Canada occurred in the context of international changes. Movements for national liberation in societies like Algeria, and the presence of post-colonial societies in the Commonwealth, for example, made Canadian politicians and intellectuals acutely aware of human rights issues. Fanon was widely read in Quebec around that time, and the American Indian Movement raised the consciousness of Canadian Aboriginal people and their leaders.

The situation in which multiculturalism policy emerged was the first stage of a morphogenetic cycle where a distribution of structural and cultural resources constrained and enabled agents to reflect on the situation and consider how to realize interests and modify the structural and cultural landscape (Carter 2000: 122, 138). This took place when the Bi-Bi Commission presented its report. The commission had interacted with leaders of organizations representing Canadians whose origins were neither English nor French; who were experiencing status anxiety amid the rhetoric of biculturalism, the two-nation society, charter groups, and founding peoples; and who were unwilling to have their part in building modern Canada overlooked (Breton 1984: 134; Ostry 1978: 106–07). The most prominent group was Ukrainian-Canadians who described multiculturalism as the distinctive characteristic of Canadian society (Royal Commission 1966: 127). One Ukrainian-Canadian, Senator Paul Yuzyk, emphasized that the "third element ethnic group" were co-builders of the West and other parts of Canada and that they should be guaranteed the right to perpetuate their mother tongues and cultures (Porter 1987: 117). That "third element" comprised 26% of the population in 1961, and Yuzyk accused the Bi-Bi Commission of ignoring it, alternatively privileging the French and English (McRoberts 1997: 122–24).

The objective of the Bi-Bi Commission was to explore how Canada's public institutions could better reflect the bilingual and bicultural nature of the country, while simultaneously recognizing the contributions of other groups at the same time (Breton 1986: 39). Advocating the integration of immigrants rather than their assimilation, the commission observed that a number of cultural groups wanted to maintain their own linguistic and cultural heritage without under-mining national unity (Innis 1973: 134–35). The Trudeau government accepted the contention of those other cultural communities "that they, too, are essential elements in Canada and deserve government assistance in order to contribute to regional and national life in ways that derive from their heritage yet are distinc-tively Canadian" (Trudeau 1971: 8545–46).

The pressure that the so-called "third-force" leaders placed on the commis-sion and the federal government came from groups in frustrating social positions who faced exigencies that they sought to eradicate (cf. Archer 1998: 83). Their promotional creativity, and the government's positive response, was facilitated by contextual processes including progress in the recognition of human rights and the rise of Quebec separatism—and the stimulus that the latter provided for develop-ment of a new Canadian identity in place of the anglo-conformist one.

While advocating multiculturalism, Trudeau was concerned that the notion of collective rights implied in the concept of biculturalism might actually encour-age separatists in Quebec (Breton 1986). In order to appease or subvert their sovereignty claims, the federal government designed the multicultural policy to redefine Canada symbolically and to redistribute social status among linguistic and ethnocultural groups (Pearson 2001: 138; Breton 1984: 134). It was clearly a nation-building measure, a symbolic act within the historical trajectory through which the Canadian nation has been, and continues to be, constructed. As Trudeau put it in 1971:

> ... national unity, if it is to mean anything in the deeply personal sense, must be founded on confidence in one's own identity; out of this can grow respect for others and a willingness to share ideas, attitudes and assumptions. A vigor-ous policy of multiculturalism will help create this initial confidence. (Trudeau 1971: 8545-46)

Therefore, this morphogenetic cycle started with prevailing structural and cul-tural conditions, primarily ethnic inequalities and a weak form of nationalism. These prevailing conditions were understood to require change after interaction involving the federal government with Quebec nationalists, representatives of the "third force," and the Bi-Bi Commission. Those conditions and interactions were part of the context that enabled the reasoning and resources of the federal government to become the causal mechanism that produced the policy of multi-culturalism. As Archer's theoretical framework suggests, social conditions lead to interaction and a new set of conditions, that is, implementation of the multicul-tural policy was elaborated. However, Archer notes that, even after a given change has been elaborated, interested parties may seek to optimize their interests under the new arrangements. It is not surprising, then, that the practices introduced by Canada's multicultural policy became an important context for the emergence of a further morphogenetic cycle, as interactions between critics of the policy and the federal government led to elaboration of other policy measures.

SECOND CYCLE: THE IMPACT AND ELABORATION OF MULTICULTURAL POLICY

The stated purposes of multicultural policy were to support the cultural development of ethnocultural groups, to help their members overcome barriers to full participation in Canadian society, to promote creative encounters and interchange among ethnocultural groups, and to assist new Canadians in acquiring at least one of Canada's official languages (Kymlicka 1998: 15). The policy was established through programs that sponsored activities such as ethnic song and dance performances, ethnic presses, language teaching, immigrant orientations, folk culture studies, and ethnic archives. Most funds were granted to local organizations for festivals, television programs, Saturday schools, literary clubs, and art exhibits (McRoberts 1997: 126). Assistance to ethnic groups for the expression and development of their cultures was, therefore, a major element in the implementation of the policy. In 1973, the Canadian Ethnocultural Council, a coalition of national ethnic organizations, was formed to provide consultation for these groups with the government (Binavince 1997: 95; Leman 1997: 5). The focus in the 1970s was clearly on fostering many kinds of cultural activities rather than on the discriminatory barriers facing minorities in Canadian society. While the government of Quebec rejected multiculturalism, all other provincial governments eventually established their own multicultural policies and agencies (Friesen 1993: 9–11).

Opinion surveys are major sources of evidence suggesting that the policy influenced subsequent interaction in the ethnic relations field. In the mid-1970s, Berry et al. (1977) demonstrated that, although Canadians were not familiar with the policy, there was fairly wide support for the multicultural notion of promoting and sharing Canada's cultural diversity. This suggests that, at least at the symbolic level, the policy's impact was effective. However, Kymlicka (1998: 17ff) vigorously argues that the success of the policy was shown by other changes. After 1971, he contends, naturalization rates were highest among "multicultural groups" and lowest among immigrants from the US and UK; ethnic populations had increased representation in Parliament; demand for English and French language classes had increased considerably; there had been an overall decline in ethnic endogamy; and permanent ethnic enclaves did not exist in Canadian cities, except among Jewish and Italian populations whose arrival preceded multiculturalism. Kymlicka (1998: 21) also notes that Canada has higher levels of immigrant integration than the US, citing a 1997 poll in which 75% of Canadians agreed that "different ethnic groups get along well here." He concluded that the multiculturalism program was working and " … achieving what it set out to do: helping to ensure that those people who wish to express their ethnic identity are respected and accommodated, while simultaneously increasing the ability of immigrants to integrate into the larger society" (Kymlicka 1998: 22).

There is other survey evidence supporting Kymlicka's case. In 1991, the Angus Reid Group (1991) interviewed a sample of over 3,000 Canadians, 95% of whom agreed with the statement "you can be proud of being Canadian and proud of your ancestry at the same time." Also, 73% of respondents believed that multicultural policy ensured that people from different backgrounds had a sense of belonging to Canada, and 89% identified as "Canadian." Furthermore, Berry (1999: 7) found that 70% of Canadians favoured having a culturally diverse society in Canada in which ethnocultural groups maintain and share their culture with others. Support for integration rather than assimilation had increased from Berry's national survey in 1974. Although there were degrees of comfort reported with people of various ethnic backgrounds, the level was high overall.

In 1996, an Environics poll found that multiculturalism was identified as a common Canadian symbol more often than Canada's national sport of hockey (Biles 2002: 3). A more recent poll conducted by that group showed that 82% of adult Canadians agree that the government should support the preservation and enhancement of the multicultural heritage of Canadians. The same poll showed that 80% believed that multiculturalism helps to ensure respect for cultural and racial diversity in Canada's institutions (ACS/Environics 2002). In 2001, a survey of Arab-Canadians reported that almost 92% agree that they take comfort in being both Arab and Canadian, and that that's what multiculturalism is all about (Khouri 2002).

Meanwhile, the Economic Council of Canada sponsored two studies in the early 1990s that found integration leads immigrants to increase their participation in Canadian society while simultaneously maintaining their cultural identity. The reports also found that Canada's multiculturalism policy "strengthens the belief that a person's confidence in his/her own individual identity and place in the Canadian mosaic facilitates his/her acceptance of the rights of members of their groups" (Economic Council 1991: 32).

Friesen (1993) described multiculturalism as delivering at least minimal results such as the process of eliminating racist elements from school textbooks and other curriculum materials. A decade ago, he anticipated that multiculturalism was part of a greater pedagogical think-tank where issues of global peace, cooperation, and human rights would become integral parts of educational systems. Other evidence pointing to the policy's positive influence on ethnic discrimination includes a decline in the proportion of members of the corporate elite who are of British origin, accompanied by an increase in those of both French and "other" origins (Ogmundson and McLaughlin 1992). There is further evidence that ethnicity, as distinct from "race," has decreased in importance in the overall pattern of social inequality (Ornstein 1998: 159; Breton 1998: 105).

While these are important factors, maintenance of ethnic ties and identities is sometimes an asset and sometimes a liability for attaining upward socio-economic mobility. A poll conducted by Bibby (1995: 38–39), for example, found that 44% of Canadians preferred the mosaic model of Canada. This is in comparison to 56% a decade earlier. Furthermore, 88% of respondents maintained that immigrants had an obligation to learn Canadian ways, up from 85% a decade earlier. This ambivalence in Canadian attitudes exemplifies "democratic" (Henry et al. 2000) or "hegemonic" racism (Winant 2001), that is, public opposition to racism accompanied by continuing covert forms of racial discrimination.

It is difficult to establish that Canada's multicultural policy is a direct cause of the above contradictory developments, if only because many other processes were involved. The latter included pressure from international opinion and the struggles of anti-racists, First Nations, and other minorities. It would, however, be unreasonable to contend that multiculturalism had no effect at all. From the realist perspective, the various practical applications of the policy were important conditions that, along with others, produced changes in attitudes and behaviour and simultaneously generated widespread and sometimes intense and bitter debates.

Turning to the ongoing struggles over optimum arrangements noted by Archer, three distinguishable areas of concern are racism, ethnic politics, and national unity and identity. In 1971, the federal government did not specifically acknowledge the existence of racism as a problem. The ethnic minorities who voiced their concerns to the Bi-Bi Commission represented European immigrants and their descendants, not racial minorities such as African- and Asian-Canadians. However, by the mid-1970s, as immigration from various Asian countries, the Caribbean, and other non-European regions increased, anti-racists and leaders of racial groups, concerned about overcoming racist barriers in employment, housing, and education, began to protest against the policy (Leman 1997: 5). Multiculturalism's emphasis on cultural barriers was understood as a code signal that racism was either not considered as a significant problem or that it had been explained in terms of conflicts between ethnocultural groups or their incompatibility with mainstream Canadians. In response to such criticisms, the federal government set up a Race Relations Unit in 1982 and a Special Committee on Visible Minorities in Canadian Society. It also began to fund conferences on racism and the law and racism and the media. A House of Commons Standing Committee on Multiculturalism was also created in 1985. In its report, the committee distinguished issues of culture from those of ethnic inequality, including race relations, immigrant settlement, official language training, education, immigrant women's issues, employment discrimination, affirmative action, and employment equity. The committee observed that, although multicultural policy had evolved from cultural preservation to the promotion of equality, it was "clearly insufficient" and needed "clear direction" (Fleras and Elliott 1992: 75).

In response to some of the committee's concerns, the Employment Equity Act of 1986 was passed on the grounds that Canada was a multicultural society (Department of Canadian Heritage 1997: 103). The act required all federal departments and agencies to adopt multicultural principles and to make their personnel more inclusive of ethnic minorities. Two years later the government gave multicultural policy legal status with its Canadian Multiculturalism Act, the first of its kind in the world. Its stated purposes were to balance cultural recognition with equal access and full participation in social, political, and economic spheres through the eradication of racism and the removal of discriminatory barriers. Also in 1988 the government established a Race Relations Foundation to foster racial harmony and cross-cultural understanding. This decision was taken during negotiations with the National Association of Japanese-Canadians over redress for anti-Japanese racist acts during World War II. The foundation sponsors anti-racist conferences and research on racism. In adopting these various measures, the federal government was responding to interested groups concerned to optimize the impact of the elaborated policy.

The above legislative and other multicultural measures were welcomed by many white second- and third-generation Canadians, including those third-force groups who had supported the policy at the outset, as well as Canadians of British origin eager for ways to distinguish Canada from the US. But dissenting voices alleged that collective rights would replace individual rights, that the Liberal Party was using the program to attract or retain the electoral support of ethnic communities, and that the program favoured better organized groups. Major objections to the policy also came from those who saw multiculturalism as failing to accomplish its objectives by creating ethnic ghettoes that impede the integration of immigrants by dividing and fragmenting Canadians (Ogmundson 1992; Bissoondath 1994). However, some of these critics appear to have overlooked the voluntary nature of the policy and its assumption that members of all ethnic communities may or may not wish to preserve their culture. The policy clearly implies that the terms on which immigrants and others integrate into Canadian society are negotiable (Kymlicka 1998).

The issue of Canadian national identity was a third arena of struggle, particularly after the election of the Parti Québécois in 1976. It was followed by intensive debates about the nature of Canada and the effects of the government's policies in the area of cultural diversity. The Charter of Rights and Freedoms was a federal government initiative that elaborated the policy by emphasizing the preservation and enhancement of the multicultural heritage of Canadians. The 1988 Multiculturalism Act was also justified in part by linking its principles to a Canadian national identity.

It is clear that the various implementations of Canada's multiculturalist policy were among the socio-cultural conditions that led to further struggles around ethnic and racist issues, ethnic political recognition, and national unity. Some of those debates were informed by deeper analyses of the policy's significance to which we now turn.

CRITIQUES BASED ON ANALYSES OF UNDERLYING STRUCTURES

Porter (1987: 121) and McAll (1990) are among the analysts who have noted that ethnicity and class in Canada are frequently so intertwined that their separate influences over people's socio-economic location are difficult to determine. The gendered and class relations in which people of diverse ethnic and racialized backgrounds live are primary elements in the underlying cultural and structural context in which multicultural policy has been practised. Epitomizing Winant's (2001) argument that, in advanced capitalist democratic societies where it has been officially proscribed, racism has moved from domination to hegemony, Bannerji (2000) conceptualizes multiculturalism in terms of ideological codes that maintain hegemonic practices. These include mechanisms with which the Canadian state manages destabilizing tendencies in order to reproduce those underlying social relations, especially the class relations of capitalism, but also gender and other relations involving ethnic or national groups (Winant 2001; on hegemony, see also Joseph 2000: 198-99). This managing process organizes socio-cultural and legal-economic space through policies like the Employment Equity Act, which encourages greater representation for four designated groups, one of which is "visible minorities," in federally funded institutions like universities.

However, Bannerji claims that multicultural policy ignores certain aspects of the structural and cultural contexts in which the Canadian society, economy, and polity have developed. It also ignores aspects that remain obscured by liberal perspectives that focus on individual people and their differences by adopting a discourse around diversity that portrays society as a horizontal space (Bannerji 2000: 50). In reading all socio-cultural forms or differences in terms of descriptive plurality and asserting the existence of cultural essences, that discourse signals heterogeneity without hierarchy. Bannerji explains the policy as providing a naturalized political language in which

> the concept of race lost its hard edges of criticality, class disappeared entirely, and colour gave a feeling of brightness, brilliance or vividness, of a celebration of a difference, which was disconnected from social relations of power, but instead perceived as diversity, as existing socio-cultural ontologies or facts. (Bannerji 2000: 32)

She accuses multiculturalists of reading the notion of difference in a socially abstract manner and of focusing on a few particularities of people's cultures and averting their gaze from underlying structures. Her observations fit into a critical realist analysis that points beneath the surface of multicultural policies to relations of power and to ideological mechanisms that serve to preserve those relations.

Bannerji's critique is supported by Li's (1988: 9) empirical research findings that the policy failed to combat racism or discriminatory practices in the labour market. This finding was supported by Lautard and Guppy (1999), who observed very small declines in ethnic differentiation and stratification between 1971 and 1991 and who noted that, despite some progress, penetration into elite groups remained limited. Other studies report "ethnic penalties," "brutal income inequality," and "financial penalties" for visible minorities (Herberg 1990; Geschwender and Guppy 1995).

Multiculturalism's silence on the issue of class is part of an ideological code that marginalizes analyses of class relations by defining them as radical, extreme, or Marxist and, consequently, as not serious. This silence is a mechanism that protects the powerful and assumes that their practices are normal, natural, necessary, and irreplaceable because any alternative to capitalism is unthinkable.

It is likely that class was part of what Kymlicka (1998: 183) meant when he observed that "Multicultural policies are situated within a much larger structure of social and political institutions that are taken as given." In addition to class and gender relations, those conditions include powerful Canadian politicians and intellectuals like Charles Taylor and Kymlicka himself who write about "the Other" among Canadians as people to whom they are willing to grant recognition (Day 2000: 210–22).

Criticisms based on underlying structures have also been raised on the basis of the notion of tolerance that is embedded in the multicultural policy. For instance, Mirchandani and Tastsoglu (2000) note the underlying assumption that acts of tolerance are unidirectional and that the majority "we" is urged to tolerate the minority "them." They point to certain limits to tolerance, such as the absence of concerns in multicultural policies about economic inequalities, fears expressed in the press of making too many concessions to homosexuals and feminists, and support for preserving freedom of speech rather than freedom from oppression.

Day and Sadik (2002) argue that the multiculturalism policy of the Canadian state perpetuates the colonial status of Aboriginal peoples by failing to acknowledge their status as diverse sovereign nations and by emphasizing individual rights in a capitalist, patriarchal, bureaucratic, and colonial nation-state that denies Aboriginal claims to sovereignty or traditional nationhood. They contend that the policy's advocacy of cultural recognition and respect, as supported by condescending mainstream intellectuals like Taylor and Kymlicka, reinforces the subordinate position of Aboriginal nations and people and thwarts the radical possibilities of the multicultural context: "the recognition of which Taylor speaks is not equal, reciprocal and freely given but a partial and grudgingly bestowed *gift* from an identity that sees itself as intrinsically valuable...." (Day and Sadik 2002: 19). The gift is to the disadvantaged from the powerful, who assume what Parekh (2000) conceptualized as a moral and cultural monopoly, rather than the result of negotiations among equals in nation-to-nation relationships.

For Day and Sadik, a traditional perspective of Aboriginal nationhood that challenges the "destructive and homogenizing force of Western liberalism and free-market capitalism" (Alfred 1999: 60) and which derides the exploitation of another person to enrich oneself (Maracle 1996: 41) offers a mechanism for decolonization. But it must be part of a strategy that also recognizes the linkages between patriarchy, racism, sexism, and capitalism.

Kamboureli (1998) notes that the Canadian Multiculturalism Act excludes governing bodies in the Yukon and Northwest Territories and those that govern Indian bands. These exclusions, together with the monarchy cited in the proclamation of the act, stand for the colonial and post-colonial condition of Canada that contradicts the ideals of multiculturalism. She quotes Brook Thomas, who said that the rhetoric of law helps to maintain order at the price of disguising or denying the conflicts produced by the *status quo*, thereby helping to legitimate it. Kamboureli reminds us that the technology of ethnicity is part and parcel of the larger systems within which it operates, particularly institutions that were created by and for anglophone and francophone elites. This point is supported by minorities who object to the notwithstanding clause in the Constitution because it privileges anglophone and francophone elites and has the potential to undermine the constitutional protection offered to ethnic or racialized minorities (Binavince

1997: 93). According to Binavince (1997: 98) the bystander status granted to ethnic minorities and First Nations at the Charlottetown deliberations was further evidence that for the politically powerful members of Canada's white majority, multiculturalism is not a priority.

The policy of multiculturalism is therefore one mechanism among many—anti-communism, the widespread belief that Marxist perspectives on class relations are invalid, and the corresponding absence of dialogue in the media in other political arenas around class issues—which have reproductive effects on Canadian society. They deflect attention away from class relations and other forms of power in Canada and make class-based and decolonizing political activities difficult. Canada as a capitalist liberal democracy is committed to individualistic values and the sanctity of private property that are fundamental features of class relations. The public "multicultural" discourse around cultural and ethnic issues is, therefore, a mechanism for protecting class differences as basic elements in our social structure by keeping them outside the political consciousness of the vast majority of Canadians. In addition to the dependent class situation of most Aboriginal people, this position is also evidenced by the disadvantaged position of lower class minorities like the blacks of Montreal who have not benefitted from multicultural policies supposed to ensure "an inclusive society, based on equality and the ability of all members of society to reach their full potential" (Warburton 1997: 119–41; Flegel 2002). A second example is Luther's (2002) explanation for how multicultural advocacy groups are not recognized as charities because they are self-interested rather than altruistic. He concludes that "group empowerment, group mobilization, group protest, and political action that could alter society's inequitable yet acceptable social order" are discouraged, suggesting that this is further evidence that the policy is societal management rather than an effort to address structural inequalities stemming from the relations between class and racialization.

CONCLUSION

The perspectives represented by Kymlicka and Bannerji address different levels of social reality and are themselves embedded in what critical realists call the strata or domains of reality which comprise Canadian social and political life. Kymlicka concludes that the policy provides opportunities for ethnic and other minorities to engage in active pursuit of certain cultural objectives, a conclusion about what Layder (1997) calls "situated activity," that is, what agents do in particular places and social positions. Bannerji's critique sees the policy as emasculating class-based politics and radical movements among racialized minorities by legitimizing state-approved individual ethno-cultural and class differences as integral to Canadian society, insights about the domain of what Layder calls "contextual resources" (Layder 1997; Pearson 2001: 141; Carter 2006). As Fleras (2002: 10) observes, multiculturalism can be empowering yet controlling as part of the same process by helping minorities to pry open opportunities while co-opting them into the very system they are challenging.

Several critical realist tools have proven useful for understanding developments in this field since the 1960s. First, there were the contextual conditions that gave rise to the policy. The programs implemented under the policy subsequently became mechanisms that, as shown by Kymlicka, contributed to some of the outcomes it sought. But they also were conditions under which intense debates occurred around matters both addressed and not addressed in that policy. Most importantly, those practices helped to reproduce social inequalities, particularly those associated with class and gender relations, the colonial position of Aboriginal peoples, and continuing ethnic and racial discrimination. Protests by anti-racist voices, using reasoning and resources, were among the mechanisms that subsequently led the federal government to take specific measures to address racism.

Multicultural policy has also become the cultural condition for ongoing debates about the Canadian identity, Canadian values, and the degree of democracy and opportunity in Canadian society. In the parliamentary debate in 1988, several speakers described multiculturalism as a key element of the Canadian identity. One referred to it as a matter of national pride and national sentiment (House of Commons Debates, 22 March 1988: 13751). Fleras and Elliott (1992: 125) described multiculturalism as "the quintessential Canadian value." However, critics of the policy allege that it is divisive, that it keeps Canadians separate from one another, and that it privileges racialized minorities. One can detect, therefore, persisting contradictory developments involving competing interests. The strategic mechanisms they deploy will lead to further outcomes as further morphogenetic processes unfold.

This chapter is a first effort to apply critical realism as a means to understand the origins of Canada's multicultural policy; its effects within the Canadian polity and society; and ongoing debates about racism, class, and Canada's post-colonial experience. The policy is one of many mechanisms, structures, and causal powers that operate on social relations in Canada. More detailed research on those many practices will adequately untangle the web in which the relations and behaviours discussed here are embedded.

There are political implications in the above analysis. The demands and struggles of Quebec and First Nations nationalists and racialized minorities, especially women, are potential mechanisms for change as they face other forces with their own causal powers. As Day (2000: 225–27) suggests, a radical imaginary response is called for which would accept the need for an ongoing negotiation of all universal horizons. However, he appropriately cautions that this could lead to renunciation of recognition by the communities involved and make impossible a community of equals that English Canada always claims to desire but does not guarantee.

Accepting the critiques of Bannerji (2000) and Dei (2000) means pursuing counter-hegemonic and anti-racist activism on all fronts and supporting the aspirations of First Nations peoples (Winant 2002). Whether at local, regional, national, or global levels, both respect for and the dignity of all human beings and First Nations communities and cultures must be protected against Eurocentrism, exploitation, opportunity hoarding, and the use of power for the accumulation of wealth at the expense of providing for people's social rights to good health, education, and a viable lifestyle. As Schwalbe (2000: 781) puts it: "... this requires a close look at who does what to whom and with whom, and how they're doing it, using what kinds of material and symbolic resources." Critical realism is a useful tool in looking for and explaining those processes. The struggle for justice must therefore not only address culture, language, and religion but also their hybrid manifestations and their intersecting relations with race, gender, class, disability, sexual orientation, and other social disadvantages (Dei 2000: 312). All of these structural and cultural conditions preceded Canada's multicultural policy, but struggles to transform them have persisted throughout the past 35 years. Among those involved are many whose consciousness remains at a level that doubts the usefulness of anti-racist, intersectional, or class- or gender-based politics and who will continue to seek social justice in the mainstream liberal context, supporting multiculturalism and working to advance equality of opportunity.

REFERENCES AND FURTHER READINGS

ACS/Environics. 2002. Public Opinion Poll in 30 Years of Multiculturalism. *Canadian Issues/ Thèmes canadiens* (February): 4–5.

Alfred, T. 1999. *Peace, Power, Righteousness: An Indigenous Manifesto*. Don Mills: Oxford University Press.

Angus, I. 1997. *A Border Within: National Identity, Cultural Plurality, and Wilderness*. Montreal and Kingston: McGill-Queen's University Press.

Angus Reid Group. 1991. Canadians and Multiculturalism: National Survey of the Attitudes of Canadians. Ottawa: Multicultural and Citizenship Canada (August).

Archer, M. 1989. *Culture and Agency: The Place of Culture in Social Theory*. Cambridge: Cambridge University Press.

——. 1995. *Realist Social Theory: A Morphogenetic Approach*. Cambridge: Cambridge University Press.

——. 1998. Social Theory and the Analysis of Society. In T. May and M. Williams, eds., *Knowing the Social World*. Buckingham: Open University Press. 69–85.

Archer, M., R. Bhaskar, A. Collier, T. Lawson, and A. Norrie (eds.). 1998. *Critical Realism: Essential Readings*. London: Routledge.

Bannerji, H. 2000. *The Dark Side of the Nation: Essays on Multiculturalism, Nationalism, and Gender*. Toronto: Canadian Scholars' Press.

Berry, J.W. 1984. Multicultural Policy in Canada: A Social Psychological Analysis. *Canadian Journal of Behavioural Science* 16(4): 353–70.

——. 1999. Intercultural Relations in Plural Societies. *Canadian Psychology* 40(1): 12–21.

Berry, J.W., R. Kalin, and D.M. Taylor. 1977. *Multiculturalism and Ethnic Attitudes in Canada*. Ottawa: Ministry of Supply and Services.

Bibby, R. 1995. *The Bibby Report: Social Trends, Canadian Style*. Toronto: Stoddart.

Biles, J. 2002. Everyone's a Critic. *Canadian Issues/Thèmes canadiens* (February): 35–38.

Binavince, E. 1997. The Role of Ethnic Minorities in the Pursuit of Equality and Multiculturalism. In A. Cardozo and L. Musto, eds., *The Battle Over Multiculturalism*. Vol. 1. Ottawa: Pearson-Shoyama Institute. 90–100.

Bissoondath, N. 1994. *Selling Illusions: The Cult of Multiculturalism in Canada*. Toronto: Penguin.

Breton, R. 1984. The Production and Allocation of Symbolic Resources: An Analysis of the Linguistic and Ethnocultural Fields in Canada. *Canadian Review of Sociology and Anthropology* 21(2): 123–44.

——. 1986. Multiculturalism and Canadian Nation-Building. In A. Cairns and C. Williams, eds., *The Politics of Gender, Ethnicity, and Language in Canada*. Vol. 34, Collected Research Studies of the Royal Commission on the Economic Union and Development Prospects for Canada. Toronto: University of Toronto Press. 27–66.

——. 1998. Ethnicity and Race in Social Organization. In R. Helmes-Hayes and J. Curtis, eds., *The Vertical Mosaic Revisited*. Toronto: University of Toronto Press. 60–115.

Bunge, M. 1997. Mechanism and Explanation. *Philosophy of the Social Sciences* 27(4): 410–46.

Carter, R. 2000. *Realism and Racism*. London: Routledge.

——. 2007. Prospects for a Post-Race Sociology. In Sean P. Hier and B. Singh Bolaria, eds., *Race and Racism in 21st-Century Canada: Continuity, Complexity, and Change*. Peterborough: Broadview.

Carter, R., and C. New. 2004. *Making Realism Work*. London: Routledge.

Day, R.J.F. 2000. *Multiculturalism and the History of Canadian Diversity*. Toronto: University of Toronto Press.

Day, R.J.F., and T. Sadik. 2002. The BC Land Question, Liberal Multiculturalism, and the Spectre of Aboriginal Nationhood. *BC Studies* 134: 5–34.

Dei, G.J.S. 2000. Contesting the Future: Anti-Racism and Diversity. In S. Nancoo, ed., *21st Century Canadian Diversity*. Mississauga: Canadian Educators' Press.

Department of Canadian Heritage. 1997. *Annual Report on the Operation of the Canadian Multicultural Act*. Ottawa: Queen's Printer.

Economic Council of Canada. 1991. *New Faces in the Crowd: Economic and Social Impacts of Immigration*. Ottawa: ECC (May).

Flegel, P. 2002. Challenges to Canadian Multiculturalism: The Case of Black Montreal. *Canadian Issues/Thèmes canadiens* (February): 39–41.

Fleras, A. 2002. Multiculturalism as Critical Discourse. *Canadian Issues/Thèmes canadiens* (February): 9–11.

Fleras, A., and J. Elliott. 1992. *The Challenge of Diversity: Multiculturalism in Canada*. Scarborough: Nelson.

Friesen, J.W. 1993. *When Cultures Clash*. Calgary: Detselig.

Geschwender, J., and N. Guppy. 1995. Ethnicity, Educational Attainment, and Earned Income Among Canadian-born Men and Women. *Canadian Ethnic Studies* 27(1): 67–83.

Hedstroem, P., and R. Swedberg. 1998. *Social Mechanisms: An Analytical Approach to Social Theory*. Cambridge: Cambridge University Press.

Henry, F., C. Tator, W. Matis, and T. Rees. 2000. *The Colour of Democracy: Racism in Canadian Society*. Toronto: Harcourt Brace.

Herberg, W. 1990. Ethno-Racial Economic Hierarchy in Canada: Theory and Analysis of the New Vertical Mosaic. *International Journal of Comparative Sociology* 31(3/4): 206–21.

Innis, H. 1973. *Bilingualism and Biculturalism: An Abridged Version of the Royal Commission Report*. Toronto: McClelland and Stewart.

Joseph, J. 2000. A Realist Theory of Hegemony. *Journal for the Theory of Social Behaviour* 30(2): 179–202.

Kamboureli, S. 1998. The Technology of Ethnicity: Canadian Multiculturalism and the Language of Law. In Davis Bennett, ed., *Multicultural States: Rethinking Difference and Identity*. New York: Routledge.

Khouri, R.G. 2002. *Arabs in Canada: Post 9/11.* Toronto: G7 Books.

Kymlicka, W. 1995. *Multicultural Citizenship: A Liberal Theory of Minority Rights.* Oxford: Oxford University Press.

—. 1998. *Finding Our Way: Rethinking Ethnocultural Relations in Canada.* Oxford: Oxford University Press.

Lautard, H., and N. Guppy. 1999. Revisiting the Vertical Mosaic. In P. Li, ed., *Race and Ethnic Relations in Canada.* 2nd ed. Toronto: Oxford University Press.

Layder, D. 1997. *Modern Social Theory.* London: UCL Press.

Leman, M. 1997. *Canadian Multiculturalism.* Current Issue Review 93-6E. Ottawa: Research Branch, Library of Parliament.

Li, P. 1988. *Ethnic Inequality in a Class Society.* Toronto: Wall and Thompson.

Luther, R. 2002. Multiculturalism, Advocacy Groups, and Charitable Tax Status. *Canadian Issues/Thèmes canadiens* (February): 20–24.

Maracle, L. 1996. *I Am Woman: A Native Perspective on Sociology and Feminism.* Vancouver: Press Gang.

McAll, C. 1990. *Class, Ethnicity, and Social Inequality.* Montreal and Kingston: McGill-Queen's University Press.

McRoberts, K. 1997. *Misconceiving Canada: The Struggle for National Unity.* Oxford: Oxford University Press.

Mirchandani, K., and E. Tastsoglu. 2000. Towards a Diversity Beyond Tolerance. *Studies in Political Economy* 61: 49–77.

Ogmundson, R. 1992. On the Right to be Canadian. In S. Hryniuk, ed., *Twenty Years of Multiculturalism.* Winnipeg: St John's College Press.

Ogmundson, R., and J. McLaughlin. 1992. Trends in the Ethnic Origins of Canadian Elites: The Decline of the Brits? *Canadian Review of Sociology and Anthropology* 29(2): 227–42.

Ornstein, M. 1998. Three Decades of Elite Research in Canada: John Porter's Unfulfilled Legacy. In R. Helmes-Hayes and J. Curtis, eds., *The Vertical Mosaic Revisited.* Toronto: University of Toronto Press. 145–79.

Ostry, B. 1978. *The Culture Connection: An Essay in Culture and Government Policy in Canada.* Toronto: McClelland and Stewart.

Parekh, B. 2000. *Rethinking Multiculturalism, Cultural Diversity and Political Theory.* Cambridge, MA: Harvard University Press.

Pawson, R. 2000. Middle-range Realism. *European Journal of Sociology* XLI(2): 283-325.

Pearson, D. 2001. *The Politics of Ethnicity in Settler Societies.* Basingstoke: Palgrave.

Porter, J. 1965. *The Vertical Mosaic.* Toronto: University of Toronto Press.

—. 1987. *The Measure of Canadian Society.* Ottawa: Carleton University Press.

Royal Commission. 1966. *Preliminary Report of the Royal Commission on Bilingualism and Biculturalism.* Ottawa: Queen's Printer.

Sayer, A. 1992. *Method in Social Science: A Realist Approach.* 2nd ed. London: Routledge.

—. 2000. *Realism in Social Science.* London: Sage.

Schwalbe, M. 2000. Charting Futures for Sociology: Inequality Mechanisms, Intersections, and Global Change. *Contemporary Sociology* 29(6): 775–81.

Stasiulis, D. 1999. Feminist Intersectional Theorizing. In P. Li, ed., *Race and Ethnic Relations in Canada.* Toronto: Oxford University Press. 347–97.

Trudeau, P.E. 1971. Statement to the House of Commons, House of Commons Debates, 8 October.

Warburton, R. 1997. Status, Class, and the Politics of Canadian Aboriginal Peoples. *Studies in Political Economy* 54: 119–41.

Winant, H. 2001. *The World is a Ghetto*. New York: Basic Books.

——. 2002. Durban, Globalization, and the World after 9/11: Toward a New Politics. *Poverty and Race* 11(1). <http://www.prrac.org/full_text.php?text_id=730&item_id=7775&newsletter_id=60&header=January/February%202002%20Newsletter>.

15 | TROUBLES WITH "ANTI-RACIST MULTICULTURALISM"
The Challenges of Anti-Racist and Feminist Activism

Sarita Srivastava[1]

Multiculturalism has become a symbol of Canada. In the last few decades, the multicultural approach to managing ethnic diversity has become central to Canada's image as a tolerant and benevolent nation. Multiculturalism officially acknowledges the wide diversity of ethnic communities in Canada and encourages cultural exchange and harmony. However, official multiculturalism barely acknowledges the historical inequities of race and ethnicity within Canada, and it does little to address systemic racism. Multiculturalism, and its liberal foundation, advocate education, cultural exchange, policy reform, and symbolic gestures as ways of addressing social inequality. It avoids more profound challenges to racist practices and institutions. On the contrary, by representing Canada as a country that values and celebrates ethnic difference, multicultural discourse only submerges more critical discussions of racism. We might say that liberal multiculturalism has taken a 3-D approach—one that celebrates dance, dress, and dining, but fails to take into account the multiple dimensions of racial and social inequality.

Anti-racist approaches, which explicitly analyze and challenge racism, and which are clearly rooted in progressive social movements, may be seen as an alternative to multiculturalism. While the term "anti-racism" encompasses a broad range of theoretical and activist approaches, it is built on the assumption that racism and racialization stem from relations of power embedded in institutions and social practices, rather than from individual attitudes, prejudices, or cultural misunderstandings. In contrast to multiculturalism, which is based on a discourse of liberal pluralism, anti-racist theory challenges liberalism and its notions of equal opportunity and reform (Henry *et al.* 1995: 41). Anti-racist practice is framed as an explicitly "action-oriented strategy aimed at institutional systemic change" (Dei 1996: 252).

While anti-racist approaches have been evolving and anti-racist activism has been strong, the multicultural approach has been pervasive and has shaped Canadian discourses on race and ethnicity. As such, it often forms the framework, either unspoken or explicit, for addressing racism in many organizations, institutions, and communities, even where anti-racism is the explicit goal. While this blend of multiculturalism and anti-racism, which is sometimes referred to as "anti-racist multiculturalism" (Nadeau 2005: 21; Bonnet 2000: 63), can be strategically useful, the results can be disappointing. Not surprisingly, multicultural and liberal approaches to challenging racism often fall spectacularly short of making fundamental changes to everyday practice and organizational structure.

In this chapter, I look at the attempts of community and social movement organizations to deal with the challenges of racism, and I argue that their efforts have often been constrained by discourses of liberal multiculturalism. I explore this argument by looking first at how organizing in the feminist movement has been shaped by multiculturalism and then by examining more closely a tool used by community organizations, that is, the anti-racist workshop. In looking at the feminist movement, we see that, while multicultural policy and discourse opened up some avenues for organizing by women of colour, it has also limited the terms and language of their participation and significantly contained their activism. The rest of the chapter details my research on anti-racist workshops, which suggests that multicultural discourse can also pervade these efforts in problematic ways. My research shows that the techniques used in anti-racist workshops often echo liberal and multicultural notions that more education and more knowledge will reduce prejudice and therefore racism. Similar to multiculturalism, these pedagogical techniques often put people of colour on display for the education of passive spectators. I argue that this emphasis on learning more about others merely reinforces, rather than transforms, racialized identities and relations of power. I begin with a brief overview of multiculturalism, liberalism, and some of the shortcomings of these approaches for challenging racism.

MULTICULTURALISM, LIBERALISM, AND RACISM

Assimilationism, multiculturalism, and anti-racism are often cited as three distinct approaches to dealing with racial diversity and racism (Henry et al. 1998: 376). Assimilationism emphasizes the homogeneity of a society or organization and encourages those who are different from the dominant mainstream culture to change their own cultural and political practices so that they simply "fit in." Ethnic diversity is seen as a problem that is best minimized. It is often said that the US, for example, has encouraged a "melting-pot" style of assimilation, in which people's ethnic differences eventually melt away in the great pot of "American identity." Multiculturalism is held up as the counterpoint to assimilationism; indeed, Canadian government publications explicitly contrast their mosaic multicultural approach to the American melting-pot (Government of Canada 1987). Rather than encouraging assimilation, official multiculturalism acknowledges and highlights Canada's ethnic diversity.

Anti-racism encompasses a diverse range of theoretical and activist directions, but it is distinguished from multiculturalism because it is rooted in political and grassroots struggles against racism and other forms of oppression rather than in state policy. Often these are not coherent, organized struggles, and they may not formally take the name "anti-racist." The term "anti-racism" itself was not widely used until the 1980s, but it shares common threads with anti-slavery, anti-colonial, and civil rights struggles. In comparison to multiculturalism, its focus on challenging racism is explicit. Much of anti-racist theory and practice, particularly anti-racist feminism, emphasizes an intersectional approach that links racism to gender and class inequalities.

Yet, in practice, the lines between multiculturalism and anti-racism are blurred. Multiculturalism, and the notions of modern liberalism and tolerance on which it is based, are pervasive in discussions about race in Canada and have undermined more radical attempts at anti-racism in many communities. As the following review of liberal multiculturalism suggests, its focus on national unity, "harmony in diversity," and educational, cultural, and symbolic responses to racism have shaped discussions of the issue in Canada.

Prime Minister Pierre Trudeau's 1971 announcement of the new multicultural policy said that it was aimed at encouraging "creative encounters and interchange among all Canadian cultural groups in the interest of national unity" (Trudeau 1971: 8545). In other words, one of its aims is to get people of diverse backgrounds to learn more about each other, so that they will get along better and produce a more unified Canada. Although Trudeau's speech cemented multiculturalism as state policy, these notions of harmony in diversity were not new to Canadian politics. As Day's genealogy of multiculturalism in Canada details, we can trace these notions to the early 20th century. The image of a Canadian ethnic "mosaic" emerged in the 1920s and formed the basis for state programs during the 1950s and 1960s (Day 2000: 149; Foster 1926). The mosaic has remained an enduring metaphor for multiculturalism: each tile in the mosaic remains distinct and important but is subordinate in the creation of an overall design—the unified Canadian nation. National unity remains the overarching principle that undergirds multiculturalism. Multiculturalism and Citizenship Canada (1985) documents refer to multiculturalism as "the great national bandage" that holds Canada together, a phrase that highlights how multiculturalism is meant to stitch together a fragmented national unity wounded by the barrage of ethnic diversity.

More recent government publications suggest that multiculturalism, particularly the 1988 Multiculturalism Act, supports the "elimination of racism and discrimination" in Canada (Multiculturalism and Citizenship Canada 1991: 6). However, Mackey's (2002: 67) close review of multicultural policy persuasively demonstrates that this interest is limited to "symbolic and emotional issues" and that the fundamental concern remains national unity (Multiculturalism and Citizenship Canada Corporate and Policy Branch 1988: 17). Its concern about racism does not extend to substantive changes in legislation, funding, or policy. As Mackey observes, despite changes to acknowledge the importance of eliminating racism, the Multiculturalism Act "is still primarily concerned with mobilizing diversity for the project of nation-building, as well as limiting that diversity to symbolic rather than political forms" (Mackey 2002: 67). In other words, this kind of multiculturalism may be described as an attempt to manage ethnic diversity while maintaining a dominant culture. Multiculturalism can be described as a strategy to *contain* rather than change difficult social relations (Henry and Tator 1999: 95).

The observation that multicultural policy is primarily "symbolic" in its intent might be interpreted as meaning that multiculturalism is therefore not significant in its impacts. On the contrary, multiculturalism has become an influential and powerful discourse in discussions of race and diversity. It is often cited in government documents, academic texts, and popular debates as an innovative, successful, and progressive model for managing the "problem" of ethnic diversity. Although surveys show that multicultural programs can be controversial, multiculturalism is nevertheless "a social value" that many Canadians share (Li 1999: 159); in a 1991 survey, 80% of Canadians agreed that "multiculturalism is vital to uniting Canada" (Angus Reid 1991). It has become one of the symbols of Canada, often cited to distinguish it as a kinder, gentler place than the US. Multiculturalism has been particularly important in propping up the representation of Canada as a tolerant, diverse nation, benevolent to newcomers. This image remains so powerful that a recent television news report about the racist head tax on Chinese immigrants,[2] began with the phrase, "Canada, the tolerant and diverse nation ..." (CBC 2006).

The pervasive effects of multiculturalism may be linked in part to its foundations in liberalism, which, as David Goldberg (1993) carefully traces, has been an overriding discourse in discussions about race. Common principles of liberalism include reason, the rational individual, and the assumption that rational reform will address social problems. Liberal approaches therefore assume that racism can be traced to individual, irrational prejudice and can be addressed through education. Liberalism's reform-oriented approach is also concerned with improving equal access to jobs, services, and benefits, but it is less concerned with transforming the inequitable social relations that make it difficult to succeed even when one is faced with so-called equal opportunity. While it is concerned about inequality, liberalism assumes equality will naturally arise from better policy, education, and legislation. The focus remains on the reform of existing frameworks and institutions, leaving little scope for more profound transformation. Because multiculturalism is founded on a discourse of liberal pluralism, it assumes that there is an equal, level playing field within which people may freely exercise their individual rights, expressing their cultural heritage as they please. The liberal approach glosses over the historical and systemic relations of racism that make this playing field less than level. These foundations of multiculturalism are repeatedly echoed in the efforts of communities and social movements confronted with questions of diversity and racism.

MULTICULTURALISM SHAPES SOCIAL MOVEMENTS

So what are the effects of this pervasive state policy and discourse? Multicultural agencies have focused on acknowledging ethnic communities in Canada through a variety of services, programs, advertising, and direct funding. If we look at diversity and racism through this multicultural lens, we find that our vision is limited to a narrow range of images. Multiculturalism produces a certain kind of whiteness, the "*Canadian*-Canadian" (Mackey 2002: 3), as the dominant centre against which "other" Canadians are measured as different. However, only certain kinds of difference are celebrated and supported through multicultural discourse and services. As Mackey (2002: 65, 66) says succinctly, "state recognition of diversity also limits diversity," and "defines acceptable forms of difference." Certain identities and forms of diversity and communities are prescribed, reinforced, and even produced, while other ways of organizing are not.

Community and social movement groups researching or organizing on issues of racism and diversity then find themselves trying to make claims in terms that are recognizable by multicultural policy and discourse in order both to be recognized as valid and to access funding. We see this in the cases, discussed in more detail below, of women of colour who are encouraged to create organizations of "visible minority" women and of anti-racist feminist organizing that uses multicultural terms to make itself more tolerable. The term "anti-racist multiculturalism" (Nadeau 2005: 21; Bonnet 2000: 63) highlights how social movements and community organizations have used multicultural frameworks to achieve anti-racist ends. However, integrating multicultural discourse into anti-racist organizing can also produce a precarious and problematic form of politics, one based on recognition of multicultural identities and ways of making sense of diversity.

Multicultural interventions in community organizing have been largely concerned with supporting ethnic diversity and ethnic participation in civic life. Because of the serious concerns with this multicultural framework, it's not surprising that many social movement groups who are attempting to deal with racism, either in their own organizations or in their communities, have explicitly subscribed to an anti-racist framework. However, multicultural discourse has nevertheless had a profound impact on community and social movement organizations in two ways: 1) through its funding of and intervention in community organizing; and 2) through its pervasive influence on discourses of racial diversity, tolerance, and diversity in unity. Here, I discuss how these effects of multiculturalism have shaped and limited the work of Canadian feminist organizations.

Women of Colour Organize Through Multiculturalism: The National Organization of Immigrant and Visible Minority Women (NOIVM) and the Ontario Coalition of Visible Minority Women (OCVMW)

There are two striking examples of state-sponsored intervention in community organizing efforts: the National Organization of Immigrant and Visible Minority Women (NOIVM) and the Ontario Coalition of Visible Minority Women (OCVMW). In both cases, the federal or provincial governments became involved in guiding discussions and even creating organizations to deal with the concerns of immigrant women and women of colour. Both cases provide examples of how multiculturalism can direct and shape organizations in ways that seem to be more about managing problematic populations than about meeting communities' goals and needs.

NOIVM and OCVMW were created in the 1980s after two conferences sponsored by the federal and Ontario governments to look at the issues facing "immigrant women" and "visible minority women." While immigrant women's organizing had been active since the 1970s in organizations such as Toronto's Women Working with Immigrant Women (WWIW), these were unique, state-initiated attempts to form provincial and national organizations, reflecting a 1978 study on immigrant women by the Multiculturalism Directorate (Das Gupta 1999). The federal government was involved in organizing the 1981 National Conference of Immigrant Women, out of which grew a national and provincial Immigrant Women's Network. In Ontario, government agencies held a similar conference in 1983 that resulted in the formation of OCVMW. In 1986, a National Conference on Immigrant and Visible Minority Women was held; NOIVM was formed as a result (Carty and Brand 1993).

Both these organizations illustrate how multiculturalism produces certain kinds of difference and organizes that difference by reinforcing particular categories of identity. In this case, state multicultural involvement in community organizing meant that the terms "visible minority" and "immigrant women" were chosen as organizing categories rather than a term such as "women of colour." The term "women of colour" arose from anti-racist writing and activism and gained broad political currency within North American feminism. Beginning in the early 1980s, there has been an exciting array of feminist writing and activist efforts organized through this relatively new political identity, such as the influential collection *This Bridge Called My Back: Writings by Radical Women of Colour* (Moraga and Anzaldua 1983). While not uncontroversial or universally accepted (Bannerji 2000), the term "women of colour" refers to a political identity rooted in this collective struggle against sexism and racism.

In contrast, terms such as "visible minority women" have been strongly linked to and perpetuated by Canadian state policy and practice. As Bannerji observes, the "visible minority woman" is "a categorical child of the state, cradled by the Ministry of Multiculturalism and the Secretary of State" (Bannerji 2000: 31). It is a term that has little connection to anti-racist feminism and its integrated analysis of racism, sexism, and classism. This becomes strikingly clear in the history of NOIVM and OCVMW. Rather than highlighting political strength and resistance, the term "visible minority" is a reflection of state multicultural policy, and it implies a weak and inferior political position. However, the presence of multicultural policy and discourse has meant that some feminist organizations, including NOIVM and OCVMW, have emphasized the term "visible minority women," which has in turn shaped the goals, structure, and practices of their anti-racist efforts. In particular, Carty and Brand (1993: 179) observe that the state-defined categories of "visible minority" and "immigrant" were used to signify only race and ethnicity, rather than gender, as the primary concerns of these communities. In other words, organizations such as NOIVM and OCVMW, concerned with "visible minorities," were expected to deal with issues such as immigration and employment that mainstream women's organizations did not, but conversely they were not supposed to deal with fundamental feminist issues. The result was that these "visible minority" organizations failed to integrate an analysis of racism and sexism and therefore failed to adequately address concerns such as reproductive choice, pay equity, and child care (Carty and Brand 1993).

Involvement by state multicultural agencies also meant that more radical, grassroots, and activist aspects of organizing by feminists of colour were undermined and circumvented. For example, in 1985 the federal multiculturalism minister held a meeting with women from immigrant and visible minority groups to consult with them about the formation of NOIVM. Das Gupta (1999) observes that by choosing individual women to invite to meetings, the minister was able to bypass the existing networks of immigrant women and women of colour. Furthermore, many of the activist and anti-racist community workers were notably not invited to this consultation process. By structuring the consultation in this way, the Ministry of Multiculturalism was, as Das Gupta (1999: 201) suggests, "retaining control of the movement through another hand-picked committee."[3] Once again, the involvement of state multiculturalism meant that certain kinds of difference and categories of identity were acknowledged in the process of building a national organization, and others were excluded.

The involvement of state multiculturalism in community organizing also distracts activists from activism, encouraging them to focus on state-defined priorities such as forming new national organizations, defining the constitution and structure of these organizations, defining who is and who is not a "visible minority" woman, and so on. For example, in the first year of its life, OCVMW spent most of its time drafting its constitution (Carty and Brand 1993: 177). In other words, the women working within NOIVM and OCVMW spent a fair bit of time on defining "visible minority women" and using limited funding to represent all the issues and all the women in this category. Furthermore, these organizations deflected activists away from the community-based work on immigration, employment, and education issues they had already been doing for years in grassroots groups such as the Cross-Cultural Communications Centre and various black women's congresses and South Asian women's groups. There were little funds or energies left for challenging racist and sexist state practices or providing alternative spaces and services for women. This outcome is not surprising. Multicultural policy and programs are usually concerned with developing the skills of individual immigrant women rather than challenging the systemic obstacles they face; for example, one multicultural discussion paper suggests that immigrant women "lack basic life skills" and should be helped to develop their "personal skills," "better knowledge of their communities," and their "rights and obligations in Canada" (Secretary of State 1982: 4). Roxana Ng's (1988: 98) extensive study of immigrant women's groups highlighted similar problems, showing that efforts often became channelled into state-funded services rather than into alternative forms of organizing.

Finally, like similar organizations, NOIVM and OCVMW did not even receive adequate funding from the federal or provincial governments. As Carty and Brand's (1993) analysis demonstrates, the state-sponsored initiative to organize women nationally under the categories "immigrant" and "visible minority" merely created poorly funded and ineffective organizations.

The Women's Movement Confronts Anti-Racism: The National Action Committee on the Status of Women (NAC)

Women of colour and immigrant women have been politically active in feminist and anti-racist issues since the 1970s; however, the mainstream feminist movement did not adequately take their activism and their anti-racist concerns into account. Since its rise in the late 1960s, the second-wave women's movement in Canada was primarily directed by white, middle-class, Canadian-born women; these were the women who ran the organizations, sat on the boards, and lobbied the provincial and federal governments.

Beginning in the 1980s, feminists of colour began to challenge the white dominant centre of North American feminism, both in the US and in Canada. Feminist scholars challenged the universality of the category "woman" and showed that by neglecting analyses of race and sexuality, feminist theory had inadequately conceptualized women's oppression, particularly in relation to immigration, reproductive issues, and the family (Carby 1982; Amos and Parmar 1984; hooks 1981; Lucas *et al.* 1991). Feminist and community organizations in Canada began confronting charges of racism from their own members and began shifting their goals, priorities, and practices in the mid-1980s and early 1990s (Egan *et al.* 1988; Henry *et al.* 1995). However, as my own research has shown, anti-racist challenges within Canadian feminist groups have often met with emotional resistance (Srivastava 2006). Controversy and conflict about racism were common threads running through the women's movement during this turbulent period in feminist history. White feminists have sometimes reacted to charges of racism by reasserting themselves as the guardians of feminism and feminist unity and purity and as the standards of what is truly feminist (Srivastava 2002, 2005). The multiculturalist discourse that centres whiteness and that uses a language of tolerance, benevolence, diversity, and national unity has strong echoes in these battles. Multicultural discourse also offers a nationalist "unity in diversity" framework that can frame feminist discussions about anti-racism. One of the prevailing responses of feminists concerned about anti-racist critiques has been that the unity and integrity of the movement will be disrupted; as in multiculturalism, the implicit assumption has been that white feminists have the responsibility of guarding this unity (Srivastava 2002). Finally, even within social movements, we often see a liberal non-racism, bolstered in part by multiculturalism, which can make it difficult to raise an anti-racist critique without being countered with an indignant, incredulous response such as "You're calling *me* a racist?"

In Canada, one of the most public examples of this kind of anti-racist battle was fought in the National Action Committee on the Status of Women (NAC), which has been one of the most significant national women's organizations in this country. NAC is an umbrella organization, at one time representing hundreds of women's groups across Canada, which made significant interventions in national political debates during the 1980s and early 1990s. During this same period, NAC was also seeing significant challenges to its overwhelmingly white history and composition. In 1991, it implemented an affirmative action policy that designed positions on the executive for underrepresented groups, such as Aboriginal women and women of colour. A significant turning-point was the election of Sunera Thobani in 1993, the first woman of colour to be president of NAC. However, these accomplishments were the culmination of years of struggle by feminists of colour within NAC; their anti-racist activism required a slow battle to overcome not only bureaucratic and structural barriers but also resistance from NAC leaders.

Multicultural discourse provided a way to gently fend off radical anti-racist changes to NAC. Mary-Jo Nadeau (2005) suggests that NAC leaders used a hierarchical multiculturalist framework to deal with and contain anti-racist challenges by activists within the organization. Like state multicultural discourse, this framework used the language of pluralism to espouse diversity. However, the multicultural language of "unity in diversity" used in NAC documents also submerged concerns about racism:

> Consistent with official multiculturalist discourse, "diversity" here obscures the dominant white feminist position, and functions as a substitute for an analysis of racism and other hegemonic relations operating in NAC. (Nadeau 2005: 24)

Multicultural discourse also allows white feminists to position themselves as the central "we" who are reaching out to "include" other women, a common dynamic in organizational discussions about diversity and racism. In a NAC funding proposal, for example, "visible minority" women were represented as new "priority targets for membership outreach" rather than integral to the direction of the organization (NAC 1985). Multicultural discourse lends another dimension of support to this form of resistance to anti-racism, as this resistance is similarly based on an imagined national history that places white "Canadian-Canadians" at the centre.

Furthermore, multicultural discourse was useful for NAC in its relations with the state. In seeking state funding, NAC was able to use multicultural discourse to legitimate itself as a diverse, equality-seeking organization that represented, as it suggested in a submission to the Secretary of State, "immigrant and visible minority women" and "multicultural groups"(NAC 1985; Nadeau 2005: 9). As a national organization with a strong orientation to government policy, NAC was well positioned to draw on the multicultural story of the progressive white nation opening its doors to welcome newcomers. At the same time as its executive was talking about the importance of increasing diversity, however, NAC's organizational history and framework was one which emphasized white women's ownership and dominance and which placed "strict limits on the participation of racialized women in NAC's political culture and its governing apparatus"(Nadeau 2006: 16).

At the same time, this crucial period of Canadian feminism was also one in which anti-racist challenges were becoming increasingly forceful. Nadeau (2006: 21; 2005: 11) uses the term "anti-racist multiculturalism" to refer to the complex and creative ways that feminists of colour within NAC used multicultural discourse to make anti-racist concerns acceptable and palatable. In particular, multiculturalism gave women of colour the space and language they needed to create a Visible Minority and Immigrant Women's Committee (1985) within NAC. While the committee originally framed its work in multiculturalist language, advocating "the need for *acceptance* of these *cultural diversities* in the women's movement" (NAC 1985), it later became a central platform for the more profound anti-racist challenges that transformed NAC by the early 1990s (Nadeau 2005; Rebick and Roach 1996: 112).

Anti-Racist Workshops and Multicultural Discourse

As we have seen, internal conflicts about racism became increasingly common in feminist and social service organizations beginning in the 1980s. These turbulent times encouraged the growth of a new educational and organizing tool: the anti-racist workshop. These workshops were—and still are—often concerned with learning more about racism, commonly using the technique of drawing out personal experiences of participants, especially people of colour. Frequently the method of choice for dealing with public charges of racism in Canadian institutions, anti-racist workshops (sometimes called equity, diversity, cross-cultural, consciousness-raising, or conflict resolution workshops) became almost commonplace in public agencies, universities, schools, and social movement organizations during the 1990s. During that decade, the provincial New Democratic Party government in Ontario created the Ontario Anti-Racism Secretariat (OARS), which funded a plethora of anti-racist initiatives by community organizations and encouraged an increase in the number of anti-racist workshops and educational initiatives. Once again, we see an overlap between anti-racism and state multiculturalism, a kind of anti-racist multiculturalism that opens possibilities for change but also limits the kinds of change that are possible.

Anti-racist workshops are often seen as a key strategy towards diversity or equity and are an important site for analyzing the trajectory and failures of anti-racist efforts. While they have helped to name the problem of racism in many institutions, we should be equally concerned with *how* racism has been named. Because liberal multiculturalist notions have had such a profound influence on these kinds of pedagogical efforts, racism is often represented as ignorance rather than as historic and systemic inequality. In my own research, I have found that this continuing influence of liberalism and multiculturalism has clearly shaped anti-racist workshops in ways that limit the potential for anti-racist change. The research I present here is based on my observations of or participation in anti-racist workshops and organizational meetings in Toronto[4] and on confidential interviews with anti-racist activists.[5]

Many anti-racist workshops have used discussion techniques that encourage personal and emotional disclosure, particularly concerning experiences of racism. I refer to this as the "let's talk" approach to anti-racist pedagogy (Srivastava 2006). This approach has clear links not only with official multicultural policy in Canada but also with multicultural and liberal traditions more generally. The value of hearing first-hand the stories of other people's lives has conventionally been considered important to multicultural or cross-cultural alliances. What Troyna (1993) calls "benevolent multiculturalism" has been primarily concerned with recognizing cultural diversity, promoting pluralism, and encouraging "inter-group tolerance" (Short 1991: 33). According to the well-known "contact hypothesis," which posits that interracial contact will reduce prejudice, this kind of cultural exchange is valuable for race relations (Cook 1978; Short 1991; McLeod 1994). As in official multiculturalism, the emphasis is on "creative encounters" in which we learn about other communities and individuals (Trudeau 1971: 8545). In the multicultural tradition, these "creative encounters" have often focused on so-called "cultural" aspects of life—food, traditions, clothes, religion, song, and dance.

However, the contact hypothesis has been challenged in part because reductions in individual prejudice towards the people one meets during cultural exchanges often do not generalize to all members of the group (Troyna and Hatcher 1992; Amir 1998; Cook 1978). In fact, in some cases contact may even worsen prejudicial attitudes (Amir 1998). More broadly, multicultural education has been criticized for its emphasis on social control and normalization (Troyna and Williams 1986; Jakubowicz 1988; Rezai-Rashti 1989); its ineffectiveness (Troyna 1987; Moore 1993; Sleeter 1993); its "rationalism" (Rattansi 1992: 33); its failure to question position, privilege, and unequal power (Walcott 1990; Thomas 1987); and the assumption that there is a relationship between knowledge and conduct (Britzman 1993).

Anti-racist education has been offered as a counter-proposal to multicultural education; however, liberal multiculturalist assumptions about how racism may be countered by better knowledge of others remain a strong influence. Whether linked to state multiculturalism or to conventional models of cross-cultural exchange, pedagogical models which emphasize the value of hearing about each other's everyday lives, experiences, and culture have been such a strong thread that, despite a number of critiques, the history and continuing influence of these forms of official, practical, and academic multiculturalism remain in present anti-racist work. In both anti-racist and liberal multicultural models of education, production of knowledge is seen as an important goal—knowledge of the experiences of people of colour, self-knowledge, or knowledge of the other's perspective. In particular, some anti-racist workshops can be characterized by the desires of some white participants for "better" knowledge of the racial Other. One result is that, despite its promise to challenge racist knowledge and practices, anti-racist pedagogy can become implicated in perpetuating inequities of race and representation.

An anti-racist discussion or workshop is often facilitated by a professional or informal facilitator who uses techniques of experience-sharing to elicit, discuss, and analyze personal experiences of racism, as well as to solicit feelings about those experiences and about co-workers. In many workshop exercises, non-whites are expected to disclose stories of racism, while whites share their feelings of being shocked, affronted, racist, not-racist, and so on. As my interviews show, workshops and meetings then become focused on the exploration of experiences of racism and feelings about racism.

A toolbox of techniques that is drawn from consciousness-raising and popular education models shapes these discussions of anti-racism. These are techniques explicitly aimed at shaping group dynamics and physical space, techniques designed to encourage a participatory and egalitarian environment to share experience. They typically include small group discussions in which participants tell personal stories and share emotions; the "go-around" in which each member of the whole group is compelled to speak in turn about their experiences of racism; the flip chart, used to record stories about racism through drawing or text; and role-plays of racist incidents. These techniques form the repertoire of the "let's talk" approach. People of colour become objects of knowledge whose utterances are meant to contribute to the self-knowledge project of the listeners—a project to create certain knowledge about racism and one's own character and one's own feelings.

This focus on personal experiences and emotional disclosure has been criticized as being especially painful for many non-white participants, limited for conducting useful discussions, and unnecessary for making anti-racist change (Razack 1993; Benjamin 1992; Ellsworth 1989; Srivastava 1994). These tools can also produce knowledge of racism and racial identities that supports individualized and emotional strategies for anti-racism rather than organizational ones. On the one hand, they provide white participants with a space for expressing their fear, guilt, or anger. On the other hand, they demand something else of people of colour. While white participants may feel encouraged to explore their feelings and self-knowledge, people of colour are generally expected to share their experiences and knowledge concerning racism. In formal meetings, informal discussions, and workshops, people of colour are expected to confront, directly persuade, or "share" their feelings with whites in their workplaces or organizations.

For example, in one account at a large women's advocacy group, Carmen, a lesbian of colour, relates how the demand for her personal experience became suddenly urgent, required by her co-workers only in the context of a diversity workshop: "I remember the facilitator just said to me, 'So Carmen, why don't you tell us what it's like to be a lesbian in a straight office?'" (interview transcripts). The knowledge of Carmen's life is newly demanded within the context of anti-racist organizational change. This parallels the suggestion by a number of women in my graduate courses that we should hold an anti-racist workshop; when the request was refused by a woman of colour, she was challenged by the women making the proposal, who confronted her after class saying, "But how are we supposed to learn? We *have* to have a dialogue." Their demand was founded on their need to learn, to educate themselves. Clearly, even when this designation as a "resource on racism" is refused, it is often demanded or "prompted." Razack (1993: 63), analyzing the problematic use of "storytelling" in her own human rights course, tells how a South African woman finally left in tears after twice "confronted" by fellow students "with a firm 'Why don't you tell us about your experiences?'" Linda Carty (1992: 15) writes that these expectations of knowledge from experience also shaped her experience as a black woman teaching university students: "What was clearly expected of me, the Black woman instructor, was to bring to class *my personal experience* of the issues being discussed (I was actually told this more than once by some participants outside of class)." Gloria Anzaldua (1990) describes a similar scene in her US Women of Colour class, in which white women either asked politely, pleaded or demanded that women-of-color teach them.

In more formal anti-racist workshops, popular education techniques may explicitly focus on the production of knowledge about racism through the experiences of people of colour. Gurnah (1984: 7), for example, describes Racism Awareness Training (RAT) workshops in the UK as "rightly concerned with people's personal experience of racism." McCaskell (1995: 256) similarly notes that anti-racist education "requires a particular type of *pedagogy*.... based on learners' real social experience." In discussing her human rights course, for example, Razack (1993: 63) writes that her goal was "to forge a politics of alliances based on this sharing of daily experiences." One model common to many workshops is the discussion, presentation, and analysis of personal experiences of racism. The analysis may be structured and formal, or form a minor part of the process. Early on, various methods such as small or large group discussions or "go-arounds" (everyone speaks one by one) are used to elicit personal experiences of racism. The facilitator may record them on a flip chart, display them, or do an oral presentation. In one anti-racist workshop I attended, we were asked to speak about our experiences in small groups, present our discussion to the larger group, and have our comments displayed on the wall. A Toronto Board of Education manual used in anti-racist workshops for adolescents prescribes very similar techniques, asking students to "share personal experiences of racism" (Ontario Ministry of Education and Training 1994: 19). Facilitators are told to use the participants' personal experiences of racism as "raw material" for social analysis. They are asked to prompt the young person of colour for details, and "get them to describe their experiences and feelings in the most vivid way possible." They then record and organize the experiences under general categories.

KNOWLEDGE OF RACISM AND RACE

Ironically, these techniques of knowledge production may reproduce the same relations they seek to "uncover." Because the "let's talk" model is influenced by a trend towards individualization, discussions of experience often glide over a concerted examination of social relations. Not only are people's experiences displayed, but they are also used to produce and reinforce a collective knowledge that often denies the power relations that produce that experience. In particular, the process by which whites might have learned racist knowledge is rarely explored, nor are strategies for challenging racism at an organizational or systemic level. The following two sections provide an elaboration of this critique.

The underlying assumption of these workshop techniques is that there is a link between ignorance and racism. In particular, the increasing personalization of the "let's talk" techniques often used in anti-racist workshops are supported by liberal multiculturalist assumptions about how racism may be countered by better knowledge of others. As David Goldberg (1993: 117) argues, the inevitable outcome of liberal analyses of racism is policies that assume that "racism can be eradicated for the most part by education." The idea that there is an "automatic" association between knowledge and conduct (Britzman 1993: 126) is influential, even within the context of more radical political efforts.

For example, some activist responses to the "war on terrorism" since September 11, 2001 have reflected these closely held notions about the associations between ignorance and racism, and between knowledge and conduct. In particular, some campus and community forums supported the popular belief that a fuller knowledge of Muslim communities would lead to more fruitful strategy. During a community forum on American military action in Afghanistan, held in Toronto the same fall, for example, there was an attempt by organizers to run an anti-racist workshop. Another common tactic, one used by organizers at the University of Toronto in the fall of 2001, has been to mount a film or lecture series about Islamic religion and culture, presumably to educate those ignorant about its "positive" aspects. As Cynthia Wright[6] wryly observes, the critical response to a terrorist attack by Christian fundamentalists would hardly be to screen *The Ten Commandments*—and yet a screening of the *History of Islam* was the response of campus activists seeking critical discussion following September 11. In the end this representational strategy merely highlights that violent actions by whites are not causally linked to ethnicity and religion.

There is an assumption, in other words, that knowledge of racism is best acquired by examining the lives of people of colour—rather than by acknowledging and challenging the array of racist knowledge and practices. Contrary to the intended outcomes of popular education, the mix of pedagogical practices and philosophies in anti-oppression or "diversity" workshops often produces people of colour, queers, and other marginalized participants as the objects of knowledge. The "equal" sharing of experiences and feelings is overshadowed by power relations of race. In most of the cases I studied, the tellers—people of colour who shared their experiences—were seen as primary resources, the "authentic" knowers. As we have seen, techniques require participants to discuss and present, role-play and analyze their personal experiences of racism. The goal becomes knowledge about race that is produced by and about people of colour—knowledge for scrutiny, rejection, or gratitude by whites. This educational approach to gaining knowledge of "the other" reconfirms static associations between racial identity and lived experience. The assumption is that people of colour who speak in workshops or discussions of race represent stable identities that reflect a global experience and that their stories will thus provide the most truthful knowledge. Organizational discussions of anti-racism may then begin to echo the "cultural" celebrations of liberal multiculturalism to which they are often contrasted, as the performance of scenes from people's lives satisfies a desire for data and drama.

The focus on people of colour as the "authentic" knowers means that this pedagogical project can then represent a treacherous space for those who are made "other." The focus begins and can remain on these individuals, the legitimacy of their story, and, by implication, the legitimacy of their identity. For example, the faith in knowledge as an antidote to racism often marks participants of colour as experts if they accept the invitation to dialogue or as angry or indifferent if they reject the demand. Anti-racist education and change efforts can then become bogged down by the way that angry or indifferent responses are linked to racial identity, reinforcing, for example, the stereotype of the "angry woman of colour."

Denial and Innocence

The "equal" sharing of experience is further subverted by the more direct denial, dismissal, and competition of stories, a phenomenon described in my interviews and observed in workshops. The ultimate denial occurs when stories are simultaneously desired and rejected. One man in an anti-racist workshop proclaimed, "It couldn't really be this racist in *Canada*." The anti-racist workshop can provide a space and format for this denial. The inevitable dismissals and denials of their stories can also put people of colour in the position of defending, reasserting, and reinforcing their identities as resources on racism.

The following example of a workshop exercise illustrates how the protestation of ignorance on the part of white participants not only constitutes people of colour as the resource for better knowledge but also relieves whites of this responsibility. It occurred in an anti-racist workshop at a large women's centre that has been attempting anti-racist change for a number of years. It is particularly useful because it is told by both a woman of colour and a white woman, each involved in anti-racist work, who have quite opposing perspectives of the same incident. Yasmin, a recently hired woman of colour, describes her irritation at the exercise, "Naming the Things You Are Proud Of," that divided the women of colour and white women into two groups:

> There was an exercise—"Naming the Things that You Are Proud Of"—asking us to name the things that we were proud of having accomplished as a group. When people reported back, the white women had almost nothing.

Even when directly asked, the white women sidestepped the question of examining their own histories and stories of "pride" and ethnicity. Yasmin pinpoints the pervasive tendency of whites to ignore the relations of power inherent in the decision not to make oneself vulnerable, in the privilege of rejecting the notion of ethnicity. At the same time, Yasmin says, the white participants think that they are challenging racism precisely because, in refusing to participate in the exercise, they have refused pride in whiteness. Samantha, a white manager at the same organization, felt that the discussion was fruitful, and she was taken aback by the anger expressed by the women of colour:

> We had a discussion about what makes us proud to be white ... and the women of colour went off and talked about what made them proud to be women of colour.... And so we decided that there was nothing that made us proud to be white, because ... anyway.... But women of colour were really pissed off that

white women couldn't come up with anything. And—imagine if we did come up with stuff! They would be saying, "How dare you take credit for stuff."

Samantha's description shows that some white women feel caught in the dichotomy of this exercise—how do they express feelings of pride without reinforcing racial superiority? "Naming the Things You are Proud Of" puts women into a competition of knowledge and emotion about race and ethnicity, a competition that seems destined to fail—or perhaps to be "won" by the white participants who choose not to participate. The exercise was likely meant to ethnicize whites, perhaps to actually *counter* the usual spectacle of women of colour as ethnic resources. Instead, it supported that problematic construction of racial identity since the participants and facilitators failed to analyze the relations of power in representations of both whiteness and ethnic pride, which became visible as the white participants chose not to make themselves vulnerable.

Once again, we see that the burden of being a teaching resource is placed on women of colour, who themselves learn nothing new about the construction of "white" or European culture from the perspective of white women. This discussion ends by merely highlighting that only non-white ethnicity is meant to be displayed and explored in these workshops and that whiteness remains the invisible ethnic norm, supposedly with no stories to "uncover."

The dead-end of this exercise reinforces the wishful myth that whites are ignorant when it comes to race. How could the white women have responded differently? What kinds of discussions of whiteness would avoid a facile equivalence between white and non-white ethnicity, a reduction of racial dominance to ethnic difference? Perhaps Samantha could have begun with a willingness to be vulnerable in discussions of whiteness, in that way acknowledging the vulnerability of women of colour and the privilege of her refusal to be vulnerable. Perhaps she could have begun with a willingness to express her critical thoughts on the notion of "pride." This line of inquiry might have led in some useful directions: Which sources of pride reflect privilege and exclusion, and which challenge dominant relations of power? What might white women's stories of ethnicity and pride tell us about constructions of racial dominance and inferiority?

These questions point to a very different kind of pedagogical project, one entirely outside liberal and multicultural approaches that see education as an antidote to prejudice or a route to cross-cultural exchange. Instead, it would ask questions about how we learn racist knowledge, how we perpetuate racist practices, and how we can change our everyday practices.

CONCLUSIONS AND ALTERNATIVES

Multiculturalism and anti-racism have often been counterpointed as distinct and mutually exclusive approaches to dealing with questions of ethnic diversity and racism. A close analysis of anti-racist efforts that have been influenced by liberal multiculturalism shows that there is instead a complex and contradictory relationship between these two ostensibly divergent approaches. In practice, they overlap, and are even intentionally brought together, in a mode we might call anti-racist multiculturalism. This raises a number of problematic situations for social movements and community organizations that are seeking profound anti-racist changes, even as it provides opportunities for activists.

As we have seen, the strong threads of liberalism and official multiculturalism mean that many anti-racist workshops focus on the supposed problem of ignorance rather than on racist knowledge and institutions. As a result, anti-racist educational efforts can often echo liberal multicultural confinements of identity. Official multiculturalism has also intervened more directly in community organizing, as evident in the organizations for "visible minority women" that were initiated and sponsored by state agencies. This intervention redirected, diffused, and contained the concerns of women of colour and immigrant women by framing their concerns within multicultural terms, by distracting activists away from their community-based work, and by excluding more radical activists and existing activist networks. On the other hand, despite her deep concerns about the multicultural framework, Das Gupta (1999: 187) suggests that multiculturalism also "provided a context in which disempowered and marginalized groupings have been able to make progressive demands from the state." Nadeau's research on NAC shows that we can draw similar conclusions about anti-racist organizing within the feminist movement. While the discourse of multiculturalism was used to submerge discussions of racism within this national women's organization, it ironically also allowed feminists of colour to create a space from which to launch more profound anti-racist challenges. In both cases, anti-racist activists patched together a kind of anti-racist multiculturalism in order to seize a crevice in which more radical anti-racist organizing could lodge itself.

Nevertheless, as Day (2005: 86) points out, "policies of state multiculturalism, as progressive as they might be, direct political and academic attention away from many more pressing concerns." While multiculturalism has provided the impetus for some projects that address the difficulties faced by marginalized communities, it has also been an effective strategy for containing activism that would more radically challenge unequal relations of race, class, and gender. Because of its enduring influence on representations of diversity, ethnic identity, and racism in Canada, multicultural discourse can also limit activists' conversations to certain categories of community and identity and certain kinds of concerns.

Yet there are many alternative ways of organizing that have been able to step entirely outside a multiculturalist and state-based framing of anti-racist change. For example, in the last few years a number of informal networks and groups have been organized across the globe to support undocumented residents and refugees and to resist immigration laws. These campaigns challenge the notion of the "illegal immigrant" by asserting that "no one is illegal" and by demanding an end to deportations and detentions of those without status. In Europe, the No Borders movement has been active at a number of levels, including raising public awareness by targeting private companies that benefit from detention and deportation (Nyers 2003). Across Canada, a variety of organizing efforts have been organized through networks such as No One is Illegal (Lakeoff and Porcello 2005; Solidarity Across Borders 2004). Anti-deportation activism has worked to block deportations, prevent detention, and improve conditions for immigrants and refugees by challenging security, policing, and immigration practices. No One is Illegal groups in Montreal, Toronto, and Vancouver have used a variety of tactics, including street demonstrations, cultural events, direct action in immigration offices, and tracking and publicizing individual cases. These anti-deportation campaigns demonstrate that contemporary anti-racist organizing is able not only to transcend the confinements of Canadian multiculturalism but also to challenge the very concept of national borders.

NOTES

1   Thanks to Richard Day and Mary-Jo Nadeau for talking about this chapter with me and offering encouragement and comments. Thanks also to Jake Burkowicz for his research assistance. The primary research in this chapter was supported in part by a grant from the Social Sciences and Humanities Research Council (SSHRC).

2   The head tax, as much as $500, was levied from 1885 to 1923 exclusively on Chinese immigrants to Canada. The Canadian government collected about $23 million in total, equivalent to $1.2 billion in today's dollars. One of the effects of the punishing head tax was to keep families separated for decades, as men worked alone to send money to families whom they couldn't afford to bring to Canada. In June 2006, the Canadian government officially apologized for the head tax and announced compensation for the handful of surviving head tax payers.

3   It is important to note, however, that the involvement of the state in these organizations was not uncontroversial or uncontested; on the contrary, the issue of state control over immigrant women's organizing has been contentious since the 1970s, when government officials were asked to leave the organization Women Working with Immigrant Women (Das Gupta 1999; Ng 1988: 98).

4   Toronto is the largest city in Canada, with one of the highest proportions of "visible minority" and "foreign-born" residents (to use Statistics Canada terms). Toronto had a population of 4,682,897 in 2001 (New York has about 7.8 million inhabitants) (Statistics Canada 2003). The percentage of "visible minority" residents is about 37%, and the percentage of "foreign-born" residents is about 44% (compared to 24% in New York) (Statistics Canada 2003: 28).

5   This research is based on 21 confidential interviews with white and non-white feminists involved in anti-racist efforts in 18 women's organizations based in Toronto, including drop-in centres, shelters, feminist advocacy groups, and feminist publications and publishers. Neither the individuals nor the organizations are named in order to preserve this confidentiality. I also draw on observations of 12 anti-racist workshops or workshop series, as well as numerous organizational meetings, in a variety of sites including feminist, environmental, social justice, and popular educational organizations, as well as an Aboriginal youth conference. In five of these workshop series, I was either participant or facilitator.

6   Cynthia Wright, personal communication, November 2001.

REFERENCES AND FURTHER READINGS

Amir, Yehuda. 1998. Contact Hypothesis in Ethnic Relations. In Eugene Weiner, ed., *The Handbook of Interethnic Coexistence*. New York: Continuum Publishing. 162–81.

Amos, Valerie, and Pratibha Parmar. 1984. Challenging Imperial Feminism. *Feminist Review* 17(3): 3–19.

Angus Reid. 1991. *Multiculturalism and Canadians: Attitude Study, 1991*. Toronto: Angus Reid Group. Submitted to Multiculturalism and Citizenship Canada.

Anthias, Floya, and Cathie Lloyd. 2002. Introduction: Fighting Racisms, Defining the Territory. In F. Anthias, and C. Lloyd, eds., *Rethinking Anti-racisms: From Theory to Practice*. New York: Routledge. 1–21.

Anzaldua, Gloria (ed.). 1990. *Making Face, Making Soul: Creative and Critical Perspectives by Feminists of Color*. San Francisco: Aunt Lute Books.

Bannerji, Himani. 2000. *The Dark Side of the Nation: Essays on Multiculturalism, Nationalism, and Gender*. Toronto: Canadian Scholars' Press.

Benjamin, Akua. 1992. Critiquing Anti-Racist Consultancy. Paper presented to the Anti-Racism and Feminism Conference, Canadian Research Institute for the Advancement of Women (CRIAW), 13-15 November, Toronto.

Bonnett, Alistair. 2000. *Anti-Racism*. London: Routledge.

Britzman, Deborah. 1993. The Ordeal of Knowledge: Rethinking the Possibilities of Multicultural Education. *Review of Education* 15: 123–35.

Carby, H. 1982. White Women Listen! In Paul Gilroy, ed., *The Empire Strikes Back*. London: Hutchinson and the Centre for Contemporary Cultural Studies. 212–35.

Carty, Linda. 1992. Women's Studies in Canada: A Discourse and Praxis of Education. *Resources for Feminist Research* 20, 3–4: 12–18.

Carty, Linda, and Dionne Brand. 1993. Visible Minority Women: A Creation of the Canadian State. In Himani Bannerji, ed., *Returning the Gaze: Essays on Racism, Feminism, and Politics*. Toronto: Sister Vision Press. 169–81.

CBC 2006. The National. 23 June.

Cook, S.W. 1978. Interpersonal and Attitudinal Outcomes in Cooperating Interracial Groups. *Journal of Research and Development in Education* 12: 97–113.

Das Gupta, Tania. 1999. The Politics of Multiculturalism: Immigrant Women and the Canadian State. In E. Dua and A. Robertson, eds., *Scratching the Surface: Canadian Anti-racist Feminist Thought*. Toronto: Women's Press.

Day, Richard. 2000. *Multiculturalism and the History of Canadian Diversity*. Toronto: University of Toronto Press.

——. 2005. *Gramsci is Dead: Anarchist Currents in the Newest Social Movements*. Toronto: Between the Lines.

Dei, George. 1996. Critical Perspectives in Anti-Racism: An Introduction. *Canadian Review of Sociology and Anthropology* 33(3): 247–67.

Egan, Carolyn, Linda Gardner, and Judy Persad. 1988. The Politics of Transformation: Struggles with Race, Class and Sexuality in the March 8th Coalition. In Frank Cunningham, Sue Findlay, Marlene Kadar, Alan Lennon, and Ed Silva, eds., *Social Movements/Social Change*. Toronto: Between the Lines. 20–47.

Ellsworth, Elizabeth. 1989. Why Doesn't This Feel Empowering? Working through the Repressive Myths of Critical Pedagogy. *Harvard Educational Review* 59(3): 297–324.

Foucault, Michel. 1990. *History of Sexuality: An Introduction*. New York: Vintage.

Foster, K. 1926. *Our Canadian Mosaic*. Toronto: YWCA.

Goldberg, David. 1993. *Racist Culture: Philosophy and the Politics of Meaning*. Cambridge: Blackwell.

Government of Canada, Standing Committee on Multiculturalism. 1987. *Multiculturalism: Building the Canadian Mosaic*. Ottawa: Supply and Services Canada.

Gurnah, Ahmed. 1984. The Politics of Racism Awareness Training. *Critical Social Policy* 10 (Summer): 6–20.

Henry, Frances, and Carol Tator. 1999. State Policy and Practices as Racialized Discourse: Multiculturalism, the Charter, and Employment Equity. In Peter Li, ed., *Race and Ethnic Relations in Canada*. Toronto: Oxford University Press, 88–115.

Henry, Frances, Carol Tator, Winston Mattis, and Tim Rees. 1995. *The Colour of Democracy: Racism in Canadian Society*. Scarborough: Nelson.

hooks, bell. 1981. *Ain't I a Woman: Black Women and Feminism*. Boston: South End Press.

Jakubowicz, A. 1988. The Celebration of (Moderate) Diversity in a Racist Society: Multiculturalism and Education in Australia. *Discourse* 8(2): 37–75.

Lakeoff, Aaron, and Seth Porcello. 2005. Status, Survival, and Solidarity: Non-status People and the Politics of Precarity. <http://toronto.nooneisillegal.org/node/72>.

Li, Peter. 1999. The Multiculturalism Debate. In Peter Li, ed., *Race and Ethnic Relations in Canada*. Toronto: Oxford University Press. 148–77.

Lucas, S., J. Persad, G. Morton, S. Albequerque, and N. el Yassir. 1991. Changing the Politics of the Women's Movement. *Resources for Feminist Research* 20(1): 3–4.

Mackey, Eva. 2002. *The House of Difference: Cultural Politics and National Identity in Canada*. Toronto: University of Toronto Press.

McCaskell, Tim. 1995. Anti-Racist Education and Practice in the School System. In S. Richer and L. Weir, eds., *Beyond Political Correctness: Toward the Inclusive University*. Toronto: University of Toronto Press. 253–72.

McLeod, Keith. 1994. Multiculturalism and the Concept of a Non-Racial Society: A Perspective on Teacher Education. *Orbit* 25(2): 18–25.

Moore, B. 1993. The Prejudice Thesis and the Depoliticization of Racism. *Discourse* 14(1): 52–65.

Moraga, Cherrie, and Gloria Anzaldua. 1983. *This Bridge Called My Back: Writings by Radical Women of Colour*. New York: Kitchen Table Press.

Multiculturalism and Citizenship Canada. 1985. *Education: Cultural Pluralism in Canada*. Ottawa: Supply and Services Canada.

——. 1988. Corporate and Policy Branch. *Canadian Multiculturalism Act* Briefing Book: Clause by Clause Analysis. Unpublished document released under Access to Information Act, quoted in Mackey 2002.

——. 1991. *Multiculturalism: What Is It Really All About?* Ottawa: Supply and Services Canada.

NAC. 1985. *Program Submission to Secretary of State for 1986-87* (September). Ottawa: Secretary of State.

Nadeau, Mary-Jo. 2005. *The Making and Unmaking of a Parliament of Women: Nation, Race and the Politics of the National Action Committee on the Status of Women (1972–1992)*. PhD dissertation, York University, Toronto.

——. 2006. Rewriting the Borders: Nation, Race, and the Politics of Writing Canadian Feminism. Departmental Seminar, Sociology Department, Queen's University, Kingston, 27 February.

Ng, Roxana. 1988. *The Politics of Community Services*. Toronto: Garamond.

Nyers, Peter. 2003. Abject Cosmopolitanism: The Politics of Protection in the Anti-Deportation Movement. *Third World Quarterly*, 24, 6: 1069–2003.

Ontario Ministry of Education and Training. 1994. *The Resource Guide for Antiracist and Ethnocultural Equity Education, JK-Grade 9*. Toronto: Ontario Ministry of Education and Training.

Rattansi, Ali. 1992. Changing the Subject? Racism, Culture, and Education. In J. Donald and A. Rattansi, eds., *Race, Culture and Difference*. London: Sage. 11–48.

Razack, Sherene. 1993. Storytelling for Social Change. *Gender and Education* 5(1): 55–70.

———. 1998. *Looking White People in the Eye*. Toronto: University of Toronto Press.

Rebick, Judy, and Kike Roach. 1996. *Politically Speaking*. Vancouver: Douglas and MacIntyre.

Rezai-Rashti, G. 1989. Multicultural Education, Anti-Racist Education, and Critical Pedagogy: Reflections on Every Day's Practice. Unpublished.

Secretary of State. 1982. Multiculturalism: Priorities. Discussion Paper, 21 December. Ottawa: Secretary of State.

Short, G. 1991. Combatting Anti-Semitism: A Dilemma for Anti-racist Education. *British Journal of Educational Studies* 34(1): 33–44.

Sleeter, C. 1993. How White Teachers Construct Race. In C. McCarthy and W. Crichlow, eds., *Race, Identity, and Representation in Education*. New York: Routledge. 157–71.

Solidarity Across Borders. 2004. *Newsletter* (Spring).

Srivastava, Sarita. 1994. Voyeurism and Vulnerability: Critiquing the Power Relations of Anti-Racist Education. *Canadian Woman Studies* 14 (2): 105–09.

———. 1996. Song and Dance? The Performance of Antiracist Workshops. *Canadian Review of Sociology and Anthropology* 33(3): 292–315.

———. 2002. Facing Race, Saving Face: Anti-racism, Emotion, and Knowledge in Social Movement Organizations. PhD dissertation, University of Toronto.

———. 2005. Facing Race, Saving Face: Moral Identity in the Face of Anti-racism. *Signs* 31(1): 29–62.

———. 2006. Tears, Fears, and Careers: Anti-racism, Emotion, and Social Movement Organizations. *Canadian Journal of Sociology* 31(1): 55–90.

Statistics Canada. 2003. *2001 Census Analysis Series. Canada's Ethnocultural Portrait: The Changing Mosaic*. Ottawa: Statistics Canada.

Thomas, Barbara. 1987. Anti-racist Education: A Response to Manicom. In J. Young, ed., *Breaking the Mosaic: Ethnic Identities in Canadian Schooling*. Toronto: Garamond.

Troyna, Barry. 1987. Beyond Multiculturalism: Towards the Enactment of Anti-racist Education in Policy, Provision, and Pedagogy. *Oxford Review of Education* 13(3): 307–20.

———. 1993. *Racism and Education: Research Perspectives*. Toronto: OISE Press.

Troyna, Barry, and Richard Hatcher. 1992. *Racism in Children's Lives: A Study of Mainly White Primary Schools*. London: Routledge.

Troyna, Barry, and J. Williams. 1986. *Racism, Education, and the State: The Racialisation of Education Policy*. Beckenham: Croom Helm.

Trudeau, Pierre. 1971. Announcement of "Federal Multicultural Policy." *House of Commons Debates* 8 October: 8545–48.

Walcott, Renaldo. 1990. Theorizing Anti-Racist Education: Decentering White Supremacy in Education. *Western Canadian Anthropologist* 7(2): 109–20.

EXPANSION OF THE CANADIAN POLIS

Replicating International Legal Norms of Indigenous Self-Determination in the Canadian Context[1]

Jennifer E. Dalton

INTRODUCTION

According to the Merriam-Webster Dictionary, the *polis* is "a state or society especially when characterized by a sense of community." This definition implies societal cohesiveness based on citizen or communal attachment to the state. Canada can be described as a community of individuals, wherein citizens may experience a sense of community or attachment to the Canadian state or *polis*. Yet, the Canadian example is unique because of its multicultural nature. Ultimately, Canadian society consists of a conglomeration of different cultural groups that fall under the umbrella of Canadian citizenship.

There is an obvious disconnect between notions of Canadian community and citizenship, on the one hand, and marginalized groups such as visible minorities and immigrants on the other. Despite the fact that Canadian culture embodies and purports to embrace multiculturalism, these same marginalized groups are often the victims of discrimination, exclusion, and isolation. Aboriginal peoples represent one of the most marginalized groups in Canada. This chapter asserts that the Canadian *polis* must be expanded to fully include international legal conceptions of Indigenous self-determination in order to facilitate greater recognition and acceptance of Aboriginal communities and their rights. The primary emphasis here is placed on what Indigenous self-determination entails in the international legal context and how this depiction might be replicated in Canada.

In international law, Indigenous self-determination is often given different meaning and content than in the Canadian context. In fact, the term "self-determination" is more often used in the former, while "self-government" is used in the latter as an expression of the right of self-determination. This neither negates nor diminishes the importance of self-determination as an overarching objective for many Aboriginal peoples in Canada. As stated by Alan Cairns:

> ... domestic developments could not have brought us to where we are now without the support offered by the international environment. Indeed, Aboriginal nationalism, cultural pride, and the pursuit of self-government would all be

much weaker in the absence of supportive messages by the international environment.... International law, which formerly "facilitate[d] empire building and colonization ... [now] provides grounds for remedying the contemporary manifestations of the oppressive past." (Cairns 2000: 40-42)

In other words, Cairns emphasizes the impact of international law on the Canadian legal and political realms. In particular, he points out the effects of international law and legal norms on Aboriginal issues and rights in the Canadian context. These issues and rights arguably include the right of self-determination for Aboriginal peoples in Canada.

There is no firm agreement on precisely what self-determination entails, either under international law or in Canada. Mary Ellen Turpel (1992: 580) argues that "Indigenous claims unite legal, historical, political, moral, and humanitarian arguments in a body of doctrine that may be viewed as a third generation of international human rights law focussing on the uniquely collective nature of Indigenous claims. This new generation of human rights has been termed the 'rights of peoples.'" In the Canadian context, Aboriginal peoples have employed the term because of its relevance for their objectives and, more importantly, due to the resonance it holds in describing their inherent and historically based rights. In these ways, the right of self-determination can be replicated in the Canadian context based on the essential meanings and goals behind the concept.

Generally speaking, Aboriginal self-determination is a philosophical principle that embodies the right of Aboriginal peoples to choose how they live their collective lives and structure their communities based on their own norms, laws, and cultures. It includes the freedom and equal human right to control one's destiny, usually in the context of groups or communities. Equally important, its actualization can occur through Aboriginal self-government. In other words, Aboriginal self-determination can be viewed as an overarching principle, while Aboriginal self-government is one way that principle can be put into practice or expressed by Aboriginal peoples.

According to S. James Anaya (2000: 97–98, 104–05, 107, 109–10), there are five fundamental characteristics embodied in self-determination: freedom from discrimination; respect for cultural integrity; social welfare and development; lands and natural resources; and self-government. The last two characteristics are highly controversial since they stress the importance of autonomy in governance based on the interplay between laws, land use, and resources (Anaya 2000: 98, 104–05, 109–10), which can conflict with jurisdictional authority at the federal, provincial, or territorial levels. Depending on what type is adopted, self-government might include decision-making, law-making capabilities, and varying degrees of autonomy, including in relation to a land base or territory. In these ways, self-government can ensure that Aboriginal peoples live according to their own norms and values, and therefore it is a significant embodiment of the right of self-determination (Turpel 1992: 593, 595; RCAP 1997: paras. 452–69, 512–18).

Anaya (2000: 75) further defines "self-determination [as giving] rise to remedies that tear at the legacies of empire, discrimination, suppression of democratic participation, and cultural suffocation." Further, Turpel (1992: 580) observes that:

> Indigenous claims are multifaceted because they bring together requests for land, requests for autonomy from the political structures and cultural hegemony of dominant "settler" societies, and pleas for respect for their distinct Indigenous cultural and spiritual world views. The claims also seek redress for systemic discrimination against Indigenous peoples in the legal (criminal justice) and political systems, the social services sector, and the workforce.

However, while self-determination may indeed seek to break from colonial practices, this does not necessarily equate with the pursuit of secession from Canada. Rather, a secessionist objective occurs only in a minority of cases. The majority of Aboriginal peoples focus on self-determination as the reinstatement of autonomy over "political, social, and cultural development" *within* Canada and freedom from state interference in order to allow the preservation and transmission of cultures to future generations (Turpel 1992: 593; Sambo 1993: 23).

In international law, self-determination is a right vested in "peoples," and this is where much of the controversy lies. How are "peoples" defined in international law? How might this definition be reproduced in the Canadian context? Should Aboriginal peoples be considered "peoples" with a right of self-determination in Canada, and, if so, does this necessitate an expansion of the Canadian *polis*, specifically with regard to the scope of applicable laws?

In this chapter, it is argued that Aboriginal peoples in Canada do indeed constitute "peoples," as that term is used in the context of self-determination. They should, therefore, be accorded the right of self-determination as defined by international law. Ultimately, as will be discussed, this does indeed require an expansion of the Canadian *polis*, specifically with regard to the laws that are applied. Nonetheless, in the Canadian context the right of self-determination focuses on *internal* forms of self-determination. While it is not assumed at this point that the question of secession might not arise at some point in the future, the quandary of the right of *external* self-determination within a federalist system such as Canada involves the exploration of other legal, jurisdictional, political, social, cultural, and economic nuances, which is beyond the scope of this forum.

Before dealing with the principal subjects outlined above, a brief historical analysis of the development of Indigenous self-determination in international law is in order. This will help situate the aforementioned debates within the relevant historical context from the perspective of international law.

SELF-DETERMINATION IN INTERNATIONAL LAW

Aboriginal peoples in Canada have found that, in some ways, international legal mechanisms have been more conducive to their goal of achieving recognition of a right of self-determination than has been the case within the domestic context. This is due, in large part, to the higher level of consideration accorded self-determination within international law. In the Canadian common law system, the possibility of self-government for Aboriginal peoples is usually raised, while self-determination receives little attention. Part of the reason for this lies in the concepts of "nations" and "peoples," which are part and parcel of self-determination as recognized under international law. Before proceeding to define "peoples," it is important to briefly review the history and development of self-determination in international law, particularly in relation to Indigenous peoples.

A History of Indigenous Self-Determination

The principle of self-determination first gained international political recognition after World War I as a result of the disintegration of the Austro-Hungarian, Russian, and Ottoman empires (Anaya 2000: 76; Anaya 1993: 134–36). The purpose of negotiating peace at the time ultimately included the specification that peoples and nations should exercise their own sovereign wills, without fear of domination by other states (Anaya, 2000: 75). Self-determination was not formally acknowledged as an international norm until the formation of the United Nations (UN) (Anaya 2000: 76–77). Such recognition appears in Articles 1 and 55 of the UN's Charter although at that time self-determination was not referred to as a "right" (Daes 1996: 47).

Since that time, international law has developed other resolutions and declarations with respect to the right of self-determination for peoples. It is clearly articulated in the International Covenant on Economic, Social and Cultural Rights (ICESCR) and the International Covenant on Civil and Political Rights (ICCPR). Two of the most recent developments in the international arena with regard to self-determination, applicable specifically to Indigenous peoples, are the Organization of American States (OAS) and the UN Draft Declaration on the Rights of Indigenous Peoples (Draft Declaration). Within the OAS, the Inter-American Commission on Human Rights approved the Proposed American Declaration on the Rights of Indigenous Peoples in February 1997, which is currently undergoing further examination at the request of the OAS General Assembly (Harrington 2004: 16). Both support the right of self-determination as a fundamental right for Indigenous peoples, but the Draft Declaration is more ambitious and less "integrationist" (Harrington 2004: 16). In particular, Article 3 of the Draft Declaration states that "Indigenous Peoples have the right to self-determination. By virtue of that right they freely determine their political status and freely pursue their economic, social and cultural development" (United Nations 1994: 3; Iorns 1992). Coulter (2002a: 3) notes that self-determination remains a "political principle but not yet a rule of international law."

Of course, despite the existence of these international legal provisions on the right of self-determination, it should be remembered that there is often a divide between the recognition of a principle and how that principle may or may not be put into practice. In other words, despite the theoretical existence of international legal principles on the right of self-determination, their application to Indigenous peoples, including in the Canadian context, is not necessarily a foregone conclusion.

Who Are "Peoples"? External *versus* Internal Self-Determination

Many critics of the right of self-determination for Indigenous peoples claim that they do not constitute "peoples" or "nations" recognized under international law, and therefore the right of self-determination cannot be applied to them, either internationally or domestically in Canada. Yet, there is no "internationally accepted [definition] of the [term] 'peoples'" (Alfredsson 1996: 71).

Uncertainty over the meaning of "peoples" often finds its roots in debates over the form that self-determination might take. Such form is often placed on a continuum of external *versus* internal concepts of how it might be put into practice. External self-determination involves independent statehood, including recognition as a nation under international law, provided that the nation in question has a permanent population, a defined territory, a government, and the capability of entering into relations with other states. Conversely, internal self-determination refers to those rights that support and preserve "Indigenous cultural difference through independent political institutions" within an existing nation-state (United Nations 1986a: 37). While internal self-determination has already been given some support at the Canadian federal and provincial levels through various self-governing arrangements, external self-determination is much more controversial (Kingsbury 2000: 25–26; Hannum 1993: 23–24). This is due, in large part, to the depiction of "independent statehood" and "the capability of entering into relations with other States," which could amount to jurisdictional conflicts or secession of Aboriginal peoples from the Canadian state.

Other conceptions of internal self-determination emphasize the importance of cultural definition and preservation, economic self-sufficiency, and political autonomy including self-government arrangements and various forms of democratic, political, and representative rights (Alfredsson, 1996: 65–66, 71–78). Essentially, these sorts of concepts are limited to self-determination powers *within* states, and thus do not require attempts at secession or absolute political independence (Iorns 1992: 215–17, 220, 222–28). However, there is still the potential for conflict in areas of overlapping jurisdictional authority.

Nevertheless, it is often because of fears of potential secession or significant jurisdictional conflict that states are hesitant to define various groups as "peoples." Many are hesitant to accord Indigenous peoples the title of "peoples" or "nations" since international law does not permit secession of Indigenous populations from larger states, and, accordingly, attempts at secession are usually viewed as both unacceptable and unfeasible by nation-states.

Furthermore, it is feared that defining "peoples" as including Indigenous peoples might result in a "slippery slope," wherein other groups will expect such recognition. There is concern that this would ultimately lead to instability and political unrest (Coulter 2002a: 13). Instead, states often prefer to define such groups, including Indigenous peoples, as "minorities." There is significant and contentious debate over whether Indigenous peoples, including Aboriginal peoples in Canada, constitute minorities rather than peoples or nations. This debate includes important cultural, historical, and territorial issues which are beyond the scope of this chapter (for further discussion, see Dalton 2006; RCAP 1997: paras. 997-1027, 5719–27; Macklem 1995–96: 211–15; Macklem 1992–93: 1353–55; Kymlicka 1995; Spaulding 1997; Borrows 2001; McDonald 1996).

Ultimately, most states need not fear the threat of secession by Indigenous peoples. While many might argue for a right to unilaterally secede under international law, "international law neither forbids nor supports secession" because it is neither proscribed nor sanctioned as a legal right (Coulter 2002b: 5). Additionally, as noted earlier, in the context of Aboriginal peoples in Canada, most groups do not seek secession or other external mechanisms of self-determination.

Anaya (2000: 79) emphasizes internal modes of self-determination, but he does so in tandem with defining "peoples." He stresses the significance attached to the interdependencies that exist among individuals, groups, and states in the contemporary realm and suggests that associations between the varying levels of society, both domestically and globally, are key to explaining "[t]he term *peoples* as it relates to a contemporary understanding of self-determination", (2000: 78). Aboriginal peoples should not be denied recognition as peoples, but recognition should not be based on issues of territory, ethnicity, or history alone:

> [A] limited conception of "peoples," accordingly, largely ignores the multiple, overlapping spheres of community, authority, and interdependency that actually exist in human experience. Humanity effectively is reduced to units of organization defined by a perpetual grip of statehood categories; the human rights character of self-determination is thereby obscured, as is the relevance of self-determination values in a world that is less and less state centered.... *Group challenges to the political structures that engulf them appear to be not so much claims of absolute political autonomy as they are efforts to secure the integrity of the group while rearranging the terms of integration or rerouting its path.* (Anaya 2000: 78-79, emphasis added)

Anaya's approach emphasizes the role played by internal forms of self-determination, not independent statehood or outright political separation. Such *interdependence* is relevant in the Canadian context, arguably reducing fears of secession as a priority of most Aboriginal groups here, but what does this mean for Indigenous populations? In light of the competing definitions of "peoples," do Indigenous groups qualify?

Indigenous groups have histories that are directly linked to the history of classical colonialism. This results in very complex and distinctive definitions of Indigenous peoples, including how their pre- and post-contact societies might be described; how their societies were and continue to be connected to their territories; and the ultimate impact of colonialism on their traditions, cultures, institutions, and laws. Essentially, their histories make defining Indigenous populations a multifaceted and complex task. Such complexity is seen in the working definition originally proposed by the UN's *Study on Indigenous Populations*. While it is lengthy, its partial inclusion is warranted due to the historical information and defining features it offers regarding who constitutes Indigenous peoples. It reads as follows:

> Indigenous communities, peoples and nations are those which, having a historical continuity with pre-invasion and pre-colonial societies that developed on their territories, consider themselves distinct from other sectors of the societies now prevailing on those territories, or parts of them....
>
> The historical continuity may consist of the continuation, for an extended period reaching into the present, of one or more of the following factors:
> (a) Occupation of ancestral lands, or at least of part of them;
> (b) Common ancestry with the original occupants of these lands;
> (c) Culture in general, or in specific manifestations (such as religion, living under a tribal system, membership of an Indigenous community, dress, means of livelihood, life-style, etc.);
> (d) Language (whether used as the only language, as mother-tongue, as the habitual means of communication at home or in the family, or as the main, preferred, habitual, general or normal language);
> (e) Residence in certain parts of the country, or in certain regions of the world;
> (f) Other relevant factors. (United Nations 1986b: 50-51)

While this working definition is very useful in its degree of detail, as noted earlier international law does not have a formal definition of who constitutes peoples. For example, the "International Indian Treaty Council describe[s] Indigenous populations as 'composed of nations and peoples, which are collective entities entitled to and requiring self-determination....'" (Macklem 1995–96: 200). Erica-Irene Daes (1996: 50) describes a "people" along the following lines:

> Whether a group constitutes a "people" for the purposes of self-determination depends, in my view, on the extent to which the group making a claim shares ethnic, linguistic, religious or cultural bonds, although the absence or weakness of one of these bonds or elements need not invalidate a claim. The extent to which members within the group perceive the group's identity as distinct from the identities of other groups should be evaluated according to a subjective standard.

According to Daes's definition, it would appear that most Indigenous peoples, including Aboriginal peoples in Canada, could fall under this depiction. However, it should be noted that this is a much more complex issue; it is beyond the scope of this chapter to discuss in detail which Indigenous peoples might be characterized as "peoples" (see Dalton 2006 for further discussion), but the above discussion is relevant for outlining some of the significant issues.

Applying the Right of Self-Determination to Indigenous Peoples under International Law

While the specific form that self-determination should take is discussed minimally in the related literature, internal forms of self-determination are usually epitomized as more feasible and appropriate than are external forms. For example, as noted above, Anaya places a great deal of emphasis on internal forms of self-determination. He argues that fears of secession are unfounded since most Indigenous peoples' goals are realistic *within* the context of "parent" states. Equally important, and as noted earlier, international law does not recognize a legal right to secession for peoples *within* a state, ultimately reducing the potential for seceding successfully.

This debate over the form that self-determination should take is part and parcel of the larger debate concerning the recognition of Indigenous peoples as holders of the right of self-determination. This broader discussion is exemplified in the Draft Declaration inasmuch as the related negotiations have sought to determine whether Indigenous peoples have a right of self-determination and to what extent that right should be recognized and protected. The mere existence of the Draft Declaration, and the fact that negotiations have been occurring for many years, indicates that under international law, Indigenous populations have made gradual progress in gaining recognition as "peoples." Even though there is no firmly established international legal definition of "peoples," and no formal recognition of Indigenous self-determination under international law, it is becoming increasingly acceptable under international law to recognize Indigenous communities as "peoples" and "nations" who are entitled to some degree of self-determination.

For example, Robert Coulter (2002a: 13) asserts this contention, providing an abundance of supporting claims for internal forms of self-determination. He seeks to demonstrate how Indigenous peoples are unique from other "minority" populations by showing that this inherent difference means that Indigenous peoples should be treated as peoples with internal self-determination rights and that, consequently, such rights are not warranted for other "minority" groups. Coulter asserts that many Indigenous peoples are legally recognized "as distinct political or social entities" with ongoing social activities, practices, norms, and institutions; they are organized as communities that are historical and current, independent, and self-governing. Most Indigenous peoples "had or still have a definite or distinct territory and legally defined membership," and they stress the importance of their connectedness to their lands. These characteristics are combined to demonstrate the distinctiveness of Indigenous peoples from other groups.

Additionally, Coulter (2002a: 13) provides further claims in support of Indigenous self-determination beyond the uniqueness of Indigenous peoples. He maintains that Indigenous ways of life, including Indigenous cultures, social institutions, languages, and spiritual traditions, are "gravely threatened by the dominant societies." Indigenous peoples experience this threat irrespective of their historical recognition as nations, despite the legally binding treaties into which they entered, and regardless of the fact that they "pre-date the states where they are located." Further, most Indigenous peoples have been excluded from constitutional state-building (Daes 1996: 53) and political participation, and they have been "forcibly or wrongfully deprived of their lands and resources..., suffered unjust warfare, discrimination, and the suppression of their political, social and cultural rights" (Coulter 2002a: 13). Finally, Coulter (2002a: 13–14) notes that Indigenous peoples are still subjected to political and economic situations that resemble former vestiges of colonialism, such as minimal power within states, high levels of discrimination, and social injustice. He maintains this set of claims to demonstrate the need for Indigenous peoples to have a right of self-determination so as to protect their rights, restore control over their lives, and rebuild the societies that were taken from them.

Daes (1996: 54) is also a strong supporter of an Indigenous right of self-determination. She argues that the Draft Declaration should include the following important paragraph:

> Indigenous peoples have the right to self-determination in accordance with international law, subject to the same criteria and limitations as applied to other peoples in accordance with the Charter of the United Nations. By virtue of this, they have the right, *inter alia*, to negotiate and agree upon their role in the conduct of public affairs, their distinct responsibilities, and the means by which they manage their own interests.

In addition to this argument, Daes (1996: 55) notes the relevance of Article 31 of the Draft Declaration in support of *internal* forms of Indigenous self-determination. She asserts that Article 31 provides general guidelines for the exercise of Indigenous self-determination rights through "*autonomy or internal self-government within existing states.*" Article 31 states the following:

> Indigenous peoples, as a specific form of exercising their right to self-determination, have the right to autonomy or self-government in matters relating to their internal and local affairs, including culture, religion, education, information, media, health, housing, employment, social welfare, economic activities, land and resource management, environment and entry by non-members, as well as ways and means for financing these autonomous functions. (United Nations 1994)

While even internal forms of Indigenous self-determination are not yet formally recognized under international law, progress can be seen, as evident in the Concluding Observations of the UN Committee on Economic, Social and Cultural Rights (CESCR) and the UN Human Rights Committee (HRC) in December 1998 and March 1999 respectively. At the time, these two committees had undertaken analyses of Canada's human rights record with regard to Aboriginal peoples. While previous assessments had occurred, this was the first time that the CESCR and HRC had applied Article 1 of both the ICESCR and the ICCPR. As argued by Andrew Orkin and Joanna Birenbaum (1999: 114), this application was significant because it applied the notion of "peoples" and the right of self-determination as embodied in Article 1 to Aboriginal peoples in Canada, adding to the currency and relevance of these terms in the Canadian context. The *Concluding Observations* included the following pertinent statement:

> The Committee notes that, as the State Party acknowledged, the situation of the Aboriginal peoples remains "the most pressing human rights issue facing Canadians." In this connection, the Committee is particularly concerned that the State Party has not yet implemented the recommendations of the Royal Commission on Aboriginal Peoples (RCAP). *With reference to the conclusion by RCAP that without a greater share of lands and resources institutions of Aboriginal self-government will fail, the Committee recommends that the right of self-determination requires,* inter alia, *that all peoples must be able to freely dispose of their natural wealth and resources* and that they may not be deprived of their own means of subsistence (art. 1, para. 2). The Committee recommends that decisive and urgent action be taken towards the full implementation of the RCAP recommendations on land and resource allocation. *The Committee also recommends that the practice of extinguishing inherent Aboriginal rights be abandoned as incompatible with article 1 of the Covenant.* (Human Rights Committee 1999; emphasis added)

Despite this apparent progress, the debate over whether Indigenous peoples constitute "peoples" under international law continues (Alfredsson 1996: 63–65). While various states are gradually supporting some internal form of self-determination powers for Indigenous populations, this right has not yet been formally recognized under international law and a consensus among states has not yet been achieved (Daes 1996: 55; Coulter 2002b). Nonetheless, the fact that some states, including Canada, are starting to emulate the international consideration of Indigenous peoples as constituting "peoples" and "nations" gives credence to Cairns's emphasis on the role of international law affecting the domestic laws of states.

However, even at the level of preliminary, informal recognition of Indigenous peoples as "peoples" under international law, the right of self-determination is still expected to be internal in nature. This is primarily due to the international legal recognition of the sovereignty of states and respect for territorial boundaries; potential secession of Indigenous populations would seriously hinder the territorial integrity of states. This does not mean that external self-determination should not be a right accorded to Indigenous peoples in appropriate circumstances, nor does it mean that the present author does not support such a right. Instead, as others have noted, the right of external self-determination may be a crucial component for some Indigenous groups, particularly those suffering from wrongful domination, oppression, and colonialism (Coulter 2002b: 6; Daes 1996: 51–55; Daes 1993: 6–7).

REPLICATING INTERNATIONAL LEGAL NORMS OF SELF-DETERMINATION IN THE CANADIAN CONTEXT

What does this mean for Aboriginal groups in Canada? Do they constitute "peoples"? Can and should international legal norms be replicated in Canada? If so, this necessitates an expansion of the Canadian *polis*, most notably in terms of the scope of applicable law to the Canadian *polis*.

Sources and Application of International Law

Applying international legal norms to the Canadian context is not necessarily a cut-and-dried affair. There are several sources of international law, such as conventional international law and treaties, customary international law, and general principles found in judicial decisions and scholarly writing, that are relevant to the Canadian context (see Harrington 2004: 6–7; Kindred *et al.* 2000).

　　While customary international law is applicable in the Canadian context, it is necessary for it to be treated as obligatory in order for it to take its full effect. "To the extent that customary law can be established, it is as binding on Canada as ratified treaties. [Fortunately,] [c]ustomary international law is thought to be the law of the land, subject of course to the right of the legislature to override it by enacting a statute" (Harrington 2004: 19). Conventional international law includes both self-implementing and non-self-implementing treaties. While Canada might be a signatory to non-self-implementing treaties, such agreements are unenforceable under Canadian domestic law unless they are legislatively implemented by Parliament (Harrington 2004: 18). Consequently, it is not possible to assume the application of conventional international law in the Canadian context. While international legal norms certainly inform Canadian law, including "statutory interpretation and judicial review," (*Baker v. Canada (Minister of Citizenship and Immigration)* 1999 [hereafter, *Baker* 1999]: para. 70) it is necessary for Canada to play an active role in adhering to international legal norms. This is relevant in the context of the right of Indigenous self-determination under international law and whether it is applicable to Aboriginal peoples in Canada.

Indian Status and Lovelace: Application of International law

The case of *Sandra Lovelace v. Canada* (hereafter, *Lovelace* 1977) is important, most notably in the way that it demonstrates the influence of international law on Canadian law. In this case, Sandra Lovelace had lost her Indian status under the Indian Act, s.12(1)(b) because she married a non-status man. Upon the dissolution of her marriage, because she had lost her Indian status, she was denied the right to return to the Tobique reserve where she had been born, raised, and spent the majority of her life.

The HRC decided that the Canadian government was in breach of Article 27 of the ICCPR, to which Canada is a signatory. Article 27 provides: "In those States in which ethnic, religious or linguistic minorities exist, persons belonging to such minorities shall not be denied the right, in community with the other members of their group, to enjoy their own culture, to profess and practise their own religion, or to use their own language." The United Nations Human Rights Committee decided that the Canadian government had breached Article 27 by continuing to deny Sandra Lovelace "the opportunity to live on the reserve, the only place that she could practice her culture in community with other members of the group" (*Lovelace* 1977: 1). Consequently, the discrimination incurred by Lovelace, and all Indian women who married non-Indian men, as a result of s. 12(1)(b) of the Indian Act was in conflict with the civil and political rights as outlined in the aforementioned ICCPR.

This decision "was considered a landmark case because there was a recognition of 'a right for minority groups and their members to define themselves'" (Jackson 1994: 182), including the significance of cultural and familial connections to one's overall identity. Most significantly, this decision helped lead to the introduction and implementation by the Canadian Parliament of Bill C-31, the main purpose of which was to reinstate Indian status to those who had lost it under the discriminatory provisions of the Indian Act. Ultimately, in acting on *Lovelace*, the Canadian government demonstrated that it concurred with the HRC's decision.

Additionally, the relevance of the *Lovelace* case is demonstrated in the effect that international law can have on Canadian law. The case demonstrates the seriousness with which the HRC viewed the violation of the rights in question, while the enactment of Bill C-31 as the government's response indicated Canada's acceptance of *Lovelace* and its provisions as set out by the UN.

Applying International Legal Norms: "Peoples" in Canada

Canada is both a member of the UN and a signatory to its Charter and relevant international covenants, such as the ICCPR and the ICESCR. Additionally, Canada supports the right of internal forms of self-determination for Aboriginal groups, as noted at the Commission on Human Rights Working Group on the Draft Declaration:

Our goal at this working group will be to develop a common understanding, consistent with evolving international law, of how this right is to apply to Indigenous collectivities, and what the content of this right includes. Once achieved, this common understanding will have to be reflected in the wording of Article 3.

[T]he Government of Canada accepts a right of self-determination for Indigenous peoples *which respects the political, constitutional and territorial integrity of democratic states.* In that context, exercise of the right involves negotiations between states and the various Indigenous peoples within these states to determine the political status of the Indigenous peoples involved, and the means of pursuing their economic, social and cultural development. (United Nations 1994; emphasis added)

This Canadian position was reiterated in 2000 at the Commission Working Group on the Draft Declaration, and it is still Canada's current position (Coulter 2002b: 4). Similar sentiments are evident in the "Statement of Reconciliation: Learning from the Past," which is part of a larger report entitled *Gathering Strength: Canada's Aboriginal Action Plan*, released by the federal government in 1997. The statement, referring to the Aboriginal peoples of Canada, notes:

For thousands of years before this country was founded, they enjoyed their own forms of government. Diverse, vibrant Aboriginal nations had ways of life rooted in fundamental values concerning their relationships to the Creator, the environment, and each other, in the role of Elders as the living memory of their ancestors, and in their responsibilities as custodians of the lands, waters and resources of their homelands.... The Government of Canada recognizes that policies that sought to assimilate Aboriginal people, women and men, were not the way to build a strong country. *We must instead continue to find ways in which Aboriginal people can participate fully in the economic, political, cultural and social life of Canada in a manner which preserves and enhances the collective identities of Aboriginal communities, and allows them to evolve and flourish in the future.* (Minister of Indian Affairs and Northern Development 1997: 4–5; emphasis added).

While the above quotation does not deal directly with the right of Aboriginal self-determination, it does indicate the attitude that the "collective identities" of Aboriginal peoples should be respected and safeguarded by the government of Canada. Arguably, when viewed together with the previous quotation made by the Canadian delegation at the Commission on Human Rights Working Group, the position of the government of Canada becomes clearer with regard to the right of Aboriginal self-determination: the government of Canada supports Aboriginal self-determination, but it must be *internal* in nature and must respect the territorial integrity of Canada. Yet, none of these statements has received formal recognition by the government, none has been embodied in government legislation, and the definition of Aboriginal populations as constituting "peoples" in the Canadian context is still unclear. A more developed definition of "peoples" would be useful in clarifying the potential place of Aboriginal peoples in Canadian society as "peoples" and "nations" with a right of self-determination.

CANADIAN LEGAL ANALYSES OF "PEOPLES" AND "SELF-DETERMINATION"

In addition to a small number of relevant judicial decisions, the Royal Commission on Aboriginal Peoples (RCAP) offers important insight into Aboriginal populations as constituting "peoples" with a right of self-determination. The following discussion will review some of the central arguments made by the RCAP to this effect, in addition to undertaking a legal analysis of two central judicial decisions related to the subject. The purpose herein is to develop a more advanced and concrete definition of Aboriginal "peoples" in the Canadian context and, by extension, to replicate international legal norms of self-determination in Canada.

Royal Commission on Aboriginal Peoples: Defining Aboriginal Peoples

One of the central sources dealing with the issue of defining Aboriginal communities as constituting "peoples" is the RCAP Report, released in 1996. Volume 2, entitled "Restructuring the Relationship," assesses various factors which can help to determine which Aboriginal peoples in Canada can be classified as "peoples" with a right of self-determination, thereby providing some insight into defining "peoples," more generally, within the Canadian federation. For instance, the RCAP (1997: para. 543) asserts the basic premise that Aboriginal peoples are nations vested with self-determination powers. The RCAP clarifies this further in the following detailed quotation:

> By Aboriginal nation, we mean a sizeable body of Aboriginal people with a shared sense of national identity that constitutes the predominant population in a certain territory or group of territories. There are 60 to 80 historically based nations in Canada at present, comprising a thousand or so local Aboriginal communities.
>
> Aboriginal peoples are entitled to identify their own national units for purposes of exercising the right of self-determination....
>
> The more specific attributes of an Aboriginal nation are that the nation has a collective sense of national identity that is evinced in a common history, language, culture, traditions, political consciousness, laws, governmental structures, spirituality, ancestry and homeland; it is of sufficient size and capacity to enable it to assume and exercise powers and responsibilities flowing from the right

of self-determination in an effective manner; and it constitutes a majority of the permanent population of a certain territory or collection of territories and, in the future, will operate from a defined territorial base. (RCAP 1997: paras. 454–55, 5757–60)

While this definition is not necessarily complete, it does allude to issues of identity and culture as discussed in earlier statements regarding the international legal context. It also incorporates the relevance of territories and a permanent and "sizeable" population as important components of Aboriginal "nationhood." It suggests that, by limiting the right of self-determination to sizeable Aboriginal nations, a balance is struck between very small Aboriginal communities and much larger Aboriginal populations:

> Which Aboriginal groups hold the right of self-determination? Is the right vested in small local communities of Aboriginal people, many numbering fewer than several hundred individuals? Were this the case, a village community would be entitled to opt for the status of an autonomous governmental unit on a par with large-scale Aboriginal groups and the federal and provincial governments. In our opinion, this would distort the right of self-determination, which as a matter of international law, is vested in "peoples." Whatever the more general meaning of that term, we consider that it refers to what we will call "Aboriginal nations." (RCAP 1997: para. 5729)

The above statements provide significant descriptive detail about how to define Aboriginal "peoples." Equally significant, the RCAP Report demonstrates support for the recognition of various Aboriginal communities as constituting peoples with a right of self-determination. However, there are some notable problems with the RCAP conception. For instance, the classification of 60 to 80 Aboriginal nations, which includes roughly 1000 communities, is noted as being historical in nature. This does not take into account that some historical Aboriginal communities no longer exist as political entities, nor does it seem to take into consideration the effects of the Indian Act or the evolution or general changes that have occurred to separate Aboriginal communities and the Aboriginal population as a whole. Neither does it consider the historical, contemporary, or developmental differences between Aboriginal peoples.

Another significant problem with the RCAP definition of Aboriginal nations is that it appears to be too exclusionary in nature. More specifically, it does not support self-determination powers for communities deemed too small. Should these groups be denied the right of self-determination simply because of their size? Additionally, RCAP does not take into consideration the fact that roughly half of Aboriginal people no longer live on reserves, with a large proportion living in urban centres. While many urban Aboriginal people are members of Aboriginal nations with a land base, this cannot be said for all. Growing levels of urban assimilation and the resultant disconnection from the "home" nations worsens this situation further. As a result, a portion of the Aboriginal population in Canada is without a defined land base. This poses a problem for the territorial component of RCAP's definition of "Aboriginal nations"—it ultimately excludes a part of the overall Aboriginal population. Despite these issues, the RCAP Report still demonstrates significant overall support for the recognition of *some* Aboriginal communities as constituting peoples with a right of self-determination.

The Quebec Secession Reference: Self-Determination and "Peoples"

Canadian common law, and in particular Supreme Court judgements, have not dealt with the right of self-determination of "peoples" to any great extent. While there are a few exceptions, the common law system has tended to treat these issues as falling under the general rubric of international law and, therefore, less relevant in Canadian cases. Despite this general inattention, it is important to assess two key rulings in order to demonstrate the ways in which international legal norms, as they relate to Indigenous peoples and the right of self-determination, have been replicated in the context of Canadian law. This, in turn, will confer further legitimacy on the claim that Aboriginal populations constitute "peoples" in Canada.

The *Reference Re Secession of Quebec* [1998] (hereafter *Quebec Secession Reference*) provides fairly recent insight into how the Supreme Court of Canada defines "peoples" and "self-determination," both under international law and in the Canadian context. While the *Quebec Secession Reference* dealt with the potential for Quebec to unilaterally secede from the Canadian state, the Court mentioned briefly that the interests of Aboriginal peoples, many of whom live in the northern regions of the province, would have to be considered in the process of negotiations on Quebec secession. The Court did spend a significant amount of time discussing the concept of self-determination and its portrayal as a right accorded to peoples. While the Court was looking at these issues as they relate to Quebec, I assert that its definitions of "peoples" and "self-determination" are also applicable to Aboriginal peoples in Canada.

Specifically, in the *Quebec Secession Reference* (1998: para. 112) the Court noted that "international law places great importance on the territorial integrity of nation states and, by and large, leaves the creation of a new state to be determined by the domestic law of the existing state of which the seceding entity presently forms a part." This statement is important in that it demonstrates one aspect of the relationship between international law and domestic law: international law defers to domestic law on questions of territorial integrity and jurisdictional issues.

The Court proceeded to note that "[t]he existence of the right of a people to self-determination is now so widely recognized in international conventions that the principle has acquired a status beyond 'convention' and is considered a general principle of international law" (*Quebec Secession Reference* 1998: para. 114). However, the Court asserted that "international law expects that the right to self-determination will be exercised by peoples *within the framework of existing sovereign states* and consistently with the maintenance of territorial integrity of those states. Where this is not possible, in ... exceptional circumstances, ... a right of secession may arise" (*Quebec Secession Reference* 1998: para. 122; emphasis added).

The Court continued with a definition of who constitutes "peoples," noting that there is uncertainty under international law. The Court's definition of "peoples" is not overly detailed, but this is partly because to do so might restrict various conceptions of the term. Instead, the Court clarified that a "people" might be just one portion of an entire population and is often bound by various factors such as a common language or common culture (*Quebec Secession Reference* 1998: paras. 123–25). In addition, it specified that the right of self-determination as accorded to "peoples" has developed as a human right:

> The right to self-determination ... is generally used in documents that simulta-neously contain references to "nation" and "state." The juxtaposition of these terms is indicative that the reference to "people" does not necessarily mean the entirety of a state's population. To restrict the definition of the term to the population of existing states would render the granting of a right to self-deter-mination largely duplicative, given the parallel emphasis within the majority of the source documents on the need to protect the territorial integrity of existing states, and would frustrate the remedial purpose. (*Quebec Secession Reference* 1998: para. 124)

Ultimately, the Court determined that internal self-determination and territorial integrity are not fundamentally at odds with each other; they are not mutually exclusive:

> While the International Covenant on Economic, Social and Cultural Rights and the International Covenant on Civil and Political Rights do not specifically refer to the protection of territorial integrity, they both define the ambit of the right to self-determination in terms that are normally attainable within the frame-work of an existing state. There is no necessary incompatibility between the maintenance of the territorial integrity of existing states, including Canada, and the right of a "people" to achieve a full measure of self-determination. A state whose government represents the whole of the people or peoples resident within its territory, on a basis of equality and without discrimination, and respects the principles of self-determination in its own internal arrangements, is entitled to the protection under international law of its territorial integrity. (*Quebec Secession Reference* 1998: para. 130)

In other words, the Supreme Court accepts the existence of various peoples *within* the Canadian federation. Aboriginal peoples arguably must be included within this framework, considering the fact that they have their own distinct and unique cul-tures, languages, practices, customs, traditions, laws, and histories—factors that, as discussed earlier, are often considered part of "peoplehood."

Indeed, the Court has recognized the fact that Aboriginal peoples lived on the land in groups from time immemorial. In the *R. v. Van der Peet* decision (hereafter, *Van der Peet*), the Court affirmed that

> when Europeans arrived in North America, aboriginal peoples *were already here*, living in communities on the land, and participating in distinctive cultures as they had done for centuries. It is this fact, and this fact above all others, which separates aboriginal peoples from all other minority groups in Canadian society and which mandates their special legal, and now constitutional, status....
>
> [T]he fact is that when the settlers came, the Indians were there, organized in societies and occupying the land as their forefathers had done for centuries. (*Van der Peet* 1996: paras. 30, 33)

This statement serves to illustrate the distinct status attached to Aboriginal peoples by the Supreme Court of Canada. Additionally, it includes various crucial components that are relevant to defining "peoples" with a right of self-determination. For example, it emphasizes that Aboriginal peoples were "living in communities on the land" and that they had "distinctive cultures." These factors speak to the importance of territory, cultural practices, and community involvement, each of which is crucial in determining whether a group constitutes a "people." It is argued, therefore, that this illustrates the potential for Canadian common law to treat Aboriginal peoples as "peoples" with the right of self-determination, albeit internal in nature.

The Powley Decision

The *R. v. Powley* (herafter *Powley*) decision helps to shed further light on how "peoples," including Aboriginal peoples, are defined under Canadian common law. *Powley* dealt with an Aboriginal right to hunt for food as held by Métis people under s. 35 of the Constitution Act, 1982. This case is a legal watershed because it represents the first opportunity for the Supreme Court of Canada to deal with the rights and inclusion of Métis peoples under s. 35.

At issue in *Powley* was subsection (1) as defining the relevant Aboriginal rights in the case, as well as subsection (2) as specifically including the Métis people as entitled to those rights. While these two subsections have been in effect since the patriation of the Canadian Constitution in 1982, s. 35 has remained largely ineffective for Métis peoples because Canadian governments have taken "the position that the Métis [have] no existing Aboriginal rights protected by s. 35, thereby refusing to negotiate or deal with the Métis people and their rights" (Métis National Council 2003: 1).

This has changed with the *Powley* decision. Steve Powley and Roddy Charles Powley, members of a Métis community near Sault Ste. Marie, had been charged for hunting contrary to the Ontario Game and Fish Act. Both pleaded not guilty because they claimed an Aboriginal right to hunt for food in the Sault Ste. Marie locality. They argued further that subjection to the relevant provision of the Game and Fish Act was a violation of their rights under s.35(1) (*Powley* 2003: para. 6). At the trial court level, the Superior Court level, and the Ontario Court of Appeal, the rulings favoured the Powleys (*Powley* 2003: para. 7). The ruling of the Supreme Court of Canada was also positive for the Powleys, reaffirming their Aboriginal right to hunt for food as Métis people.

The Supreme Court has dealt with a few issues that are relevant for the purposes of this chapter. These issues relate to the task of defining "peoples," including more specifically, Métis peoples. While defining Métis peoples is potentially too limited to apply to all Aboriginal peoples due to the characteristic differences between the Métis and other Aboriginal groups, it is nevertheless fruitful to assess the Court's approach to defining the Métis as "peoples." The Court was careful to note that it could not attempt to "enumerate the various Métis peoples that may exist" (*Powley* 2003: para. 12), but it did emphasize the need to be able to identify a claimant as Métis for the purposes of entitlement to an Aboriginal right under s. 35(1). The Court limited its analysis to "indicating the important components of a future definition [of Métis peoples], while affirming that the creation of appropriate membership tests *before* disputes arise is an urgent priority" (*Powley* 2003: para. 30).

There were three central aspects that the Court enumerated in defining Métis identity for the purpose of claiming rights under s. 35: self-identification, ancestral connection, and community acceptance. Self-identification requires that an individual identify as a member of a Métis community. Such self-identification should not be of "recent vintage" or simply for the purposes of benefiting from a s. 35 right. In other words, genuine self-identification as a member of a Métis community is expected (*Powley* 2003: para. 31). While ancestral connection does not require a minimum blood quantum level, it does require that an individual demonstrate that his or her "ancestors belonged to the historical Métis community by birth, adoption, or other means" (*Powley* 2003: para. 32). Finally, in demonstrating Métis identity, it is important for an individual to be "*accepted by the modern community whose continuity with the historic community provides the legal foundation for the right being claimed*" (*Powley* 2003: para. 33; emphasis added).

This last requirement was more vague, as the Court opined that the Métis should determine acceptance for themselves. However, the Court did emphasize the importance of involvement in the community; a shared culture, customs, and traditions; and overall "contextual understanding" of the community (*Powley* 2003: para. 33). Once again, the relevance of genuine involvement in and acceptance by a Métis community was argued as crucial in defining Métis identity.

In addition to outlining the requirements for recognition of Métis identity, the Court provided a general definition for the Métis Nation as a whole:

> The term Métis in s. 35 of the *Constitution Act, 1982* does not encompass all individuals with mixed Indian and European heritage; rather, *it refers to distinctive peoples who, in addition to their mixed ancestry, developed their own*

customs, and recognizable group identity separate from their Indian or Inuit and European forebears....

A Métis community is a group of Métis with a distinctive collective identity, living together in the same geographical area and sharing a common way of life. (*Powley* 2003: para. 1; emphasis added)

This quotation, along with the defining features of individual Métis identity, demonstrates the importance of several factors that were discussed earlier as having relevance when defining "peoples." For example, self-identification, ancestral connection, and community acceptance, along with a shared "common way of life" and "geographical area," accentuate community, collective identity, and culture. In addition, the importance of territory is apparent, while the overall emphasis on community ultimately includes communal activities such as customs and traditions. These aspects are strikingly similar to those included in Daes's definition of "peoples" and to the definition of Aboriginal peoples as constituting "nations," as discussed in the RCAP Report.

Ultimately, these characteristics are indicative, not only of how the Court defines peoples, but also of the conditions under which certain groups might be recognized as peoples. This is arguably applicable to Métis peoples as well as other Aboriginal groups. While none of these specifications constitute formal recognition of Aboriginal peoples as constituting "peoples," they certainly allow for a more detailed and thorough conception of how Aboriginal populations, including the Métis, constitute "peoples." This, in turn, supports the argument that, as "peoples," Aboriginal peoples in Canada should have a right of self-determination, as provided for under international law. Ultimately, this requires the replication of international legal norms of Indigenous self-determination in the Canadian context.

CONCLUSION

Many Aboriginal people, including Métis people, live off reserve in urban centres or away from their communities, and therefore their attachment to a land base or shared territory may be uncertain. It becomes very challenging to define these people as constituting "peoples" if some sort of land base or territorial attachment is a requirement, as posited in several of the discussions above. In such circumstances, one option might be to look to national Aboriginal organizations or home communities to speak for one's interests and to embody the principle of self-determination. Of course, this option does not deal with other issues such as isolation from one's community, difficult personal circumstances, loss of culture, loss of language, or other factors which may diminish the likelihood of involvement in one's own Aboriginal community. Consequently, even the best attempts at defining Aboriginal "peoples" with a right of self-determination may fall short, ultimately excluding individual members for a variety of reasons. This serves to demonstrate the complexity of these issues.

Nevertheless, this chapter has shed light on a number of important issues relating to the difficult task of defining Aboriginal "peoples" with an accompanying right of self-determination. The form that the right of self-determination should take has been evaluated, ultimately demonstrating that *internal* forms of self-determination are largely workable *within* nation-states. This does not preclude the right of *external* self-determination for peoples under certain circumstances, but this issue was beyond the scope of this chapter.

This chapter has also discussed various approaches to defining "peoples" under international law, with an eye to determining whether Indigenous groups qualify as "peoples" entitled to the right of self-determination. Various assertions have been made supporting the claim that Indigenous groups are indeed "peoples" with a right of internal self-determination. International law has gradually started to define Indigenous peoples as constituting "peoples" and therefore as entitled to a right of self-determination. This gradual acceptance is still developing and there is still a great deal of debate surrounding the issue.

Progress has also occurred in the Canadian context, but formal legal recognition of Aboriginal groups as constituting "peoples" has not yet occurred either through statute law or common law. At the same time, while the government of Canada has recognized an internal right of self-determination for Aboriginal peoples in various statements, it has not released any formal legislation or written policies recognizing a right of Aboriginal self-determination; it has not taken a formal stance on Aboriginal peoples as constituting "peoples"; and it has not determined *which* groups constitute "peoples." The Supreme Court of Canada and the RCAP have provided some explication of "peoples," but the former has not applied it to Aboriginal peoples, nor has it yet defined which Aboriginal peoples might constitute "peoples," while the latter has provided a fairly limited conception.

Ultimately, it is apparent that the Canadian *polis* currently does not fully embrace international legal conceptions of Indigenous self-determination. In other words, while international legal norms on Indigenous self-determination are gradually advancing to embrace Indigenous communities as constituting "peoples" with a right of self-determination, the Canadian *polis* is "lagging behind," with an equal level of progress not yet achieved. Instead, the current scope of applicable laws in the context of the Canadian *polis* is not broad enough to encompass recent developments in international law on the issue. This does not mean that developments and progress to match international legal norms on Indigenous self-determination are not possible. Instead, the Canadian *polis* must be expanded to include a larger scope of applicable legal norms. In this case, the Canadian *polis* must be expanded to allow the full replication in the Canadian context of international legal norms on Indigenous self-determination, including formal recognition of Aboriginal communities as constituting "peoples" with a right of self-determination. Once this has been achieved, then the difficult task of determining which Aboriginal communities constitute "peoples" with a right of self-determination can be undertaken.

NOTES

1   As always, my deepest appreciation and gratitude are held for my mother, Janet E. Dalton, for her continual support, encouragement, and helpful editorial suggestions. Thanks to Kent McNeil for useful comments on an earlier draft of this chapter. I also would like to acknowledge the generous financial support of the Social Sciences and Humanities Research Council of Canada (SSHRC) by way of a SSHRC Canada Graduate Scholarship (Doctoral Studies).

REFERENCES AND FURTHER READINGS

Alfredsson, Gudmundur. 1996. Different Forms of and Claims to the Right of Self-Determination. In Donald Clark and Robert Williamson, eds., *Self-Determination: International Perspectives*. New York: St. Martin's Press. 58–86.

Anaya, S. James. 1993. A Contemporary Definition of the International Norm of Self-Determination. *Transnational Law and Contemporary Problems* 3: 131–64.

——. 2000. *Indigenous Peoples in International Law*. 2nd ed. New York: Oxford University Press.

Borrows, John. 2001. Uncertain Citizens: Aboriginal Peoples and the Supreme Court. *Canadian Bar Review* 80: 15–41.

Cairns, Alan. 2000. *Citizens Plus: Aboriginal Peoples and the Canadian State*. Vancouver: University of British Columbia Press.

Canadian Charter of Rights and Freedoms. 1982. Part I, Constitution Act, 1982, being Schedule B to the Canada Act 1982 (UK) 1982, c.11.

Charter of the United Nations. 1945. 59 Stat. 1031, TS no. 993, 3 Bevans 1153, 1976 YBUN 1043.

Chartrand, Paul L.A.H., and John Giokas. 2002. Defining "The Métis People": The Hard Case of Canadian Aboriginal Law. In Paul L.A.H. Chartrand, ed., *Who are Canada's Aboriginal Peoples?: Recognition, Definition, and Jurisdiction*. Saskatoon: Purich Publishing. 268–304.

Commission on Human Rights Working Group. 1996. *Statements of the Canadian Delegation on Article 3, the Right to Self-Determination*. 53rd Session. Geneva: Office of the United Nations High Commissioner for Human Rights.

Constitution Act, 1982. 1982. Schedule B to the *Canada Act 1982* (UK), 1982, c.11.

Coulter, Robert. 2002a. Indigenous Peoples and the Law of Self-Determination: A Possible Consensus. Helena, MO: Indian Law Resource Center. 1–22.

——. 2002b. The Possibility of Consensus on the Right of Self-Determination in The UN and OAS Declarations on the Rights of Indigenous Peoples. Draft Discussion Paper. Helena, MO: Indian Law Resource Center. 1–7.

Daes, Erica-Irene. 1993. Some Considerations on the Right of Indigenous Peoples to Self-Determination. *Transnational Law & Contemporary Problems*: 1–11.

——. 1996. The Right of Indigenous Peoples to "Self-Determination" in the Contemporary World Order. In Donald Clark and Robert Williamson, eds., *Self-Determination: International Perspectives*. New York: St. Martin's Press. 47–57.

Dalton, Jennifer E. 2006. *Aboriginal Self-Determination: Protection and Accommodation under Canadian Constitutional Law*. LLM Thesis. Osgoode Hall Law School, York University.

Game and Fish Act. 1990. R.S.O. 1990, c. G.1.

Giokas, John, and Paul L.A.H Chartrand. 2002. Who are the Métis in Section 35?: A Review of the Law and Policy Relating to Métis and "Mixed-Blood" People in Canada. In Paul L.A.H. Chartrand, ed. *Who are Canada's Aboriginal Peoples?: Recognition, Definition, and Jurisdiction.* Saskatoon: Purich Publishing. 83–125.

Hannum, Hurst. 1993. Rethinking Self-Determination. *Virginia Journal of International Law* 34: 1–70.

Harrington, Joanna. 2004. Canada's Obligations under International Law in Relation to Aboriginal Rights. Paper presented at the Pacific Business and Law Institute, Ottawa, Ontario, 1–31.

Human Rights Committee. 1999. *Concluding Observations on Canada.* 65th Session, CCPR/C/79/Add.105.

Indian Act. 1970. R.S.C. 1970, c.I-6.

International Covenant on Civil and Political Rights. 1967. 6 ILM 368.

International Covenant on Economic, Social and Cultural Rights. 1967. 6 ILM 360.

Iorns, Catherine. 1992. Indigenous Peoples and Self-Determination: Challenging State Sovereignty. *Case West Reserve Journal of International Law* 24: 199–348.

Jackson, Margaret. 1994. Aboriginal Women and Self-Government. In John Hylton, ed., *Aboriginal Self-Government in Canada: Current Trends and Issues.* Saskatoon: Purich Publishing. 180–98.

Kindred, Hugh, Karen Mickelson, Ted McDorman, Armand De Mestral, René Provost, Linda Reif, and Sharon Williams. 2000. *International Law: Chiefly as Interpreted and Applied in Canada.* 6th ed. Toronto: Emond Montgomery Publications.

Kingsbury, Benedict. 2000. Reconstructing Self-Determination: A Relational Approach. In Pekka Aikio and Martin Scheinin, eds., *Operationalizing the Right of Indigenous Peoples to Self-Determination.* Turku/Abo, Finland: Institute for Human Rights, Abo Akademi University. 19–37.

Kymlicka, Will. 1995. *Multicultural Citizenship: A Liberal Theory of Minority Rights.* Oxford: Clarendon Press.

Macklem, Patrick. 1992-93. Distributing Sovereignty: Indian Nations and Equality of Peoples. *Stanford Law Review* 45: 1311–67.

——. 1995-96. Normative Dimensions of an Aboriginal Right of Self-Government. *Queen's Law Journal* 21: 173–219.

——. 2001. *Indigenous Difference and the Constitution of Canada.* Toronto: University of Toronto Press.

McDonald, Leighton. 1996. Regrouping in Defence of Minority Rights: Kymlicka's Multicultural Citizenship. *Osgoode Hall Law Journal* 34(2): 291–319.

Merriam-Webster Dictionary. <http://www.m-w.com/>.

Métis National Council. 2003. *Fulfilling Canada's Promise: Métis Rights Recognized and Affirmed.* Ottawa: Métis National Council.

Minister of Indian Affairs and Northern Development. 1997. *Gathering Strength: Canada's Aboriginal Action Plan.* Ottawa: Public Works and Government Services Canada.

Orkin, Andrew, and Joanna Birenbaum. 1999. Aboriginal Self-Determination within Canada: Recent Developments in International Human Rights Law. *Constitutional Forum* 10(4): 112–19.

RCAP (Royal Commission on Aboriginal Peoples). 1997. Vol. 2: Restructuring the Relationship. In *For Seven Generations: An Information Legacy of the Royal Commission on Aboriginal Peoples* (CD-ROM). Ottawa: Libraxus Inc.

Sambo, Dalee. 1993. Indigenous Peoples and International Standard-Setting Processes: Are State Governments Listening? *Transnational Law and Contemporary Problems* 3(1): 13–47.

Spaulding, Richard. 1997. Peoples as National Minorities: A Review of Will Kymlicka's Arguments for Aboriginal Rights from a Self-Determination Perspective. *University of Toronto Law Journal* 47(1): 35–113.

Turpel, Mary Ellen. 1992. Indigenous Peoples' Rights of Political Participation and Self-Determination: Recent International Legal Developments and the Continuing Struggle for Recognition. *Cornell International Law Journal* 25: 579–602.

United Nations. 1960. *Declaration on the Granting of Independence to Colonial Countries and Peoples.* UNGA Res. 1514 (XV), 15 UN GAOR, Suppl. (no. 16), UN Doc. A/4684.

——. 1986a. *Declaration by the International NGO Conference on Discrimination Against Indigenous Populations in the Americas.* UN Doc. E/Cn/.4/Sub.2/1986/7.

——. 1986b. *Study on Indigenous Populations.* UN Doc. E/CN.4/Sub.2/1986/7/Add.4.

——. 1994. *Draft Declaration on the Rights of Indigenous Peoples.* UN Doc.E/CN-4/Sub.2/1994/2/Add.1.

United Nations General Assembly. 1970. *Declaration on Principles of International Law Concerning Friendly Relations and Co-operation among States in accordance with the Charter of the United Nations.* GA Res. 2625 (XXV).

Vienna Convention on the Law of Treaties. 1969. 1155 U.N.T.S. 331, Can. T.S. 1980 No. 37.

CASES CITED

Baker v. Canada (Minister of Citizenship and Immigration). [1999] 2 S.C.R. 817.

Calder v. A.G.B.C. [1973] 34 D.L.R. (3d) 145.

R. v. Powley [2003] 2 S.C.R. 207.

Reference Re Secession of Quebec [1998] 2 S.C.R. 217.

R. v. Van der Peet [1996] 2 S.C.R. 507.

Sandra Lovelace v. Canada [1977]. Communication No. R.6/24, Report of the Human Rights Committee, UN GOAR, 36th Sess., Supp. No. 40, at 166, U.N. Doc. A/36/40, Annex 18 (1977) (views adopted 29 December 1977).

NOTES ON CONTRIBUTORS

B. SINGH BOLARIA is currently Professor Emeritus, University of Saskatchewan, and Adjunct Professor, University of Victoria. Over 40 years, he has authored and edited many books, articles, and chapters in the areas of medical sociology, racism and social inequality, immigration, and social issues.

BOB CARTER is Associate Professor of Sociology, University of Warwick. He has published widely on the politics of racism and immigration and on social theory and sociolinguistics. He is the author of *Realism and Racism: Concepts of Race in Sociological Research* (Routledge 2000) and the co-author (with Alison Sealey) of *Applied Linguistics as Social Science* (Continuum 2004). He also co-edited (with Caroline New) *Making Realism Work* (Routledge 2004). He is currently completing a book for Sage provisionally entitled *De-racializing Sociology* (2008).

JENNIFER E. DALTON is a Ph.D. candidate at Osgoode Hall Law School and a SSHRC Canada Graduate Scholar. Her primary research interests are interdisciplinary in nature, encompassing Aboriginal law and politics in Canada, Indigenous self-determination under international law, Aboriginal comprehensive and self-government agreements, quantitative data analysis and survey research, Canadian constitutional law and reform, and Canadian electoral politics. Recent publications appear in *Windsor Review of Law and Social Issues* and *Canadian Journal of Law and Society*.

GEORGE J. SEFA DEI is Professor and Chair, Department of Sociology and Equity Studies, Ontario Institute for Studies in Education of the University of Toronto. His teaching and research interests are in the areas of anti-racism, minority schooling, international development, and anti-colonial thought. He is the co-author, with Alireza Asgharzadeh, Sharon Eblaghie-Bahador, and Riyad Shahjahan, of *Schooling and Difference in Africa: Democratic Challenges in Contemporary Context* (University of Toronto Press 2006); and has co-edited, with Gurpreet Singh Johal, *Critical Issues in Anti-Racist Research Methodologies* (Peter Lang 2005); with Arlo Kempf, *Anti-Colonialism and Education: The Politics of*

Resistance (Sense Publishers 2006); with Ali Abdi and K. Puplampu, *African Education and Globalization: Critical Perspectives* (Lexington Books 2006); and with Nuzhat Amin, *The Poetics of Anti-Racism* (Fernwood 2006).

ENAKSHI DUA is Associate Professor in the School of Women's Studies at York University, Toronto. She is co-editor, with A. Robertson, of *Scratching the Surface: Canadian Anti-Racist Feminist Thought* (Women's Educational Press 1999); and, with M. Fitzgerald, L. Gardner Taylor, and L. Wyndel, *On Women Healthsharing* (Women's Educational Press 1994). She has also published articles on Indian migrants and racism in Canada in *Canadian Women's Studies, Sociologie et société*, and the *Economic and Political Weekly*.

SEAN P. HIER's recent publications appear in such journals as *Socialist Studies, Canadian Ethnic Studies, Theoretical Criminology, Media Culture and Society*, and *New Media and Society*. He recently edited *Contemporary Social Thought: Themes and Theories* (Canadian Scholars' Press 2005) and co-edited, with B. Singh Bolaria, *Identity and Belonging: Rethinking Race and Ethnicity in Canadian Society* (Canadian Scholars' Press 2006) and, with Josh Greenberg, *The Surveillance Studies Reader* (Open University Press 2007).

DEREK HUM is Professor of Economics and Fellow of St John's College, University of Manitoba and is a member of the National Statistics Council of Statistics Canada. He has published articles in many areas of economics as well as public administration, statistics, sociology, anthropology, and history. He has written or edited seven books, 20 monographs, and more than 100 journal articles and book chapters.

GUIDA MAN teaches at the Atkinson School of Social Sciences, York University. Her current research examines how immigrant women from Mainland China and India navigate the Canadian labour market. She recently published articles in the journals *Environment and Planning A* (with Audrey Kobayashi and Valerie Preston) and *Women's Studies International Forum* and contributed a chapter to *Canadian Woman Studies: An Introductory Reader* (Inanna 2006).

PATRICIA MONTURE is a Mohawk woman, lawyer, and Professor of Native Studies at the University of Saskatchewan. She is author of *Thunder in my Soul: A Mohawk Woman Speaks* (Fernwood 1995).

DHIRU PATEL lived and worked in Africa, India, and Europe before joining the Canadian federal government in 1982 to develop race relations policies, programs, and research. He has presented papers at national and international forums on identity, belonging, globalization, citizenship, and transnationalism, particularly as it relates to younger generations. He has published *Dealing with Interracial Conflict: Policy Alternatives* (Institute for Research on Public Policy 1980) and has contributed chapters to *Transnational Identities and Practices in Canada*

(University of British Columbia Press 2006) and a forthcoming edited volume on racism and social inequality in Canada.

VIC SATZEWICH is Professor of Sociology at McMaster University. He is author of *Racism and the Incorporation of Foreign Labour* (Routledge 1991) and *The Ukrainian Diaspora* (Routledge 2002). He is co-author, with Terry Wotherspoon, of *First Nations: Race, Class, and Gender Relations* (Canadian Plains Research Centre 2000) and co-editor, with Lloyd Wong, of *Transnational Identities and Practices in Canada* (University of British Columbia Press 2006).

WAYNE SIMPSON is Professor and Head of the Department of Economics, University of Manitoba. A specialist in labour economics, applied microeconomics, quantitative methods, and social policy, he has worked for the Bank of Canada and Economic Council of Canada. He is the author of *Urban Structure and the Labour Market: Analysis of Worker Mobility, Commuting, and Underemployment in Cities* (Oxford University Press 1992) and co-author, with Derek Hum, of *Income Maintenance, Work Effort, and the Canadian Mincome Experiment* (Economic Council of Canada 1991) and *Maintaining a Competitive Workforce* (Institute for Research on Public Policy 1996). He has also published more than 40 refereed articles in economics and policy journals and numerous technical and research reports, book chapters, and other articles.

A Professor of Sociology at Queen's University, **SARITA SRIVASTAVA**'s research has focussed on social movements, the sociology of gender and race, and the sociology of emotions. Her primary research interest is the interdisciplinary, historical, and organizational study of race and gender. Recent publications include articles in *SIGNS: Journal of Women and Culture in Society* and the *Canadian Journal of Sociology*, March 2006. Her forthcoming book, *Facing Race, Saving Face: Antiracism, Emotion and Knowledge in Social Movements*, will explore the historical debates, emotional responses, and pedagogical practices that arise when social movements such as feminism are faced with anti-racist challenges.

CHERYL SUZACK is an Assistant Professor of English at the University of Victoria and a member of the Batchewana First Nations. She has guest edited (with Gary Boire) a special issue of *ARIEL* entitled "Law, Literature, Postcoloniality" and has published a review essay entitled "Theorizing the Politics of Common Ground" in *Postcolonial Text*.

RICARDO TRUMPER is Associate Professor of Sociology in the Irving K. Barber School of Arts and Sciences at the University of British Columbia, Okanagan. His recent publications appear in *Race and Class*, *ANTIPODE*, and *Canadian Geographer*.

RENNIE WARBURTON taught sociology from 1965 to 2003 at the University of Victoria, where he is Professor Emeritus. He is author and co-author of articles and book chapters on homlessness religion, nationalism in Canada and Switzerland, nurses and teachers in British Columbia, Asian racialization in British Columbia, Indigenous Canadians, and various other topics. He co-edited, with David Coburn, *Workers, Capital, and the State in British Columbia* (University of British Columbia Press 1988).

LLOYD WONG is an Associate Professor of Sociology at the University of Calgary and the Social and Cultural Domain leader at the Prairie Centre of Excellence for Research on Immigration and Integration. His research interests include transnationalism, citizenship, racism and ethnic discrimination, and Chinese ethnic entrepreneurship. He has recently published articles in *International Migration, Asian and Pacific Migration Journal,* and the *International Journal of Urban and Regional Research.* As well as co-editing, with V. Satzewich, and contributing to *Transnational Identities and Practices in Canada* (University of British Columbia Press 2006), he has published book chapters in *Changing Canada: Political Economy as Transformation,* with V. Satzewich (McGill-Queen's University Press 2003) and *Street Protests and Fantasy Parks: Globalization, Culture, and the State* (University of British Columbia Press 2002).

TERRY WOTHERSPOON is Professor of Sociology at the University of Saskatchewan. He has published several books, including: *The Sociology of Education in Canada: Critical Perspectives* (Oxford University Press 1998), *The Legacy of School for Aboriginal People: Education, Oppression, and Emancipation* (with Bernard Schissel, Oxford University Press 2003), *First Nations: Race, Class and Gender Relations* (with Vic Satzewich, recently reissued by the Canadian Plains Research Centre), and *Multicultural Education in a Changing Global Economy: Canada and the Netherlands* (edited with Paul Jungbluth, Waxmann 1995). His recent research and publications address issues related to teachers' work in Aboriginal communities and education and work prospects for diverse social groups in the context of major social and economic transformations.

LI ZONG is an Associate Professor of Sociology at the University of Saskatchewan and an affiliated researcher of the Prairie Centre of Excellence for Research on Immigration and Integration in Canada. He is also Adjunct Professor for the Tianjin Academy of Educational Science, Xi'an Jiaotong University, and Lanzhou University in China. He co-authored, with Xinheng Yang, *Introduction to Sociology* (Qunzhong Press 1986) and has published many journal articles, book chapters, and reviews on the issues of Chinese professional immigrants, new racism, multiculturalism, transnational Chinese business, civil society and social transformation, and race and ethnic relations.

INDEX

To better explain the lived, interrelated realities of race and racism, Dei presents five "conversations" currently taking place in discourses of race. Ranging from 19th-century representations of race and intelligence to 21st-century media discourses on race, criminality, and terrorism, he identifies a common cultural thread linking the present to the past. The politics of anti-racism, he concludes, cannot successfully negotiate the obstacles of post-colonial Canada in the absence of race identities, and he argues that the liberating potential of anti-racist work is to be realized in embodied forms of knowing.

In the final chapter, Vic Satzewich introduces the concept of whiteness, which has become an important area of inquiry over the last several years. The problem with studies of whiteness, Satzewich contends, is that they increasingly fail to break from representational patterns appearing in the present. He acknowledges that a number of important studies of the present have explained whiteness as an objective cultural condition to acknowledge, address, and fight against, but he nevertheless finds a new strand of race essentialism emerging in this line of critique that works against the development of progressive scholarship.

To bring conceptual clarity to whiteness studies, Satzewich identifies two general perspectives that are informed by a number of interrelated analytical assumptions. The first, the historical perspective, conceptualizes whiteness as a contingent identity that is neither fixed nor stable. Satzewich explains that over the past 100 years, European groups that today would be classified as "white" were neither understood nor represented in this way and that it is inaccurate to use current understandings of whiteness to explain representational patterns in the not-so-distant past. By contrast, the experiential approach to whiteness conceptualizes white identities as objective conditions that need to be exposed and critically interrogated. Whiteness is conceptualized, implicitly or explicitly, on the basis of socially constructed notions of the white body, and the social category of white is essentialized as a universal condition of privilege. Through an exploration of both perspectives, Satzewich advocates an understanding of whiteness as historically specific *and* socially negotiated.

Taken together, these first four chapters highlight some of the nuances in the study of race and racism. All contributors agree that race is a social construct whose origins as a cultural signifier trace to developments in 19th-century science, and all contributors recognize race as a fluid historical identity. The authors differ, however, in the ways that they believe race should be studied and known. Thus, these chapters introduce some of the complexity that needs to be addressed in analyses of race and racism in 21st-century Canada.

REFERENCES

Thomas, W.I., and D. Thomas. 1928. *The Child in America: Behavior Problems and Programs.* New York: Knopf.